British Social Welfare in the Twentieth Century

Also by Robert M. Page:

Stigma
Altruism and the British Welfare State
Social Policy in Transition (edited with John Ferris)
The Costs of Welfare (edited with Nicholas Deakin)
Modern Thinkers on Welfare (edited with Vic George)

Also by Richard Silburn:

Poverty: the Forgotten Englishmen (with Ken Coates)

British Social Welfare in the Twentieth Century

Edited by

Robert M. Page

and

Richard Silburn

palgrave
macmillan

Published by
PALGRAVE
Houndmills, Basingstoke, Hampshire RG21 6XS and
175 Fifth Avenue, New York, N. Y. 10010
Companies and representatives throughout the world

PALGRAVE is the new global academic imprint of
St. Martin's Press LLC Scholarly and Reference Division and
Palgrave Publishers Ltd (formerly Macmillan Press Ltd).

ISBN 0–333–67770–6 hardback
ISBN 0–333–67771–4 paperback

This book is printed on paper suitable for recycling and
made from fully managed and sustained forest sources.

A catalogue record for this book is available
from the British Library.

Printed and bound in Great Britain by
Antony Rowe Ltd, Chippenham and Eastbourne

Editing and origination by
Aardvark Editorial, Mendham, Suffolk.

Transferred to digital printing 2003

Contents

List of Tables and Figures		viii
Acknowledgements		ix
Notes on the Contributors		x

Introduction		1
by *Richard Silburn*		

PART I   The Century Surveyed — 13

1	**The Twentieth Century: an Overview**	15
	by *John Stewart*	
2	**Paying for Welfare in the Twentieth Century**	33
	by *Jim Tomlinson*	

PART II   Political Ideas — 53

3	**Neoclassicism, the New Right and British Social Welfare**	55
	by *Norman Barry*	
4	**New Liberalism and the Middle Way**	80
	by *Robert Pinker*	
5	**Democratic Socialism and Social Policy**	105
	by *Michael Sullivan*	

PART III   Welfare and the State — 131

6	**Education**	133
	by *Michael Sanderson*	
7	**Health**	159
	by *Helen Jones*	
8	**Employment, Unemployment and the Labour Market**	179
	by *Sean Glynn*	
9	**Poverty and Social Security**	199
	by *Pete Alcock*	
10	**Housing**	223
	by *Norman Ginsburg*	

For Baron Duckham – a truly noble professor

and

For Pat, Luke, Ben and Tom, with love

PART IV   Welfare Outside the State   247

11   **Voluntary and Informal Welfare**   249
       by *Jane Lewis*

12   **Commercial and Occupational Welfare**   271
       by *Margaret May and Edward Brunsdon*

PART V   The Future   299

13   **The Prospects for Social Welfare**   301
       by *Robert M. Page*

Notes   316
Bibliography   319
Index   351

List of Tables and Figures

Tables

2.1   Expenditure and revenue in the 'new' welfare state
        of the 1940s   41

6.1   Percentage of children attending grammar and
        independent schools c.1900–c.1940   141
6.2   Percentage of children attending universities   141
6.3   Percentage of children entering university 1930s–1970s   142
6.4   Percentage of students in subject areas   145
6.5   Contribution of education to annual growth rates   146

Figures

2.1   Public expenditure on welfare in the twentieth century   34

Acknowledgements

We are both once again indebted to the indefatigable Ros Kirk – Senior Administrator in the Centre for Social Work at the University of Nottingham – who has prepared the manuscript for Macmillan. Her help, advice and unfailing good humour is much appreciated.

At a time when the barbarians appear to have taken up permanent residence in some of our higher education institutions, most distressingly in what used to be thought of as positions of senior academic leadership, we would like to take this opportunity to thank the Nottingham 'Martyrs of 1997' for their collegiality, decency and intellectual commitment over the years. The denigration of scholarship and the contempt shown for good teaching in some of our self-styled 'research-led universities' mean that we are unlikely to see the like of them again, to the great impoverishment of our once great seats of learning.

Finally, we are extremely grateful to our editor Catherine Gray at Macmillan, who has been so supportive of this collection from inception to publication.

Notes on the Contributors

Pete Alcock	is Professor of Social Policy and Administration at the University of Birmingham.
Norman Barry	is Professor of Politics at the University of Buckingham.
Edward Brunsdon	is Principal Lecturer in Social Policy at London Guildhall University.
Norman Ginsburg	is Professor of Social Policy, University of North London.
Sean Glynn	is Professor of Economic History at London Guildhall University.
Helen Jones	is Lecturer in Social Policy, Goldsmiths College, London.
Jane Lewis	is Professor of Social Policy, University of Nottingham.
Margaret May	is Principal Lecturer in Social Policy at London Guildhall University.
Robert M. Page	is a Senior Lecturer in Social Policy in the School of Social Work at the University of Leicester.
Robert Pinker	is Professor Emeritus of Social Administration at the London School of Economics and Political Science.
Michael Sanderson	is Reader in Economic and Social History at the University of East Anglia.
Richard Silburn	was for many years Senior Lecturer in Social Policy at the University of Nottingham and is now an independent scholar and researcher.
John Stewart	is Senior Lecturer in History at Oxford Brookes University.
Michael Sullivan	is Reader in Social Policy at the University of Wales, Swansea and Director of the National Centre for Public Policy.
Jim Tomlinson	is Professor of Economic History at Brunel University.

Introduction

Richard Silburn

Social policy as a specialist area of academic study and debate is a relatively recent development in the intellectual division of labour. Social administration, as it was usually called until the 1970s, had its late nineteenth-century origins in the development of the profession of social work. It was recognised that the growing interest and concern with social work activity required more expert, trained personnel, if it was to establish itself as a serious professional activity. This gave social administration in its earlier years a marked practical and vocational bias. To some extent this bias remains, although as the subject has evolved and matured so has its scope and the range of interests which it addresses, and hence its appeal to a much wider constituency of students and scholars.

Social policy and administration has always prided itself, perhaps rather complacently, on its intellectual eclecticism. Not so much an academic discipline with its own distinctive body of theory or methods of study, it sees itself more as a defined area of intellectual interest, drawing as appropriate on the methods and theoretical standpoints of a wide range of social science and humanities perspectives.

Paul Wilding has published two perceptive articles on the evolution of social administration as an academic subject (Wilding, 1983, 1992). In the first he contrasts the 'traditional' social administration of the 1950s and 60s with the much more analytical and critical shape of the subject as it developed in the 1970s; in the second article he traces the major movements of the 1980s which raised new problems and issues, and imposed new perspectives. He characterised the 'traditional social administration' as being 'particular, prescriptive and parochial' (Wilding, 1983 p. 3), and 'seldom, if ever, firmly located in the context of the kind of society revealed by economic, sociological and political analysis' (Wilding, 1983 p. 4). To this might be added another comment, that it was firmly located in the present. The heart of the subject was, in Richard Titmuss's famous if misleading phrase, 'the study of the social services' (Titmuss, 1958, p. 14), their legislative framework, their administrative structure, broad policy goals and issues of day-to-day implementation. The historical context within which the social services had developed and evolved was not ignored, but it was seen essentially as 'background' to the pressing and distinct concerns of the present, and drew exclusively on the British experience without reference to events and developments in other countries. For Ramesh Mishra, 'The over-arching idea that gave meaning to

1

this historical exploration was the rise of *laissez-faire* in the nineteenth century, with the Poor Law Reform of 1834 as a major signpost, and its subsequent decline which culminated in the arrival of the welfare state. The triumph of collectivism over individualism was generally seen as due to a growing social conscience, although a variety of influences was recognised' (Mishra in Bulmer *et al.*, 1989 p. 66)

This can be seen very clearly if we reread what was a core textbook throughout the 1950s and for some considerable period of time thereafter. Penelope Hall's *Social Services of Modern England* was first published in 1952; and was regularly revised and reissued thereafter. Penelope Hall was herself responsible for the first six revisions between 1952 and 1963. Thereafter the task was undertaken by a group of Penelope Hall's colleagues at Liverpool University. The early editions reveal a great deal about the approach to the subject that characterised the 1950s and on into the 1960s. The defining moment for the book is 5 July 1948, the day the major postwar social policy reforms came into effect. The subject matter was confined to an examination of the major state-organised social services as they operated in England and Wales (both particular and parochial); the principal source materials were the enabling legislation and regulations that governed their administration (prescriptive). The text was detailed and painstaking and essentially descriptive; there was little reference to a wider intellectual context, whether that was to be found in political theory, sociology, social philosophy or history. The approach was practical and matter-of-fact, it intended to inform rather than explain. Penelope Hall's readers were likely to become public service professionals and practitioners, and they needed to know, quite concretely, the legislative and administrative parameters within which they would operate.

There are some brief references to the historical evolution of social policy. Penelope Hall's introductory chapter includes a few paragraphs where she acknowledges the role of philanthropic individuals and social investigators in the nineteenth century, and her recommendations for further reading include such well-known texts as Trevelyan's *English Social History* and the work of the Hammonds (Hammond and Hammond, 1911, 1917; Trevelyan, 1944); she also recommends biographical studies of the great and the good. Later editions have little more to say on the historical background, although the recommended reading reflects the slowly growing historical literature. In the 1969 edition, the first one to be edited by Anthony Forder, the entire period between 1834 and 1939 is summarised in four brief pages of text. This actually tells us a great deal about the mood and preoccupations of the period. Many people were still prepared to believe that 5 July 1948 truly was a defining moment, that in important respects a new social order had been introduced, that an escape had been made from an often ugly past, and that in this new environment there was little to be learned from the experience of that past, apart from awful warnings. The challenge of social administration was to understand the processes by which an immediate policy goal could best be achieved, to perfect the techniques which would facilitate this achievement and to train up successive cadres of, predominantly, public sector workers. The goals and purposes of social policy, the ultimate objectives, were determined through political dialogue and debate, the social administration task was to translate political goals into process, policy and practice. In the main, this now-centredness meant that the past added colour rather than substance, at most it offered clues about why some stubborn obstacles to social improvement were so persistent. Essentially, 1948 represented a moment of rupture, a new and hopeful beginning, in which historical context was at best a fore-echo, a prologue or an overture to the new reality. Howard Glennerster describes it, gently, as 'historical descriptions of the development of services mostly in the Whig tradition, explaining how the 1944–48 legislation had reached the summit of human achievement' (Glennerster in Bulmer *et al.*, 1989, p. 110)

Two powerful intellectual trends can be detected here. The first was a rejection of ideologically based analysis and explanation, in favour of a practical empiricism, and the second was a commitment to a positivist perspective in which there was no obvious limit to the capacity of a society to re-engineer itself in any ways it chose by general agreement and consensus, surely guided by a gently Fabian belief in rational social progress and the technocratic skills of social planners and administrators.

This has made social policy and administration an essentially applied subject, interested in understanding the world as it is perceived to be, and committed not only to trying to understand, but where necessary to change that reality. Sociological theory did not at this time figure largely in the social administration debate, although the functionalist bias of academic sociology of the time was as much corroborative of this approach as challenging. If anything, there may even have been a mistrust of theory, as encouraging endless debate about issues that can never be finally resolved, and in the meanwhile diverting energy from the more important tasks of initiating action. There is however one further distinctive feature of social policy and administration at this time, a feature which is perhaps more contested than once it was, but which still permeates, and for some people remains an important defining strand to the subject. This is a strong normative element. Although not often spelled out explicitly, social policy rests on a core of values involving ideas about equity and social justice, of fairness, on views about the nature of citizenship in a democratic society. If social policy is about action, about choices and about social change, it is these values which give a critical sense of direction. For some the origin of these values may be traced to the tradition of Christian Socialism, for others they are essentially secular and are more likely to be rooted in socialist or social democratic ideas.

This approach both to social policy as a political process and as a subject of academic study was soon to be severely challenged, in ways that reflected a wider intellectual reorientation affecting most of the social sciences and humanities. Paul Wilding's two articles identify some of the strands that helped to refocus social administration. First, there was an increasing dissatisfaction among some social administration scholars with the descriptive nature of the subject and the lack of a coherent underlying social theory. Second there was a sharpening of the wider political debates about the role and competence of the state, which challenged the more consensual atmosphere of the 1950s and 60s. These political divisions and their underlying ideological roots became central to the social policy debates of the 1980s, and remain central to the ongoing debates in the 1990s. There was growing concern about sluggish economic growth limiting revenue, while rising levels of unemployment imposed increasing, perhaps unsustainable costs, on the welfare budget. There was growing anxiety that welfare goals were in practice not being achieved and may actually be unachievable, despite ever-greater expenditure, larger staffs and administrative reorganisation.

A powerful resurgence of interest in Marxist ideas among social scientists, including economists, sociologists and historians, encouraged a perspective that gave greater emphasis to social conflict rather than consensus as a driving force for social change, and posed awkward questions for students of social policy about the neutrality of the state, and the integrity of the supposed welfare ethic. Simultaneously, feminist ideas forefronted gender rather than class relationships as a focal point of conflict, in which traditional social policy measures could be seen as reproducing oppressive gendered roles and functions. There were also the first tentative suggestions, later to become a source of major concern, that there might be environmental limits to endlessly continued economic growth and consumption. Finally, more recently, and partly as a result of ever-closer links with our European neighbours, there was a greater interest in, and willingness to learn from, the experience of other partner nations and beyond, who have evolved welfare systems of their own.

These are very large changes in intellectual focus and direction, which extended far beyond the specialist interests of the student of social policy. Certainly they forced a re-examination of the traditional assumptions of social administration, but so they did across the entire spectrum of the social sciences and the humanities.

One reflection of these new concerns among students of social policy has been a growing interest in a much more critical and analytical exploration of the historical roots of social policy. This was both an important and a difficult change of emphasis. 'Certainly the optimistic Whiggish history favoured by so many social administrators, charting the growth of government toward the nirvana of postwar Beveridgean/Keynsian consensus, contributed to the ill-preparedness of many for the recent transformation in the focus of social policy debates' (Bulmer *et al.*, 1989, p. 7). Important as the legislative programme of the 1940s was in restructuring the postwar welfare state, the roots of social policy can and should be traced much farther back in time and the experience of the 1940s and beyond must be located in a broader canvas of long-term social change and development. If social divisions and conflict are an abiding feature of social systems, then should we not try to understand them better by tracing their origins and evolutions? Social policy is no longer narrowly concerned with the organisation and administration of a range of state social services, essentially for operational reasons, but by an 'attempt to understand the roles and functions, the latent and manifest purposes, of social policy, in different kinds of society at different stages of development' (Wilding, 1983) and one might add, at different times. Many of the contemporary controversies and debates surrounding for example the Victorian Poor Law, or the Liberal reforms before the First World War, are no longer to be thought of as of minor arcane interest to the antiquarian, but are now seen to focus on fundamental issues and dilemmas that are as difficult today as ever they were. The year 1948 is perceived to be as much a continuation as a new start.

In short then, starting rather slowly in the late 1960s, but rapidly gathering force, the study of social policy (and of sociology, and politics, and history) has been transformed, as new or rediscovered social and intellectual movements emerged and came to prominence. The links between social policy and sociological and political theory are now much clearer and deeper than they were; social policy no longer works in what Hilary Rose once described as 'regal isolation' (Rose, 1981) but is now grounded in one or another theoretical and analytical framework of contemporary social science. There is less confidence in the essentially consensual nature of society and more understanding of deeply rooted social conflicts, conflicts between individuals or groups of people distinguished by class, race or gender, and conflicts of goal or purpose, for example, of reconciling the goal of improved living standards with a concern for environmental protection and sustainability.

Over the past 30 years there has amassed a substantial body of historical knowledge about the evolution of social policy, and about the underlying ideas that drove it. To a large extent this reflects changes of interest and emphasis among academic historians themselves, driven by many of the same public anxieties and concerns that were moving the social sciences. The historian Gareth Stedman-Jones, author of an important study of ideas (including social policy ideas) in late Victorian England describes his own intellectual development thus:

> 1964–5, the time at which I began research, coincided with the early stages of a leftward movement, both among students and among parts of the intelligentsia... (which) encouraged a more combative and innovative stance, both in politics and intellectual work. Of particular importance, in my own case, were the political and cultural positions pioneered and developed by the New Left Review... in intellectual approach it set its face against most indigenous traditions and styles of thought... and deliberately opened itself to heterodox theoretical currents in France, Italy and Germany... having spent some time in Paris before going to Oxford, I was

already more sympathetic to the cultural iconoclasm of the Review and its engage-
ment with continental theoretical idioms. As a historian I was already more excited
by the approaches associated with the Annales than by most of the work being
produced at the same time in Britain... in general, it seemed to me that the task of
a historian on the left was not to confine attention to the history of labour movements, oppressed classes or parties of the left, but rather to reconstruct historical
totalities. (Stedman-Jones, 1984, pp. xiii–xiv)

Here we see a repositioning of the subject-matter of historical study, asking
different questions, seeking different kinds of evidence and engaging with a
wide range of philosophical and social theory. It is one particular illustrative
example of 'a massive shift of interest on the part of historians all over the world
away from traditional political history (the narrative of the actions and policies
of rulers) and towards social history' (Burke, 1992, p. 19). Social and economic
history now have a much higher profile and credibility among historians than
they ever did. The narrow preoccupation with political history, with kings and
wars, has given ground somewhat to a broader concern with wider patterns of
social life. This in turn has required the discovery and recognition of sources of
historical evidence additional to public archives and official papers.

There has been an increasing convergence of interests between historians and
social scientists which is still at times uneasy, but where there is at least a
shared or overlapping intellectual terrain, to the great benefit of both parties
and their readers. What has been taking place is a substantial breaking down
of traditional academic boundaries, which is by no means confined to historians and sociologists. Peter Burke talks of 'a sense of common purpose
among social theorists and social historians... the terms 'historical sociology',
'historical anthropology', 'historical geography', and (rather less frequently)
'historical economics' have come into use to describe both the incorporation
of history into those disciplines and their incorporation into history'. Burke
goes on to add the cautionary note that 'convergence on the same intellectual
territory occasionally leads to border disputes... and sometimes to the coining
of different terms to describe the same phenomena' but concludes that 'it also
allows different skills and points of view to be exploited in a common enterprise' (Burke, 1992, p. 18).

Indeed some of us would argue that whereas the development of sociological theory since the late nineteenth century has helped to transform our
understanding of social processes, in recent years the baton has passed back
to those historians who have been able to absorb some of the conceptual and
methodological frameworks of the sociologists, and whose writings are
among the most stimulating and suggestive intellectual products of our time.

It is clear that the maturing of social policy and administration as a subject
of study was only one part of a much broader reorientation of academic interests and preoccupations since the 1960s, running right across the social
sciences and humanities.

Among historians we have seen the growth of interest in social and economic history, and among some of these scholars a concern with the development of social policy and of welfare states. Some have focused on the political alignments and realignments, others on political philosophies and ideas, the ideological underpinning of action. Yet others are concerned with how policy has been implemented, and the administrative machines that have been created for that purpose. All of these interests are of course shared by the social policy specialist.

There has also been a surge of historical interest in events of the relatively recent past. It is a moot point how far back into the past you have to go to become safely History, but it is certainly the case that History now boldly claims a legitimate interest in the greater part of the twentieth century. While the Victorian Poor Law has for many years been a well-researched field, the task of examining its gradual erosion during the first half of the twentieth century has been embarked upon much more recently, and there is still a great deal of work to be done. There is now a substantial body of work on the period before the First World War; the great Liberal social reforms of 1906–11 have now been extensively explored as something more than some sort of a preamble or overture to the 'real' reforms of the 1940s. Similarly the inter-war years, which were once a veritable dark age for those too young to remember them directly, are now much better appreciated, and although there is still much more work to be done on the 1930s, it is apparent how many of the reforming ideas that prevailed in the 1940s were widely discussed in that earlier period. Again, the 1940s themselves have for some years now been a subject of keen debate among historians and social scientists alike, the so-called Consensus controversy, with one viewpoint originally suggested by Titmuss (1950) and later elaborated and developed by Paul Addison (1975), and more recently contested, especially by 'revisionist' historians linked with the Society of Contemporary History (see, for example Pimlott, 1988, or Smith, 1986a). Even more recently, a refereed academic journal called *Twentieth Century British History* has started to be published, and from the outset has been publishing lengthy and highly specialised articles on a wide range of social policy questions.

An indication of how far and how fast things have moved can be gained from examining the bibliographies of two major early contributions to the history of social policy. David Roberts, an American scholar, published an important and original book in 1960 on the *Victorian Origins of the British Welfare State*. In the Preface, he notes that the Victorian period was 'alive with social reforms and bureaucratic growth', and the four tasks he set himself were 'to describe this growth, to analyze its powers and organisation, to discuss the men who became its civil servants, and to show in detail how well it worked'. But whereas studies of government, and especially parliamentary government were 'long and distinguished', studies of the welfare state were 'meager indeed'. On the first of his four themes he acknowledges the work of such authors as the Webbs and the Hammonds, and cites a number of useful biographical studies. But 'few historians have yet dealt with the second of the above aspects... No historian has dealt with the third'. As for the fourth task, Roberts suggests that the opening up of the public records of the Poor Law authorities 'has given the historian a remarkable opportunity to observe administrative conflicts in detail' (Roberts, 1960, pp. vii–ix).

It is clear that at the time Roberts felt that he was moving into largely uncharted territory; as it transpired his own book was to be an early and major contribution to what was to become an important debate among historians on the nineteenth-century Administrative Revolution, its origins, evolution and its ideological and political roots.

Compare this with the situation confronting Derek Fraser, the author of one of the first, and still the best, of the historical textbooks for an undergraduate readership, *The Evolution of the British Welfare State*. First published in 1973, a revised second edition was published in 1984. The basic structure of the first edition was retained, and the bibliographies are also arranged in a broadly similar fashion, with books and articles grouped under 23 subheadings. The 1973 edition refers to 274 books and 54 articles; the 1984 edition to 362 books and 127 articles. This gives some indication of the rapid expansion of source material over this brief period. Even more remarkable is the fact that 35 per cent of the books cited in 1984, and 59 per cent of the articles were first published during the eleven years between the first and second editions.

This suggests that just as social policy specialists were discovering an interest in the history of their own subject-matter, so this appetite was being fed by the ever-richer output from historian colleagues. This work was, and is, to be found in the form of articles in the academic learned journals; these are often on highly specialised themes and issues, but as their mass grows, so a wider and wider spectrum of social policy has become the subject of sustained and detailed historical enquiry. Then there are the historical monographs; book-length treatment usually with a bigger sweep, and covering a longer time-period. There are biographies of key figures in the history of social policy, which focus on both the life and the work. There are Marxist histories, there are feminist histories. Finally there are a number of textbooks which draw on this now rich body of source material, in an attempt to synthesise a broad overview.

At their best they incorporate a professional historian's concern with primary source materials, carefully documented and sensitively interpreted to provide the most accurate possible record of events. But the best of them are also sensitive to the key policy issues, the central dilemmas of social policy, issues of rights and responsibilities, the nature of citizenship, the juxtaposition of needs and means, of freedom and compulsion, of the public and the private. As we shall see these great dilemmas are the constant preoccupations of the social policy specialist, revisited and reworked by each successive generation, but never finally resolved.

The enrichment that this has given to the subject of social policy is hard to exaggerate. Indeed to many of the key social policy debates of recent years historians have been vital contributors. The extent to which social class conflicts have been a stimulant (or should it be a depressant?) for social policy has been explored in detail by historians. What part do changing ideas play, what are the ideological cornerstones of social policy; where do they originate, how have they changed? All of these questions have been approached by historians.

For students of social policy, getting to grips with these big issues for the first time, it can be both helpful and instructive to be able to do so by revisiting some of the great social policy debates of the past. The student discovers that there is sufficient of similarity for the eternal nature of the issues at stake to be clearly grasped, but that there are also important contrasts, differences of emphasis and of understanding, clashes of values, prejudices and preferences, differences that give the historical example its unique tone and colour. It also helps to sharpen the appreciation of the unique tone and colour of the present day, and to see the present as another refraction which will in turn be reviewed (critically, maybe caustically, certainly condescendingly) by generations of students to come.

The growing recognition of the importance of a historical understanding of the roots and development of social policy ideas and practice does not, of course, mean that the study of social policy is no more than the study of its own history. Students of social policy have interests and concerns that are the defining characteristics of their subject. The critical questions for the social policy specialist relate, as we have already indicated, to a range of core values, which are in turn reflected in the debates about the goals of social policy and the preferred methods for approaching those goals. At the most abstract level are the 'big issues', the core values that give social policy its critical sense of direction, values such as social justice, equity, or equality. These are then reflected in policy proposals, and their organising principles; who should receive services, how should they be paid for, how should they be administered, to whom are service providers accountable, and so on. Here are some of the permanent areas of policy debate, around such issues as universality or selectivity, citizen's rights or earned entitlements, contributory or means-tested systems, top-down or bottom-up systems of service delivery and accountability and so on. Here issues of social class, of gender and of race create additional cross-cutting tensions. Finally, and drawing very much on the practical and applied legacy of the 'traditional' social administration, there will still be a proper concern with the minutiae of entitlement, on the terms and conditions that may be attached, on the legal frameworks which legitimise policy and so forth. Needless to say, there is scope for disagreement, argument and debate at all stages and at all levels.

Historians may vary very considerably one from another in how much interest they take in the distinctively social policy issues of this kind. But where they do take such an interest and are sensitive to the different perspectives and viewpoints that are involved, and then can, as historians, locate these debates within the wider historical canvas, then they are able to make a very substantial contribution indeed to both areas of study.

It is with very much this vision that we set about the task of compiling this book. We wanted to locate the pressing social policy concerns of our times firmly into their historical context, as a means to a better understanding of the central issues at stake and their possible evolution during the years ahead. Our aim was to recruit a team of contributors, some of whom would be historians with a specialist interest in the evolution of social policy, while others would be social policy specialists with a keen sense of the value of grounding social policy within its history. In this way we hoped to achieve the best possible synthesis of the two academic perspectives, each informing and enriching the other, each giving the other guidelines and a sense of direction.

Each contributor has been charged with a different specific task, but the very structure of the book reveals some of the broadening of the subject that we have referred to throughout this introduction. While there are of course chapters which look carefully at each major service area in turn, they go far beyond a descriptive account of the enabling legislation, or even the supposed intentions of the lawmakers, to probe for more elusive social goals and agendas, and to acknowledge a wider range of opportunities and constraints. While there is some discussion of administrative systems, it is not assumed that such systems always achieve what they set out to achieve, or even that it is always clear what it is that they hope to achieve.

But the first half of the book is not centrally concerned with 'the study of the social services' at all, but is intended to establish the broader framework of ideas and institutions within which the services are set. Part 1 attempts an introductory overview of the entire century. John Stewart covers the unravelling of social policy from the perspectives of 'the party political context, including the role of social class; gender and age; the local state and the voluntary sector; ideological influences; and the international sector' (Stewart, below). Jim Tomlinson then covers the same period, but is essentially concerned with discussions about how welfare has been paid for, and the tensions between welfare costs and other pressures on economic resources. He brings to bear not only a keen sense of the fundamental issues of social policy, and a sensitive grasp of history, but has the added skill of the economist.

Part II comprises three chapters on the wide range of different political ideas and ideological perspectives that underlie thinking on social welfare. Norman Barry examines what are often thought of as Conservative ideas, rooted in neo-classical thought, Robert Pinker is concerned with the Liberal alternative, and especially the New Liberal thought that flowered in the late nineteenth century, and Michael Sullivan looks at the tradition of democratic socialist thought. It is never easy, and usually misleading to try to force complex bodies of ideas into rigidly separate boxes. As these chapters reveal very clearly, political ideas constitute a very tangled skein, and exploring their exposition over time helps us to unpick areas where ideas overlap and others where they conflict more sharply.

The chapters on specific service areas comprises Part III; Michael Sanderson writes about education, Helen Jones about health, Sean Glynn on employment and unemployment (an often-overlooked theme in the social policy literature), Pete Alcock on poverty and social security, and finally Norman Ginsburg on housing.

The contributors to Part IV reflect another major shift of emphasis from the social administration of the 1960s. Jane Lewis discusses the long tradition of voluntary and informal welfare systems, while Margaret May and Edward Brunsdon examine welfare services provided by commercial organisations, and another often-neglected theme in the mainstream social policy literature, the role of occupational welfare.

The book concludes with a speculative overview including the prospects and challenges facing social policy as we move into the new millennium.

PART I

The Century
Surveyed

1

The Twentieth Century: an Overview

John Stewart

Introduction

In a now famous front-page article in May 1996, the *Guardian* announced 'The End of the Welfare State'. Alongside photographs of William Beveridge and government and opposition spokesmen, the piece claimed that Conservative and Labour parties had both 'declared an end to the welfare state as it has been known for fifty years, foreshadowing a new and looser compact between the individual and the government' (the *Guardian* 8 May 1996). Mark Twain-like, this report may be premature. But it does raise questions about what we mean by 'the welfare state', and what sort of welfare provision preceded it. Hence the historical context this chapter seeks to provide. It is organised around particular themes focusing in the first instance on state policy, although it will be emphasised that this can take a number of forms; and that welfare is also provided by non-state bodies and by families and individuals.

Issues, Debates, and Contexts in Twentieth-century British Social Welfare

The formation and realisation of social policy is a complex process. It involves interactions between social institutions such as the central state and families or voluntary associations; and is further shaped and influenced by social factors such as gender, class, and age. This might suggest that welfare provision is a highly contested area, given the divergent interests of the various actors and institutions involved. These complexities are echoed in the public debate over welfare; and the academic debate over the history, nature, and aims of social policy. One important dimension of such debates is how, and to what ends, resources are to be allocated within society. Social policy is, in other words, closely bound up with economic policy. The economic dimensions of welfare are dealt with in this volume by Jim Tomlinson. It is worth reminding ourselves, however, of three important economic matters which impinge directly on the issues discussed in this chapter.

First, the adoption of particular economic strategies – such as Keynesianism or monetarism – may crucially affect the volume of resources made available for welfare. Second, one of the century's most obvious characteristics – outside the two world wars and the quarter of a century after 1945 – has been the persistence of high levels of unemployment. The perceived need to provide the unemployed with at least a subsistence-level standard of living has implications for the amount of resources available for other welfare functions. Third, one consequence of the Edwardian Liberal welfare reforms was the creation of a symbiotic link between the central state's economic policy and its social policy (Crowther, 1988, p. 14). This was a shift away from the previous situation whereby social welfare was, for the most part, the responsibility of local bodies – such as Poor Law Boards of Guardians – with revenue-raising powers for this purpose. Furthermore, this century has seen an apparently inexorable rise in welfare expenditure, both in absolute terms and as a proportion of Gross Domestic Product (GNP) (Glennerster, 1995, pp. 221–2; Middleton, 1996a, p. 98). Welfare provision has, therefore, undoubtedly become a central feature of both society and economy.

With these general economic points in mind, the following categories have been adopted as a means of unravelling modern British social policy: the party political context, including the role of social class; gender and age; the local state and the voluntary sector; ideological influences; and the international context. This is not to suggest that no other analytical categories might be employed. It is increasingly evident, for example, that race and ethnicity have played an important role in welfare, particularly since the Second World War. The National Health Service, for instance, has depended largely on immigrant labour, usually on low wages; and concepts which may influence social welfare attitudes, such as 'the underclass', can clearly have racial overtones. Hence, argues Law, the 'racialised construction of the British welfare state'. More work is needed, as Helen Jones points out, by historians and other social scientists in this area for a fuller understanding of the modern welfare system (Jones, 1994, p. 193; Law, 1996, pp. 154, 59, Ch. 2 and *passim*).

Having examined factors central to social policy formation, we then discuss the problems of definition inherent in the term 'welfare state'; and the notion of 'consensus' when applied to post-Second World War welfare policies and institutions. The issues raised have considerable contemporary relevance, given the current wide-ranging debate on the aims and future of British social welfare.

Party Politics and Social Class

The period from the 1867 Reform Act to the final achievement of full adult suffrage in 1928 saw the progressive enfranchisement of the mass of the population. This made the working class and its condition and concerns increasingly central in social discourse: for example in the last two decades of the nineteenth century 'unemployment' came to be formally defined and took on its contemporary meaning. Of particular note was the 1918 Representation of the People Act which, in addition to granting full manhood and partial female suffrage, also gave paupers, previously a politically stigmatised group, the vote. So ended the principle that those receiving public money be denied the franchise (Harris, 1990a, p. 74, 1972, p. 4).

The political rise of the working class – organisationally manifested by the Labour Party's formation in 1900 – was a significant factor in the development of twentieth-century social welfare. It was significant, moreover, not only in itself, but also in its effect on the other major political parties. The Liberal welfare reforms of 1906–14, for example, may be partly explained as a response by one party of the 'left' to the emergence of another (Hay, 1983, pp. 25–9).

By the end of the First World War Labour was effectively the main opposition party, forming minority governments in 1924 and 1929/31. The Labour Party was part of Churchill's wartime coalition – successfully having the term 'social security' inserted into the Allies' declaration of war aims, the Atlantic Charter – and after the 1945 election formed its first majority administration. The Labour administrations of 1945–51 inaugurated some of the principal institutions of the 'welfare state'; it was primarily under Labour, in other words, that what has been described as the 'classic welfare state' was created (Digby, 1989, Ch. 4). Until recently, when matters have become increasingly fluid, the Labour Party has broadly subscribed to the principles of the 1942 Beveridge Report, conventionally viewed as the 'founding document' of the welfare state. Consequently the governments of 1964–70 and 1974–79 attempted, with varying degrees of success, to consolidate the achievements of 1945–51.

It is therefore tempting to see modern welfare provision as primarily developed by parties of the left – the Liberals in the early part of the century and Labour since – in response to a politically rising working class. While a persuasive argument, which has had a huge impact on the historiography of British social welfare, this temptation needs to be resisted. Politically, this century has been dominated by the Conservative Party. Conservative governments have, therefore, been responsible for the enactment and administration of much of the century's social welfare.

Conservatism has, historically, encompassed two main strands – paternalism and *laissez-faire*. Broadly speaking, the former is in favour of state intervention in order to achieve or maintain social stability. This was important in the nineteenth century, and should not be discounted in the twentieth. The 1944 Butler Education Act, for example, can be seen as enhancing and expanding state educational provision while fending off more radical proposals from both left and right – a triumph of both reform and conservatism (Lowe, 1993, pp. 196–203). *Laissez-faire*, on the other hand, is hostile to state welfare and in favour of 'free market' solutions to social problems. Hence the significance of the 'New Right' gaining the initiative in the Conservative Party in the 1970s, and the accompanying shift in attitude towards state-provided welfare.

Social groups other than the working class have, furthermore, an interest in social policy, and have often benefited disproportionately from its implementation. It is not only the working class which manifests or is a beneficiary of 'social solidarity' (Baldwin, 1990, pp. 8ff.). As was quickly recognised by analysts such as Richard Titmuss, the British middle class has done well out of postwar welfare reforms. This has political implications, especially for the Conservatives, who draw much of their support from this social group. Government policy between 1979 and 1997, for instance, attempted to favour services 'extensively used by the middle classes' thereby conflicting with and in practice attenuating 'other policy goals', including that of reduced government expenditure (Titmuss, 1976b, pp. 208–9; Le Grand and Winter, 1986, p. 427).

The middle class has played a further role in shaping twentieth-century welfare provision through the operation of professional groups such as the British Medical Association. These have vested interests in how particular policies are decided and implemented, and how administrative power is subsequently distributed. Hence the BMA's oppositional attitude to the 1911 National Insurance Act and the 1946 National Health Service Act and, given its professional power, its ability to win on both occasions concessions from elected governments (Gilbert, 1966, Ch. 6; Perkin, 1989, pp. 343–8).

We also need to acknowledge that social policy is 'not just a matter of government legislation. Inaction is just as definite a policy as action' (Glennerster, 1995, p. 149). Clearly this could be applied to administrations of any political persuasion. However, given that the Conservative Party has dominated modern politics, and given its ideological strand disinclined to intervene in economy and society, this observation has particular resonance for Britain's party of the right. In the 1930s the Conservative-dominated National Government was frequently criticised for its failure to address social problems. It defended its (in)actions by stressing the inefficacy of government intervention and the need to allow the economy to recover through the working of its own mechanisms.

Important theoretical and comparative work – notably by Esping-Andersen – further suggests that any 'social democratic' explanation of the origins of 'welfare states' is problematic in its adoption of a linear and monocausal approach. As already noted in the British context, the middle class too has an interest in state welfare, and this is borne out by comparable developments in other countries. Comparisons also reveal that Britain's welfare system has features more often associated with 'liberal' welfare regimes, such as that of the United States, than with 'social democratic' welfare regimes, such as those of Scandinavia. The predominant characteristics of the former are 'means-tested assistance, modest universal transfers, or modest social insurance plans'. Great emphasis is placed on the market's role in satisfying needs, with welfare aimed primarily at the very poor. The latter, by contrast, seek to dispense with the market as a means of allocating social resources, place great emphasis on universal programmes of welfare and full employment policy, and pursue a welfare state promoting 'an equality of the highest standards, not an equality of minimal needs' (Esping-Andersen, 1990, pp. 26–9). It is therefore evident that any simple correlation of the 'rise' of the working class and the 'rise' of the 'welfare state' is in need of considerable qualification.

Gender and Age

Politics is not, moreover, simply a matter of the role of parties or particular social classes. Women's emergence on to the national political stage has been a notable feature of the last 100 years. While the full female parliamentary franchise was not achieved until 1928, women were already active on local bodies with important welfare functions. Female Poor Law Guardians took 'a particular interest in improving workhouse sick wards'; and women councillors, through their concern with infant mortality, had by 1918 'assisted in the creation of nearly a thousand maternity and infant clinics'. Women were also numerically preponderant in expanding occupations such as teaching, and central to the wide range of nineteenth-century philanthropic organisations with welfare functions. They had, therefore, a key role as welfare 'providers' (Prochaska, 1980; Digby, 1996, pp. 221–2). In terms of provision, gender remains highly significant, not least in occupational terms in services such as health and education, where lower paid and lower status workers have always tended to be women. Of even greater significance is that most welfare provision by women has historically been through the institution of the family, and thereby unpaid. During the Edwardian era, for example, pressure was exerted on working-class women to take greater care of the 'children of the nation' in order to stem the widely feared impact of 'racial deterioration' (Davin, 1978).

Women may also be targeted as welfare 'consumers'. With the expansion of the parliamentary franchise in 1918, for instance, the major political parties sought to use social policy to enhance their appeal to this new part of the electorate (Stewart, 1996, pp. 169–70). As with the provision of welfare, therefore, so too is consumption shaped by gender concerns. In important instances these have reinforced, deliberately or otherwise, power relations and perceptions of women's 'proper role'. Prior to the 1940s, welfare's overt discrimination – one notable instance being state health insurance – disadvantaged most women. This became apparent with the introduction of the NHS, and had in turn implications for that service's costs. Even the apparently 'universalist' welfare policies since the 1940s might be seen as having inbuilt assumptions about women's role and status. State family allowances, first enacted in 1945, assumed a domestic role for mothers while reinforcing the 'male breadwinner logic' whereby policy was to be geared towards assuring that under most circumstances it was the husband and father's responsibility to provide for his dependants. Consequently, family allowances were always perceived as a subordinate part of the welfare system (Pedersen, 1993, Conclusion).

It would be wrong, however, to suggest that women are simply passive recipients of social policy. Their historic role as 'providers' and their increasing political involvement from the end of the last century suggest a more complex situation. Gender analyses have added considerably to our understanding of modern social welfare, although its exact relationship with other causal factors is controversial and still to be fully worked out, as the case of old-age pensions noted below illustrates. What is clear, however, is that perceptions of gender roles have historically played a powerful role in social policy. Assumptions about women's role in the family have helped structure particular welfare policies. Furthermore, such policies in themselves have helped reinforce society's views on gender by, for example, suggesting that childcare is the particular responsibility of women. Ascribed gender roles therefore shape, and are shaped by, social welfare.

Alongside rapidly expanding studies of gender can be noted another social 'division' with ramifications for welfare, but which has received much less historiographical attention – age. One characteristic of this century's social policy has, since the 1908 Old-Age Pensions Act, been provision for the elderly in the form of state pensions. At the other end of the spectrum, it has been argued that the histories of children and of social policy are inseparable, and that each cannot be properly understood without reference to the other (Hendrick, 1994, p. xi). More generally, the age structure of the population can have welfare implications, as in contemporary concerns over an ageing population and its consequences for pensions and medical care. The weight of social policy directed at particular age groups therefore depends on their perceived 'value' at any particular time. During the First World War, for instance, the Local Government Board, partly through the prompting of organisations such as the Babies of the Empire Society, offered local authorities large subsidies to enhance their infant welfare provision. This was clearly motivated by concerns over future 'racial fitness' (Jones, 1994, pp. 40–1). The central point is that from around the late nineteenth century society became increasingly age-stratified. In this process social policy was both cause, through its separating out of particular age groups for particular attention; and consequence, through the perceived need to cater for specific age groups for broader social ends.

Age, it might therefore be suggested, is a factor in social policy in its own right. It can, however, be usefully put alongside gender, for two reasons. First, the introduction of state old-age pensions provides a case study of welfare provision where it is argued that gender was not a prime causal factor, despite the majority of pension recipients being women. This again stresses the need to tease out the nuances of social policy formation and implementation (Thane, 1996).

Second, the care of both the young and the elderly inevitably raises the question of the family, and of women's place therein. This, it should be noted, is despite the logical distinction which can be made between each of these social categories. Families have historically cared for more young and old people than the state. Hence any governmental assumption that families will take on this welfare responsibility is in itself a policy strategy, a further example of the point made earlier about state 'inaction'. Such 'informal care' has always been undertaken primarily by women, hence its strong gender dimension. Informal care plays a crucial welfare role, and is almost certainly expanding as demographic and political changes affect existing state welfare systems. The complex interactions between young people, women and the family have led to an historiographical debate about 'maternalist' – as opposed to patriarchal – welfare states, particularly in the earlier part of the century when women's role in influencing state policy has been increasingly recognised. Equally there has been an emphasis on the centrality of family policy in welfare provision throughout the century as a whole (Crowther, 1982; Bock and Thane, 1991; Koven and Michel, 1993; Pedersen, 1993; Glennerster, 1995, pp. 152–3). Debates about the role and future of the family, and how social policy should cater for it, are, therefore, nothing new. In such debates, deep-rooted and longstanding assumptions are clearly evident.

The Local State and the Voluntary Sector

Gender analysis has also proved invaluable in illuminating the relationship between the central state and other providers of welfare. Older accounts of British social policy tended to stress the rise of 'collectivism'. One aspect of this was the role played by reforming civil servants and, at certain points, academics, in an expanding state bureaucracy. Such considerations should not be entirely discounted. William Beveridge, both civil servant and academic, is famed as one of the 'founders' of the 'welfare state'. The historical nature of women's welfare activities, however, provides a useful qualification to this rather 'Whiggish' interpretation, and to an overemphasis on the role of the central state.

As earlier suggested, women were important providers of welfare through local politics, philanthropic organisations, or both. This in turn illustrates the historically 'weak' nature of the British central state. At least until the Second World War, local authorities and institutions – such as the Poor Law in its various guises – provided a wide range of social services. In some fields this continued after the apparently centralising tendencies of the 1940s: the housing programme, for example, was carried out by local authorities, just as it had been after the First World War. Of course as Jim Tomlinson shows elsewhere in this volume, it is evident that the financing of welfare has shifted from the locality to the centre in the course of the century, and this has restricted the ability of local bodies to either supply welfare or to act autonomously in welfare provision. Nonetheless, local government retains administrative control of important welfare functions such as education and the personal social services, and a proportion of their funding continues to derive from local taxation. This too is a corrective to overemphasis on the central state's role.

Furthermore, Britain has – in marked contrast to many other European societies – a long tradition of welfare 'voluntarism', of a 'mixed economy of welfare'. Beveridge is best known for his part in the creation of the postwar 'welfare state', but was also a committed advocate of voluntarism. His *Voluntary Action* appeared in 1948, the very year in which the 'welfare state' formally came into being. Prior to the First World War, annual contributions to registered charities exceeded annual expenditure on the principal institution of public welfare, the Poor Law; and the Great War itself saw a rapid expansion of charitable activity (Beveridge, 1948; Harris, 1990a, p. 68; Lewis, 1996, p. 175). Within the mixed economy of welfare non-governmental organisations continue to play a crucial part. The National Society for the Prevention of Cruelty to Children, founded in the late nineteenth century, has always played a key part in providing and coordinating child welfare services (Hendrick, 1994, pp. 50–60). Voluntary bodies can also act as pressure groups for particular causes. The 'rediscovery of poverty' of the 1960s saw the formation of organisations more concerned with campaigning than with direct provision. Among these were the Child Poverty Action Group, another influential player in child welfare policy; and Shelter, which sought to raise public awareness of the hitherto undiscovered or ignored housing problem (Timmins, 1995, pp. 256–8).

Relations between the voluntary sector and the state have certainly fluctuated over time. The century as a whole has seen both the persistence of voluntarism and a tendency for it to react to a 'growing and more positive state presence' by cooperation and convergence. However voluntarism has recently undergone a further 'revival', alongside the informal and private sectors, the latter most notably in pensions and health care. Post-1979 Conservative governments have committed themselves to welfare provision through not only the market and the family, but also voluntary bodies. Each of these was highly acceptable to New Right ideology although in the event the matter has proved more problematical than anticipated. There is little doubt, for example, that the state sector remains predominant; that there are inherent contradictions in New Right approaches to non-state welfare; and that leaders of certain voluntary organisations have been among the most vociferous opponents of New Right welfare ideology (Finlayson, 1994, pp. 6, 166, Ch. 4, Conclusion; Lewis, 1996, p. 155).

Ideological Influences

The state's relationship with other welfare providers, and its willingness or otherwise to act in particular circumstances, raises the question of ideology's role in welfare. It is a crude caricature to suggest that the nineteenth century was simply and entirely dominated by *laissez-faire*, with its emphasis on individualism and hostility to state intervention (Taylor, 1972). Nonetheless *laissez-faire* did have a powerful impact on social policy, especially the Poor Law, the century's central piece of welfare legislation; and on the related preoccupation with self-help and voluntarism. These attitudes retained their hold into the twentieth century. The National Insurance Scheme introduced in 1911, for example, involved contributions from the state, employers, and employees. One way of viewing employee contributions is as institutionalised, and compulsory, saving: in other words, self-help (Gilbert, 1966, Ch. 5). However 'Victorian values' have also had other, more subtle, influences on subsequent policy formation – for instance in the collectivism of the Friendly Societies, key players in shaping and providing welfare in the early part of the century (Harris, 1992, pp. 174ff.).

From around the 1870s intellectual challenges to *laissez-faire* began to emerge. Among these were 'New Liberalism', stressing a more 'organic' view of society and an increased role for the state in ensuring that individuals were not overly disadvantaged by circumstances not of their own making. Welfare measures aimed at particular groups were part of New Liberalism's agenda, although there was no fundamental questioning of property rights. Rather, New Liberalism sought to ameliorate the 'social problem', so making British capitalism more efficient in an increasingly hostile and competitive world, as well as acting as an antidote to the 'rise of socialism'. The zenith of New Liberalism – at least in a party sense – was the Edwardian era when the Liberal governments introduced wide-ranging social reforms. These were innovative not least in their circumvention of the Poor Law, an institution which was not going to die easily but which henceforth was increasingly restricted as to the sectors of the population with which it dealt. It is also noteworthy that many early Labour leaders did not disagree with the 'progressive' ideology of New Liberalism, only how, and by whom, it was to be carried out (Freeden, 1978; Pugh, 1993, Ch. 6).

Liberalism in the party sense was in severe trouble after the First World War while Labour, although the main opposition party, never formed a majority administration before 1945. It was therefore the Conservatives who shaped inter-war social policy and did so largely, although by no means entirely, under the influence of the 'Treasury View'. This stressed 'traditional' – and very nineteenth-century – policies of retrenchment and public expenditure cuts in the face of economic depression. The extent to which this was successful is another matter – welfare expenditure continued to rise in the inter-war period. Similarly, Conservative administrations did not seriously attempt to dismantle existing welfare systems, and although the overall picture is one of inertia, in some areas – for example housing – improvements were made (Peden, 1988, pp. 27–9; Digby, 1989, p. 49; Middleton, 1996a, p. 98).

However, despite the Conservatives' political dominance, Liberalism continued to have considerable impact on welfare thought, notably through John Maynard Keynes and William Beveridge. The former's economic theories questioned whether the free market economy truly was a self-regulating mechanism. This implied the need for government intervention to 'save' capitalism, for example by 'managing' the economy to reduce unemployment. Beveridge's ideas – at least as expressed in his famous 1942 Report (Cmd 6404) – stressed the desirability of more comprehensive social security coverage to protect all individuals from misfortunes such as unemployment, and were crucially underpinned by the Keynesian strategy of economic management to ensure full employment (Harris, 1977, Ch. 16; Peden, 1988). Together, the arguments of Keynes and Beveridge were embraced by the Labour Party during the 1940s, forming the intellectual foundations of its postwar 'New Jerusalem'.

The extent to which the Keynes/Beveridge paradigm became a consensus is a matter of considerable debate, and is dealt with separately below. By the 1970s the New Right, rejecting social and economic interventionism, sought to 'roll back the frontiers of the state' in the field of welfare by promoting the role of, for example, private sector and family provision. This has proved more difficult than anticipated. However, the related phenomena of an economic crisis throughout the western world – exemplified by the Labour government's appeal to the International Monetary Fund in 1976; and the advance among the major western states of New Right ideas – as witnessed by the election of the Thatcher government in 1979 – pushed attitudes to social policy into a new era.

The International Context

The British experience is not, therefore, isolated from the wider international context. Approaches to welfare have, for example, been influenced by other countries' experiences. The Liberal welfare reforms of 1906–14 owed a debt to German precedents – Lloyd George famously visited Germany to examine its welfare system – most obviously in the area of health insurance. More recently, New Right ideas on 'workfare' have gained inspiration from the United States (Hennock, 1987; King, 1995). Concerns about international competitiveness – economic, imperial, and military – and the impact of 'foreign' ideologies have also been important in certain periods. In the Edwardian era, fears over the lessons of the Boer War and the related issue of 'racial deterioration' influenced those Liberal welfare reforms targeting health and children. During the late 1930s, a period of high international tension, debates about physical education in schools were informed by schemes undertaken by foreign dictatorships, although the actual outcome was highly ambiguous (Hay, 1983, pp. 43, 54; Welshman, 1996, pp. 39–47).

A number of commentators, most famously Titmuss, have argued that war has been central to social policy formation (Titmuss, 1950). This interpretation has suggested that the state has felt it necessary to enact welfare reforms during, or in the immediate aftermath of, major conflicts: to enhance current or future military efficiency; to 'reward' citizens for their participation in the war effort; as a result of rising expectations on the part of particular groups, especially the working class; as a consequence of increased 'social solidarity' during wartime throughout society as a whole. The Boer War and the First World War led to wide-ranging debates about welfare, and in certain areas new policies were implemented – for example local authority housing after 1918 (Hay, 1983, p. 18; Crowther, 1988, Ch. 3). During the 1940s – the decade of both the creation of the 'welfare state' and the Second World War – a strong case can be made for a 'close association between warfare and welfare' (Briggs, 1961a, p. 221). And, as has recently been argued, there is scope for historical investigation into the impact of the 'Cold War' on domestic politics, and thereby on social policy. It may be that postwar welfare policies in Britain, and in other European states, had as part of their agenda the creation of internal stability to counter what was perceived, until very recently, as the external threat of Communism (Jones, 1996, p. 47).

Nonetheless, issues remain to be resolved in relating war and peace to welfare programmes. The emergence of 'welfare states' in the 1940s – in both Britain and certain other European countries – does not necessarily mean that their origins lie in that decade, nor that they were brought about by war. The obvious counter-example is neutral Sweden's highly developed welfare system. Furthermore, a number of historians of social policy have drawn attention to 'the considerable continuity between wartime policies and pre-war thinking' (Smith, 1986a, p. x). This in turn has implications for the idea of a postwar 'consensus'.

The 'Welfare State' and 'Consensus'

Debates such as that over the impact of war on welfare emphasise the highly contested nature of social policy. This leads us to directly address matters which previously have been only implied. We have seen that welfare can be provided not just by the central state, but also by the local state, voluntary organisations, the market, and informal care. Similarly, it has been argued that a range of factors must be taken into account for a historical understanding of welfare policy. This suggests that there is no simple, linear process resulting in the creation of a 'welfare state', nor any monocausal explanation.

It is therefore now difficult to agree with some older welfare histories – such as Maurice Bruce's *The Coming of the Welfare State*, first published in 1961 – which emphasised evolution towards state collective action embracing the whole community (Bruce, 1968, pp. 7, 13). Similarly, there are problems in fully accepting theories of welfare, such as those of Marshall, which see the 'welfare state' as the final achievement of full citizen rights. Marshall argued that British society had moved through certain 'stages', each characterised by the gaining of particular 'rights'. Specifically, these were 'civil rights', such as those of individuals to freedom of speech and a fair trial; 'political rights', principally participation in elections; and 'social rights', that is, access to some form of basic social security. The achievement of social rights would lead to the abolition of poverty, and allow individuals to fully participate in the activities of their society. In the late twentieth century, and given the issues discussed in this chapter, it is difficult to take quite such an optimistic view of the development of modern British history (Marshall, 1950).

And, as is generally acknowledged, we need to examine closely the premises on which analyses of twentieth-century British social welfare were based, and the historical period from which they derive: in the case of Marshall, in the optimism about the 'welfare state' in the immediate aftermath of its creation. Similarly, Asa Briggs, writing in the early 1960s, distinguished between a 'social service state' employing 'communal resources... to abate poverty and to assist those in distress'; and a 'welfare state', concerned 'not merely with the abatement of class differences or needs of scheduled groups but with equality of treatment and the aspirations of citizens as voters with equal shares of electoral power'. For Briggs, the Second World War had been crucial in shifting the balance from the selectivity of the former to the universality of the latter. While an influential attempt to arrive at a definition of the 'welfare state', many would now question the notions of universality and citizen rights central to this argument (Briggs, 1961a, pp. 228, 257; Thane, 1990a, pp. 12–13).

To further complicate matters, it is also necessary to ask what exactly we mean by 'welfare state', an expression impossible to avoid in any discussion of modern social policy. Originally a term of abuse directed against the Weimar Republic's social programme, the phrase began to be used more positively in Britain from the early 1940s, so making the contrast with her 'warfare' opponents. However, it was only later in that decade that politicians began to systematically employ the term. What they had in mind, therefore, were the reforms and institutions of the 1940s – Anne Digby's 'classic welfare state' (Lowe, 1993, pp. 10–11).

While the expression's historical origins are important, it is still necessary to seek a more precise meaning. We have already encountered one definition, that of Briggs. Rodney Lowe suggests that there have always been 'five core social services' central to the welfare state: social security, education, health, housing, and the personal social services (Lowe, 1994, pp. 2–3). Emphasis on these should not obscure the point made by Pat Thane, that 'a high proportion of the activities of the modern state has some welfare content'. In particular, the state may also pursue welfare policies through labour market regulation and through the fiscal system, and has done so at least since the Edwardian era when, as noted, the economic and social policies of the central state became intimately linked (Thane, 1989b, p. 143). In respect of taxation, this point was forcibly made by Titmuss, who traced the rise of 'fiscal welfare' back to the early part of the century. He further noted taxation policy's relationship to changing perceptions of the relationship between the state, the family, and the individual; and that fiscal policy could no longer be thought of 'simply as a means of benefiting the poor at the expense of the rich' (Titmuss, 1976a, pp. 45–50).

In truth, however, there is, as Lowe and others argue, 'no agreement over what a welfare state is'. How the 'welfare state' is both defined and analysed will depend to a considerable extent on the ideological and historical position of the analyst (Fraser, 1984, Foreword; Lowe, 1993, part I; Lowe, 1994a, p. 1). Definitions of the 'welfare state' also feed into debates about the level of continuity between social policy prior to and after the 1940s; the exact nature of the 'classic welfare state'; and its relationship to the events of the last two decades. Do we, for example, still have a 'welfare state' as defined by the social welfare institutions of the late 1940s? Is this question no longer particularly relevant? Has concern with the nature of the 'classic welfare state' made us over-preoccupied with the past at the expense of asking what kind of welfare policies should be pursued for current and future generations?

One way of approaching such issues is through the debate over 'consensus', another notoriously difficult term to define. In a useful commentary, Kavanagh suggests that 'consensus' is not a 'precise concept', but rather a convenient way of referring to a number of overlapping phenomena:

> shared values among elites, continuity of policies in government, consultation between government and groups, and agreement on which policies are 'non-

starters' or to be excluded, as well as elite accord on policy objectives and means. (Kavanagh, 1992, pp. 178–9)

Specifically in the field of social welfare, proponents of the idea of consensus argue that during the 1940s agreement on the need to reform British society became common political currency. Although it was the Labour governments of 1945–51 which created most of the institutions of the 'welfare state', this was something with which Conservatives did not fundamentally disagree. While there continued to be disputes between the major parties, both nonetheless subscribed to the Keynes/Beveridge paradigm – a managed economy and universal, comprehensive social services. As perhaps its most persuasive advocate, Paul Addison, puts it: 'the new consensus of the war years was positive and purposeful' and: 'the postwar consensus… was real enough while it lasted, and admirable in its consequences' (Addison, 1994, pp. 14, 292).

Historiographical problems began to arise, however, for example in attempting to fix the chronological boundaries of 'consensus'. Lowe concludes that 'consensus – defined as an historically unusual degree of agreement – was not a mirage in the 1940s', but is sceptical about its continuance in any real sense into the 1950s and beyond (Lowe, 1990, pp. 180–2, 156–7). Other commentators argue that consensus persisted down to the 1970s, when a combination of economic crisis and the advent of a radical Conservative administration shattered the postwar consensus, a view supported by Margaret Thatcher herself.

This powerful notion of consensus in postwar welfare – in itself partly a product of the socioeconomic and political upheavals of the 1970s – therefore has both contemporary and historical meaning, and continues to have its supporters, although most commentators are aware of its inherent problems. Nicholas Timmins, for example, while accepting the need to challenge any view of 'a Golden Age in which a lavishly funded welfare system operated in a glow of consensus', is equally concerned to question 'the obverse view… that there never was any real agreement about ends and means, and that the Conservatives always did have a blueprint for breaking the thing up'. He adds that even before 1979 the Conservatives had controlled the welfare state for a similar length of time to Labour, and been responsible for 'some of its most expansionary phases' (Timmins, 1995, pp. 3–4). Timmins' qualifications nonetheless suggest that the idea of consensus is now highly contested.

Charles Webster questions the concept's usefulness in his work on the historical development of one of the welfare state's central institutions, the NHS. He suggests that a 'good case can be made for a coalition between labour and the senior civil service' at the time of the service's creation; that these two groups interacted; and that their commitment to some form of national health service pre-dated the Second World War. Webster further argues, however, that 'it is difficult to sustain the argument for a more wide-spread consensus in the evolution of the NHS'. Ultimately the consensus view lacks 'historical credibility' (Webster, 1990, pp. 149, 151).

Webster extends this argument to a crucial era of Conservative control of the NHS, 1951–64. Here he finds 'little support for the idea of a sustained consensus of support for the NHS as the principal pillar of the welfare state'. On the contrary, the period saw a 'substantial attack' on the service, although pragmatic political considerations prevented the implementation of some of the more far-reaching proposals. Consequently a critical analysis of the Conservative governments' record is essential to an understanding of current predicaments in the NHS, and the welfare state generally. Webster's analysis can be usefully contrasted with that of Rudolf Klein, who emphasises the strong consensual elements in postwar health policy, at least until the advent of the Thatcher administration (Webster, 1994, pp. 69–72; Klein, 1995, pp. xii–xiii).

The debate over 'consensus' is therefore unresolved, but despite criticisms it is a concept still widely employed in political science and history texts (for example Childs, 1995, p. 97; H. Jones, 1996, pp. 44–5). For the purposes of this chapter it raises important, and interrelated, questions about modern British social welfare. Overemphasis on consensus can, by stressing the particular circumstances of postwar Britain, obscure longer-term continuities. The Beveridge Report, for example, was largely predicated on the need to consolidate the existing system of national insurance, initiated before the First World War. Similarly, it has been argued that the steps taken towards a National Health Service in the 1940s were the 'natural continuation of a pre-existing trend' (Webster, 1988a, p. 2; Lowe, 1993, p. 126). Hence it is crucial not to understate pre-1939 developments in welfare provision, which in turn calls into question the Second World War's transformative effect on social policy.

The idea of consensus may also obscure the nature of provision after 1945 by implying that through political agreement most of postwar Britain's social problems were resolved. But however much the 'classic welfare state' may have aimed at universalism and non-selectivity, these were never fully achieved. Law suggests that even the most apparently 'universalist' welfare state institution, the NHS, has failed to meet 'the health needs of black minority groups', and that the 'normalisation of racism in welfare state policies' is part of a wider historical process of racial and ethnic exclusion (Law, 1996, pp. 154, 160).

National Assistance was originally assumed to be a short-term measure – a final 'safety net' – for those who fell outside the national insurance system. Instead National Assistance, and its various successors, have been a permanent feature of postwar social policy, catering to growing numbers of welfare recipients. Their expansion, and their adherence to a means-testing ethos stretching back to the nineteenth century, in themselves undermine the alleged universalism and insurance base of the postwar welfare state. Unsurprisingly, therefore, the stigma associated with poor relief has carried over into certain parts of the 'welfare state'. Similarly, the 'rediscovery of poverty' during the 1960s raised profound issues about the efficacy and coverage of supposedly universalist social welfare (Lowe, 1993, pp. 47–8; Timmins, 1995, pp. 255ff.). All this again stresses the idea of longer-term continuities.

Defences of, and attacks on, the 'welfare state' have evoked the notion of consensus. The Fabian academic and policy advisor Brian Abel-Smith supported consensus, and deprecated its erosion. In 1980, shortly after the formation of the first Thatcher administration, he suggested that proposed government spending plans would 'end the postwar Butskellite consensus on the welfare state' wherein debate had been about 'how much to spend on further developments'. The proposed social services cuts would 'polarise the nation' (Abel-Smith, 1980, pp. 17, 21).

The New Right, by contrast, argued that consensus had weakened Britain's postwar performance and created a 'dependency culture', for example by the introduction of universal benefits. Hence the need to reject full employment as an aim of government policy and to introduce greater selectivity into the welfare system. Such analysis received support from some historians, most notably Correlli Barnett in works such as *The Audit of War*. This argued that resources allocated to welfare after 1945 by governments of both major parties were responsible for Britain's postwar decline as a world power. Consequently generous social policies, far from aiding international competitiveness, actually hindered it (Barnett, 1996; for a critique, Harris, 1990b).

One example of how this was addressed politically concerns the already-noted postwar trend towards greater use of means-tested benefits, and the consequent questioning of the universalism and insurance base of the 'welfare state'. This has been accelerated by the 'attack on national insurance' of the 1980s, particularly in the wake of the Fowler Review, with the ending of Treasury contributions to the National Insurance Fund in 1988 – a notable milestone in British social welfare history. The shift away from national insurance has involved, as a corollary, an even greater significance for means-tested benefits: many unemployed claimants, for example, have either exhausted insurance benefits or never been entitled to them, a situation strikingly similar to that of the interwar period (Hill, 1990, pp. 58–64).

The notion of consensus has therefore been used since the 1970s to promote particular political agenda with specific policy implications. The welfare strategy of post-1979 Conservative governments has been largely predicated on the need for the abolition of consensus. From a very different political standpoint it has been argued – from the perspective of the mid-1990s – that over-concentration on consensus resulted in an 'informed opinion unprepared to react to the radical policy initiatives' after 1979. Associated with this was a neglect of the historic roots of Thatcherism, namely late

1940s Conservative policy (Webster, 1994, p. 72). Consensus is, therefore, more than an esoteric academic debate, a reminder of how perceptions of history can shape current politics and policies.

Emphasis on consensus, as Webster's work on the NHS has shown, can also lead to an underestimation of the highly contested nature of social policy formation. The resolving of such conflicts represents 'consensus' only inasmuch as all disputes in a democratic society have, ultimately, to find a politically acceptable solution. It does not mean that those 'defeated' will necessarily come to support the adopted policy. Conflict was not confined to the early years of the 'welfare state', nor did it simply take place between government and opposition. In the mid-1950s, a bitter battle occurred within the Conservative administration over welfare expenditure, resulting in the resignation of the proto-monetarist Chancellor, Peter Thorneycroft, in 1958. On one level this might suggest that Macmillan's government was committed to the continuance and consolidation of the welfare state. But as historical examination has shown, the episode illustrates the limitations of postwar consensus, which was both fragile and 'essentially passive, evading rather than addressing the country's fundamental problems'. In the longer term, it was the welfare state's destruction rather than construction which was to become 'the object of 'conviction' politics' (Lowe, 1989, pp. 524–5 and *passim*).

Conclusion

This chapter began by quoting a newspaper article. As will now be apparent, the terms and chronology the latter employed are subject to historical debate and analysis, in itself an indicator of social policy's highly contested and politicised nature. As has also been stressed, in its actual realisation welfare provision is shaped by the complex interaction of a range of factors and institutions. The development of modern British social welfare has not simply been a linear progression towards increasingly collectivist provision: on the contrary, periods of reaction against state welfare – such as that since 1979 – are as important and as characteristic of the century as the great 'advances' of the Edwardian era and of the 1940s. Welfare provision is not divorced from the broader historical context but, on the contrary, helps shape it and is shaped by it. The specific policy outcomes and practices which derive from the interactions of various factors and the contexts in which they operate for the most part display elements of both continuity and change, albeit in different proportions in different circumstances.

The welfare state of the 1990s is not the same as that of the 1940s – even allowing for problems of definition; far less is it congruent with the pre-welfare state provision of 1900. Nor, however, is it completely divorced from these earlier forms. Certain attitudes of our Victorian predecessors remain embedded in welfare policies, and may even be experiencing something of a revival, at least in their cruder manifestations. This in turn reminds us that some contemporary arguments hostile to state welfare have a long historical lineage (Johnson, 1986). Hence the need for an understanding of both change, and why it occurs; and the persistence of certain attitudes and practices. Hence, that is, the need for an understanding of historical context.

2

Paying for Welfare in the Twentieth Century

Jim Tomlinson

Introduction

Welfare is taken here in a broad sense to mean provision of health care, education, and social services plus income in unemployment, sickness and old age. A significant part of this is provided without being financed – most obviously, the 'informal' care of the sick, disabled and elderly by relatives who receive little or no recompense for their services. But it is the 'formal' sector of welfare which is concentrated upon here, where finance has to be found to pay either for provision of services (for example health care) or income at a time of loss or impairment of earning power or the occurrence of some expensive event, such as maternity. Such provision can be financed by charity, by individuals (for example via health insurance or private pensions), and by corporations (by occupational benefits for those who work for them). In all three cases tax exemptions may be given, or in other words, financial assistance from the general body of tax payers. This complex mix of tax breaks and occupational welfare has long been identified as a significant aspect of British welfare provision, to be put alongside the traditional focus on the directly government-financed components (Titmuss, 1958; see also Sinfield, 1978, Pond, 1980). Some further brief comments on the growth and significance of this 'private' welfare provision is offered below, but in practice we know very much less about it than we know about the 'welfare state' as traditionally defined, financed by general taxation or quasi-taxes like national insurance. Most of this chapter will focus on the financing of that traditional welfare state, which is undoubtedly the larger part of the story, but the incompleteness of that picture should always be kept in mind.

The issue of financing the welfare state cannot be treated apart from many other aspects of the development of provision. Decisions have never been made on the scope and organisation of welfare without finance having been an integral, and usually crucial, part of the discussion. How welfare is paid for has shaped the pattern of eligibility, the organisation and the outcomes of provision. After an overview of the scale and pattern of financing, this chapter analyses those interactions, showing how financing issues have played a crucial role in the evolution of welfare in twentieth-century Britain.

The Pattern of Financing

In 1900 the publicly financed provision of welfare cost a sum equivalent to about 2.6 per cent of GNP, by 1996 this figure was roughly ten times as large, at 25 per cent (see Figure 2.1). The growth over that period has been irregular, with a rising trend during the period of 'New Liberal' reforms before the First World War, sharp increases at the end of that war, followed by retrenchment. The early 1930s saw substantial increases, mainly due to unemployment, and abstracting from that, the interwar trend appears quite flat. There was a notable increase in the 1940s, although not perhaps as large as common perceptions of 'the creation of the welfare state' in this period might suggest.

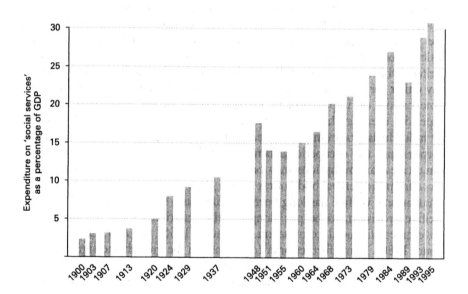

Source: Middleton (1996a) Table 3.2; UK National Accounts (Blue Book).

Figure 2.1   Public expenditure on welfare in the twentieth century

Partly this reflects the sharp fall in unemployment post-1945, this fall providing a significant offset to the rise in costs elsewhere, most notably in health. Expenditure as a proportion of GNP stabilised in the 1950s, but saw a major, sustained upsurge in the 1960s and 70s, before being reined back by the Labour government in the economic crisis of 1975/76. Thereafter the trend growth was resumed, but at a lower rate, and this continued to be the case under both the Thatcher (1979–90) and Major (1990–97) Conservative governments, despite their anti-welfare rhetoric.

Compared with Britain's Western European neighbours, the surprising fact is the broad similarity of the pattern of growth, although for most of the postwar period the British level of expenditure has been slightly lower (Heald, 1983, pp. 29–32; Johnson, 1994a; Hill, 1996, pp. 40–1, Ch. 6). At this level of generality it seems clear that similar forces have shaped the level of welfare provision across the rich countries of Western Europe. On the other hand, the pattern of finance has been significantly different in Britain, and the implications of this point will be returned to below.

In 1900 almost all expenditure on welfare was by local authorities, and most of the finance for welfare was raised locally. Peacock and Wiseman (1967) estimated that 73 per cent of all welfare spending at that date was by local bodies, largely on Poor Relief, and almost all of this came from the local property tax, the rates. Since that date the share of spending on welfare by local authorities has declined, and within that declining share, a much larger proportion has been paid for by central government grants. This pattern of centralisation has been driven by a number of forces including the abolition of the Poor Law, the nationalisation of health provision in the 1940s, and the fact that pensions, a very large and growing category of expenditure throughout the period, have always been based on national provision. In the 1980s and 90s this trend continued and was reinforced by the Conservative government's distaste for any challenge to its powers from local bodies. However, rather paradoxically, the policy of community care went against this trend and expanded the role of local authorities. This only happened after a prolonged debate in government circles, and was accepted only as part of a policy of giving local authorities a *purchasing* role, but emphasising the scope for private and voluntary *provision* of the service. (Deakin, 1994, pp. 171–3). Indeed this purchaser/provider split eventually emerged as perhaps the most distinctive general theme of welfare reorganisation in the Thatcher/Major years. In addition to limiting the scope of their activities in this way, central government has encouraged them to maximise the user charges applied to their services. Overall, community care provided only a small blip in what otherwise has been a very striking long-term trend to centralise provision of most welfare in Britain and to finance more of that provision from central sources.

Another broad trend to be noted is the source of that increasingly centralised finance. It should be emphasised that the overwhelming bulk of finance has come from tax *not* borrowing. While in serious economic down-turns such as in the early 1930s, mid-1970s and early 1990s, governments have borrowed on a large scale to pay for immediate demands for relief of unemployment, the long-term trend is clearly one of matching increased expenditure by increased taxation. Taxation here is taken to include national insurance contributions, and these were the major financing innovation of the first part of the twentieth century. Introduced under the 1911 National Insurance Act to pay for health and unemployment provision, their scope was greatly extended over the next three decades, and after the reforms of the 1940s, insurance contributions financed the great bulk of the transfer payments aspect of the welfare state (though notably *not* the National Assistance 'safety net' nor the new family allowances). On the other hand, the reforms in health during the 1940s, left this service almost wholly financed from the general tax revenue pool, and education from local rates and that same pool. The latter feature distinguished the British from most continental European systems, where contributions play a large role in financing health care. In the period since the Second World War national insurance has continued to be a major source of finance for transfer payments, but to do this it had to be changed (from 1961 onwards) from the flat-rate system to an earnings-related basis. Without this change it could never have turned into the great engine for raising revenue it had become by the 1990s, in 1997/98 raising £49 billion, compared with £72 billion from income tax.

By the late 1990s publicly financed welfare was absorbing a larger than ever proportion of both GNP and total public expenditure. Debate about the 'burden' of taxation to pay for public spending was therefore inescapably tied to the issue of paying for welfare. Government policy in the 1980s and 90s was to try and encourage private provision of welfare and in this way to attempt to respond to continuing strong demand for such provision while delivering cuts in taxation. This strategy seemed to have made little progress by 1997, with the underlying trend in public spending on welfare (abstracting from the impact of the economic cycle) still clearly upwards.

The Implications of the Pattern of Finance

In this section a detailed account is given of the major developments in the finance of the welfare state since 1900. The aim is not to cover every facet of the growth of welfare provision, but to focus on the debates and policies with major financing aspects.

The significant expansion of welfare provision under the Liberal government after 1906 must be seen in the context of a growing fiscal crisis with ramifications well beyond welfare. Broadly speaking, both Liberal and Conservative Parties in this period had come to believe that increased welfare provision for the growing ranks of the enfranchised working class would pay political dividends, while also potentially strengthening 'national efficiency', meaning the human base of the British Empire, in a period of growing inter-imperial rivalry. However, that rivalry involved growing military expenditure which also had to be financed. Tax revenue at that time was largely raised from a small number of consumption taxes on goods such as alcohol, sugar, tea and coffee which fell largely on the working class, and income tax which was paid only by the better-off. Neither political party wanted a major expansion of these tax sources, so looked for ways to raise money which would be less politically damaging. On the Conservative side a popular strategy was to go for tariff protection, aiding the protected industries, but setting the tariffs at a rate that would still generate large revenues. The Liberals were adamantly opposed to any such interference with free trade, and so chose to try and raise money by raising income tax, but especially from taxes on capital, notably land, in an attempt not to undermine the party's traditional support from the middle classes. This was the strategy that led to the great crisis surrounding the 'People's budget' of 1909, which could eventually only be passed after a major reform of the House of Lords (Murray, 1980).

The major welfare provision at stake in this budget debate was pensions, although it may be argued that the new trend of policy was initiated by the provision of free school meals begun in 1906 (Gilbert, 1966, Ch. 3). These pensions were introduced in 1908, on a non-contributory basis. There had been growing pressure for some provision for the 'aged poor' since the 1870s, especially aimed at reducing the numbers dependent on the highly unpopular Poor Law, but previous proposals had largely been rejected for financial reasons, as pensions for the current elderly population would inevitably have to be paid for by those currently in work (Thane, 1978). The 1908 Act made provision, with a very low pension, only for those who were very poor and of good character. It was not intended to be a universal system, and may be seen as a continuation of the idea of 'residual', means-tested welfare embodied in the Poor Law, but without the same stigma of pauperisation.

In the debates leading up to the 1908 Act one of the controversial issues was how far a state-funded pension would remove the incentive for private saving, and hence have a detrimental effect both in increasing 'dependency' on the state, and depressing total savings in the economy. Both of these issues were to recur throughout twentieth-century debates on welfare. The first issue, of dependency, cannot be discussed here (see Johnson, 1986; Waine, 1993) but the issue of savings is closely related to finance and needs some attention.

Johnson (1985, Ch. 7) has analysed in detail the arguments about the impact of pension and other welfare provision on the savings of the working class. He concludes that there is no evidence from the data that savings fell as the state stepped in. He also makes the general point that saving for long-run contingencies among the working class was constrained not only by the low level of income but also by the high degree of uncertainty in working-class life (pp. 200–2; see also Llewellyn-Smith, 1910). What is the point in scratching together small savings for retirement if they could be wiped overnight out by unemployment and sickness? From this perspective, a basic level of provision by the state might *increase* private efforts as these were now more likely to bear long-term fruit.

The payment of non-contributory pensions from 1909 obviously added to the direct costs of welfare to ordinary tax revenue. These costs were greater than expected, as large numbers claimed, despite the restrictive conditions and low level of benefits (Thane, 1978). These higher than expected costs encouraged the Treasury and others to seek to reduce the Exchequer costs of future welfare provision by using contributory insurance. The other major welfare reforms in this period introduced this principle, which was to be of abiding importance.

Under the 1911 National Insurance Act employers, employees and the government each contributed to two separate funds for health and unemployment. But while the health scheme embraced all wage earners up to an income limit of £160 per annum, the unemployment scheme was for only a small number (approx. 2.75 million) of workers in skilled trades especially prone to cyclical unemployment. While unemployment insurance was aimed at giving short-term help to the well-paid worker to prevent his (only men were employed in the insured trades) destitution at times of trade depression, the health scheme was aimed at a reduction of pauperism among the generality of the male working class. The insurance method of financing was by no means universally popular. The friendly societies which provided sickness benefits to perhaps six million members, and the industrial assurance societies which provided burial insurance[1] to the great bulk of the working class were unenthusiastic about a system of contributions which might erode their own inflows. These pressures were accommodated by giving friendly societies the administration of sickness benefit, and excluding the costs of burial from state welfare, an exclusion retained until 1948. The trade unions and Labour Party were also generally opposed to this method of financing, wanting finance to come from general taxation, and unhappy at the bureaucracy of national insurance. They had generally supported the non-contributory basis of the 1908 Pensions Act. However, some of the representatives of better paid workers saw the attraction of insurance in creating an inalienable right to benefit (Brown, 1971, Ch. 7). Unions were conciliated by being given a role in the administration of the unemployment insurance system.

The new schemes of national insurance were based on flat rate contributions for flat rate benefits. From the beginning it was recognised that flat rate contributions posed serious problems about the level of benefits which could be financed from such a source, given that the contribution had to be affordable to the lowest paid. This had been a key reason why pensions had been given on a non-contributory basis. Lloyd George, the politician in charge of the health insurance scheme coined the slogan 'ninepence for fourpence' to try and persuade workers of the attractions of his health insurance proposals, ninepence representing the combined contributions of employer, employee and the state, fourpence the workers contribution. But, as he recognised, fourpence was not a trivial sum to those earning a few shillings a week, and in an early draft of the scheme the lowest paid were to contribute less, although this provision was later dropped (Lloyd George, 1911 pp. 9, 178–9).

Lloyd George, despite his key political role in introducing national insurance in Britain, did not believe in it as the long-term basis of social welfare finance, because of the problem of affordability for the lowest paid (Bunbury, 1970, p. 48). This problem was exacerbated by the fact that contributions to the 1911 Scheme were calculated to make the National Insurance Fund actuarially viable. That is to say, the initial ninepence and fourpence included an amount towards paying the costs to the fund arising from the fact that by admitting people over the age of sixteen to the scheme, benefits were paid which had not been financed by past contributions. This was again to be an important long-term problem of social insurance – how to maintain their actuarial soundness in the face of rapidly changing circumstances.

National insurance for unemployment was greatly expanded during and just after the First World War. Again this was not done without opposition, part of this arising from the desire of those least subject to unemployment not to subsidise those likely to be big claimants on the Unemployment Insurance Scheme (Whiteside, 1980). But the attractions of a scheme which removed the stigma of the Poor Law while getting the working class to pay a large share of the cost proved attractive to governments faced with both demands for social reform and clamours for reduction in general taxation.[2] However, insurance as a mechanism for dealing with unemployment proved unworkable in the interwar depression. To be financially sound the Insurance Fund relied on unemployment not exceeding a certain level, if contributions were to pay for benefits. This level had been set at 8.5 per cent in 1911, but this figure was exceeded in every interwar year after 1920. The government was therefore faced with either forcing large numbers of unemployed workers on to the Poor Law or providing benefits without enforcing the conditions attached to insurance. The latter was deemed politically expedient, and down to the mid-1930s unemployment insurance was effectively suspended by a variety of expedients. In 1935 the government re-established a self-supporting Fund by placing responsibility for those who had exhausted their benefit entitlement under Unemployment Assistance Boards (Booth, 1978). The operations of the latter served greatly to reinforce support for the insurance principle among the organised working class by its use of a household means test, which made many previous recipients of insurance benefits effectively dependent on other members of their household (Crowther, 1988, pp. 40–50, 59–72).

The scale of expenditure on unemployment relief, and the breakdown of the insurance scheme, was one powerful force against major extensions of welfare provision in the interwar period. Thus in 1925 the Secretary of the Ministry of Labour wrote that 'the cost of Unemployment Insurance is so great that the country cannot afford to embark upon fresh schemes of social insurance involving the collection of further contributions from employers and employed' (Public Records Office, 1925). But in fact fresh schemes were embarked upon, notably pensions, where a new, slightly more generous scheme was introduced in 1925 and extended to widows and orphans, this time on a contributory basis, covering all those who were members of the health insurance scheme. So while the insurance principle was coming under enormous pressure in dealing with unemployment, support for this method of finance was strengthening in both government and other circles.

This generality of support is indicated by the fact that the Labour Party's plans for postwar social reform, drawn up *prior* to the 1942 Beveridge Report, supported this principle, both in order to escape the conditions attached to non-contributory benefits and as useful method of financing a major extension of welfare provision (Brooke, 1992, Ch. 4).[3] Beveridge, of course, proposed a flat-rate insurance scheme as the core of his rationalisation and extension of welfare, although the report notably lacked an extended defence of the principle, relying largely on an appeal to the 'sentiments of the British people' (Cmd 6404, 1942, p. 293).

Despite the central place of Beveridge and social insurance in discussion of the welfare reforms of the 1940s it is important to note that most of the new expenditure inaugurated by those reforms was not financed by insurance contributions. As Table 2.1 shows, the big increases in expenditure in this period were in health and to a lesser extent in other services also financed almost entirely out of general taxation.[4] Much of the increase in social insurance entitlement was effectively paid for by the decline in payments to the unemployed as postwar full employment took effect. By the late 1940s the National Insurance Fund was yielding large surpluses, and the Exchequer was reducing its contributions in response. This was ironic, given that the scale of benefits under the extended National Insurance Scheme had been set at less than generous levels because of the need to limit benefits to what was affordable from flat rate contributions. The 'austerity' of the 1940s welfare provision, especially national insurance benefit levels, therefore owed a great deal to the combination of flat-rate insurance with overly pessimistic views about the economic future (Tomlinson, 1998).

Table 2.1 also suggests that financing the new welfare state was less of an economic 'burden' than commonly suggested, even if we accept that provision of welfare should be seen in that way, rather than, at least in part, as a way of keeping the working population healthy, educating them to make them more productive, and boosting their morale and so yielding economic benefits as well as imposing costs. It is a striking feature of recent attacks on postwar welfare provision that they do not even try to show in any detail that the new higher taxes to pay for postwar welfare had a detrimental economic effect. Barnett (1986), for example, for all his vitriol, makes no effort to specify the mechanism by which the alleged 'New Jerusalem' of the 1940s depressed investment (Tomlinson, 1995).

Table 2.1 Expenditure and revenue in the 'new' welfare state of the 1940s

| | 1938/9 | | 1951/2 | |
Expenditure	£m	per cent of GDP	£m	per cent of GDP
Social Security	310.5	5.4	709.0	4.8
Education	111.8	2.0	328.2	2.2
Health	74.4	1.3	489.2	3.3
Training	6.0	0.1	5.5	0.0
Housing Subsidies	23.7	0.4	77.6	0.5
Nutrition	1.0	0.0	70.4	0.5
Total	527.4	9.2	1679.9	11.3
Food Subsidies	331.1	2.3		
Revenues (per cent of total)				
Central Government	50.1	70.3 (64.4*)		
Local Government	29.3	9.7 (11.6*)		
National Insurance Contributions	20.6	20.0 (29.3*)* excluding food subsidies		

Source: Political and Economic Planning, (1953), pp. 4, 11.

The immediate postwar extension of welfare provision was matched or even exceeded in other Western European countries, but the methods of paying for this were significantly different in Britain. Continental European countries put much greater reliance on contributions from employers and employees to pay for such things as health care (Harris, 1992). This was linked to a much greater administrative decentralisation, where welfare was organised by local government and employer and trade union bodies, with central government providing a framework and some of the funding, but distancing itself from administration. In Britain, by contrast, the reforms of the 1940s were much more of a *nationalisation* of welfare, both in administrative and financial terms. Where the original 1911 Act had devolved the administration of health insurance on to friendly societies, and unemployment insurance on to trade unions, from the 1940s the whole system was administered by central government bodies. Nationalisation was equally apparent in the NHS, where hospitals provided by either charity or local authorities were brought into a national hospital system. National insurance was also made a comprehensive, truly national system with uniform contributions and benefits. But, as noted above, most new expenditure on welfare was paid for out of the national general tax pool, not from insurance contributions.

Despite their austere character, in the 1950s there was considerable distaste for the new welfare provisions of the previous decade, notably among Conservative politicians and the Treasury. Much of this opposition focused on the costs of the new system. On the one hand, the NHS proved much more costly in public expenditure terms than had been initially expected (Webster, 1988a, p. 133), and this had already provoked a major political crisis under Labour. The new Conservative government launched an enquiry into the costs of the NHS chaired by the economist Guillebaud, but this to a large extent backfired, as the report tended to show how efficiently the service was run, but also that in key areas, especially capital spending, it had been underfunded (Lowe, 1989).

Concern about the finances of national insurance focused not on the immediate situation, where full employment continued to yield its bounties, but the prospective future costs arising from the ageing of the population and the consequent demand for pensions. Pensions have in fact been at the centre of debate about financing welfare almost throughout this century (Titmuss, 1955; Thane, 1989a). This arises from two broad points about pensions. First, if they are to be financed on a contributory basis then they necessarily have a very long 'lead-time'; to build up sufficient contributions to yield a decent pension entitlement takes, even for those with consistent and reasonably well-paid employment, a very long time. Hence immediate response to political pressure for new or improved pensions has always been at odds with the insurance principle. As noted above, in 1908 this principle was not yet widely adhered to, and a non-contributory scheme was introduced. In 1925, when the first contributory scheme was introduced, the pension level was extremely austere, but even so the fears about future liabilities were evident. Beveridge proposed to deal with the problem by phasing in the new 'subsistence pension' over twenty years. The political pressures of the 1940s led to most of the new pensions being paid immediately, but below the rates advocated by Beveridge, leading to the well-known expansion of claims for National Assistance which he had hoped to minimise.

This general tension between insurance and pension provision was added to in the interwar period by the ageing of the population, and this process was seized on in discussion of pensions in the 1940s and 50s (Thane, 1990a). Beveridge had recognised the potential costs of an older population in expenditure on pensions, and advocated that working beyond current retirement age be encouraged to reduce this cost. Nevertheless he envisaged a sharply rising contribution to the National Insurance Fund by the Exchequer in the future to finance these pension payments. The Treasury in the 1940s used these prospective costs as an argument both for restricting the level of pensions, and then for cutting its current insurance contribution as the Fund benefited from full employment. Treasury pressure on this issue continued through the 1950s, and the Phillips committee in 1954 accepted the Treasury pessimism on this question, and advocated an end to raising the basic pension in line with inflation (Cmd 9333). However, political pressure led to pension levels rising broadly in line with the new affluence of the working population. In the late 1950s there was a major struggle over pension provision, one outcome of which was the switch in 1961 to graduated insurance contributions, which obviously greatly eased the finances of a Fund previously constrained by the need to make employees contributions affordable by the lowest paid.

The pessimism about future demographic trends of the 1940s proved exaggerated in the face of the postwar 'baby-boom', although the proportion of the population over the normal pensionable age has risen as the large cohorts born before the First World War have aged. In the 1960s and 70s this demographic shift was accompanied by a parallel 'bulge' among those in the pre-working age groups, giving overall a high ratio between the working and non-working population. This was a major reason for the expansion of state welfare spending in those two decades. However, this expansion did not on the face of it prove difficult to finance. Full employment, at least until towards the end of the period, proved a boon to both general tax revenue and the earnings related contributions to national insurance. A prosperous economy appeared able to support both its young and its old. But this optimistic picture needs to be qualified. First, there were a significant number of old people and others who remained poor, and whose poverty was 'rediscovered' in the early 1960s. Second, financing welfare (as well as other components of public spending) was increasingly achieved by lowering the income tax threshold. Before 1939 income tax had been essentially a tax on the middle classes. In the war it was extended to be paid by better paid workers. But in the postwar period it was extended down to include the poor, so that income tax liabilities fell even on those whose incomes fell below 'subsistence' supplementary benefit levels (Field *et al.*, 1977, Ch. 4). Third, the coverage of welfare provision on the basis of insurance was increasingly seen to fit poorly with changing economic and social realities. This last point requires some amplification.

Insurance systems by definition restrict entitlement to contributors (and possibly their dependents). In this way finance is tied directly to benefits. A tripartite contributory system as built up in Britain tied contributions (and hence benefits) to employment status – participation in the labour market (including self-employment) has been the pre-condition for participation in the system. Benefit was, in Beveridge's phrase, payable to cover 'interruption of earnings', on the presumption that jobs would be available to all those who wanted them. Beveridge has often been seen as having a crude 'male breadwinner' approach to this issue, assuming that men (and unmarried women) would work, but that married women and children would be dependents, and so reliant on the husband's insurance record. In fact Beveridge tried to deal with what he recognised was the significant minority of married women who worked, but ultimately they were anomalous in his system (Glennerster and Evans, 1994, pp. 62–5). While women's participation in the labour market increased in the 1960s and 70s, much of this increase was in part-time work, and most women had interrupted insurance contribution records. Similarly, this period saw a growth in the number of divorces leading in turn to a rising number of single-parent families with little involvement with the labour market. Coupled to the low level of insurance benefits, these changes in social and labour market patterns led to increasing levels of dependence on non-contributory benefits, which had to be financed by general taxation.

Despite these problems and pressures few saw a major financial problem with the welfare state until the mid-1970s. In this period a number of forces combined to produce a widespread view that the current and prospective size of welfare provision could not be financed without major damaging repercussions for the rest of the economy. First was the OPEC oil price rise of 1973/74 which inaugurated (although it did not necessarily cause) a slow-down in economic growth in all major Western European countries. In the long boom after 1945 growing social welfare provision had partly been paid for from economic growth, although as Table 2.1 makes clear, welfare spending rose faster than total output. Nevertheless, economic growth, which was rapid even in Britain by historic standards, enabled that spending to be financed with less strain than in succeeding years when growth slowed down.[5] Second, unemployment, which began to edge up in the late 1960s, rose sharply in the early 1970s, increasing demands on welfare provision while reducing the income base on which it was financed. Third, the trend rise in public expenditure of the 1960s and early 1970s coalesced in the mid-1970s with the recession-induced deterioration in public finances, creating unparalleled levels of public borrowing. At the same time, the increasing international mobility of capital meant much greater vulnerability of governments to any loss of confidence in international financial markets. Levels of confidence were increasingly linked to the scale of a government's borrowing, and so in 1975/76 there unfolded in Britain a 'fiscal crisis' in which the weakness of the currency led to the government wishing to borrow abroad, but finding that any such borrowing could only be done on the basis of fiscal retrenchment. In fact the Labour government began the process of public spending cuts before the currency crisis came to a head, but two further rounds of cuts were necessary before confidence was restored and funds from abroad made available (Cairncross and Burk, 1992).[6] The cuts in public spending in the late 1970s were by far the largest in the postwar period (and much greater than any in the Thatcher years), and public spending in general and social spending in particular reached a gently sloping plateau.

From both ends of the political spectrum dire warnings were issued, before the mid-1970s cuts in spending, that current levels of welfare spending were undermining the dynamism and even the viability of British capitalism. Marxists and adherents of the New Right together foresaw a cataclysm if the expansion of welfare was not reversed. But while the rapid expansion of the 1960s and early 1970s was halted in its tracks in 1975–77, there was no return to levels of expenditure of the 1950s. For all their rhetoric of 'rolling back the state', the Conservatives under Thatcher and Major presided over a level of expenditure which continued to rise in almost every year, even if, on trend, the rise in share of GDP seems to have slowed, although the trend became more difficult to discern as the cycles in the level of activity became more violent. This rise in total spending was largely driven by demand-side factors which the Conservatives felt unable to resist, rather than by policies which were designed to deliberately expand the scope of welfare. Increased demand and greater sophistication in health care raised NHS expenditure year by year. An increase in the numbers of the very old also raised demand for health provision and on other welfare services. The weakness of the demand for labour underpinned a steady increase in benefit claims, and also added to the withdrawal of most under-18s from the jobs market and their movement into education. The increase in participation rates in post-16 education was also deliberately encouraged by the government in its dramatic expansion of university education from the late 1980s. Cuts in benefit levels, such as tying pensions to price rather than wage increases, and squeezes on the incomes of public sector workers were used to try and contain rising expenditure, but except perhaps by the sale of council houses[7] the Conservatives did not change the basic shape of the core welfare state in their search for economies.

Most of this expansion had to be financed from general tax revenues. As in the 1920s and 30s, most of the unemployed were not eligible for insurance benefits and as in those decades the governments of the 1980s and 90s squeezed the incomes of the unemployed, but failed to prevent a huge rise in the total of benefits paid to them (from £3.7 billion in 1978/79 to £10.8 billion in 1995/96). But in a new departure, the government also increasingly subsidised low wages by the payment of housing benefit and Family Credit to those in work. The latter benefit, paid exclusively to low-income working households, cost £1.7 billion by 1995/96. (Department of Social Security, 1996). This rise in spending was a most paradoxical outcome of the attempt to 'price people back into work', and in terms of social policy meant a return to a pattern of 'outdoor relief' prevalent before the 1834 Poor Law Amendment Act. One implication of this trend would be that a minimum wage which effectively raised the incomes of the low paid could have a significant effect on saving public spending on such wage subsidies.[8]

The 'burden' of supporting the old with pensions did *not*, it should be noted, increase in the 1980s, when the number of pensioners was stable. Unfortunately from a financial point of view, this occurred precisely at the time when the numbers of unemployed rose most sharply. Not only did this increase claims for Unemployment Insurance Benefit (although many of the unemployed soon exhausted their entitlements, as noted above) but also narrowed the general tax base of the economy. The result was that while total tax revenue had to be increased through most of the 1980s and 90s to pay for higher expenditure, the Conservative commitment to reduce income tax, especially for the better-off, led to a switch to more indirect taxation which tended to fall more heavily on those on low incomes.[9] Overall, the Conservatives in the 1980s and 90s found it impossible to escape the pressures to increase total welfare spending, however much particular groups might be squeezed and however much rhetoric might be expended on the need to reduce the costs of state welfare.

Some Policy Issues

The first and perhaps most important policy point to be made about financing the welfare state in the twentieth century is that, while there have been almost continuous claims about its unaffordability, and the severe damage that will follow from further expansion, expansion has been sustained without any evidence of such damage having been done. Partly this has flowed from the legitimacy that the welfare state has generally retained in the eyes of the insurance contributor and tax payer, so that, for example, despite both the 'fiscal panic' of the mid-1970s and the New Right rhetoric of later years the broad shape of welfare provision established in the 1940s has not been seriously threatened by a 'tax-payers revolt'.

Leaving aside the question of aggregate expenditure on welfare, how far have the specific methods of financing affected the outcomes of the welfare state? One feature of the system has been that, within the income maintenance part, heavy reliance has been placed on insurance. If things had worked out as hoped and anticipated by Beveridge in the 1940s, and insurance had eventually paid for almost all benefits, the reliance on insurance might be seen as largely unproblematic in terms at least of its effects on entitlements. But as we have seen above, insurance based on labour market participation is inherently unable to cope in a world where life-long full-time employment of the whole adult population is not the norm. The result is that national insurance continually throws up gaps in provision which either leads to exclusion from benefit or has to be filled by other systems of entitlement, with non-contributory benefits usually given on less advantageous terms than those paid for by insurance contributions. While the attractions of insurance to those who wanted non-means-tested benefits given as of right is understandable, as a method of finance it has serious limitations. However it may be that insurance helps to sustain support for the financing of welfare because it is, in effect, an earmarked tax, and the idea of such taxes seems to be gaining support. Traditionally the Treasury has been strongly hostile to such earmarking, in order to retain flexibility in expenditure. But it may be that the electorate increasingly wants to reduce the flexibility in the hands of distrusted governments, and earmarked taxes might be a way of protecting and legitimising at least some welfare expenditure. The fact that Western European systems rely more heavily on explicit taxes may have aided their faster expansion through much of the postwar years. On the other hand, a more explicit link between public willingness to pay and specific parts of welfare provision would be likely, for example, to accentuate the squeeze on the position of the unemployed. Public opinion evidence shows that, while a sizeable majority of the population are in principle in favour of more spending on health, education and pensions, this is not true for unemployment (Central Statistical Office, 1996 p. 127).

Because a large part (approximately 70 per cent in the mid-1990s) of the British welfare state is paid for out of the general tax pool, the impact of welfare state financing on its distributional consequences depends in large part on the general pattern of tax incidence, although the structure of national insurance contributions as well as the pattern of entitlement will also shape these consequences. This is not the place to discuss the latter issue, which has been the object of much scholarly attention in recent years, and which has shown the difficulties of assessing the impact of expenditure patterns, especially of services provided in kind, like education and the NHS (Le Grand, 1982; Goodin and Le Grand, 1987). On the general tax pattern, this has been crucial since the 1940s, since when most welfare expansion has been paid for from this source. Nominally the British tax system in the postwar years has, at least until the 1980s, been highly redistributive, with high nominal rates of tax at the top end of the income scale. However, this progressivity was considerably reduced by the growth of a wide range of exemptions and allowances, such as for pensions, house purchase and other expenditures. Some of these tax breaks were reduced in the 1980s and 90s as general tax rates on higher incomes were reduced, although a new break for contributions for health insurance was introduced. Generally such allowances were worth more to higher-rate tax payers. Alongside this complicated pattern of taxpaying at the top end of the income distribution was the fall in the threshold for income tax which brought huge swathes of the poorly paid increasingly into the tax net. This obviously reduced the progressivity of the system as well. Overall, therefore, insofar as it is determined by the general pattern of British taxation, the welfare state has been mildly redistributive, although some *elements* of the system have had much more of that character, for example the funding from general revenues of non-contributory benefits which to a substantial extent are targeted on the poor. Comparative evidence on this part of welfare provision suggests Britain has achieved a relatively high level of efficiency in raising the incomes of those to whom the benefits are aimed (Mitchell, 1991). The redistributive impact of postwar tax (and spending) policies are, it should be emphasised, inherently complex and controversial, and this is especially so if the impact of occupational and fiscal welfare are taken into account. For example, although some official data on the revenue costs of various tax allowances has been published since the end of the 1970s, the figures remain sparse, and are largely ignored in discussions of the costs of welfare. For some discussion of the issues see, for example, Field *et al.*, 1977; Lowe, 1993, pp. 281–93; Hills, 1993, pp. 15–7.

Prior to the Second World War a greater proportion of welfare expenditure was financed from national insurance contributions, and these, being at the time flat rate, were regressive in their incidence. Such schemes mainly redistributed money over an individual's life cycle (most obviously from working to retirement years), or from those less prone to those more prone to such contingencies as unemployment and ill-health. Partly because of this flat rate structure of social insurance, it was estimated that in the 1930s the welfare state as a whole only redistributed about 2 per cent of national income from the rich to the poor (Clark, 1937, pp. 142–4). The early postwar expansion in provision and the increased role of general tax revenues increased the progressive impact of the system, although by precisely how much was hotly disputed in the 1940s and 50s (for example Weaver, 1950).

In principle, as Beveridge pointed out, an interruptions of earnings model could suggest an income maintenance system based on no vertical redistribution of income, with contributions from one part of the life-cycle simply being redistributed 'horizontally' to another part. But Beveridge did not advocate this and it did not happen. National insurance, even if wholly employee-funded, would have some redistributive effects because of the greater likelihood of those at the bottom end of the income distribution falling into unemployment and ill-health. Because of the Exchequer contribution to the National Insurance Fund, financed from general taxation, that impact is increased, although, as suggested above, to a controversial extent. Nevertheless, in considering the redistributive impact of welfare provision, it is important to stress that the life-cycle aspect remains important. The welfare state smooths out considerably the sharp cycles in income that occur over most people's lifetime (Hills, 1993, pp. 17–19).

This smoothing operates from the interaction of all aspects of the welfare state, but was probably made less strong relative to the pattern of vertical redistribution when insurance contributions moved from a flat rate to an income-related basis from the 1960s, although the application of a ceiling on graduated contributions in the British system has reduced the progressivity of its impact. Clearly, a move to earmarked taxes rather than insurance as a base for social welfare funding would seem likely to involve abolition of that ceiling, which seems to have no logic, and currently leads to a quite sharp fall in the marginal rate of tax (income tax plus insurance contributions) at twice the average level of income.

An important implication of the British practice of drawing most welfare finance from the general tax pool has been that employers contributions have been much lower than is typical in continental Europe, although the scale of the difference is disputed (House of Commons, 1995, p. 101). Harris (1992) has suggested this continental pattern may have led to higher levels of expenditure on those in the working age groups, and is therefore inclined to suggest this may have had economic benefits. However, while an argument for Britain switching revenue sources in this way might have had some force in the era of postwar full employment, today any measure which on the face of it would raise the costs of employment is hardly likely to attract governments anxious to reduce labour costs.

Prospects

The fears about the future costs of pensions arising from the ageing of the population have re-emerged in the 1990s, and have figured strongly in recent debates about the costs of social welfare (see Department of Social Security, 1993; House of Commons, 1995). In part this, as before, is a tactical device by those unsympathetic to the welfare state to try and raise fears about its cost in the future. Expenditure on social security has been focused upon partly because it is the fastest rising component of welfare spending, but also because, unlike the case of education and health, some of the beneficiaries are politically weak and unpopular, notably the unemployed and single mother, and perhaps also the sick and disabled.

But there is a genuine issue about the future scale of requirements for pensions, an issue which is common to all advanced industrial countries which all have broadly similar demographic profiles. However, on a comparative basis Britain faces much less of a financing problem than most countries, much of the ageing of the British population having already taken place. Hills calculates that raising the basic state pension in line with average earnings would increase spending on pensions by 0.32 per cent of GDP in each year until 2041. This is a significant amount, but hardly justifies talk of a 'demographic time bomb' (Hills, 1993, pp. 11–13). In fact scares about future pension costs led to the detachment of the basic state pension levels from earnings in the 1980s, so that the ratio of that pension to the incomes of those in work has declined sharply, alongside a severe reduction in the future benefits from the State Earnings Related Pension Scheme. This has had the striking effect of *reducing* state expenditure on pensions as a share of GDP from 4.7 per cent in 1982/83 to 4.0 per cent by 1994/95 (House of Commons, 1995, p. lxvi). Of course, this trend has been accompanied by the governmental encouragement of both occupational and private pensions to boost total retirement income, both with significant exchequer costs. But neither of these is a satisfactory solution to the future of pensions for the population as a whole. The casualisation of work, especially at the lower end of the income and skill range undermines the basis of occupational schemes. The figures suggest that such pensions have reached a plateau in their proportion of the population covered, at about 37 per cent (House of Commons, 1995, p. xxii). Personal pensions suffer from high costs of administration and are not a sensible way for most people to acquire retirement income. So the future prospects for financing pension provision are much less serious than scaremongerers are suggesting if we simply project forward current entitlements and population trends.

One response to this alleged crisis of pension provision is worth further note – that of funding as opposed to Pay-As-You-Go (PAYG) schemes. Some commentators, especially economists, have argued that by building provision on asset accumulation, funding will generate higher economic growth, although the evidence for this is weak (Mabbett, 1997). Equally, the idea that funding will *guarantee* better future pension entitlement than existing PAYG schemes (for example Field, 1996a) begs the question of what kind of regulatory framework would accompany such schemes to prevent fiascos such as that in private pensions in the early 1990s.

On the overall issue of social security funding, as Andrew Dilnot has argued:

> The problem in a nutshell is that there is really no problem with financing social security if we go on as we are now. But if we go on as we are now with benefits going up in line with prices, we shall have benefits which are less and less acceptable. We shall be driving the living standards of those at the bottom of the income distribution further and further away from the living standards of the rest of the population and that seems unacceptable. (House of Commons, 1995, Evidence of A. Dilnot, p. 2)

By reforms of social security the Conservatives after 1979 stemmed the growth of spending in that area without halting it. While the unemployed and the recipients of basic state pensions were squeezed, their numbers continued to increase. But the most rapid rises in benefit expenditure in the 1978/79–1996/97 period were to invalids, in rent allowances (because of the deregulation of rent levels) and in Family Credit. In all, benefits rose in real terms by 3.1 per cent per annum, significantly faster than the rate of growth of the economy, or than expenditure increases on other parts of the welfare state. A major part of this increase stemmed from the deterioration of the economy over this period. Not only was this obviously true of benefits paid to the unemployed, but, although to an unknowable extent, the rise in claims for sickness and invalidity benefit have also in part reflected the weakness in the demand for labour, as they have done in the past (Whiteside, 1987). But in addition, the sharp rise in wage subsidies in the form of Family Credit shows another aspect of that deterioration, with many more jobs being supplied with wages deemed, even by the government, as having unacceptably low wage levels.

In looking at the future financing of welfare, it is this condition of the economy which appears the crucial problem. As the Parliamentary Social Security Committee argued:

> The numbers of people of working age as a proportion of the population, or in comparison with the numbers of elderly, are almost irrelevant unless we know the proportion within that group who are actually working and contributing through tax and National Insurance. It is the growth in the number of people of working age who are outside the workforce that may cause difficulties with the financial equation (House of Commons, 1995, para. 33). This, of course, is simply to re-iterate what Beveridge emphasised in the 1940s: without a fully-employed economy the costs of financing a welfare state are always going to be so large as to constantly put its viability under threat.

Of course, the state of the labour market has altered markedly since Beveridge's time. The gender balance has moved sharply towards women, and simultaneously part-time work and, recently, short-term contracts have multiplied. These processes in themselves do not create a funding problem for state welfare. Indeed, insofar as they facilitate higher levels of employment, they underpin an increase in GDP per head which, through all the fluctuations of the 1980s and 1990s, has seen the average household income rise by 30 per cent. This point is not made in ignorance of the radical changes in the *distribution* of that income which has occurred, but rather to make the point that all the arguments about our ability to afford the welfare state need to be set against that expansionary trend. The financing problem is not that we are in aggregate too poor to afford current or future demands for provision, but a political problem of finding mechanisms which will allow public opinion on welfare to be translated into government policy. Equally, the idea that such provision will inevitably be forced down by so-called globalisation is to a large extent a disabling myth (Hirst and Thompson, 1996). Too much discussion of welfare provision has historically been driven by such scaremongering. A little more optimism of the intelligence, as well as of the will, would seem appropriate at the end of this century.

Select Bibliography

The issues surrounding the development of the financing of the welfare state lie on the borderlands between social policy, economics and economic and social history. As a result there is a dearth of literature dealing directly and in detail with this subject. Most historical works on the welfare state deal to some extent with this topic. For the period before 1914 Gilbert (1966) remains unchallenged in its depth. Similarly for the interwar period, Gilbert (1970), supplemented by Crowther's survey (1988), and in addition Political and Economic Planning (1937) offers an excellent contemporary summary. For the period of the 'classic welfare state' *c.* 1945–75, Lowe (1993) is invaluable. For the period from 1974 until the late 1980s, Hills *et al.* (1990) is crucial. For the 1990s, Hills (1993) and Glennerster and Hills (1998) provide a summary of a great deal of recent research.

Works on public spending inevitably involve lots of discussion of financing the welfare state. Middleton (1996a) deals with the whole of the century in detail, Heald (1983) has great breadth and depth on the postwar period, while Thain and Wright (1995) cover the period of Conservative rule after 1979.

For works more focused on financing issues in the area of welfare, Field *et al.* (1977) offer a unique assessment of aspects of the postwar tax system, and Sandford *et al.* (1980) include essays on a range of aspects of tax and welfare at the end of the 1970s. The debates of the 1990s are covered by Glennerster (1992) and Deakin and Page (1993), and dramatically portrayed in House of Commons (1995), which includes evidence from an unusually diverse range of ideological positions. The future of welfare, including financing issues is covered by Glennerster (1992). Titmuss (1958) remains a classic for its combination of originality and analytical bite, and Johnson (1986) demonstrates how great is the continuity in arguments about the financial and other aspects of the welfare state.

PART II

Political Ideas

Neoclassicism, the New Right and British Social Welfare

Norman Barry

The growing disquiet about the British welfare state has, not surprisingly, been articulated by various versions of conservative thought. However, it should be stressed that there is no homogeneous body of ideas that can be labelled uncontroversially as conservative, neoclassical liberal, or New Right. The criticisms of the modern welfare state are varied and the nuances evinced by various authors can be traced to fundamentally rival philosophical predispositions. However, they do seem to form a perhaps unnatural, but convenient, coalition in opposition to prevailing social democratic sentiments.

The scepticism about the welfare state is more complex in relation to traditional conservatives than it is with neoclassical liberals (see Barry, 1997). After all, conservative thinkers have never been hostile to some collective action to aid the deprived and, indeed, Conservative political leaders often claim credit for their more than *sotto voce* role in the creation of the postwar welfare state (the Beveridge Report emerged from deliberations of the wartime coalition government) and, despite their protestations at the growth of the system, they have never openly questioned, for example, the National Health Service or the system of social insurance (first established in 1911). In distancing themselves from the more radical economists of the neoclassical school, they have often cautiously praised the communitarian features of the welfare state; not only as expressions of social solidarity but also as valuable correctives to the potentially rampant individualism of market society

If anything, conservative criticisms of the welfare state relate more to changes in 'character', and to a corrosion of moral standards that a too generous welfare system might produce, than to the problems of efficiency and cost that seem to concern the neoclassical economists and classical liberal critics. I use the latter terms to distinguish all types of individualism from most varieties of conservatism: it is their explicit reliance on marginalist economic theory that makes classical liberal criticism of welfare policy distinctive. The label New Right tends to describe those conservatives who have adapted market economics to the traditionalist political value structure; although their reverence for the conventional moral code marks them off from the economists on some important issues.

The classical liberal criticisms of excessive collective welfare provisions derive almost exclusively from the orthodoxy of neoclassical economics. Although, as we shall see, they are not opposed to some welfare provision for the deprived,[1] the form that it should take derives almost exclusively from the theoretical orientations of orthodox microeconomics. This is a view of social science that is irrevocably rooted in a rigorous individualism. Persons are abstracted from their social environment and treated as utility-maximisers and their behaviour is more or less predictable from this assumption and from our knowledge of the incentive structure that faces them. Thus, if welfare is supplied at zero price by the state then demand for it will rise almost automatically. Those forms of self-restraint and communally enforced standards of behaviour, which are often valued as important methods of social control by traditional conservatives, are assumed to be powerless to prevent the emergence of certain forms of socially harmful behaviour in the context of virtually costless (to the recipients) welfare.

Despite the motivation of self-interest, people are assumed to have some concern for others in their utility functions. Their sense of well-being is lowered if their societies are disfigured by the presence of avoidable poverty. Thus the relief of poverty contributes to the well-being of the donors as well as the beneficiaries. It is only the 'public good trap'[2] that prevents these benevolent sentiments being expressed through entirely voluntary activity.

Part of the neoclassical objection to the comprehensive welfare state is that the suppliers of collective services are themselves utility-maximisers. The professional classes that work in the welfare system are not motivated by altruistic sentiments and can be assumed to press for the expansion of the services irrespective of the findings of social science that might cast doubt on their necessity. While neoclassical theorists might concede that in the voluntary sector (the expansion of which they continually press for) people are motivated by altruistic concerns, this cannot be relied on to be a feature of heavily bureaucratised state services. In their analysis of the modern welfare state neoclassical liberals have been heavily influenced by public choice theory, which assumes that public officials strive to maximise their own utility, even though they are not faced with the familiar profit opportunities of the private market sector. Public officials simply maximise the size of their bureaux, their salaries and so on (see Niskanen, 1978).

If there is a moral principle at work in the neoclassical theory of welfare it is the belief in liberty. This dominates the work of all the thinkers in the field. The implication of this concern is that forms of welfare should be designed in a way that preserves the maximum freedom of choice for the recipients of other people's generosity. Ideally, poverty relief should be delivered in the form of cash and the beneficiaries permitted to spend it on whatever welfare goods they desire. There is perhaps an optimistic assumption in all this, that is, that individuals can be relied on to spend cash on, for example, private health insurance, saving for old age and even unemployment insurance. There is a deep distrust of the paternalism that is said to underlie all welfare schemes that involve the state in the supply of the familiar welfare goods, and their compulsory consumption.

Closely linked to this respect for personal liberty is a philosophical objection to comprehensive welfare states which derives from the relentless subjectivism of the ethics that informs neoclassicism. There are no objective moral values which could validate a heavy role for the state in the supply of compulsory welfare. Furthermore, the uncompromising individualism of the doctrine is a serious impediment to the invocation of communal values in the justification for the common consumption of, say, health, pensions and education. This does not mean that the neoclassical theorists are *immoralists*; that they do not believe that moral values are important for stable societies. In fact, they frequently stress that it is the existence of comprehensive welfare states which has done the most to undermine personal autonomy and individual responsibility for action. However, there is perhaps an optimistic faith in the capacity of persons to organise their lives in a rational manner in the absence of state direction and control. But the doctrine also holds firmly to the view that it would be wrong to cede to the state authority to enforce moral standards and prudent consumption habits.

It is here that there is a real difference between neoclassical liberalism and conservatism. For exponents of the latter doctrine have been most critical of that cash-based form of welfare which leaves individuals free to spend money on whatever they like (strictly speaking, neoclassicism does not require that the aid should be spent on welfare goods at all). For this merely transfers the self-interest of the market to the public sphere; producing a fractured community of 'dutiless egoists' who recognise no obligations to society. In conservative thought there is belief in the idea of *reciprocity*, that people have an obligation to the community that takes care of them in times of distress and thus they have a duty to observe standards of appropriate behaviour. It is an idea that underlies the policy of workfare; which requires that welfare recipients perform some social function (if no market-based employment is available) in return for cash. This has long been a feature of social democratic regimes (for example, Sweden) and has recently been made obligatory in the US. It is increasingly an aim of British conservative welfare thought.

It would not be true to say that all British welfare state critics adopt the extreme version of the neoclassical doctrine outlined above. This really belongs to the Chicago tradition of free market economics and is best exemplified in Milton Friedman's theory of welfare; especially his idea of the

Negative Income Tax (see Barry, 1995). However, it has had an influence on thinkers anxious to avoid the moralism that is implicit in overtly conservative welfare doctrines and some versions of a guaranteed minimum income continue to be attractive (see Brittan and Webb, 1993). Furthermore, the desire, which is common to neoclassical and conservative thinkers, to return many public welfare services to the private sector derives from reasoning associated with neoclassical economics. Certainly, the analysis of particular welfare issues, especially health care and pensions, is very much influenced by the economic style of reasoning.

Perhaps it is the competing ideas of *causation* in social affairs that really distinguishes the two schools of thought. The neoclassical liberals seem to believe that welfare problems, for example unmarried motherhood, voluntary unemployment and so on are rational responses to the incentive structures that face individuals. Social harmony will emerge spontaneously only if the appropriate market-based signals are operative. There is a recognition by some neoclassical theorists that there is a certain insolubility about welfare problems: given what we know about human nature, and the relative ease with which welfare benefits can normally be obtained, people are likely to become permanent dependents in extensive welfare states.

Conservatives, perhaps unusually, are less pessimistic and tend to think that social values such as sobriety, prudence and the recognition of duty, can be promoted if welfare policies are formulated in certain ways and are made consistent with prevailing cultural values. They tend to believe that the withdrawal of familiar benefits, which is a neoclassical strategy, would not automatically generate good behaviour: as well as producing considerable distress it might result in an increase in crime and other dysfunctional behaviour. Furthermore, conservatives might also stress that the form the welfare state has taken in Britain (and especially Europe) has not produced the kind of social pathologies that have occurred in the US, for example widespread unmarried motherhood and an alienated underclass that reproduces itself through the generations. Although as we shall see, there is evidence that similar phenomena are beginning to emerge in Britain.

In this country there is a much wider range of welfare services than in the US and the problems here are over the economic sustainability of the system and the reduction in choice that it produces. In mainland Europe there is an even more comprehensive array of social services and the welfare state is thought to be under even greater economic threat than in Britain. In dealing with these issues conservatives have been very much influenced by neoclassical thinking, despite the philosophical differences between the two doctrines.

The Meaning of Welfare

A large part of the neoclassical critique of the welfare system in Britain depends on a particular meaning of welfare. In a purely theoretical sense welfare is defined subjectively as the satisfactions individuals experience from uncoerced actions – pre-eminently from market exchanges. Because welfare is defined subjectively there is very little that collective action can do (except in carefully defined circumstances[3]) to make welfare improvements in society. It is this which underlies the claim that the collective delivery of the familiar welfare services does not normally result in an increase in social well-being because particular individuals will be harmed, especially those compelled to pay for them, and because compulsion reduces freedom of choice.

For a neoclassical liberal, state involvement in welfare is legitimate only if it increases the opportunities for individual want-satisfaction and this can better be done by cash redistribution rather than through the direct delivery of a good or service. Of course, the cash has to be raised by taxation, but people's willingness to pay for it is thought to flow from the altruistic preferences that we are thought to have. What is distinctive about the neoclassical liberal theory of welfare is the claim that there are no objective criteria of 'need' which could validate the collective supply of, say, health care or education. The neoclassical liberal would have great difficulty in accepting that anyone could have a better idea of needs (which are interpreted as wants) than the person themselves. Yet, of course, we do speak of there being objective needs which the person may not be subjectively aware of, as when a doctor says that a patient is in need of medical treatment even when she does not express a want for it. Some orthodox conservatives do not shy away from a limited paternalism and are therefore more amenable to the claim that a welfare state can meet with people's objective needs, not just their wants.

However, as we have seen, this does not mean that there is no case for some state welfare. This is recognised by most classical liberals as being straightforward redistribution from the better-off to the deprived. What is important here is the distinction that neoclassical liberals make between the welfare principle and the insurance principle. Most of the welfare state in Britain is based on social insurance – the idea that individuals have paid for unemployment benefit, health care and pensions through regular contributions to a fund on which they draw on in times of distress. Although all this is associated with the postwar Labour government it really began in 1911 when the then Liberal government introduced health and unemployment insurance to a range of workers (old-age pensions were introduced in 1908, although they were then a modest form of redistribution and not based on insurance). But most neoclassical liberals have not accepted this because they think that insurance can be supplied by the market whereas redistributive welfare cannot.

In principle, insurance-based welfare payments are not redistributive but constitute entitlements for which the recipient has paid through past contributions. They are not subject to the indignity of means-testing – which is obviously the main feature of neoclassical orthodoxy with regard to welfare. To an extent it could be claimed that the Beveridge system is consistent with traditional liberal principles. It is just that the omnipresence of market failure in private insurance systems means that it has to be done by the state. Purist neoclassical liberals deny that there is market failure, although some moderate liberals, and many orthodox conservatives, believe that there is. Although there were straightforward redistributive elements in the original Beveridge system (especially Family Allowances, now called Child Benefit, and National Assistance, now known as Income Support) he wanted these to be a minor feature of the welfare state.

A lot of neoclassical liberal research has been concerned with demonstrating that social insurance (which was copied from Bismark's Germany) was not actually required. People had made arrangements through friendly societies and other private schemes for unemployment benefit, health care and even education (see Green, 1996) before government got involved. The major neoclassical liberal argument is that the growth of the comprehensive welfare state is a result of the confusion between the welfare principle and the insurance principle, producing poor insurance for the bulk of the population and inadequate welfare for the really deprived.

However, some New Right thinkers have reluctantly accepted that there is a case for some state involvement here and they have tried to justify this by appealing to an extension of liberalism itself. The argument here is that in certain markets the phenomenon of 'adverse selection' (see Jackson, 1994) makes private insurance infeasible. Adverse selection occurs when those most likely, say, to be ill or unemployed, take out cover against these contingencies and those least likely to be affected will not. Thus the pooling of resources and the spreading of risk, on which insurance depends, cannot take place. It is difficult for private insurance companies to acquire the requisite knowledge of risks and so they cannot adjust the premiums accordingly. There is the further problem that certain people are simply uninsurable (although for neoclassical purists that is simply a matter for a properly formulated redistributive welfare policy).

Of course, one of the major justifications for state organised unemployment insurance is that the private market would be highly vulnerable in the event of a cataclysmic economic downturn, such as the Great Depression. It is also probable that private insurers against unemployment would not be able to distinguish between voluntary and involuntary manifestations of the phenomenon and would be adversely affected by 'opportunism' (the deliberate exploitation of the systems for purely personal gain). It is for these reasons that the state has to act on ostensibly classical liberal grounds. Even that staunch advocate of the doctrine, Hayek, showed some approval of national insurance, as long as it was genuine insurance: although he looked forward to the gradual winding up of state schemes (Hayek, 1960, p. 300).

However, it is not absolutely clear that the problem of adverse selection requires the state to nationalise insurance. If there is a problem of people's reluctance to insure, this could be solved by requiring citizens to insure privately, by analogy with third-party motor insurance, without compelling them to join a uniform public monopoly (which was the basis of Hayek's doubts about social insurance). Also relevant to the neoclassical critique is the fear that social insurance will be used as an instrument for income redistribution rather than as proper insurance for those who might be unable to participate private schemes, if these were viable.

But nowadays the New Right is less sure of the supposed non-viability of private unemployment insurance. It has been argued (Beenstock, 1994) that only in the early stages of industrial development is there a rationale for collectivised unemployment insurance, with uniform contributions and benefits. As a country becomes richer its citizens are able to purchase privately whatever cover they desire. It would also be possible for insurance companies to spread the risk in the global market if there should be any doubt about their ability to cope with macroeconomic vagaries in particular countries. Furthermore, neoclassical liberals claim that private insurance companies would be better equipped to monitor the claimants and eliminate fraudulent applications than the state is. Beenstock (1994) argues that under nationalised insurance, unemployment benefits are 'open-ended', that is, the state is under an obligation to pay out for potentially indefinite periods whatever the circumstances. Private companies would impose more rigorous tests and would presumably impose a time limit on the receipt of unemployment benefit.

What the neoclassical liberals object to in social insurance and other welfare state benefits is the comprehensive nature of the coverage; which means that there is in an inbuilt tendency for them to grow. Not only that but they 'crowd out' alternative forms of protection and effectively prohibit experimentation. Their guarantee also leads to a view of the state as the agent responsible for curing all social ills. Indeed, however modest these systems might appear to their admirers, welfare states involve a form of 'rational' planning in which government becomes actively involved in most aspects of social and economic life. A conservative philosopher not normally associated with neoclassical economics, Michael Oakeshott, produced an important criticism of this rationalism by using a distinction between 'civil association' and the 'enterprise state' (Oakeshott, 1975). It has become an important intellectual weapon in the battle against an extensive welfare state. In a civil association individuals order their affairs in the context of general rules which have no overall purpose. They are 'adverbial' rules which tell us how to do, in a procedural sense, whatever it is that we wish to do: they do not impose any pattern or purpose on society as a whole. To construct a welfare system, almost from first principles, which has the specific purpose or telos of maximising welfare, happiness or social justice, would be an example of 'rationalism in politics'; that baleful attempt to make a spontaneous order conform to a pre-conceived plan. For Oakeshott, a collectivised welfare system is a version of the 'state as an all-embracing, compulsory corporate association... and its government the manager of an enterprise' (Oakeshott, 1975, p. 311). It is charged with the responsibility of organising every aspect of people's lives and has the duty of taking care of every grievance.

It may seem extreme to categorise Beveridge as a rationalist. After all, was not his system little more than a natural extension and completion of an inchoate welfare arrangement that was already acquiring some rationale from recent history and economics? And, anyway, did not Beveridge himself regard his 'plan' as a necessary adjunct to voluntary arrangements (which he, Beveridge, [1948] favoured throughout his life)? This may be true but it is undoubtedly the case that his postwar welfare state has been criticised by both conservatives and neoclassical economists for virtually obliterating those private and voluntary arrangements that had a long history of coping with the variety of welfare needs that people have. What is more, it is because of his influence that the meaning of welfare inexorably shifted from being a minimal set of policies designed to help a *minority* which is unable, for various reasons, to cope with the problems of personal responsibility for action in a free society, to an all-embracing plan covering health, education, pensions, unemployment and so on for everyone.[4]

The rise of comprehensive welfare states throughout this century has clearly brought about a shift in the meaning of welfare. For what neoclassical thinkers (and some conservatives) are objecting to is the 'institutional' welfare state: a system which organises most details of people's lives and which incorporates all citizens within its provisions. This contrasts with the 'residual' welfare state which is primarily concerned with identifying the poor and taking measures aimed solely at relieving their poverty. Of course, neoclassical liberals are exclusively concerned with the latter and all but the most communitarian conservatives would insist that people should be able to opt out of the state system, even though they are not opposed to its existence.

The major rationale for this private world of welfare would be freedom but its justification would also involve a comparison between the state and the market in terms of efficiency. For almost all New Right thinkers are highly sceptical of the capacity of the voting mechanism to transmit accurately people's preferences for, say, health care or old-age pensions. Indeed, a common complaint about nationalised health care, especially of the British type, is that it regularly underspends on health in comparison to a private insurance system, for example in the US (although that country has had a form of nationalised medical care for the poor and the over-65s since 1965).[5] New Right thinkers are normally unmoved by the argument that the emergence of a kind of 'two tier' system of welfare as a consequence of 'privatisation' will result in the public sector being starved of funds in the absence of middle-class pressure for higher standards. In fact, they argue (Marsland, 1996, p. 142) that lower standards in the public sector will be a powerful incentive for people to exit. Indeed, there is an argument that the existence of both a public and private system of welfare would actually benefit the public sector for it would be continually under competitive pressure to maintain standards. A protected monopoly would have little incentive to respond to consumer choice, for the latter is only possible within the framework of civil society.

The Problem of Moral Hazard

Although they are less concerned with the rather heady issues examined by conservative philosophers, neoclassical economists have produced a critique of the Beveridge conception of welfare which is by no means incompatible with Oakeshott's anti-rationalism. However, the criticism here has tended to derive from certain well-established features of human behaviour and from some orthodoxies of market economics which are directly applicable to welfare policy. The most important phenomenon identified by neoclassical economists is 'moral hazard'. This occurs when a measure designed to deal with the problems of a deprived group encourages the size of that group to grow. Human nature is presumed to be pretty much unchanging so that individuals will always adjust their behaviour to better themselves. In the welfare state they will do so at other people's expense. Thus, too generous unemployment benefit will discourage people from seeking work and unmarried motherhood will increase as the economic differences between marriage and remaining single diminish through state aid. An example in recent British welfare history is the remarkable increase in the claims for invalidity benefit that occurred when the payments here were more favourable than unemployment benefit.[6] This increase in disability and physical unfitness took place at a time when the general health of the population was improving. Madsen Pirie summarised the problem of moral hazard clearly with this comment: 'Anything you do to relieve distress will instigate more of the behaviour which caused the distress' (1994, p. 25).

Of course, private insurance markets are prone to the same phenomenon. People take less care of their property once they are insured (they might even act recklessly with the deliberate intention of securing an insurance payout). However, in the private market there are various devices which insurance companies have developed to mitigate the worst effects of human behaviour. In a state welfare system it is difficult to devise protective measures against 'opportunism', without at the same time hurting the people whom the welfare system wishes to aid.

In fact, although the welfare state creates moral hazard, the very existence of the phenomena could be used, in some interpretations of neoclassical theory, to validate compulsory saving, for example for old age. If people know that they will be taken care of in their retirement this may encourage them *not* to save, or to save very little, thus presenting future generations with a large welfare bill. This phenomenon, if it exists, could be used to justify compulsory saving for old age. Still, it is doubtful whether many classical liberals take such a depressing view of people's likely behaviour in free markets. Most writers in this tradition do not doubt the capacity of individuals to spread their earnings over a lifetime so that they do not become a burden on others in their old age.

Most neoclassical liberal thinkers, then, believe that moral hazard is exclusively a consequence of extensive and collectivised social welfare, including its social insurance elements. A satisfactory solution to the problem has never been discovered by classical liberals or orthodox conservatives. Historically, it was only effectively dealt with by the 1834 Poor Law Amendment Act which introduced the harsh 'less eligibility' principle into the welfare system. The legislation was provoked by the notorious 'Speenhamland' system which had subsidised wages (according to the price of bread). This not only turned out to be very costly but also, its critics maintained, produced a kind of moral disorder.[7]

The 1834 Poor Law Amendment Act abolished 'outdoor' relief and made the poor live under authoritarian conditions in the workhouse where the standard of well-being was made deliberately less favourable than that of the lowest paid labourer outside. This was entirely a result of the application of utilitarian social philosophy, with its attempt to calibrate exactly the human response to welfare policies. But it was a utilitarianism significantly different from modern neoclassical thinking. For exponents of the latter normally try to devise welfare systems which preserve, as much as possible, personal liberty. Indeed, if aid to the deprived is mainly a function of our benevolent sentiments then it would be immoral to impose heavy duties on the recipients of welfare.

Although no New Right theorist wishes to restore the Poor Law system, the opprobrium with which it was once treated has lessened somewhat in recent years (see, for example, Gertrude Himmelfarb, 1995) and the logic behind the Poor Law has been partially accepted even though its particular solution to the moral hazard problem obviously has not. Workfare schemes, which make cash payments dependent on compulsory work, are implicitly drawing on the theory of human nature that inspired the designers of the 1834 Poor Law.

Indeed, in the US, workfare schemes are now a major part of federal and state welfare law. The philosophy that underlies it is curiously redolent of Poor Law thinking. A leading American welfare theorist, Lawrence Mead (1986, 1992) has specifically blamed the permissive nature of the welfare system for the social dysfunctioning that is so apparent there, for example the emergence of a drug culture, a permanent underclass and, most important, the dramatic rise in unmarried motherhood. He believes that easily available welfare has reduced the competence of the new poor (who are different from the old underprivileged working class) and rendered them incapable of normal functioning in civil society. He therefore recommends a mild authoritarianism to instil the values of proper citizenship in welfare recipients: workfare forms a major element in his scheme. He claims that the solution to the work problem 'lies not in freedom but in governance' (1992, p. 181).

It is noticeable that Mead does not recommend reducing the size of the welfare state very much, which is the strategy of classical liberals and market economists, but stresses that its character and form should be changed. His work is now beginning to be incorporated into conservative welfare thought in Britain precisely because his reform proposals require a kind of reciprocity between the donors of welfare benefits (the taxpayers) and the recipients. This is clearly different from almost all varieties of economic liberalism.

In the contemporary world the greatest influence of Poor Law type thinking has been on conservatives rather than on classical liberals. This is because the former believe that the real effect of the Poor Law, and Victorian morality in general, was to entrench certain valuable social and personal virtues – sobriety, prudence and a relative far-sightedness. An important adjunct to this was the sense of stigma and shame that was attached to the recipient of welfare (Himmelfarb, 1995, Ch. 4 and Epilogue) and these functioned as necessary discouragements to dysfunctional behaviour. It is no surprise that this moralism should have a growing influence on conservative thinking.

But it is not an attitude that features strongly in neoclassical liberal social thought. Here the emphasis is on liberty and the aim of policy is to produce an efficient form of welfare which does not deprive individuals of their freedom; hence the attractiveness of the Negative Income Tax scheme or some version of the Guaranteed Minimum Income. It is these measures that have provoked the wrath of conservatives and the internecine debate in the New Right here is in some sense a replay of the Speenhamland versus the Poor Law controversy. Indeed, given the behavioural/causal mechanisms that feature strongly in neoclassical liberal thought, the only solution they can recommend to the moral hazard problem is to lower cash payments to deter potential shirkers: but this would adversely affect the 'deserving' poor. Because of this, some New Right conservative thinkers (Willetts, 1992, p. 140) are willing to accept the consequences of moral hazard if an attempt to prevent them would victimise the deprived, although presumably there are limits to their tolerance of it.

However, neoclassical liberals would normally take action to reduce the attractiveness of possibly over-generous welfare payments and, since they tend to adopt a more or less deterministic view of human nature, they would maintain that people's behaviour would respond rationally to a change in the incentives structure that faces them. If that were the case then the result of a fall in the value of benefits would be a reduction in the numbers on welfare to a very small proportion of the population. They could be targeted more effectively than under the prevailing arrangements.

Social Justice and Welfare

A criticism which is common to conservative and neoclassical liberal writing on the welfare state and welfare policy in general is that the meaning of welfare has shifted perceptibly throughout the twentieth century from a concern with the deprived, who are so either for genetic reasons or because of some adverse and unpredictable developments in the labour market, to an obsession with social justice or equality. These critics have identified certain crucial developments in the understanding of welfare which have led to deprivation being measured not by the numbers of people who fail to reach an acceptable level of absolute well-being but by their *relative* place in the overall distribution of income. Thus poverty is not understood to be the failure of some to secure adequate housing, nutrition and so on (which, it is admitted, should be assessed by reference to the level of a country's overall economic well-being and not according to some measure of mere subsistence) but by how distant the poor are from the average wage. In Britain, therefore, a person's absolute level of well-being should be obviously higher than someone's in the Third World (and government has an obligation to make it so) but it should not be evaluated according to some criterion of social justice.

There are both philosophical and practical reasons why this position should be so rigorously adhered to. For neoclassical liberals, the rejection of egalitarianism depends upon a distinction between 'end-state' and procedural justice. In the former conception, a society is just if the outcome (for example the distribution of income) of a social and economic process is consistent with a preconceived pattern. For a socialist welfare theorist, this pattern is validated by such principles as desert and need, or sometimes equality for its own sake. An income distribution is just only if it reflects these moral values. Public welfare policy should be designed to reproduce such an end-state.

The neoclassical liberal objects to this for at least three reasons. First, the outcome of a market process can never be known in advance and it is folly to attempt to point the exchange system in some preconceived direction. Second, in a world of subjective value there is never going to be agreement on what is a just distribution of income and wealth and therefore any pattern of reward, derived from a notion of desert or an expanded concept of need, will simply be an arbitrary command of a centralised authority (the state). The only relevant consideration here is people's economic *value*, and that can only be determined by the market. Thus it is often the case that some people's incomes will appear not to concur with popularly held views of desert but this, according to neoclassical liberals, is of no relevance to social welfare or income distribution. Third, any attempt to use the welfare system to implement some desired distribution will have an adverse effect on productivity. By interfering with the labour market, a state desirous of generating some (arbitrary) distribution of income will reduce total output, therefore making less wealth available for allocation to the genuinely deprived.

Closely linked to all this is a belief in the 'trickle-down' effect: that is, despite the inequality that the market produces, the higher earnings of the successful will gradually filter down, through their consumption and investment expenditure, to improve the condition of the worse off. Although the communitarian instincts of some conservatives may cause them to dissent at the sometimes arbitrary distributions of income thrown up by a completely undirected market economy, this distaste has never provoked them to embrace doctrines of social justice. They do think that overall well-being will be increased, and inequality reduced, by 'natural processes'.

The efficacy of the 'trickle-down' effect has been the least persuasive of neoclassical welfare theories. Indeed, it has been suggested in a recent report (Joseph Rowntree Foundation, 1995) that during the period 1979–90 in Britain there was, in fact, no evidence of it: the income of a small percentage of the population actually fell in real terms. However, this is a very complex statistical debate and the figures that are used in it are by no means unambiguous. If actual *expenditure* by various social classes is considered there is apparently no fall in real income at the bottom but a significant increase (see Green, 1996, pp. 58–62). A further important point is that the composition of the group at the bottom varies over time; very few people stay in that position for long periods (Marsland, 1996, pp. 57–8).

Still, neither the orthodox conservatives nor the neoclassical liberals have made too much of the trickle-down argument. They have preferred to concentrate on the incoherencies of the demands for social justice and on the inefficiencies and inequities that occur when it is made an object of public welfare policy. Certain crucially important research on the capacity of the welfare state to promote equality has added credence to this aspect of general New Right thinking. It has been shown that the attempt to produce equality by the methods of the welfare state actually produces inequity.

Ironically, neoclassical liberal writers (see Barry, 1990, Ch. 6) have exploited the work of basically pro-welfare state writers (Le Grand, 1982; Goodin and Le Grand, 1987) who have demonstrated that the tendency of most of the familiar welfare policies is not to generate equality but to produce a redistribution towards the better-off.[8] What is crucial here is that these critics use a methodology which is almost identical to that of the neoclassical liberals.

The key point is that, although some services, for example the National Health Service, are nominally available equally to all, their consumption is unequal because the middle classes are in a better position to take advantage of them. Thus Le Grand (1982, p. 46) writes: 'Policies involving subsidies whose distribution is dependent upon people's decision to consume the good or use the service favour the better off.' People's decisions to consume will depend on opportunity cost, that is, what they have to give up in order to consume. Thus the salaried better-off use the Health Service more frequently than hourly paid workers since they will not normally lose as much money through absence from work.

A more spectacular example is higher education where the loss of income to a middle-class family when their children go to university is nowhere near as great as it is for poorer people. In fact, the proportion of working-class children attending university has changed very little over the years despite a formally expanding higher education system. A feature of the welfare state is what Goodin and Le Grand (1987, Ch. 4) call 'beneficial involvement', a strategy through which the better-off arrange their lives so that they qualify for the benefits of social policies that were not intended for them.

Evidence such as this has not persuaded supporters of the welfare state that it should be substantially reduced. The fact that collective provision produces unequal outcomes is regarded as an unavoidable cost. The general argument is that the inequality here at least assures that higher standards for the worst off, especially in health, are maintained precisely because of middle-class involvement, although this argument is much harder to apply to university education, which many children of the working class do not consume at all.

Much of argument reinforces the traditional conservative and neoclassical liberal claim that welfare policies should not be universal or part of an all-embracing welfare plan but should be directed at the genuinely needy, irrespective of the fact that this strategy produces a two-tier system. Indeed, neoclassical writers argue that in a democratic system (Barry, 1990, pp. 105–6) a redistribution towards the middle is what one would expect. Political leaders are vote-maximisers rather than welfare maximisers and since the majority of the voters are not poor it is not surprising that redistribution should produce a perverse effect. All critics maintain that only direct cash payments can produce a genuine welfare redistribution but since a large part of welfare policy in Britain and Europe (although less so in the US) consists of in-kind services and 'entitlements' the scope for equalisation is strictly limited. Indeed, empirical research has shown that in times of welfare retrenchment it is the services and benefits that mainly go to the poor that suffer the most (Glennerster, 1991, p. 168). Because of its vast array of in-kind services (the consumption of which does not depend on income) the welfare state has been described as a 'middle-class racket' (Gray, 1992, p. 87).

However, although the middle classes appear to gain from many aspects of the welfare state, a large part of New Right thinking has emphasised the fact that much of this gain is illusory. This is because so much of welfare provision involves 'churning' (see Jackson, 1994). People pay taxes and social security contributions in order to receive from the state services which they could provide for themselves if more of their income were left in their own hands. Naturally, neoclassical theorists maintain that there is a significant efficiency loss in the cumbersome state process as well as an unconscionable reduction in personal liberty. This has fuelled the already strident demands from the New Right that the bulk of these services should be privatised.

Although at one time some conservatives were prepared to tolerate the inefficiencies of collective supply, on the grounds that at least some commonly consumed welfare services produced an essential spirit of community in an otherwise individualistic social order, this argument has much less resonance today. Under the influence of public choice theory most New Right thinkers now take the view that the same maximising behaviour that we observe in the free market is reproduced in the public welfare sector: with less than optimal results in the latter. The very notion of a 'common good', that can be reproduced by government, and which embraces all members of society, is explicitly repudiated. The favoured realistic (or cynical) view of the welfare state is that it is a system which is riven by pressure groups. These sectional groups use the public purse as a kind of common resource which is available for plunder. This is probably too extreme a view but it does remind us of the fact that the existence of a complex welfare system has not produced that spirit of altruism for which some of its early proponents had hoped.

Means-Testing and the Debate on Welfare Rights

It follows from all the above that whatever welfare activity it is permissible for the state to engage in, for most New Right thinkers this must be *selective*: that is to say, the bulk of the population should not be the concern of welfare policy and the welfare that remains should be restricted to those who 'qualify', normally by criteria confined to income and other easily assessed resources. Thus means-testing is an essential feature of New Right thinking; although economic liberals, who are worried about moral hazard, are much stricter in their specification of these criteria than are conservatives.

The British welfare system is more like that of the US than it is of Europe, since in the latter a wider range of entitlements, especially through social security, precludes the need for as much means-testing as Britain has. In very comprehensive welfare states, such as those of Sweden and Germany, there is a different form of redistribution, that is, between social groups, such as the healthy and the sick, the employed and the unemployed and the young and the old. In this country we have an inefficient, indeed often perverse, redistribution based on a combination of income and common services. It is the case that most (although not all) varieties of New Right thinking in Britain do not accept the doctrine of 'citizenship' that seems to validate the European approach to welfare. Those social democrats influenced by the citizenship theory of Marshall (1963a) would like to move the country in that direction.

The citizenship approach explicitly repudiates the idea of means-testing because it is based primarily on a revised doctrine of rights. In classical liberal political thought for a person to have a right meant that they had a claim *not* to be arbitrarily interfered with by others (and, of course, the state). The rights claims here encompass the traditional civil liberties of free expression, free movement, and the opportunity to accumulate wealth through legitimate exchange, and so on. They do not require much positive action by the state. Rights claims are rather strong; they normally defeat all counter-arguments derived from utility and depend for their validity on a rather abstract moral philosophy.

However, in social democratic welfare thought the notion of a right has been extended to enjoin the state to act positively to promote the good of individuals: there is a symmetrical structure of rights so that claims to welfare have the same moral force as claims to non-interference.[9] The possession of welfare rights, then, is as unconditional as is the claim to the traditional civil rights; it does not, in principle at least, require any qualification, such as the duty to work.

When they are translated into public policy proposals welfare rights become entitlements to certain goods thought necessary for a purposeful life and, in the European context, they are not dependent on such things as means-testing (although, as a consequence of a more communitarian-based notion of rights, a work requirement is often a condition for their conferment). The absence of means-testing is specifically designed to avoid the stigma and shame that so often accompany welfare systems that are solely concerned with the elimination of deprivation. Thus while welfare rights policies are not as unconditional as the theory that validates them might imply, they have a quite different rationale from the policy suggestions of neoclassical liberals, and, indeed, many conservatives. They are primarily addressed to questions of genuine need and are not at all concerned with integrating their recipients into the community, or guaranteeing a certain level of unemployment benefit, health care, education or old-age provision. In other words, for neoclassical liberals welfare is limited to the relief of poverty. It is obvious that it should be accompanied by serious means-testing – which must be designed so as to discourage beneficiaries from falling into that state again.

From a New Right perspective, no one is entitled to welfare merely because they occupy a certain *status*, such as being a mother or being made unpredictably redundant from a particular occupation. The only thing that is relevant to a welfare payment is income and present assets. Neoclassical liberals, ever mindful of the potential for 'opportunism' that is said to be a feature of all human action, are particularly critical of the attempt to guarantee a level of well-being to people who might have certain disadvantages, for which compensation might be thought to be owed to them irrespective of income. This might simply encourage people to acquire those disadvantages. We have noticed earlier a possible example of this opportunism in the case of the British invalidity payment system.

In fact, the translation of welfare demands into rights is perhaps the phenomenon that has provoked the most hostility from New Right thinkers. While neoclassical liberals have railed against the costs that social rights have imposed on market economies, and the disincentives to work that they are said to produce (indeed, the costs of European-style welfare arrangements are beginning to be realised by almost all observers), conservatives have been as much concerned with the kind of welfare culture that their implementation is said to produce. It is a culture of dependency, reduced personal autonomy and the prevalence of a kind of 'victim' status. The detachment of welfare rights from any notion of duty (although the New Right has undoubtedly exaggerated the ease with which such benefits can be secured, and indeed their generosity) has produced, or threatens to produce, a society of dutiless egoists. Furthermore, the attempt to guarantee individuals a certain level of well-being is an example of rationalism in politics, or the transformation of a civil association into a directed order in which the state has the duty of meeting every need that comes on to the political agenda.

Despite the theoretical approval for means tests, New Right thinkers have become a little concerned in recent years with their effects. They might not fulfil the purpose for which they were designed, that is, to get people off welfare. They fail to do this because of 'poverty traps': these occur when individuals in receipt of a range of means-tested benefits stand to lose them if they take paid employment. Sometimes the effective 'marginal tax rates' in such circumstances can be as high as a 100 per cent. This obviously explains why certain groups of people, for example unmarried mothers, have every incentive to stay out of the labour force for long periods of time. Furthermore, the existence of poverty traps is a great encouragement to fraud: a phenomenon which has actually been highlighted by left-wing thinkers (Field, 1995) but it is not something that would surprise most New Right theorists.

Neoclassical liberals are in something of a dilemma here, for they do not want a welfare system that encourages indolence and fraud, yet they cannot support a policy agenda which would impose a set of comprehensive and vastly expanded social insurance arrangements (to avoid poverty traps); it would be both costly and liberty-reducing. Of course, a short answer would be to make the means-testing so rigorous that very few people would be tempted to go on welfare. But, as we have noted earlier, this may very well adversely affect the very groups of people to whom New Right thinkers (especially orthodox conservatives) feel that 'society' at large owes a special duty.

One possible solution, now increasingly favoured by neoclassical thinkers (and some conservatives worried by the decay of civil society), is the return of a range of welfare services to the voluntary sector. This does not mean just the reinstatement of private insurance (supplemented by charitable activities) but the revival of friendly societies (Green, 1996, Ch. 6) which had, before the rise of the social insurance state, catered adequately for most working-class needs. Their very 'intimacy', and the access to local knowledge that their officials have, are thought to produce admirable mechanisms for the prevention of fraud. Such a revolution in social welfare is hard to imagine, although the inexorable rise in the cost of the conventional welfare state is certainly encouraging intense speculation on these lines (see Butler and Young, 1996).

Even this would not sufficiently deal with cases of those who, for reasons beyond their control (such as permanent disability) cannot adequately take part in civil society; although presumably their numbers would fall dramatically in a neoclassical welfare utopia that completely eliminated opportunism. Should those that remain unavoidably deprived be compensated for their disadvantage so that they have at least the opportunity to achieve a standard of living equivalent to their more fortunate fellow citizens? To guarantee this would surely not necessarily provoke the 'behavioural' problems that agitate neoclassical liberals and conservatives. Should they have to rely on private charity or be left to depend on some rigorously means-tested state benefit? It must be conceded that none of the writers from the New Right has a satisfactory answer to these particular welfare problems.

Health, Pensions and the Logic of Neoclassical Liberalism

Although neoclassical liberals have had a significant impact on thinking about welfare it is perhaps in their analyses of particular subject areas that their contributions have been most direct. This is because their discussions of *the* welfare state or *the* general welfare problem tend to be clouded by intractable ideological issues which, to some extent, defy rational analysis. However, in such areas as health care and pensions their analyses, and even policy recommendations, can be said to be conceptually linked to social science rather than to a particular political predisposition. Certainly, the contentious problems of moral hazard, and the morally and emotionally charged discussions of personal behaviour under state welfare regimes, are less likely to occur in the discussion of a rational design of policies to deal with sickness and old age. These two areas have come to dominate the welfare debate in Britain almost as much as poverty and unemployment. They perhaps pose the most serious long-term problems for the welfare state.

Although the question of health is capable of rational analysis, and for which rival policy proposals can be evaluated in a more or less non-political manner, such an approach has been hampered in Britain by the emotional appeal which collectivised health care has. It is an attraction that even Mrs

Thatcher found irresistible: witness her famous claim that 'the National Health Service is safe in our hands'. That attraction undoubtedly derives from the claim that the Beveridge reforms provided a health service that was comprehensive and 'free at the point of consumption'. Neoclassical liberals have been determined to penetrate what they regard as the moral and economic miasma that surrounds the debate about health care. It is a debate to which orthodox conservatives have contributed very little of fundamental significance. They have supported the National Health Service (NHS) since its inception in 1948 and what reforms they have introduced are all said to be consistent with its foundational principles.

The real innovations have been made by neoclassical liberals who start from the assumption that health care must be viewed as a normal service and subject to the same analysis in supply and demand terms (see Lees, 1969; Seldon, 1981). There must be a market for health care: it should be based on consumer choice and its prices must be consistent with the laws of scarcity. Although it is occasionally conceded that there are minor differences between the demand for health and the demand for other goods and services, they are thought not to be significant enough to justify the wholesale nationalisation of the medical system (although in Britain the NHS is not a technical monopoly since the private supply of health has always been allowed and it is now thriving).

Much of the criticism of the NHS stems from the claim that it is under-funded and in comparison to private insurance systems, or combined public and private systems, it certainly is. In the US[10] the proportion of GDP spent on health is a staggering 14 per cent and in Germany and France, countries that have systems much less subject to direct state control and which also involve some patient charging, it is normally about 8 per cent or 9 per cent. In Britain the figure is scarcely 7 per cent. The neoclassical liberals maintain that this shortfall is due mainly to the fact that government decides the amount of expenditure and for complex public choice reasons (see Buchanan, 1968) a democratically elected government will not transmit accurately people's desire for health care.

However, they also point out that since the service is zero-priced, the demand for it will be infinite. Unlike in a market, where there are natural checking mechanisms, a centrally determined health system will always be facing intractable problems. With rapid improvements in medical technology demand will rise in a 'free' system, yet politicians will not be able satisfy it. Like all scarce goods and services, it will have to be rationed; but instead of price determining the supply (which happens in a market) in a socialised system, doctors themselves (or bureaucrats) will have to take the decisions about allocation. They will make judgements based on such criteria as the person's likely contribution to national output (dialysis treatment is thought to be allocated in this way), age and, occasionally, their lifestyles which may have contributed to their condition.

Neoclassical liberals are not unaware of some theoretical problems with a purely insurance-based health care system. There is obviously an informational asymmetry between doctor and patient and this could encourage opportunism on the part of health providers. There is a temptation for patients to demand unnecessary care since once they have paid their premiums the marginal cost of treatment is zero (a form of moral hazard). Both these factors have been used to explain escalating health costs in the US. The market provides no automatic adjustment; it is not in the interests of any one person to reduce demand since she cannot be sure that others will be so enlightened (a version of the public good trap). It is for this reason that about 30 million Americans are not privately insured; they are simply priced out of the market.

However, neoclassical liberals are convinced that these problems are soluble. In the US, Health Maintenance Organisations offer a more or less comprehensive service at a fixed price and insurance companies are beginning to monitor health providers more effectively. In any case, these inadequacies are certainly no worse than the efficiency problems of nationalised systems. It is admitted even by some critics of private insurance that the standard of health care in the US is higher than in Britain. Although infant mortality and longevity figures are roughly comparable, the waiting time for treatment in the US and the provision of ancillary services are much more favourable. With regard to the problem of patient ignorance, it is claimed that this is not unique to health, as any motorist knows whenever he takes his car to the garage for repair. According to neoclassical liberals it can only be overcome by a market in health care which is continually transmitting information to patients.

There is, of course, the problem of the long-term (uninsurable) sick but this is a feature of all health care systems: market societies have always had quite extensive charitable institutions and throughout history private enterprise hospitals and medical practitioners have delivered services at zero price for special cases. Anyway, there is always a justification for a welfare safety net arrangement in New Right thought, even in its most 'economistic' form.

In Britain, the influence of neoclassical liberal thought on public policy has not been very effective in health care, although it has been in the theoretical debate. The purist's agenda is simply politically infeasible. The introduction of an 'internal market',[11] in which purchasers of health (the statutory health authorities) are separated from the providers (the hospitals, which are now more or less autonomous Trusts), is regarded as a pale reflection of a genuine market system. It is true that competition between the Trusts is likely to reveal more information about relative costs of treatment (money will tend to follow the patient) and the introduction of a number of 'fundholding' general practitioners (who can now go into the market and buy services) will increase the independence of doctors and widen consumer choice. But as long as the financing of health remains ultimately in the hands of central government the reality of underfunding will remain.

Perhaps the most serious long-term welfare problem for all advanced societies is provision for old age. With increasing improvements in medical care, and rising general standards of living, extended longevity is imposing escalating costs on those in work. The problem is compounded by two further factors: the decline in the birthrate which all industrial societies are experiencing and the weakening of those bonds of reciprocity between the young and the old which once imposed a strict moral obligation on children to look after parents in their retirement. Indeed, under prevailing welfare state arrangements, the young are more likely to resent the imposition of these burdens on them through the state system since they cannot guarantee that they will be so favourably treated when they retire. The original justification for state provision of pensions, that being old meant being poor, is no longer as compelling as it was when (then non-contributory) pensions were introduced in Britain in 1908. The spread of private (occupational) pensions, now embracing over 60 per cent of the workforce, and the accumulation of assets over a lifetime mean that although the very poorest in society are old, they constitute a diminishing proportion of the poorest in the population (see Barry, 1993).

An original argument for the inadequacy of the market in effectively handling the old-age problem was based on the claim that individuals had too high time preferences, that is, they would heavily discount the future and not save for their old age. It was not merely the specific problem of poverty in old age that influenced interventionists, there was also the feeling that people's incomes should be 'smoothly spread' over a lifetime; they should not experience a catastrophic drop in their standard of living on retirement. Apparently, individuals working through the market, with all its vagaries and unpredictability of employment, could not be sure of such a desirable security. In Britain, and elsewhere, pensions eventually became part of social insurance so that the old would not suffer the indignity of means-testing.

Unfortunately, things did not work out as intended, largely because the state proved to be an inadequate supplier of old-age pensions. It is true that if demographic data were perfectly stable and predictable (so that the birthrate and the age of death remained constant) and stable economic growth were achievable, the state (either through taxation or national insurance) could guarantee a specified standard of living to the old without burdening the young. There could be a kind of 'contract between the generations' (see Barry, 1985). However, this proved to be an illusion since little of the above data were stable and predictable. In Britain the 'support ratio', that is, the number of workers required to keep a pensioner at a guaranteed standard of living, has begun to decline significantly and is likely to fall below 2.4:1 in the first two decades of the twenty-first century.[12] In the US, Germany (and the rest of Europe) and Japan the situation is even worse than Britain's because these countries have less well-developed private pension provision.

But this country is only comparatively better situated, there is still a looming problem here (and, of course, Britain is significantly less economically productive than the US). The problem was compounded by the introduction of earnings related pensions in 1975. They came about because there was a genuine fear that Britain was generating a 'two nations' pension system: there were those on adequate private occupational schemes and the rest, who were dependent on the state basic payment, which was (and still is) meagre. Private pensions were not spreading fast enough to avert problems of poverty in old age. However, the State Earnings Related Pension Scheme (SERPS), introduced by Barbara Castle, is not funded (see Peacock and Barry, 1986): it is a 'Pay-As-You-Go' (PAYG) system which depends on income transfers from young to old. Very soon neoclassical economists began to worry about the future costs of this in the light of unfavourable demographic data. The neoclassical liberals, of course, always favoured the complete privatisation of pensions. They denied that there was a problem of people's unwillingness (or incapacity) to save for their old age. It was government that has too high a time preference. Political parties are influenced primarily by the date of the next election and since the immediate imposition of higher taxes (or social insurance) is a vote loser, they will be tempted to pass off the cost of generous pensions to future generations. It is an attraction that has proved to be irresistible.

The Conservative government[13] under Mrs Thatcher did attempt to grapple with the problem but, as with health care, not in a way that satisfied the neoclassical liberals. The generosity of SERPS was diminished and people were offered inducements to withdraw from it and go private (see Barry, 1993). The original intention was to abolish SERPS but interest groups (not least, the pensions industry itself) prevented the adoption of the radical solution.

An important reform was the decision to raise the basic old-age pension in line with prices rather than wages. Its *relative* value fell significantly (in fact, it is one of the few examples of welfare saving that successive Conservative governments have achieved). Old-age pensioners who rely solely on the state payment now depend on Income Support for necessary supplements. Neoclassical theorists had always maintained that if the state had not introduced earnings related provisions in the first place it could have increased the value of the basic pension. Indeed, in a fully privatised system there would be no 'bogus' state insurance and the penurious elderly could be treated as a simple welfare problem requiring genuine redistribution.

A genuine private pension system would have the additional advantage that it would generate savings for economic investment. It is sometimes said that the fall in the birthrate will have an adverse effect whether pensions are fully funded or paid under a PAYG arrangement: there would still not be sufficient workers to produce the goods which pensioners would need to buy (and they would have the nominal resources to make the purchases). However, this gloomy scenario is mistaken, for a fully funded pension system would lead to a 'deepening' of the capital structure: capital would be substituted for labour so that the optimal production of goods and services could be achieved. This is related to the point, often made by American neoclassical liberal economists, that if the tax contributions of workers are invested in stocks and bonds they would produce a significantly greater return than that achieved under compulsory PAYG systems. Neoclassical thinkers in Britain have recently been attracted to the example of Chile which has completely privatised its state pensions (see Butler and Pirie, 1995). There citizens are compelled to save a portion of their income for old age but have considerable freedom in their choice of investment.

Although the particular policy prescriptions for health and pensions of the neoclassical liberals have not been adopted by any British government they have achieved a certain intellectual credibility, more so than what they have said about poverty and the more general welfare issues. The reason is that they have used powerful weapons derived from orthodox economics in their analyses of health care and pensions. And these are untainted by the contentious moralism that tends to accompany orthodox conservatism in its appraisal of the welfare state as a total social system. Obviously, critical analysis of a state pension system is not going to be influenced by claims that it produces an 'underclass' or a generation of welfare dependents.

Neoclassical Liberalism, Conservatism and the Future of Welfare

Welfare policy in Britain is invariably about the welfare state and increasingly discussion of the latter is critical of those institutions and practices which were once accepted as politically unalterable and, if not always desirable, at least roughly consistent with what most people felt were their social duties; the performance of which properly belonged to government. Now there is open criticism of familiar policies. The assault has been led by the intellectual spokesmen of the New Right and has been quite radical: recommendations for the almost complete winding up of the system are not uncommon (Marsland, 1996). Still, the analytical effects of all this have been distorted by the sometimes populist and authoritarian attitudes of right-wing politicians.

However, we should be clear about the bases of these radical suggestions. Although there is some cross-fertilisation of ideas, there are two distinct strands in the thought of the New Right; the economic and the moral. The former generates policy prescriptions that are almost direct inferences from neoclassical economics (and the individualistic methodology on which it is founded) while the latter derives from a complex network of social and ethical ideas and is distinctly less individualistic.

The economic critique is perhaps the easiest to summarise. In principle, the claim is that recent Conservative governments have done nothing to curb the growth of public spending on welfare. It has increased sevenfold in real terms since 1949 (Butler and Young, 1996, p. 10) and all forms of welfare together now constitute about 70 per cent of the government's budget. Forty per cent of this is devoted to social security, which is now an aggregate total of £90 billion per year; also, 10 million heads of households receive some means-tested benefits. The only area in which the Conservatives in office managed an absolute reduction in spending was council housing, but even here the gains were paid for by a great increase in the means-tested housing benefit: that has generated a kind of opportunism (or implicit collusion between land-lord and prospective tenant) since claimants have little incentive to search for the cheapest accommodation and landlords do not have to compete much in offering lower rents – the government will pay.

As was noted earlier, some of these services are not strictly speaking welfare; they constitute an inefficient form of insurance, a perverse type of redistribution, or sometimes sheer waste. The most spectacular example of the last is Child Benefit, which goes to the mother irrespective of the income and wealth of her family. Neoclassical liberals have no sympathy with the argument that motherhood is a kind of status which is worthy of special treat-ment irrespective of other highly relevant economic circumstances.

The main beneficiaries of the welfare system are the unemployed, long-term sick, families with dependent children (often headed by unmarried mothers) and the elderly but such is the illogicality of the system that neoclassical liberals argue that it is difficult to distinguish between the deserving poor (who should be the concern of our altruistic sentiments) and the undeserving poor, who must be presented with an incentive structure that discourages them from becoming welfare claimants. Although some writers (Hills, 1993) have argued that the present system can be sustained with only a 5 per cent increase in the proportion of GDP spent on its various services, neoclassical liberals (see Pirie, 1994, p. 24) have carefully calculated the extra income tax and Value Added Tax that this would require. The cost in these terms is significant.

The moral critique of welfare by the New Right is difficult to summarise but it basically rests on a belief that a stable society, and an efficient market system, depend on the 'internalisation' of appropriate norms of behaviour by all citizens. This moral education is provided by the family, the community and groups smaller than the state. Although an extensive welfare state has done much to undermine the moral culture of a civil society, the conserva-tives do not think that it can be re-established by a simple withdrawal of state benefits.

An American observer of Britain, Gertrude Himmelfarb, is acutely aware of the interaction between economics and ethics. She remarked that: 'Unless we can restore a moral perspective to the lives of the poor, the alienated underclass will grow larger' (1995, p. 2). What she would like to see is a revival of Victorian values (or virtues, as she instructively calls them), and the construction of a welfare system that sustains them rather than one which encourages the rampant individualism of neoclassical liberal thinking.

Another American commentator on Britain, Charles Murray (1990), is more associated with neoclassical liberalism but what he says about the growth of the underclass in the US, which he now sees occurring in Britain, is not incompatible with orthodox conservatism. There has been a fraying of the moral fabric of British society and this is mainly a consequence of too easily obtainable welfare. The welfare state not only generates an adverse incentive structure it also conveys the wrong moral message. Murray claims that three features of the underclass that he originally detected in the US are now present in Britain. They are illegitimacy, increases in violent crime and voluntary unemployment.

Murray claims that to avoid generalised deprivation and social dysfunctioning it is necessary not only to reform the welfare system but it is also essential to inculcate certain habits: people should finish school, get and keep a job (whatever the pay), and get married (and stay married). What is of obvious importance is the preservation, indeed revival, of the conventional two-parent family. In his view it is this institution which has been the major casualty of inadequate welfare schemes.

The specific moral message of writers like Himmelfarb and Murray is not necessarily ideological for they are invoking long-forgotten virtues of civil society. The implicitly non-political source of their critique is revealed by the fact that writers from the Left (Field, 1995; Dennis, 1997) have said some remarkably similar things about the connections between welfare, economics and morals. After decades of fractious argument between the Right and the Left about welfare it looks as if some common ground may be emerging. If this is so then it might be possible, at last, to take some of the heat out the welfare issue. Most varieties of New Right thinking can take a little credit for this.

New Liberalism and the Middle Way

Robert Pinker

The Intellectual Heritage

The history of modern liberalism – like that of all the great traditions of Western political philosophy – is a record of continuous interaction between the theories and concepts developed by its leading thinkers, the institutions of party politics and governments through which activists seek to put their ideas into practice, and the processes of economic and social change.

More than any other philosopher of his time, John Locke stands out as the founding father of English liberalism (Cranston, 1969, pp. 67–8). Locke believed in a framework of basic human rights to life, liberty and property but he did not consider these rights to be absolute or unconditional. They were created, protected and subject to change by law, and it is in Locke that we find an articulated defence of the notions of both representative government and an independent judiciary. We also find in his writings an acknowledgement that the claims of liberty must always be reconciled as far as possible with those of order and constitutional continuity. The rights to property and personal freedom may be indivisible and mutually interdependent but property ownership carried responsibilities as well as rights (Locke, [1690] 1960).

By taking into account the diverse and divergent character of human aspirations Locke provided a philosophical framework for the growth of pluralism in Western democratic societies. Pluralism, as a political tradition, has always 'rested on the premise that, in a free society, compromises have to be made between competing political objectives that may all be equally desirable, but cannot be resolved to the general satisfaction on the basis of any single criterion' (Pinker, 1992, p. 274).

If Locke laid the philosophical foundations of modern liberalism, the theories of classical political economy provided its commercial rationale and vindication. Adam Smith, Thomas Malthus and David Ricardo set out the case for the liberalisation of trade and the benefits of competitive markets. Smith's optimism regarding the 'progress of improvement' challenged the central tenets underpinning conventional beliefs about poverty and the character of the poor, namely, that poverty was an ineradicable feature of civil society.

It was, however, Benthamite utilitarianism which provided the intellectual and normative links between poetical economy and the making of economic and social policy. If the doctrines of political economy set out a reasoned apologia for competitive capitalism, the teachings of Jeremy Bentham provided a framework of philosophical and psychological principles on which the efficient government of such a society could be based and which would make it possible to deal with the problem of poverty in an efficient and rational manner. Three key assumptions underpinned Bentham's conceptualisation of the role of the state in the advancement of welfare. He thought that governments ought to make it as easy as possible for individuals to satisfy their wants through their own efforts. Bentham hated tyranny, especially the tyranny of 'do-gooders' who felt that they could legislate for other people's wants. Second, he believed that human beings were motivated by two innate dispositions – the pursuit of pleasure and the avoidance of pain (Himmelfarb, 1985, pp. 78–84). Third, he maintained that the primary duty of government was to secure the greatest good of the greatest number.

Many utilitarians were attracted to classical political economy because it provided, in the model of the competitive market, an effective means of ascertaining relative individual wants. Many classical political economists, for their part, saw the utilitarian model of a deterrent Poor Law as an essential complement to the creation of a competitive market economy and the free movement of labour. Taken together, these two doctrines constituted what Halevy has described as 'philosophical radicalism' (Halevy, 1928). The individualistic elements in the doctrines informed the popular teachings of the Manchester School of reforming liberals, headed by Cobden and Bright in their political campaigns for the internationalisation of free trade, the moral reformation of the poor, the extension of the franchise and the repeal of the Corn Law. It is these precepts and causes – with their *emphasis* on the *ideals* of a minimal state, the internationalisation of competition *and a negative concept of freedom* – that have come to be described as the 'old liberalism'. In their own time, however, they were considered to be both novel and radical.

As Richard Bellamy points out, the Liberal ideal was never entirely consonant with 'those of egoistic, possessive individualism'. Much of the intellectual history of liberalism is best seen as a sustained attempt to reconcile competitive and cooperative aims and values within the framework of a free society (Bellamy, 1990, p. 2). John Robertson reminds us that Adam Smith's greatest contribution to Victorian liberalism was to conceptualise a political economy in which competition and the creation of wealth could be reconciled with the 'indigenous British constitutional principles of parliamentary sovereignty. In Smith's political economy the government plays a vital role as the provider of certain public goods (Bellamy, 1990, p. 35).

Notwithstanding Bentham's dictum that individuals are better judges than government where their own interests are concerned, the Benthamist disposition to judge political actions by their collective outcomes meant that government intervention was supported if it appeared to be the best way of maximising welfare (Bellamy, 1990, pp. 71–90). John Stuart Mill followed similarly pragmatic procedures in his application of the principle of utility to political, economic and social issues. He saw nothing unduly contradictory in supporting government intervention where market forces were ineffectual, notably in the case of elementary education, public works and hospitals. In his willingness to countenance competition between private and public sector services Mill was a Victorian apostle of welfare pluralism.

Mill supported social reform, as well as female emancipation and enfranchisement in order to assist in the moral elevation and political integration of working people into the institutions of capitalist society. Mill's radicalism, like that of other mid-twentieth-century Liberals, was directed towards moralising capitalism and the working classes. Mill revised the basic tenets of Benthamist utilitarianism with particular reference to the treatment of minority needs and the 'disturbing causes' of poverty which could neither be explained nor remedied within the terms of classical political economy. In the course of his revisions he came to the conclusion that there was no necessary antipathy between individualism and collectivism and that proposals for statutory intervention should be considered pragmatically on their merits (Mill, 1976, p. 969).

Halevy has described how political economy and utilitarianism gave intellectual unity and coherence to the great reforming movement of philosophical radicalism which exerted such a profound influence on the development of British social policy in the early part of the nineteenth century. In the years following the ending of the Napoleonic Wars these reforms found 'a public to listen to them', and they proceeded thereafter to attack 'systematically and *en bloc* all the fallacies of the conservative parties' of the time (Halevy, 1928, p. 313).

There were, however, some conflicts of principle between the various political theories that shaped the evolution of twentieth-century liberal thought. Locke's political philosophy, for example, was grounded in natural law theory and the notion of a social contract. Bentham wanted to replace all notions of natural rights with his single principle of utility. The classical political economists, for their part, looked to the 'invisible hand' of market forces to reconcile the claims of egoism and altruism. John Stuart Mill strove, albeit with only partial success, to reconcile the individualist and collectivist aspects of both utilitarianism and classical political economy.

There were other inconsistencies and ambivalences in the key tenets of the English school of philosophical idealism which also had a profound and lasting influence on the evolution of modem liberalism. In this tradition, the Oxford scholar Green stands out as the philosopher whose teaching encouraged many of his best students to dedicate their lives to the advancement of social welfare. Some of them were attracted to the individualist and others to the collectivist implications of his idealist philosophy.

Green's philosophical approach rested on a combination of moral theories derived from Hegelian and Christian idealism. From the idealist perspective, whatever we know or discover about the world is created by our own minds. Idealism rejects the positivist and empiricist approaches to knowledge. It emphasises instead the power of the individual and human mind and the notion of a common, or universal, good which transcends individual societies and can be apprehended by the intelligent application of reason (McBriar, 1987, p. 368).

Green's Hegelianism was firmly grounded in the ethical teachings of Christianity. He thought that the ultimate test of a good social institution was whether or not it contributed to the development of the moral character of the citizen. Conversely men found their freedom and self-realisation by involving themselves in civil and public duties, which constituted the institutional basis of political obligation and the pursuit of the 'common good'. As the highest level of institutional integration, the good state symbolised this combination of individual strivings towards the common good in the form of a 'general will' (Nicholson, 1990, p. 4). He maintained that issues concerning the role of the state in regulating the enjoyment of rights and the provision of services should be decided in the light of particular times and circumstances. The test should always be whether or not state intervention would remove impediments to moral development and self-determination.

For Green, the idealist notion of the common good embodied a commitment to the 'universal realisation of human capacities' and an 'imperative to will the Good Will, that is, to do what is right for its own sake'. He thought that this approach was superior to that of the utilitarians, who reduced morality to the individual sensations of psychological hedonism. At the same time Green was willing to consider the pros and cons of state intervention regarding particular social issues on their merits and with as much pragmatism as that of any utilitarian (Nicholson, 1990, pp. 190–1). He also believed that the prospects for moral and material improvement were interdependent and he therefore accepted, as Mill had done, that the state should ensure a basic level of subsistence for its citizens (Green, 1986, pp. 203–4).

Bernard Bosanquet, who studied under Green at Oxford went on to become a founder member and the first Secretary of the Charity Organization Society (COS). Bosanquet formulated an idealist theory of the state based on a conceptualisation of the 'general will', which owed as much to Rousseau and to Hegel as to his former tutor, Green. Insofar as Bosanquet and the COS endorsed the virtues of self-help and thrift, they supported the dominant values of the competitive market economy. Insofar as they held to an organic view of society as a moral community they identified with Green's idealism and rejected the individualist and atomistic aspects of political economy and Benthamite utilitarianism.

In Bosanquet's approach, the role of the state was strictly limited to one of creating the conditions in which individual citizens would be able to develop their own characters and thereby discover a collective sense of purpose. The potential power of the human mind was such, in his opinion, that, given the right incentives, it would usually enable the individual to rise above adverse circumstances. Social policies encouraging dependency on the state would destroy these incentives and compound the problem of pauperism. Lack of character was a far more significant cause of poverty than structural disadvantages and adverse social trends (Bosanquet, 1899, pp. 181–200). The tasks of charity and the poor law were to separate the helpable from the unhelpable and to provide for the latter a minimal subsistence under conditions of less-eligibility. There were close affinity between Bosanquet's views on the role of the state in social welfare and the values of old style *laissez-faire* Liberalism.

The New Liberals

During the latter part of the nineteenth century an increasing number of liberal thinkers, politicians, and policy makers came to share Green's idealistic outlook on social issues while attaching much greater importance to its collectivist implications. Vincent and Plant claim that nearly all the British idealists, apart from Bradley, were active liberals (Vincent and Plant, 1984, p. 75). Arnold Toynbee, a pupil and friend of Green, gave a distinctly radical and collectivist emphasis to his philosophical idealism arguing for a greater degree of statutory involvement in welfare and market regulation. Men like Asquith, Samuel and Grey, all destined to become eminent Liberal politicians, were former pupils of Green, and Haldane, another future Liberal minister, edited a memorial volume of his works.

Tawney was influenced by Green during his time at Balliol where he became a close of friend of Beveridge. In Harris's opinion, Beveridge was much less impressed by Green's idealism and the emerging 'policies of conscience' of the time than by the scientific empiricism of T.H. Huxley (Richter, 1964, p. 294; Harris, 1977, p. 2). Hobhouse, who was to develop his own liberalistic theory of social evolution, owed much more to Green's developmental idealism.

These were some of the leading thinkers and political activists who began to redefine the relationship between the individual citizen, civil society and the state towards the end of the nineteenth century. Within the Liberal tradition they laid the foundations of a more interventionist theory of social justice based on a concept of positive liberty which made provision for greater equality in welfare as a precondition for the equal enjoyment of personal freedom. The notions of individual responsibility and personal morality expressed in the form of self-discipline and public service were also central and distinctive features of the political movement that we know today as the 'new liberalism. By the 1890s, this coterie of New Liberals with decidedly collectivist leanings had gained ascendancy in the Liberal Party and began to attract a widening measure of public support. The rise of the New Liberalism was coincident with the political decline of Gladstonian Liberalism. Nevertheless there were some continuities between Gladstonian Liberals and their successors, such as the idea of moral improvement as the cultural dynamic of social progress.

The great poverty surveys of Booth and Rowntree dramatically revealed the extent to which adverse social conditions were preventing any kind of advancement for some sections of the labouring poor (Booth, 1889b, Rowntree, 1901). Both men were liberals in their belief that the competitive market economy was far superior to socialism in its potential for raising the living standards of all classes of citizens, including the poor, subject to a greater measure of state intervention and provision. And both men, by upbringing and temperament, were disposed to redefine all political questions in moral terms (Simey and Simey, 1960; Briggs, 1961b).

Opinions about the role of the state in the relief of poverty were also changing in the tradition of classical economic theory. Writing in 1890, Alfred Marshall, the most eminent neoclassical economist of his time, contended that 'There is no real necessary, and therefore no moral justification, for extreme poverty side by side with great wealth. The inequalities of wealth, although less than they are often represented to be, are a serious flaw in our economic organisation' (Marshall, 1907, pp. 713–19). Marshall, therefore, came to support the idea of modest income transfers from rich to poor, where such transfers did not adversely affect the size of the national dividend (Durbin, 1985, p. 28). Marshall's views were endorsed in the advice that his distinguished pupil, Pigou, gave to the Royal Commission on the Poor Laws in which he argued that transfers from rich to poor through the agencies of poor relief could be justified – provided that they did not weaken work incentives. In any event the poorest paid workers could not reasonably be expected to insure themselves against sickness and old age, and treating them punitively would do nothing to improve economic efficiency (McBriar, 1987, pp. 256–9).

Some of the new liberals, notably Hobson and Hobhouse, took a much more positive view of the role of the state. Both writers thought it was essential to reconcile the capitalist ethic with an organic model of society in which the state would be the main agent in improving the quality of life through policies of social reform (Freeden, 1978, 1990, pp. 1–10). Masterman, who held similar views, thought that the rationale of statutory social services lay in their potential for improving the condition and 'social efficiency' of England (Masterman, 1909, 1920).

Hobhouse's sociology was based on a theory of social evolution and an organic model of society. He claimed that the evidence of human history revealed a gradual progress from competitive self-interest towards cooperative altruism and the growth of organic forms of social solidarity. Governmental intervention in the fields of economic and social policy played a crucial role in furthering this progress (Hobhouse, 1898). The causes of poverty, he argued, were far more closely related to the workings of free-market capitalism than to the character of individuals. Hobhouse strongly supported the Liberal government's programme of social reform but he wanted far more radical changes, which would guarantee a decent standard of life for everyone. This objective, he thought, could only be realised by a radical policy of redistributive taxation that would transfer some of the 'unearned surplus' of wealth from the rich to the poor.

In his writings on economic and social policy Hobhouse drew on the advice of his close friend, Hobson. Hobson was a journalist and one of the most influential writers on the economic, political and social issues of his time. He argued that unregulated capitalism generated unemployment and gross social inequality, which led in turn to under-consumption at home and imperialism abroad. The solution to under-consumption lay in redistributing wealth and purchasing power from rich to poor, which would solve the problem of unemployment and create new opportunities for international cooperation (Hobson, 1909, 1938b). Hobson's economic unorthodoxy brought him into conflict with both the neoclassical economists and the young John Maynard Keynes. As Roger Backhouse points out, Hobson's error lay in the fact that he 'neglected the possibility of hoarding' and that consequently 'his monetary theory remains separate from his theory of savings and investment' (Freeden, 1990, p. 134). His total rejection of the multiplier concept, originally formulated by Kahn and subsequently developed by Keynes, meant that Hobson never came to accept that changes in investment could have a multiple effect on income and employment.

The Impact of Liberal Ideas on Social Policy

Eccleshall provides a useful summary of the development of liberalism as a political philosophy and movement. He traces its origins from the English Civil War, the Settlement of 1688 and the genesis of the Whigs as a political party. The Whigs were the party that opposed James II's succession to the throne. They supported the Glorious Revolution of 1688 and the supremacy of Parliament. The more radical and populist Levellers had wanted to abolish the monarchy and the Lords and also to extent the franchise.

The Whigs remained committed to the idea of an aristocratic society. Many leading Whigs were themselves aristocrats. Throughout the eighteenth century, however, various alliances developed between the landed Whig families and the wealthier representatives of the rising commercial classes. These alliances were held together, not by the old egalitarian ideal of 'a community of masterless and self-governing citizens' that had inspired the Levellers but by a different kind of radicalism committed to the liberalisation of trade and a modest extension of the franchise.

The term 'Liberal' came into popular usage as early as the 1830s. During the 1840s and 50s the old Whig families, committed as they were to an alliance between the landed and commercial classes, began losing their political ascendancy. In 1859 the Liberal Party was formally inaugurated. Gladstone formed his first ministry in 1868 and some years later the National Liberal Federation was established. Thereafter the Party became firmly identified with the Gladstonian policies of free trade, financial retrenchment, political reform and eventually Irish Home Rule (Eccleshall, 1986, pp. 8–26).

The first great period of Liberal political ascendancy ended with the defection of many of the old Whig families and other anti-Irish Home Rulers to the Conservatives in 1886. Joseph Chamberlain, who might have become a leading political figure among the 'New Liberals' was one of these defectors and a prime mover in precipitating the split within the Party, which led to the fall of Gladstone's third ministry (Powell, 1977). Further defections to the Conservatives took place at the time of the Boer War which some Liberals supported and others opposed.

Throughout the latter half of the century the Liberal Party began attracting more support from lower-middle-class voters and some sections of the working class and the trade union movement. The extension of the franchise in 1867 gave added impetus to the appeal of collectivism in the competition for votes and political office. The traditional radicalism of the Liberal Party gradually became more interventionist in key areas of economic and social policy.

As Biagnini and Reid (1991) point out, there was 'a substantial continuity in popular radicalism throughout the nineteenth century and into the twentieth century', which drew its guiding principles from a wide range of political doctrines, including working-class liberalism and populist conservatism as well as Marxism and English ethical socialism. Most working-class movements of the time were wary of the state and of central government intervention, although Thane points out that a closer relationship between grassroots radicalism and municipal socialism was emerging by the turn of the century (Biagnini and Reid, 1991, pp. 244–70; Thane, 1982, pp. 46–7).

Many of the local alliances that were established between trade unions and the Liberal Party lasted into the twentieth century, partly because of the politically diverse nature of British radicalism and partly because of electoral necessity. As late as 1910 over a third of the adult male population – and all of the women – were still without the vote. The pressure for a separate Labour Party grew stronger only partly because the Liberals seemed reluctant to increase its number of working-class candidates. Shortly after the TUC resolution of 1899 to form an independent Labour Representation Committee, the Taff Vale Judgement strengthened the separatist case.

The schism over Irish Home Rule in 1886 left the Liberals a weak and divided party in opposition for the rest of the century. Further conflicts over the party's policy regarding the Boer War were subsequently resolved by Campbell-Bannerman who, with the support of Asquith, rallied the party around a radical programme of social reform which was largely based on the policies developed and advocated by the New Liberals.

In 1903 Chamberlain founded his Tariff Reform League in which he linked the objectives of imperial preference and social reform together in one programme. His subsequent campaigning on behalf of Tariff Reform caused a major rift within the Conservative Party and brought down the government. In the following general election of 1906 the Liberals were returned to office with a substantial majority and a mandate for social reform.

It is worth noting that all the successful 'Lib-Lab' and Labour candidates were unopposed by Liberals. The Liberal approach to social reform was now sufficiently radical to sustain a common approach between the two parliamentary parties. This tacit alliance between Labour and the Liberals survived both the decision of the Labour Representation Committee MPs to call themselves the Labour Party and the two general elections of 1910. The final break did not come until the 'Coupon Election' of 1918, when Lloyd George carried most of his party into an alliance with the Conservatives, and the Labour Party became a dual federation of trade unions and constituency parties, with Clause Four enshrined in its constitution. From that time onwards the path towards a middle way of progressive social reform was closed.

The closure took place because there were increasingly influential elements within the Labour and trade union movements whose political aims went beyond those of ameliorative social reform. British trade unionism during the second half of the nineteenth century had been a politically diverse and fragmented movement. The Liberal Party had been generally sympathetic to trade union aspirations, notably with regard to the passing of the 1906 Trade Disputes Act and the 1913 Trade Union Act.

By this time, however, radical changes had occurred in the composition and political agendas of the British trade union movement. The new liberalism of the time was matched by a new unionism which looked to increased parliamentary representation as the best means of achieving the overthrow rather than the reform of capitalism and thereby achieving a more just form of society and social welfare (Clegg, 1985).

The 'new model' craft unions of skilled workers which emerged after the collapse of Chartism gave high priority to protecting the social welfare of their members. From the 1850s onwards many of them established local benefit and friendly societies to provide strike pay or benefits in times of hardship. Given the complete lack of statutory social services, apart from the Poor Law, the craft unions were well advised to plan for the welfare needs of their members. The unskilled unions, in contrast, were doubly impaired in all their activities – their members were too poor to accumulate regular savings and their capacity for effective strike action was circumscribed by the permanent availability of unemployed non-unionised labourers who were ready to take their jobs.

As the employers drew closer together in the face of mounting labour unrest during the 1870s and 80s, the growth of the unskilled unions added to the number and complexity of sectional union interests based on industries, occupations, levels of skill and locality. The new unionism which emerged from this period of uncompromising industrial strife was characterised by a degree of political radicalism that could not find common ground with any form of liberalism, old or new. Some leading trade unionists, such as Tom Mann looked to direct industrial action as the only way forward. In the years leading up to the First World War bitter industrial disputes occurred throughout the British docks, notably in Ireland. At the onset of war, however, the unions accepted an embargo on disputes and wage claims. Most of their leaders supported the war, and were carried along on the patriotic tide of the time (Dangerfield, 1966, pp. 178–269, 312–21; Coates and Topham, 1991).

There were other issues that beset the Liberal government between 1906 and 1914, notably the campaign for women's suffrage and the Ulster crisis. In 1903 Mrs Emmeline Pankhurst, and her daughters Christabel and Sylvia, established the Womens' Social and Political Union and launched a militant campaign for female suffrage. The government refused to consider this claim except as part of a wider programme of electoral reform. The subsequent harsh treatment of hunger strikers involved forced feeding and the recurrent release and re-imprisonment of suffragettes which brought discredit on the government and its supporters (Holton, 1986; Dangerfield, 1996, pp. 121–78).

When the Liberal government introduced a Home Rule Bill for Ireland in 1912, Sir Edward Carson's Unionist Council formed the Ulster Volunteers to resist the measure, if necessary, by force. Subsequent efforts by the Liberal government to reach a compromise were opposed by Carson and both the delayed implementation of Home Rule and the exclusion of Ulster had brought Ireland to the edge of civil war by 1914 (Dangerfield, 1966, pp. 281–92).

Both of these crises damaged the credibility and reputation of the Liberal government as a reforming administration. With the benefit of hindsight it is difficult to exonerate the Liberals for their mishandling of the suffragette issue. With regard to Ulster they did neither better nor worse than subsequent British governments.

The New Liberalism and Social Reform

The new Liberal government, on taking office in 1906, faced a number of pressing welfare issues, some of them longstanding and highly contentious in character. During the 1890s the debate about poverty had focused on finding policy alternatives to Poor Relief and on the future of the Poor Law itself. By the turn of the century the issues of poverty and ill-health were being discussed within the broader framework of the 'condition of England' question and a mounting concern over the problem of 'national efficiency'. Collectivist reformers, including the New Liberals, were challenging the deterrent principles of 1834, while their defenders were arguing that the rising costs of Poor Relief were the result of failure to enforce those principles. The decision to establish a Royal Commission on the future of the Poor Laws was taken in 1905, during the last days of Balfour's Conservative administration.

After five years of deliberation the Commission could not agree and produced two separate reports. Although there was consensus on many issues, the sticking-point proved to be the future of the Poor Law itself. The Majority Report, written largely by Helen Bosanquet, favoured transferring the functions of the Poor Law *en bloc* to the local authorities. The Minority Report, written entirely by the Webbs, argued for the break-up of the Poor Law and the transfer of its various functions to separate local authority committees. In the event – partly because both sets of proposals raised complex and costly issues of tax reform and partly because the leading ministers had moved on to more urgent matters such as national insurance – the Liberal government received both reports and did nothing (MacBriar, 1987, p. 368).

While the Royal Commission was sitting, a number of major policy developments had taken place under the new Liberal government which bypassed the Poor Law and added new statutory dimensions to British welfare provision. These developments included the provision of free school meals for necessitous children, school medical inspections, new child care services, the setting up of labour exchanges, the Old-Age Pensions Act of 1908, and the National Insurance Act of 1911 (Thane, 1982, pp. 51–100).

The 1908 Act provided non-contributory weekly pensions of up to 5 shillings for old people aged seventy or over, subject to tests of means and character. The 1911 Act covered the contingencies of sickness and unemployment. The sickness scheme was run as a partnership between the state, the big insurance companies and the smaller friendly societies who administered the scheme as approved societies under the Act.

The 1911 Act was modified on German lines, but with some important differences. The British scheme was fully funded across the board, while the German scheme was funded for old-age and invalidity pensions but unfunded for sickness benefits (Hennock, 1987, pp. 176–7). The most important difference between the two schemes lay in the fact that the British one provided flat-rate benefits, while the German scheme was graduated. In Germany the lower-paid workers received very meagre benefits.

The differences in methods of funding, coverage and administration between the German and British schemes were important but the fact that the British scheme was firmly based on a compulsory insurance principle after so

many years of delay was of overriding significance. It represented a fundamental change not only in the philosophical character of British liberalism but
in the relationship between the state and civil society. The insurance principle
represented a compromise between the traditions of individualism and collectivism in the history of British social policy and liberal thought insofar as it
had connotations of both self-help and mutual aid.

The Political Decline of the Liberal Party

The period between 1906 and 1914 marked the apogee of the Liberal Party
as a political force in Britain. The year 1906 was to be the last general election which the Liberals won with an outright majority. After 1914 the longstanding antipathy between Lloyd George and Asquith grew more
acrimonious as they came to disagree about the conduct of the war. In 1916
Lloyd George joined with the Conservatives to overthrow Asquith and
become Prime Minister in his place at the head of the second wartime coalition government. Thereafter Lloyd George became increasingly isolated. He
had lost the support of Asquith's allies in his own party and he was never
really trusted by the Conservatives in the second wartime coalition.

The conflict between Lloyd George and Asquith inflicted irreparable
damage on the Liberal Party. In parliament the Party was effectively split
between Lloyd George's coalition Liberals and Asquith's supporters. In 1923
the two factions came together again but three years later they split once
more after failing to agree on a common policy regarding the General Strike.
Asquith gave up the party leadership and was succeeded by Lloyd George.

By 1932 the Party had fragmented into three parliamentary groups. In the
1935 General Election, the Samuelites and Lloyd George Liberals together
won 21 seats and the National Liberals who supported the Conservatives
won 33. The following year a new Party organization was established which
was supported by all Liberals except the Samuelites who stayed in coalition
with the Conservatives. From 1922 onwards Labour became the second
largest party in Britain and remained so until it won its first overall majority
in the 1945 General Election when the Liberals returned only 12 successful
candidates. How then do we account for the dramatic demise of the Liberal
Party throughout the interwar years?

It has been argued that the decline had already set in during the years of
Liberal ascendancy between 1906 and 1914 when as Bradley suggests 'the
distinctly illiberal creeds of imperialism and collectivism began to take hold of
many younger Liberal minds' (Bradley, 1985, p. 76). Only a few of the New
Liberals were advocates of imperialism but their collectivism might, under
different circumstances, have provided the basis for an alliance with some
elements of the emergent Labour Party.

The majority of Liberals – old and new alike – however, were committed to finding a middle way between the more radical class-based ideologies of *laissez-faire* industrial interests on the one hand and an increasingly militant labour movement on the other. They wanted to civilize capitalism and not destroy it and reduce but not abolish class inequalities through the agencies of social reform. These aspirations, however, were thwarted because of what Henry Pelling describes as 'the long-term social and economic changes which were simultaneously uniting Britain geographically and dividing her inhabitants in terms of class' (Pelling, 1968a, p. 120).

In his controversial thesis on *The Strange Death of Liberal England*, Dangerfield argues that the decline began between 1906 and 1914 when the Liberal government failed to respond effectively to the Conservative rebellion over Ulster, the challenge of the suffragette movement and the increasing militancy of organised labour (Dangerfield, 1966). The outbreak of the First World War temporarily diverted attention from these issues that threatened the stability of the Liberal government. Yet in another crucial respect it can be argued that it was the outbreak of the war that eventually destroyed the Liberal Party itself as a major political force. Under the Defence of the Realm Act of 1914 the Liberal government assumed a sweeping range of new powers including press censorship, the internment of aliens, and the banning of public meetings. In 1915 it introduced compulsory conscription.

As Bradley writes, the coming of the First World War 'brought to the fore many of the values which Liberals most abhorred: militarism protectionism and narrow nationalism in foreign affairs, and increased governmental power and suppression of liberties at home. To make matters worse, it was a Liberal government which was banging the jingoistic drum and introducing compulsory conscription and censorship' (Bradley, 1985, p. 75).

The Political and Social Legacy of the New Liberalism

The interwar years

Paradoxically the decline of liberalism as a political party was complemented by a vigorous and creative renaissance of reformist political debate throughout the interwar years. This intellectual revival owed much to the normative legacy of the New Liberals. As Eccleshall observes, the 'classless image of the party' kept its appeal for 'intellectuals anxious to make capitalism both more productive and more just'. Their goal was a conflict-free and technically efficient society, where people could make the best of themselves in a context of economic growth and ample consumer choice (Eccleshall, 1986, p. 46). The search for a middle way of economic and social reform that was begun by the New Liberals continued throughout the 1920s and 30s in the party's annual summer schools and other gatherings (Greenleaf, 1983, pp. 142–85).

John Maynard Keynes and Lloyd George were regular attenders and supporters of these schools. Both men were committed to the pluralist vision of a mixed economy of welfare combining the best features of competitive market capitalism, state planning and statutory welfare. Despite his increasingly equivocal and isolated position in parliament, Lloyd George remained a key figure in attracting and utilising the support of other leading liberal thinkers like Fisher, Harrod, Rowntree and Scott (Eccleshall, 1986, pp. 45–51).

These were the years in which the Liberal Party published a number of highly innovative and radical plans for economic recovery and social reform including Lloyd George's Yellow Book on *Britain's Industrial Future* (Liberal Party, 1928) and the Party's election manifesto *We Can Conquer Unemployment* (Liberal Party, 1928). Keynes published his critique of unregulated capitalism, *The End of Laissez-faire* in 1926, in which he argued that a revived Liberal Party was the only political movement capable of leading the country along a middle way between the ideological extremes of reactionary Conservatism and revolutionary socialism (Keynes, 1926).

Ten years later Keynes published his *General Theory of Employment, Interest and Money* in which he set out the coherent theoretical rationale for a mixed economy of welfare that the pre-1914 New Liberals had always lacked (Keynes, 1936). Keynes thought that mass-employment was the major political challenge of his time. If capitalism was to survive this challenge had to be faced and overcome. As a liberal economist, Keynes believed that capitalism was 'the most reliable basis for his transcending values of liberty.' As a liberal collectivist, he favoured 'as much liberalism – and as little collectivism – as possible' (Williams and Williams, 1995, pp. 73–5).

In his *General Theory* Keynes challenged the neoclassical thesis that the causes of high unemployment were high wages and interest rates and that the remedy lay in cutting both. There was, in his view, no automatic process at work in unregulated market economies which would ensure that the level of investment was sufficient to ensure full employment. On the contrary, the free play of market forces was much more likely to produce a state of equilibrium at less than full employment. The goal of full employment could only be achieved if government intervened and stimulated both investment and aggregate demand by raising levels of public expenditure and playing a direct role in economic planning and management.

As Moggridge remarks, 'the *General Theory* fell among the economists of the day with a very big bang. Nothing for them was ever quite the same again' (Moggridge, 1976, p. 108). The practical implications of Keynes' analysis extended beyond the world of theoretical economics to all the other applied social sciences. Keynes himself was to play a major advisory role in the making of economic and social policies during the years of the Second World War and the postwar settlement.

Every attempt at find a middle way between the paradigms of unregulated *laissez-faire* and *dirigiste* central planning and the imperatives of competition and social justice still starts and ends with Keynes. Since he was, himself, a liberal in political outlook it is not surprising that his writings had a profound and lasting influence on the Liberal Party. What is more remarkable is the extent to which some sections of the Conservative and Labour Parties were subsequently won over to his views.

The Conservatives were the dominant political party through the interwar years – apart from two brief periods of minority Labour government in 1924 and from 1929 to 1931. Conservative policies during this period were a pragmatic mix of safety-first economic orthodoxy and cautious social reform. The sharpest conflicts between the Conservatives and Labour occurred in the fields of economic and industrial relations policy, notably with regard to the breaking of the 1926 General Strike and the provisions of the 1927 Trades Dispute and Trade Union Act. In their responses to the crises of the early 1930s neither Labour nor the Conservatives were disposed to go beyond the boundaries of conventional economic wisdom. The April 1931 budget of MacDonald's minority Labour government was uncompromisingly free trade in its provisions. When the parliamentary party split over the government's decision to cut unemployment benefits and public expenditure, MacDonald and his small band of supporters formed a coalition with the Conservatives and some breakaway Liberals and won a decisive electoral victory.

Thereafter, Britain was ruled by coalition National Governments. The decade of the 1930s was perhaps the longest period in recent British history during which the semblance of a middle way of government prevailed. It was, however, a middle way dominated by Conservative majorities and opposed throughout by a reduced Labour opposition committed to socialism and purged of most of its moderates. Throughout the 1930s the two National Governments continued following social policies that conformed with the prevailing economic orthodoxies.

More radical versions of the middle way were emerging on the left wing of the Conservative Party during the interwar period. In 1938, Macmillan published *The Middle Way* in which he set out a comprehensive plan for national reconstruction and recovery (Macmillan, 1938). Macmillan explicitly acknowledged his intellectual debt to Keynes in his chapter on financial policy. He called for the provision of major development grants in depressed areas, the introduction of a minimum wage policy and family allowances, the extension of home ownership, direct governmental involvement in the fuel and transport industries and the establishment of a central planning council to oversee the implementation of economic and social policies.

As Ritschel points out, 'Macmillan declared public spending on welfare as not only a "humanitarian thing", but also as "a vital tool of Keynesian economic management"' (Ritschel, 1995, p. 63). In this and other respects his approach might be described as 'a philosophy of business corporatism'. Macmillan himself described it as a form of 'planned capitalism' that would ensure the survival of competitive markets (Ritschel, 1995, pp. 55–6).

Macmillan's search for a middle way brought him close to sharing the middle ground of politics with the intellectual inheritors of the 'New Liberalism'. Changes of a different kind had been taking place within the Labour Party.

From 1918 onwards the Labour Party committed itself to policies of full employment, a national minimum wage, and a financial programme of radically progressive taxation designed to produce 'a surplus for the common good'. Shortly afterwards, with the advice and help of Sidney Webb, an explicit commitment to securing the 'common ownership of the means of production' was written in as Clause 4 of the Party's constitution, The words 'distribution and exchange' were added to this clause in 1929 (Durbin, 1985, p. 47).

Taken at face value, these commitments drew a clear ideological line between the explicitly social objectives of the Labour Party and the more moderate collectivist aims of the Liberal and Conservative reformers. Many of the democratic socialists who supported the Labour Party did so because they were unequivocably opposed to the institutions of capitalism and the competitive market. They supported Clause 4 because they wanted to replace capitalism with socialism. In contrast, the Liberal and Conservative collectivists wanted more government intervention and better social services in order to save capitalism. Like Keynes, they believed that competitive markets were essential to the enhancement of economic prosperity and social welfare.

The membership of the interwar Labour Party, however, encompassed a diversity of views about the ends and means of democratic socialism. It included the Webbs and their Fabian sympathisers who vested their hopes in gradual social reform, national and municipal ownership, central planning and sound administration. It also included Guild Socialists like G.D.H. Cole and Margaret Cole who wanted to create a dispersed network of syndicalist associations with direct workers' control. Other leading socialist intellectuals like Joan Robinson were influenced by both Marx and Keynes while John Hicks, Nicholas Kaldor and James Meade were already committed Keynesians. Douglas Jay and Evan Durbin had reservations about both Marxist and Keynesian economic theory (Durbin, 1985, pp. 149–50 and pp. 176–7).

In his *Politics of Democratic Socialism* Durbin argued his case for 'a collectivist approach to economic and social policy which gave equal importance to the considerations of freedom and welfare' (Durbin, 1940; Pinker, 1995b, p. 233). Durbin was convinced that the future success of socialism was dependent on the extension of choice and market efficiency as well as central planning (Durbin, 1985, pp. 290–4). Yet there were some democratic socialists who rejected such compromises. The Independent Labour Party (ILP) disaffiliated from the Labour Party in 1931. Other radical socialists like Stafford Cripps remained, and for a time, tried to construct a 'Popular Front' with both the ILP and the Communist Party (Pelling, 1968b, pp. 76–84).

The discussions that took place within the Labour movement during the interwar years helped to shape the policies of the first postwar Labour government between 1945 and 1950. They set out much of the agenda for nationalising key industries and creating a universalist welfare state. They also marked the beginning of future debates about the viability of different models of market socialism and mixed economies of welfare which might create a middle way between the extremes of socialism and capitalism.

The Second World War

With the outbreak of war in 1939, the coalition government became directly involved in the management of economic and social policy at every level. Beveridge was asked by the government to prepare an agenda for postwar social reform. When his report was published in 1942 it was widely received as a radically collectivist document (Cmd 6404, 1942). Beveridge, however, 'is easily misinterpreted if his advocacy of universalism is equated with commitment to an institutional model of welfare' (Pinker, 1992, p. 275). In the field of social security his notion of universalism was linked to a subsistence level of statutory provision and the insurance principle. As I have written elsewhere, 'The model outlined in his Report is best described as a horizontally layered, mixed economy of welfare, in which the state guarantees a basic level of provision. This certainly applies in the case of social security. In all the other major social service sectors, notably in health, education and housing, Beveridge left ample scope for the development of the voluntary and private sectors' (Pinker, 1992, p. 276).

As Beveridge himself went on to claim 'The plan is a move neither towards Socialism nor towards Capitalism. It goes straight down the middle of the road between them to a practical end. It is needed in any form of social organization' (Beveridge, 1943, p. 77). He saw state intervention, voluntary service and self-help as different expressions of personal responsibility. In all of these respects he was essentially a welfare pluralist.

Beveridge had been a life-long Liberal although he had never been a particularly active member of the party or any of its policy groups or 'think-tanks' (Harris, 1972, p. 11; Silburn, 1995a, p. 88). Although he sympathised with the Keynesian liberals, 'he found their economic policies not merely objectionable, but virtually incomprehensible' (Silburn, 1995a, p. 87). As Silburn observes, Beveridge held 'an enabling view of state activity' and was concerned more 'to preserve and reinforce existing key values rather than to replace them' (Silburn, 1995a, p. 91).

Keynes, who had little academic interest in social policy, encouraged Beveridge while he was writing his Report, welcomed its publication and recognised the extent to which its welfare proposals complemented the economic policies he was advocating. He played a vitally important role in overcoming Treasury opposition to Beveridge's main proposals (Williams and Williams, 1995, pp. 74–5).

With the publication of Beveridge's *Social Insurance and Allied Services* in 1942 (Cmd 6404, 1942) a new set of social policy proposals was added to the political agenda. Beveridge's Report was designed to appeal across party interests to those of the nation as a whole. Its basic principles and aims, however, were essentially 'New Liberal' ones pointing towards a middle way to welfare between the paths of capitalism and socialism. Taken together, Keynes's economic and Beveridge's social policy proposals were sufficient to provide a coherent social democratic manifesto for a major party holding the centre-ground of British politics.

In 1945 no such political party existed, least of all in the form of the Liberals who had ironically contributed so much to the revival of welfare pluralism in British economic and social policy. The task of implementing these policies fell to a Labour government committed to a programme of nationalisation, full employment, income redistribution and the creation of a universalist welfare state. Soon afterwards, the onset of the Cold War added rearmament to this programme.

The postwar years

Keynes died in 1946 but it was his ideas that informed and shaped both the restructuring of the postwar international economy and the Labour government's policies of social reconstruction. For the next twenty-five years a broad measure of consensus on social policy issues prevailed across the main political parties. Opinions differ regarding the strength and sincerity of this consensus (Jones and Kandiah, 1996). Nevertheless, the basic structures of the postwar welfare settlement remained substantially intact until the late 1970s. The sharpest disagreements on social policy issues arose not so much between but within the two main parties.

The Conservative Political Centre sponsored a major policy review in the late 1940s. This task was assigned to the One Nation Group and undertaken by Enoch Powell, Iain Macleod and Angus Maude. Their proposals, which were endorsed at the Party's Annual Conference in 1950, committed the Party to supporting the NHS, maintaining full employment and extending the public sector house-building programme. They also recommended a greater use of means-testing in social security provision (Macleod and Powell, 1949; One Nation, 1950; Greenleaf, 1983, pp. 313–17).

The One Nation Group wanted to check the growth of collectivism and encourage more choice in welfare. It did not, however, recommend any radical changes in the structure of the postwar settlement. Nevertheless, the genesis of the New Right reaction against central planning and welfare collectivism dates from this period. The Institute of Economic Affairs was established in 1957 and was soon followed by the creation of other right-wing policy 'think-tanks' committed to rolling back the frontiers of the state. The philosophical tenets of these New Right policy analysts were exemplified in the writings of scholars like Hayek, Friedman, Lees, Seldon and Jewkes. They owed far more to the traditions of old-style nineteenth-century Liberalism than to the policies that were being followed at that time by the Conservative Party (Hayek, 1944, 1967; Jewkes, 1947; Lees, 1961; Seldon and Gray, 1967; Green, 1987; Seldon, 1990).

The Conservatives left the basic structures of the British welfare state unchanged after their return to office in 1951. During his years as Prime Minister from 1957 to 1963, Macmillan sustained a broadly corporatist approach to planning, full employment, incomes policy and social welfare. He did so, however, in a context of recurring economic crises and mounting disagreements within his own party. In 1958 his team of Treasury ministers resigned in protest against the rising levels of public expenditure. These resignations were a clear sign that the policy consensus within the Conservative Party was breaking down.

When Edward Heath took office in 1970, his policies briefly reflected the growing influence of neo-liberalism within the Conservative Party before they were moved back to the centre ground in the face of rising unemployment. It was not until Margaret Thatcher became leader of the Conservatives in 1975 that the neo-liberal theories of the New Right came into their years of ascendancy. These changes marked the end of what was left of the welfare consensus. The search for a middle way between individualism and collectivism was, for the time being, suspended (King, 1987; Kavanagh and Seldon, 1989).

The postwar history of the Labour Party was characterised by similar ideological fluctuations and conflicts. The legislation passed by the Labour governments of 1945 to 1950 and 1950 to 1951 marked the political apogee of democratic socialist economic planning and welfare collectivism. During its years in opposition between 1951 and 1964, the party was riven with conflicts over the retention of Clause 4, nuclear disarmament and defence policy, and the future of nationalisation. Revisionists like Gaitskell and Crosland were opposed by more radical party members on all of these policy issues. In his *Future of Socialism* which was published in 1956, Crosland set out the case for a new kind of Labour Party which was both sympathetic to competitive markets and committed to greater equality and the abolition of poverty (Crosland, 1956).

During Harold Wilson's years of government between 1964 and 1970 much new legislation was enacted in the fields of education, social security and criminal and civil justice. Wilson's plans for the reform of industrial relations were, however, defeated by the unions and the left wing of the parliamentary party. After the party was returned to office in 1974 as a minority government, Wilson entered into a 'social contract' with the unions in default of a statutory incomes policy. A second general election later in the same year gave Labour a small overall majority. Britain voted to join the EEC in 1975 and the following year Wilson was succeeded as Prime Minister by James

Callaghan. By 1977, his government had lost its majority and formed a coalition with the Liberals and the Scottish Nationalists. Thereafter, the 'social contract' with the unions was swiftly undermined by industrial disputes. After the 1978–79 'winter of discontent' the government was defeated on a vote of confidence and went on to lose the general election of 1979.

The brief Lib-Lab pact of 1977–78 was the product of political necessity rather than ideological enthusiasm although the two parties shared very similar views on social policy issues. It was the ideological conflicts within the Labour Party that eventually destroyed its electoral credibility. In many important respects, all of the Labour governments from 1964 onwards strove to find a consensual middle way on issues of economic policy, industrial relations, wage restraint through statutory incomes policies and a social contract. This sporadic corporatist endeavour failed, in part, because it was opposed by the shifting coalition of left-wing trade union leaders and constituency party members. The unions were able to exert considerable influence on the movement at conference level through their exercise of the 'block vote' and through their sponsorship of MPs.

There was always a degree of consensus between the left and right wings of the party on matters of social policy although the left wanted to cut the defence budget in order to spend more on social services. They opposed the revisionists' search for a corporatist middle way on other major policy issues because they thought it was a betrayal of socialism. The deaths of Gaitskell in 1963 and Crosland in 1977 deprived the revisionists in the party of their two most powerful representatives.

After its election defeat in 1979, Callaghan was succeeded as leader by Michael Foot and the Labour Party entered a period of bitter internecine conflict. Both major parties had, in effect, abandoned the middle ground of politics but with dramatically different consequences. The Conservatives, having shifted markedly towards the neo-liberal right, won the election and became the governing party for the next 18 years. The Labour Party, in defeat, moved so far to the left that it seemed destined for permanent opposition. The struggle to expel Trotskyist militants, and defeat in the 1983 general election compounded the party's difficulties. Later the same year Neil Kinnock succeeded Foot as leader and launched a sustained attack on the Militant Tendency starting with an enquiry into its activities. Despite a third election defeat in 1987, we can date the party's gradual move back to the centre ground of British politics from this period.

This movement, however, had already been pre-empted in 1981 when a small group of leading Labour MPs broke away and formed a Social Democratic Party which subsequently entered into an electoral pact with the Liberals. In 1988, the Social Democrats voted in favour of merging with the Liberals and becoming members of a new Social and Liberal Democratic Party which has since evolved into the present Liberal Democrat Party. From the start of their association, these two parties shared much in common in their approaches to economic and social policy and the Liberal Democrats today can claim with some authority, that their intellectual and ideological lineages go back to aims and values that inspired the 'new liberals' of the pre-1914 and interwar years.

Unitarism, pluralism and the middle way

These recent ideological disputes and shifts in normative outlook have been reflected in the academic debate about the future of the welfare state since the end of the Second World War. The early period of this debate was dominated to a remarkable degree by the writings of Richard Titmuss who set out an ethically grounded defence of the postwar welfare settlement and played an active role in its extension and improvement.

Titmuss redefined the values, ways and means of the Beveridgean welfare state in uncompromisingly unitarist terms. He opposed the growth of what we now call a pluralist mixed economy of welfare on the moral grounds that it was socially inegalitarian and divisive. He was especially critical of the growth of the private and occupational welfare sectors. He defined the statutory social services in terms of their aims which he identified with the fostering of social integration and the discouragement of alienation (Titmuss, 1968, pp. 20–3). He contrasted the altruism of the statutory sector with the egoism of the private sector and went on to argue that 'the state should be the main funder and provider of social services, and only the state had the authority to implement, without fear or favour, the redistributive policies that he considered necessary' (Pinker, 1993, p. 59).

Titmuss wrote little of substance about economic policy and seldom referred to competitive markets except to disparage their aims and outcomes (Titmuss, 1974, pp. 68–9). He thought that one of the roles of statutory social services was to compensate people for the 'disservices' they suffered as a consequence of economic change (Titmuss, 1974, pp. 70–6). In more positive terms, he believed that redistributive social policies had a major part to play in the transformation of capitalism into socialism (Titmuss, 1968, pp. 116, 151).

Titmuss' approach to social policy commanded considerable respect and support across the disciplinary field in the 1950s and 60s. It became, of course, a main target of attack from the emergent groups of neo-liberal and New Right scholars who attributed the persistence of poverty within capitalism not to competition but to high taxes, inflation and excessive state expenditure. But Titmuss and his democratic socialist sympathisers were also criticised by the scholars of the New Left who rose to transient prominence in the academic debate from the 1960s onwards.

The New Left embraced a variety of socialist ideologies. It included libertarian Marxists, Black Power and radical feminist theorists and elements of the anti-psychiatry movement. It also attracted a group of 'critical social policy' analysts who challenged the Titmussian thesis that capitalism could be replaced with socialism through a process of gradual social welfare reform. They argued that the Titmussian tradition had failed 'to address the conflict between the aims and means of production and distribution' that was intrinsic to capitalism (Pinker, 1993, p. 63). The influence of the critical social policy approach proved, however, to be shortlived and it has steadily lost influence since the collapse of state socialism in Eastern Europe (Anderson and Blackburn, 1965; Williams, 1968; Miliband, 1969; Gough, 1979; Taylor-Gooby and Dale, 1981).

It is to the work of Titmuss' contemporary, Marshall, that we must turn for one of the first modern theories of welfare and citizenship that was explicitly pluralist in character. Marshall had been much involved in the debates about the future of democratic socialism during the 1930s. He was a close friend of Evan Durbin and had once stood unsuccessfully as a Labour candidate. It is, nevertheless, difficult to place him unequivocally in any distinctive political tradition.

Marshall's essay on *Value Problems in Capitalism*, which was first published in 1972, explored the problem of reconciling the claims of democracy, socialism and welfare in a free society (Marshall, 1981). In contrast to Titmuss' unitary model of society, Marshall sets out a pluralist model of 'democratic welfare capitalism' in which 'the rights of citizenship inhibit the inegalitarian tendencies of the free economic market, but the market and some degree of economic inequality remain functionally necessary to the production of wealth and the preservation of political rights' (Pinker, 1995a, p. 119).

Marshall goes on to distinguish between poverty, which he describes as 'a tumour which should be cut out' and inequality as 'a vital organ which is functioning badly' (Marshall, 1981, p. 119). He is in no doubt at all that the task of abolishing poverty must be 'undertaken jointly by welfare and capitalism; there is no other way' (Marshall, 1981, p. 117). In Marshall's ideal mixed economy of welfare the aims of collective social policies and the operation of competitive markets will, at times, conflict but in his view these 'apparent inconsistencies are, in fact, a source of stability, achieved through a compromise that is not dictated by logic' (Marshall, 1981, p. 49).

George and Wilding describe Marshall as a 'Fabian Socialist' and Dennis and Halsey choose him as one of their six exemplars of 'ethical socialism' (George and Wilding, 1976, pp. 62–84; Dennis and Halsey, 1988, pp. 122–48). If he was a socialist, then his acceptance of capitalism must make him some kind of 'market socialist'. His commitment to a libertarian concept of citizenship also suggests close normative difficulties with the ideals of social democracy and the traditions of New Liberalism. As a social policy analyst, he was a consistent advocate of the middle way. He believed that 'economic, political and social rights all expressed different dimensions of welfare, and that it was not possible to go on extending any of these rights at the expense of the others without crossing the critical threshold at which the relationship between freedom and security becomes one of diminishing marginal utility' (Pinker, 1995a, p. 113).

Since Marshall's death in 1981, major policy changes have occurred under the auspices of successive Conservative governments. The institutional map of social welfare had been transformed with the introduction of internal markets and purchaser/provider contracts within the statutory sector. These developments have been matched by a notable growth of academic interest in the dynamics and effectiveness of these new pluralist arrangements in nearly all of the main contexts of service provision.

It is difficult to do justice to the range and diversity of the recent literature which has transformed the debate about the ends of means of social welfare policy. The following salient features, however, merit particular attention. First, there has been a fundamental paradigm shift away from the dichotomous institutional and residualist models that influenced the debate in the Titmuss years towards the normative middle ground between the extremes of collectivism and individualism (Hadley and Hatch, 1981; Johnson, 1987; Gray, 1989; Pinker, 1993).

Hadley and Hatch explored the voluntary 'participative alternatives to centralised social services' within the terms of a pluralist and post-Keynesian framework (Hadley and Hatch, 1981, pp. 170–5). Klein and O'Higgins' reader on *The Future of Welfare* included a seminal essay by Judge and Knapp in which they set out a model of welfare pluralism and applied it to a discrete group of social services in order to analyse and compare the effectiveness of the different care sectors (Klein and O'Higgins, 1985, pp. 131–49). The work of the Personal Social Services Research Unit at Kent has added to our understanding of the dynamics of the mixed welfare economy with particular reference to the interactions that take place between the formal and informal dimensions of care as well as the evaluation of outcomes (Knapp, 1984; Challis and Davies, 1986; Davies and Challis, 1986). More recent reviews and studies of welfare pluralism include the work of Wistow *et al.* (1994) and Ham and Hill *et al.* (1993a, 1993b).

A second complementary development has been the growth of interest in the nature and effectiveness of quasi-markets and their implications for the continuing search for equity in the allocation of welfare resources. These developments are exemplified in the work of Le Grand (1982, 1991), Le Grand *et al.* (1992), Goodin and Le Grand (1987) and Le Grand and Bartlett (1993). The essays published in John Hills' *The State of Welfare*, and the publication of the recently completed ESRC/Suntory Welfare State Programme have carried forward the theoretical and institutional reappraisal of the key policy developments that have taken place in recent years (Hills *et al.*, 1993).

Third, the range and diversity of these theoretical and analytical enquiries into the phenomenon of welfare pluralism have been greatly enriched by the growth of comparative research and a quickening of interest in the issues of gender and race. A whole new dimension of European and Third World focused scholar-ship had been added to the debate (Pinker, 1993; Wistow *et al.*, 1994).

Conclusion

These new models of welfare pluralism have much in common, not only with what was once termed the New Liberalism but with the 'ethical socialism' of Hobhouse, Tawney and Marshall (George and Wilding, 1976, pp. 62–84; Dennis and Halsey, 1988, pp. 122–69). Like the New Liberals, Tawney emphasised the moral as well as the material preconditions for radical social reform. Nevertheless, as George and Page argue, 'what obviously separates Fabian and other socialist groups from the New Liberals is not merely their greater acceptance of State collectivism but their belief that capitalism had to be supplanted by socialism for the maximum realisation of human welfare' (George and Page, 1995, p. 5). In this respect, Tawney was a socialist although he was more an advocate of industrial democracy than of outright nationalisation.

When viewed in historical perspective, we can see how the manner of conceptualising and defining the middle way in social welfare had changed continuously over time. It has always been a concept without a fixed centre of party-political gravity. The policies expounded by Macmillan in the 1930s and Beveridge in the 1940s would probably be considered too radical by the leadership of today's Labour Party. For the time being at least, the consensus points at which reforming parties of the collectivist left and centre right find common ground have shifted to the right of the political spectrum. Nation-alisation and full employment have disappeared from the political agenda. The arguments in favour of greater equality and a minimum wage remain at the centre of the debate but those advocating higher taxation are looked on with general disfavour.

In these respects, it can be argued that the triumph of Mrs Thatcher's old-style free-market liberalism has had as profound an effect on the Labour and Liberal Democrat Parties as it has had on the Conservatives. There are clear signs that New Labour is becoming a social democratic party of the centre and is bidding for the high moral ground as a political movement. As Andrew Adonis observes, Labour now faces 'the challenge of reconciling the supremacy of private enterprise with the appropriate forms of state regulation and welfare to mitigate social ills and equip citizens to succeed' (Adonis, 1996, p. 27). Mr Blair's New Labour Party no longer has a special relation-ship of an exclusive kind with the trade union movement. And much poten-tially common ground is emerging between Labour and the Liberal Democrats on issues of social welfare.

Party politicians, however, seek power and in its pursuit they naturally emphasise their distinctiveness rather than their similarities with other parties.

To do otherwise would open up the prospect of coalition governments and the obligation to share political power. Nevertheless, there is much historical evidence that, in the context of representative democracy, there has been a continuous interplay and exchange of ideas between the major traditions of political thought. Ideas traverse party boundaries with impunity.

Today the true intellectual heirs of the old Liberalism are the theorists of the New Right and the modern Conservative Party. It remains to be seen whether or not the New Labour Party will inherit the tradition of what was once called the New Liberalism, with or without the support of the Liberal Democrats (Jones, 1996; McSmith, 1996; Wright, 1996). New Labour is clearly committed to a welfare pluralist agenda but such agendas can take many different forms. They can give more or less salience to the statutory social services. They can be more or less redistributive in their objectives. These are some of the policy choices that will have to be taken over the next five years.

Welfare pluralists, social democrats – and 'New Liberals' – have always recognised that there are no ultimate solutions of any kind in political life. As Isaiah Berlin observes, 'The world that we encounter is one in which we are faced with choices between ends equally ultimate, and claims equally absolute, the realization of some of which must inevitably involve the sacrifice of others' (Berlin, 1969, p. 168).

Politicians and policy makers, however, need practical criteria to help them in making the necessary choices. Sometimes it is sufficient to consider the public interest and do what seems most likely to produce the greatest good for the greatest number. But the public interest is seldom unitary in character – more often it encompasses a diversity of interests. As John Stuart Mill acknowledged, there is always a risk that minority interests are overlooked when policies are designed to maximise the greatest good of the greatest number.

The middle way of welfare pluralism reflects the rich diversity of values, interests and needs that are intrinsic to our human nature and can only find expression in the tolerant institutions of representative democracies. It is a way that has been followed consistently, but never exclusively, by the 'New Liberals' and their intellectual successors. Yet it also bears the footprints of a diversity of political travellers, including revisionary Conservatives and socialists, as well as collectively minded Liberals. Indeed, the middle way is rather a misleadingly grandiose term to describe what is, in fact, more a mosaic of intersecting paths pointing in roughly the same direction. It provides no fast lanes for the juggernauts of ideological history. It does, however, offer a few vantage points from which travellers can occasionally admire the view without the risk of being run over.

Democratic Socialism and Social Policy

Michael Sullivan

The twentieth century is conventionally seen as a century of social reform. That perception rests on the expansion of state social policy as a result of the early-century reforms initiated by the Liberal administrations and particularly as a consequence of the 'postwar settlement' which established a welfare state sustained and succoured in part by the social philosophy of Beveridge and the demand-management economics of Keynes. The purpose of this chapter is to map the development of democratic socialist political ideas in the UK this century and to analyse their development into a justification for welfare statism. This is done by means of a historical narrative which is concerned not only with the growth of democratic socialist or social democratic orthodoxies on social policy in the interwar and postwar years but also with the transformation of, or retreat from, social democratic nostrums in the late twentieth century.

A definitional word is necessary here. The terms, *democratic socialism* and *social democracy*, are often used interchangeably in the social policy literature and with good reason. Both terms refer to a set of political ideas that suggest that the goal of socialism is achievable through the means of parliamentary democracy. Both democratic socialism and social democracy are, then, parts of what Miliband (1973) has called *parliamentary socialism* . In Labour party political practice the terms have often come to take on different meanings: they were, especially during the early postwar years, often used to distinguish between those party left wingers, like the postwar health minister Aneurin Bevan, who held the view that parliamentary means could achieve anti-capitalist ends and those, like the Labour intellectual Crosland, who saw the goal of social democracy as humanising capitalism. From the vantage point of the 1990s, as the Labour party moves unambiguously to a redefinition of social democracy, this debate might appear theological but needs to be acknowledged in order to develop a full understanding of social and economic policy in the twentieth century.

Democratic Socialism: the Political Source of Social Reform?

British democratic socialism has been inseparably connected with the development of the Labour Party. Since its inception in 1906, Labour appears to have been more indebted to social democratic political traditions than to any other apparently more radical socialist traditions. In the early part of this century, instead of adopting the class-war strategies of some of its European counterparts, the party opted for democratic socialism as a political means and moderate, rather than extensive, egalitarianism as a political goal, with its attendant concern with the gradual reform of state structures and the introduction of social and economic strategies to 'civilise capitalism' (Crossman, 1952).

That democratic socialism, which was later to form the bedrock of welfare statism, was not however the only – or indeed the major – influence on Labour. Initially, at least, two particular strands of thought and action posed threats to any ideas of Labour as the party of social democratic welfarism.

Marxism and Labourism: Twin Threats to Welfare Statism

The threat presented by Marxism

Towards the end of the last century, the dominance of the labour movement by social democratic and welfarist approaches seemed less likely than the adoption of Marxist understandings of politics and the social world.

In the thirty years before the formation of the Labour Party in 1906, the Marxism of the, for our purposes confusingly named, Social Democratic Federation (SDF) had the potential to influence nascent leaders of the Labour Party. The Federation, perhaps the most important of the multiplicity of socialist societies in late nineteenth-century Britain, had adopted classical Marxist understandings of economics and politics. Specifically, it was committed to the idea that as a social, economic and political system, capitalism was seriously flawed. Following Marx, the SDF believed that the ultimate fate of capitalist organisation was that it would implode as a result of the tensions existing between capitalist values on the one hand and the operation of democracy on the other. The road to its final demise would be littered with political and economic crises, each of which would leave capitalism in a more vulnerable state than it had been before (see Marx, 1974 for Marx's own formulation of the nature and future of capitalism).

The SDF's early adaptation of Marxist political theory to the British situation contained elements that both linked it to and separated it from the later social democratic traditions. Under the leadership of Hyndman, an amateur cricketer turned Marxist, it developed a crude and dogmatic approach. It rejected cooperation with the trade unions on the basis that they were simply reactionary labourist organisations and believed that capitalism would be overthrown and socialism installed, as it must inevitably be, through a process of class warfare. This sort of political trajectory, of course, proved to be unacceptable to later social democrats within the Labour Party. The link between nineteenth-century SDF Marxism and twentieth-century social democratic approaches in the Labour Party was that Hyndman believed that, notwithstanding a commitment to class warfare, the British state could be bent to the job of administering socialism once it had been won by the proletarian class. Had the SDF become an influential forerunner of the Labour Party, then the party's development as a reformist political force, both in its wider reformation of Marxism and in its association with social reform is unlikely to have progressed beyond still birth.

A number of factors, however, contributed to the SDF's relative unimportance as an influence on the political direction of the Labour Party. In the first place, the SDF's militant programme and its autocratic leadership contributed to it remaining, in Engels' words, 'purely a sect. It has ossified Marxism into a dogma and, by rejecting every labour movement which is not orthodox Marxism... it renders itself incapable of becoming anything else but a sect' (Marx and Engels, 1968). Engels' words were, as we now know, prophetic. The SDF was to withdraw from the Labour Party just one year after the Party had been formed in exasperation at its failure to present itself as a class party. It was also to fail to win support in the wider reaches of the labour movement. In essence, the SDF came, with the encouragement of Hyndman, to see British trade unionism as a reactionary political force incapable of playing its part in a socialist revolution. It was so because, during the last decades of the nineteenth century, it appeared more concerned with allegedly defensive battles in support of better working conditions of its members and self-help strategies, such as the support of friendly societies, to provide some security for trades union members during times of income interruption (see Thane, 1982). Such strategies could not, for the SDF at least, replace the positive and socialist strategy of direct action by the labour movement to bring the British capitalist system to its knees. The Federation thus came to be seen as anachronistic and its influence in the labour movement decreased as the British working class came to appreciate the crudity of its political position. Its influence on the political direction of the nascent Labour Party was hardly increased by its expulsion of members like William Morris and Tom Mann (Foote, 1986, pp. 22–3) who later threw their hand in with the Labour Party. If the torch of Marxism was to be carried into the emerging Labour Party, the SDF ensured, by its sectarian approach to individuals and organisations within the labour movement, that it would not be the torch bearer.

One of the effects of the demise of the SDF was to minimise the potential authority that Marxism might have developed in the early Labour Party. Although Morris and Mann attempted to develop a Labour Marxist approach in the early Labour Party, the experience of the sectarianism of the SDF proved to be a dead-weight around the Labour Marxists' necks (Pelling, 1954; Foote, 1986; Laybourn, 1988).

The labourist threat

Despite the hostility it engendered among the SDF Marxists, the other early threat to the development of Labour as a welfarist party was *Labourism*. By this I am referring to the strand of thinking and action within the British labour that saw the role of working-class movements as solely the defence of the interests of the working class rather than as including more positive or socialist ideals. Indeed, the best evidence suggests that at the beginning of this century welfarism was seen by working-class people and their representatives in the labour movement as a threat to their attempts to create a better quality of life for themselves (Pelling, 1954, 1968a; Thane, 1984). The labourist response to the extension of state powers under the reforming Liberal government in the early years of the century was to oppose the development of an embryonic welfare state (Pelling, 1968a; Laybourn and Reynolds, 1984). Part of that hostility appears to have stemmed from experience of state institutions that had been the expression of national social policy in the nineteenth century. Pelling produces clear evidence that the responses of ordinary people to the idea of expanded state welfare was to fear an extension of the work-house solution to poverty (Pelling, 1968a, p. 2). Indeed when the Royal Commission on the Poor Law (1905–9) invited the diocesan bishops of the Church of England to collect evidence about popular feeling in respect of the Poor Law, the clerics concluded that it was almost universally loathed. They found that the idea and experience of indoor relief were repugnant to the poor who had experienced its operation as meaning the loss of home and liberty. As a consequence, the bishops found 'a great reluctance on the part of the poor to enter the [Poor Law] union' (Pelling, 1968a, p. 3). Although outdoor relief did not involve the loss of either home or liberty, ordinary people resented it, the bishops found, because of the loss of respect and the sense of social stigma perceived by its recipients.

Experience of state poverty policies were one factor in the hostility of the working class to the idea of state welfare at the turn of the century. Their experience of intervention in education served to reinforce the view that welfarism could prove an additional burden rather than a boon. Compulsory education to the end of elementary school engendered feelings of hostility or indifference among many of the working people who would be the future constituency of a social democratic Labour Party. One of the major grounds for objection was that compulsory state education involved loss of earnings for many families, some or all of whose children became wage-earners long before they would now leave school (Simon, 1974). Despite the view expressed in the report of the Royal Commission on the Elementary Education Acts that:

> the indifference of parents to education for its own sake must, we fear, be reckoned as an obstacle which has perhaps been aggravated by compulsion, and has presumably not yet reached its worst. (Royal Commission on Elementary Education, 1888)

The reality was that many families were dependent on the earnings of their school-aged children as a bulwark against starvation. One concrete example of this opposition to state welfare policy was resistance to the abolition of the *half-time system* in the textile industries. As late as 1909, a plebiscite of the members of the Cotton Operatives Amalgamation resulted in a four to one vote against the proposal to raise the school-leaving age to 13 years (Sullivan, 1991). Although general opposition to state education had moderated after the abolition of fees for schooling in 1891, this particular area of social reform, like the drive for an eight-hour working day, remained substantially unsupported by ordinary working people in the late nineteenth century (see Pelling, 1968a, pp. 3–5).

In Pelling's view, this late nineteenth-century labourist hostility to welfare, notwithstanding official trades union support for an extension in state education barely a generation later, was grounded in an anti-statist philosophy: a belief that the state was run by and for the wealthy (Pelling, 1968a, p. 5). Although the empirical reality of working-class opposition to state welfare seems incontrovertible, Pelling's interpretation of the sources of hostility are questioned, or at least refined, by Thane (1984). Whereas Pelling appears to emphasise the sources of working-class hostility as a desire for independence and a suspicion of the complex and interweaving institutions of the state, Thane is more inclined to see the origins of hostility, or indifference, as stemming from other factors. Chief among these is, according to Thane, the fact that the working class had already created an alternative form of welfare provision. This alternative to state welfare was built on the solid foundation of friendly society activity. These societies, which had a membership of over five million people at the turn of the century, were centrally concerned with mutual insurance against sickness and old age. Opposition to state social security plans seems, according to Thane, to have originated from the belief that self-help was socially and morally preferable to redistributive provision implemented by state functionaries whose activities would, no doubt, involve intrusion into the private lives of recipients (Thane, 1984, p. 879). Be that as it may, one thing seemed obvious. A clearly welfarist party, appealing for the votes of working people in the early years of this century, might have faced extinction shortly after birth. Indeed, psephological evidence, such as it is, suggests that neither Labour nor the Liberals (who were responsible for the early century reforms in income maintenance) attempted to foster their electoral fortunes by appealing to the 'welfare vote' (Pelling, 1968a; Thane, 1984; Lloyd, 1986). Indeed, a fairly respectable argument can be mounted to suggest that the Liberal social reforms were exceptional pieces of legislation rather than reflecting the general political direction of that party in government (Lloyd, 1986, pp. 1–25).

If the analysis presented so far has any validity, how might we seek to explain the growth of democratic socialism and the translation of Labour into a welfarist party by the middle of the century?

Fabianism, Ethical Socialism and Democratic Socialism

A straightforward answer to the question posed above is that, like SDF Marxism before it, Labourism failed to achieve dominance as a strategic political position within the Labour Party. The eclipse of Labourism was associated temporally, and possibly in more direct ways, with the development of Fabian and ethical socialist strands of thinking.

Fabianism: a social democratic creed for Labour

Marx's belief had been that social revolution in Europe would follow the formation of revolutionary parties of the working class (Marx, 1974). Those parties, although made up of a ballast of proletarians, would attract sections of the middle class and the intelligentsia. That analysis, although valid in many European countries, reckoned without the pragmatic traditions of the British! Instead, a number of progressive intellectuals established the Fabian Society, a think-tank before the days of think-tanks, to reform or revise the socialist ideas that were starting to make an impression in Continental Europe (see Foote, 1986). The Society, formed in 1884, is said by some to have been named after the Roman general Fabius Maximus, whom some wags credit as having never lost a battle simply because he refused to engage in any. The political purpose and influence of the Fabian Society over the 60 years between its inception and the coming of the welfare state was, however, rather more complex than the apocryphal inaction of its ancient patron.

The Society, although initially attracting quasi-Marxists like George Bernard Shaw, soon came to be dominated by the political and social ideas emanating from a circle around Sidney Webb. This one-time civil servant, who was to become a Labour MP, had been fascinated in his early life by positivist philosophical thought. Positivism's belief in a well-ordered and harmonious society guided by an educated élite appealed to this lower middle-class civil servant *manqué*. The philosophical approach offered by Positivism was supplemented by his own belief in the importance of collectivist politics which would inform a political ethic based on the idea that the individual must submit to the common good. As he was to write, his theory of life was 'to feel at every moment that I am acting as a member of a committee... I aspire never to act alone or for myself' (cited in Woolfe, 1975, p. 276). This secular Protestantism was never allowed to ossify into dogma as Marxism had been in the SDF. Shaw, Besant, Oliver and other leading Fabians acted as counterbalances to Webb's cranial and rather joyless political creed. Nonetheless, Webb's emphasis on collectivism was to permeate the Society's thinking and that of the Labour Party for much of the following century.

Fabianism's contribution to Labour thinking

Fabianism's major contributions were as follows. First, and in contrast to Marxists, Fabians argued that socialism was entirely compatible with political institutions and modes of behaviour which were peculiarly British. Socialism could be and should be achieved through a parliamentary route and, once this had been realised, a politically neutral civil service could be left to administer it. Marx and Marxists had called for the abolition of the capitalist state if socialism was to be achieved. Fabians, on the other hand, saw, in socialism, an extension of the existing British state (including parliament, the military and the monarch). Socialism for the Fabians was a sort of collectivism, the rules of which would be guaranteed, and if necessary enforced, by a set of neutral umpires, who would include state functionaries, the law and the Royals. In Shaw's words, 'the socialism advocated by the Fabian Society is state socialism exclusively'. Fabian political thought diverged fundamentally from orthodox Marxism in this respect. For Fabians, unlike their Marxist half-siblings, the capitalist state was not, in itself, a hindrance to the achievement of socialism. Early Fabians saw it as controlled, *pro tempore*, by the bourgeoisie but as capable of transformation. The state was, in other words, essentially neutral.

The problem with the state was merely a problem of which class controlled its functions. That problem would be resolved if the class composition of the House of Commons, seen by Fabians as the source of state authority, was changed. Put crudely, the election of a Labour government would, or so Fabians believed, resolve the problem of the state. Some of the Fabian rhetoric, especially that flowing from the pen of Shaw, had a distinctly revolutionary flavour '...[The state] will continue to be used against the people by the classes until it is used by the people against the classes with equal ability and equal resolution' (Shaw, 1893, p. 27). The reality was, however, that Fabian state socialism was based on the idea of Labour's control of Westminster and, via Westminster, of Whitehall. Webb was to describe this view thus:

For the Labour Party, it must be plain. Socialism is rooted in political democracy; which necessarily compels us to recognise that every step towards our goal is dependent on gaining the assent and support of at least a numerical majority of the whole people. (Labour Party Annual Conference Report, 1923)

This is an excerpt of a speech made by Webb to the annual Labour Party conference. In it we see not only Fabianism's constitutional road to socialism but also a hint of what such a road might require in policy terms. Essentially, Webb and the Fabians were to argue that, in order to get the parliamentary power necessary to take over the state and use it for the people, Labour would need to promote policies that appealed to a wider audience than its 'natural' working-class constituency. This claim prefigured later arguments between the right of the party, which was to adopt an essentially Fabian position in this respect, especially over nationalisation and welfare state proposals, and the party's left wing who were less than completely convinced.

Fabianism's second major contribution to Labour thinking is one which seems to have etched itself into the fabric of Labour policy-making procedures. The Society, while concerned to theorise the ways in which the state could be captured for the people, seems to have had a low estimation of the people for whom the state was to be captured. Although Labour socialism was to be based on parliamentary democracy, Fabians appeared to hope that democracy would permeate little further than parliament. In Fabian eyes, representative democracy appeared to rule out the direct participation in policy making by the producer, consumer or welfare recipient:

the utmost function that can be allotted to a mass meeting in the machinery of democracy is the ratification or rejection of a policy already prepared for it, and the publication of decisions to those concerned. (Fabian Society, 1896, p. 35)

Fabianism's faith in the *expert administrator* as the guarantor of British socialism was an early part of its programme. The civil service was to be the guiding hand of socialism with the elected parliament acting as a check on its activities. If the parliament could also be well endowed with experts, then so much the better: a body of expert representatives is the only way of coping with expert administrators. The only way to choose expert representatives is popular election, but that is just the worst way to obtain expert administrators (Fabian Society, 1896, p. 43).

The contribution of Fabianism considered

Fabian thinking, then, might be summarised in the following way. Socialism, or more accurately democratic socialism, required not that the state be smashed but that it is fashioned into an instrument of social change. This would be possible because the state *per se* was not the creature of any particular social class but the politically neutral administrative arm of government. Nonetheless, the expertise possessed by state personnel made them ideally placed to be guarantors of socialism won through the ballot box. As we shall see later, Fabian political theory had a significant effect on the Labour Party in the 1940s and 50s. That it was able to develop such a position of influence was in no small part because it was able to square a circle that the SDF had preferred to leave circular. Although fundamentally anti-labourist in their inclinations 'the working classes [seem to us] stupid, and in large sections sottish, with no interest except in racing odds' (Webb, 1948), Fabians developed a way of separating out personal prejudice from practical politics. For the Webbs, trade unionism had a vital part to play in any well-ordered and humane society. It was concerned with the 'regulation of conditions of employment in such a way as to ward off from the manual working producers the evil effects of industrial competition' (Webb and Webb, 1897). The beauty of this formulation, of course, was that it avoided the dismissive attitude of the SDF to the trade unions, although many senior Fabians appeared to hold their members in equal contempt, while constructing a role for trade unionism compatible with capitalist or socialist government – an equally important consideration as turn-of-the-century Fabians were unclear as to whether they should throw their lot in with the Labour Party or allow their opinions to permeate all of the major political parties.

What the Fabians gave the early Labour Party, particularly after the decision to affiliate to it, was an intellectual framework that was congruent with, and sometimes supplemented, the labourist structure of the Party. The idea of gradual progress towards collectivist social and economic policies is one that has remained with the Party. Fabianism, particularly in this period, was however a pretty cranial business. Although it might have provided the Labour Party with a theoretical rationale for social reformism, it hardly guaranteed the future of Labour as a popular political force.

Ethical socialism: the heart of Labour democratic socialism?

If Fabianism was the head of Labour during this period, then it seems that ethical socialism was its heart. Ethical socialism is here defined as that strand within the Labour Party for which the social deprivation experienced by large sections of the working class before the Second World War was seen as reason enough to support a movement for social reform. At the centre of this reform coalition was the Independent Labour Party (ILP) (formed in 1893 and later to affiliate to the Labour Party), but its adherents included many individuals driven by a sense of Christian obligation or moral outrage at the appalling conditions of many citizens' lives. In many ways the ethical socialists emerged to fill an emotional gap left by the Fabians. But they also often combined this politico-emotional approach with an acceptance and a humanising of Marxist ideas about class cleavages. Their commitment to the creation of a 'New Jerusalem' contributed passion and commitment to the Labour party in the first half of this century.

Ethical socialism's roots reached back into Victorian Christian socialism. It shared with the latter a hostility to capitalism, which it saw as the worship of money, and to private property which, it seemed to many, distorted the spiritual beauty of mankind. More than this, ethical socialism as an ideology emphasised a sort of non-comformist collectivism.

Although ethical socialists were committed, like the ILP, to the collective ownership of the means of production, distribution and exchange, a non-conformist notion of social morality rather than a Marxist passion for class conflict often fired that commitment. Thinkers like Tawney, author of the now famous *Religion and the Rise of Capitalism* (1977, first published in 1922), can be categorised as belonging to this grouping. He, like other ethical socialists, was clear that the *raison d'être* of the Labour Party was the achievement of a more equal society. Like many Labour politicians who followed him, Tawney was concerned not only with the achievement of greater equality but also with the development of a philosophy to underpin this egalitarian drive. For him, as for many social reformers, socialism was merely the expression of a Christian or quasi-Christian morality (Winter and Joslin, 1972). In *The Acquisitive Society* (1921), Tawney located the sources of poverty and inequality in the capitalist emphasis on individual rights to the exclusion of individual obligation. Such an emphasis allowed the wealthy to exercise rights under law in order to accrue wealth. Its corollary was that it understressed the responsibility persons should feel to act in ways which ensured that the acquisition of wealth for some did not lead to the immiseration of others. Capitalist societies like Britain in the 1920s 'may be called *acquisitive societies* because their whole tendency and interest and preoccupation is to promote the acquisition of wealth' (Tawney, cited in Winter and Joslin, 1972, p. 32). Driven by the development of an ethical socialist morality that saw Labour's justification for social reform as the abolition of the mean-mindedness of capitalism, Tawney looked for vehicles capable of carrying this morality forward into practical politics. One of these vehicles was Fabian political economy and especially the Webbian formulation of the relationship between the individual and the collective. The marriage of an ethical socialist morality with Fabian political theory led Tawney to call for a functional society based on the performance of duties rather than the maintenance of rights. This is particularly clear in his *Equality* (1952, originally published in 1931). This book, rightly seen as presenting a philosophy for Labour's democratic socialism, mounted a blistering attack on the inequalities seemingly inherent in an unbridled capitalist system. Within its pages we find an attack on the British upper classes for practising a form of class war by their determination to amass wealth through the exploitation of a labouring class. Rather than regard such inequalities as natural or inevitable, Tawney believed them to be grotesque and barbarous (Tawney, 1952, p. 38). This led him to promote a notion of equality which emphasised equality of esteem and dignity based on common humanity, a definition of equality which allowed for disparities in income and wealth which were not the result of crude exploitation and which placed him at the head of a tradition of thought later expanded by the Labour academic-cum-politician Crosland (1956) and the sociologist Marshall (1963a).

This idea was the rationale for a Labour Party committed to a package of social reform that would eliminate the most blatant excesses of inequality. It was, if you will, a manifesto for the principle and practice of greater equality. While accepting that it was unrealistic to conceive of a society characterised by equality of outcome, Tawney believed that the touchstone for Labour policy should be that:

> men are men, social institutions – property rights and the organisation of industry, and the system of public health and education – should be planned… to emphasise and strengthen, not the class differences which divide but the common humanity which unites them. (Tawney, 1952, p. 38)

Tawney's aspirations were not for total equality but for as much equality as was consistent with individual differences and economic growth. He accepted that differences in education, health and background would be the hallmarks of any conceivable society. But he rejected the idea that these differences should carry with them attributions of social superiority or social inferiority. More than this, his philosophy for Labour was that it should develop economic and social policies (especially relating to education, employment and health) which would lead to the diminution of artificially created differences (1952, pp. 86–7).

Tawney's ethical socialism: Labour and social policy

Of most concern to Tawney were inequalities in education and health where he found them to be all too present. Ill-health and high rates of morbidity and mortality were concentrated in working-class areas. Public schooling ensured that privilege was passed on from one generation to another and, as a corollary, social deprivation appeared to take on a hereditary nature. His argument was that the remedy lay in greater collective action to end or minimise inequalities in education and health. This would result in the creation of a health service free at the point of use and in high-quality free state education for all. The vehicle to carry these aspirations would be a welfare state introduced by a Labour government. Nor was he alone in this. During the 1920s and 30s, a reform coalition loosely centred on the Labour Party pushed for seismic shifts in the perception of the state's role in meeting social need. This is obvious in the pressure mounted by the trades union movement for revamping the social insurance system and in the Socialist Medical Association's plans for the creation of a National Health Service which would be free at the point of use (for example Sullivan, 1996).

Throughout the 50 year period before the Second World War, the labour movement, the emerging Labour Party and leading Labour members had been nourished by Fabian politics and the political philosophy of the ethical socialists and particularly of Tawney. It is one of the implicit arguments of this chapter that Labour's social reform policies in the period following the Second World War are heirs to the pre-war marriage of Fabianism and ethical socialism.

Labour and social reform: democratic socialism comes of age?

By 1945 when Labour gained a landslide general election victory, the hostility of the labour movement to state social welfare appears to have evaporated. In part, this appears to have been the result of workers' experience of the protracted slump in the 1920s and 30s. During that period, privilege and privation appeared to exist side by side: on the one hand the continued drive for profit by entrepreneurial and corporate capitalists, on the other the crushing poverty for the many of the interwar years. During this period the hostility of ordinary people to state intervention to improve living conditions understandably diminished (Cronin, 1984). Trade union opposition to the imposition of a social wage became less strident as many trade union members found themselves without a real wage to be increased by trade union activity. In these circumstances Labour plans like those for a National Health Service, originating from the Socialist Medical Association in 1930 but becoming Party policy by 1934, looked increasingly attractive (see Sullivan, 1992). The call by Keynes, Beveridge and others for a full-employment policy and a welfare state (see Harris, 1977; Thane, 1982; Sullivan, 1992) were similarly attractive. Labour's plans during the 1930s to administer a planned economy should it be returned to government and its emerging championing of a welfare state package made it identifiable with the crucial social issues of the day and was responsible, according to one commentator, for it reaching its zenith as a working-class party (Cronin, 1984). It was, however, undoubtedly the experience of war that set the seal on Labour as a social democratic party and on social reformism as an electoral advantage.

War and social policy: democratic socialism in action?

For many social democrats, the experience of war is seen as a crucial element in the process of building a social democratic consensus within and without the Labour Party. An early and influential analysis provided by Titmuss in both a semi-official publication (Titmuss, 1950) and in an essay in a later academic collection (Titmuss, 1958) has been influential. That analysis suggested that the influence of war can be discerned at three levels: popular attitudes, information about social problems and government response (see, *inter alia*, Harris, 1981, pp. 247–8; Thane, 1982, pp. 223–4 as well as Titmuss, 1950, p. 508, 1958, pp. 75–87). At the level of popular attitudes, the war – or so Titmuss believed – helped to create a hitherto absent sense of social solidarity which was both the bedrock of a social democratic consensus and a step on the road to acceptance of egalitarian social and economic policies.

War had also been a non-partisan provider of information about social problems and their scope. It had exposed social disadvantage and social ills that had remained hidden hitherto. Problems of family poverty, malnutrition and the unequal geographical distribution of health services were stripped bare, in large part as a result of evidence that a large number of armed forces recruits had proved to be unfit for war duty (Addison, 1975, pp. 171–4). Similarly, the failure of the pre-war education system to provide opportunities to working-class children was uncovered by war. Again, the war recruitment process disclosed high levels of illiteracy and innumeracy in the population (Addison, 1975, pp. 237–9). More than this, for Titmuss at least, the combination of changed public attitudes and available new information led to changes at a third level: the level of government response. Attitudes and information combined to convince government of the moral desirability and strategic necessity of intervention to provide welfare services that would meet the social needs exposed by the war.

What we have here, then, is an orthodox Fabian understanding of policy development applied to a specific set of circumstances. A moral–rational consensus on the development of a welfare state was built, or at least its foundations laid, by the provision of hitherto unavailable information about social conditions and by changes in public attitudes to social and political issues, themselves created by an awareness of those conditions (for more detailed accounts of this approach see George and Wilding, 1985, pp. 69–94; Sullivan, 1987, pp. 64–9). Titmuss himself expressed the approach thus:

> for five years of war the pressures for a higher standard of welfare and a deeper comprehension of social justice steadily gained in strength... the mood of the people changed and, in sympathetic response, values changed as well. (1950, p. 508)

This is an interpretation that finds resonances in many accounts. Academics, adult educators and political activists seemed to have witnessed, at first hand, the translation of one kind of social system into another as a result of changed attitudes and shared experience. This evidence arises not only from retrospective reports of an imagined golden age, like Foot's record of wartime revealed in a radio interview in 1983, as the recent British experience nearest to socialism. It emerges also from comments made and written at the time. Foot, like Calder (see below), is thus attributing to the Second World War a catalytic effect more profound than that effected by the First World War. The argument here appears to be that war, coming after a period of mass and extremely visible deprivation, together with the administration of the home front by Labour ministers drawn into the coalition, created a perception – and to some extent a reality – of shared sacrifice. More than this, the experience of the war was also an experience of the success of central planning of the economy and of social policy. Witness for instance the creation and operation of the Emergency Medical Service. This is seen as leading to expectations that wartime 'socialism' might live on into the peace.

Public interest in, and commitment to, a more collective postwar future is evidenced by first-hand accounts of wartime experience. The late Barbara (later, Baroness) Wooton, for instance, commented on the content of adult education classes she led during the war. The classes were, she said, concerned with a large number of social issues but 'postwar reconstruction played a considerable part in those that I took because it was all that seemed important at the time' (Harrington and Young, 1978, p. 120). The Communist leader, Harry Pollitt, pointed to a sort of equality of esteem relating to all sections of the population that accompanied a call to equality of sacrifice in wartime (Harrington and Young, 1978, p. 122).

Further supportive evidence is offered by Mass Observation surveys of public opinion during wartime (Addison, 1975, pp. 206–7, 250; Marwick, 1982, p. 127) which appeared to find that the majority of the population was concerned that postwar society should be characterised by greater economic and social security and that collectivist means were favoured to achieve this end. Marwick (1982) goes further and suggests, like Titmuss, that the experience of war was the experience of collective organisation (p. 180) and that a majority consensus emerged in favour of social reform and a sort of democratic socialism (pp. 181–6). Certainly this appearance is reinforced by the growth of opinion in the armed services that radical reform was necessary and desirable, an opinion encouraged, according to some accounts, by the Army Bureau for Social Affairs. This organisation had, in the eyes of one critic, a tendency 'towards the soft life and total reliance on the State to provide everything from the womb to the tomb' (cited in Marwick, 1982, p. 127).

Clearly, then, this sort of interpretation provides a particular view of the history, nature and provenance of wartime social policy. The history of a postwar consensus politics inclined in the direction of democratic socialism and of a collectivist social policy can be traced back to social policy developments during the war. The provenance of these activities was the war itself or, more accurately, ordinary peoples' experience of all facets of war. That experience included and led to collective organisation to meet the demands that war placed on the population, and to a wish that such collective action, with government as guarantor, might be continued into the peace. In other words the pro-welfarist activities of the war years were not imposed as the result of a top-down process in which government or opinion-formers presumed to speak for the people. Rather it grew from the bottom up. The nature of that pro-welfare politics was itself collectivist and ethical socialist in its nature. It was that individual needs should be met through a process of collective responsibility.

This sort of interpretation had, and still has, considerable currency. Many have regarded the Second World War as, in more senses than one, a 'people's war' (Calder, 1965).

A social democratic welfare politics?

Although I, among others, have argued that the analysis presented by Titmuss is deficient in some respects (Sullivan, 1992), it is clear that the contribution of wartime democratic socialism to the development of social policy was immense. This period of enforced shared sacrifice, of embryonic welfare statism – characterised as it was by the operation of a planned economy – demonstrated that democratic socialism could work and that it could work for a wider constituency than those convinced by more radical approaches to socialism. In many senses, the Second World War acted as a catalyst, paving the way for the election of a majority Labour government and the operation of social democratic social policies sustained by a Keynesian approach to economic policy. In a very real sense the war had also given sustenance to Fabian social theory and particularly to its analysis of the relationship between evidence of inequality and rational and moral responses intended to ameliorate that inequality. The experience of war was among many other things an encounter with the viability of democratic socialism to deliver greater social equality within the confines of a capitalist economy. This social democratic welfare politics found postwar expression in the establishment of a welfare state and in its growth throughout 30 postwar years.

This period of welfare statism was built on an accommodation between labour and capital. The welfare state settlement, while accepting the inevitability of capitalist social organisation and of a degree of social inequality, was built on the foundations of a particular notion of citizenship. That notion of citizenship was refined during the 1950s within the context of a wider redefinition of democratic socialism by the revisionist Labour intellectual-cum-politician, Anthony Crosland.

Redefining Socialism: Crosland and the Welfare State

The late Tony Crosland, initially an Oxford politics don and later a Labour politician, is often credited as being Labour's chief theoretician of democratic socialism. He is, in the demonology of the political left – both inside and outside that party – also credited with being Labour's chief revisionist thinker.

During the early postwar period he was preoccupied with questions about the means of best achieving the Labour party's goal of *more* equality. That is to say, he believed that the aims of a party like the Labour party should include the mitigation of inequality without accepting that its role was the creation of an egalitarian society. This distinction is, as we shall see, crucial in understanding both the development of democratic socialism, on the one hand, and the justification of the welfare state from the assaults of the right, on the other.

As early as 1952, Crosland was arguing that the capitalism to which Marx and Marxists had referred was dead or, at the very least, had been transformed out of all recognition. The welfare state and the mixed economy were themselves evidence of the transformation of capitalism away from a form of social and political organisation sustained through the exploitation of a labouring class. Capitalism, in the words of another Labour intellectual and politician, 'had been civilised' (Crossman, 1952). For Crosland:

> while capitalism has not collapsed as a result of internal contradictions, it is possible to see a transformation of capitalism occurring. Since 1945, capitalism has been undergoing a metamorphosis into a different system. (Crosland, 1952, p. 34)

It had changed, and was changing, for a number of reasons. First, the development of powerful anti-capitalist power blocs, like the trade union movement and the Labour party, in the early twentieth century had placed policy changes on the political agenda that could not be ignored by conservative or radical governments. Second, or so Crosland believed, the political aspirations of the labour movement were, coincidentally, shared by the British business class. In effect, that class came to support the idea of interventionist economic and social policy because it benefited from so doing. Full employment, one of the bases of welfare politics, meant guaranteed high levels of production and consumption which in turn meant the generation of high profit levels. The transformation of capitalism and the development of an interventionist state therefore occurred with the support, or the acquiescence, of the capitalist class. Fourth, a dispersion of ownership of the means of production and an increasing separation between ownership and management had occurred in twentieth-century Britain and, partly as a result, entrepreneurial capitalism had evolved into a system in which the dispersal of ownership had led to the diminution of exploitation. Finally, according to this thesis, the level of central planning that had developed during the Second World War had made a return to free market capitalism impossible. For Crosland and other revisionist thinkers, capitalism had given birth to a new economic and social system. The metamorphosis amounted to no less than the adoption by the state of the regulation of social and economic relationships, a role previously occupied by the market (Crosland, 1952). The revisionist thesis, then, assumed welfare statism to have been part and parcel of the transformation of an economic and social system and the revision of ideas about the appropriate relationship between the state and civil society in the UK.

It is clear that for Crosland, as for other revisionist thinkers, the political project for postwar social democrats did not include the overthrow of capitalism! Capitalism had already tamed itself and the main concern of social democrats was to work within the framework of post-capitalist politics to ensure the maximum benefits of transformed capitalism for all citizens. This view had clear implications for the postwar Labour party's economic and social politics as well a for the wider politics of welfare. He drew out these implications in a series of books and political tracts, the most influential of which, *The Future of Socialism*, was published in 1956.

The positive aspects of his arguments were that, in place of a concern with the overthrow of capitalism, Labour should be concerned with the advantages that post-capitalist politics, properly executed, could bring to ordinary people. In this, he saw a crucial role for government in intervening in the economy at a macroeconomic level to ensure economic growth. That growth was a necessary condition for achieving what Crosland believed to be Labour's most important objective, *greater* equality. Here the line of argument is quite straightforward. First, government should use Keynesian methods to stimulate consistent growth in the economy. If growth is sustainable then it is, in itself, redistributive: increases in the general level of real income having an equalising effect (such increases, for example gave access to goods such as motor cars which had previously been the privilege of the few). Crosland, then, believed that, if incomes were to rise steadily for the mass of people, the consumption cleavages between rich and poor would become much less visible. Second, he argued, growth would play a critical role in

> achieving equality without intolerable social stress and a probable curtailment of liberty... it requires the better off to accept with reasonable equanimity a decline in their *relative* standard of living because growth has enabled them [almost] to maintain their *absolute* standard of living despite redistribution. (Crosland, 1975, p. 6)

Third, growth, and government action to ensure growth, was necessary in order to fund public services without overburdening the taxpayer. Crosland was, and remained, a firm advocate of developing public services. He took the view that part of the process aimed at getting more equality, or as he was to describe it later (Crosland, 1975), equality of opportunity, was aided through the public services. Education services, provided by the state gave, and would give, access to opportunities in education hitherto not experienced by the mass of ordinary people and so on. Without economic growth more social equality was a vain hope (Crosland, 1956).

Two further questions are posed and answered in Crosland's work: how was growth to be assured and what would be the nature of the welfare state funded out of that growth?

His answer to the first question was straightforward even if, viewed from the 1990s, it appears controversial. In essence he argued that growth could be guaranteed by the following:

1. A substantial market sector where price governed what was produced.
2. A privately owned and managerially run productive sector working alongside a state sector and responding to existing levels of profits and incentives in its production and investment plans.
3. A Keynesian state prepared to use its regulatory, fiscal and monetary powers to support growth and sustain full employment.
4. A free trades union movement which pursued its objectives of protecting and improving its members' standard of living in a way compatible with such a mixed economy (see Crosland, 1956).

Fundamentally, the argument being rehearsed here is for what Furniss and Tilton term a 'social security state' (Furniss and Tilton, 1979). In abstract terms, the elements of acceptable activity that make up Crosland's conception of such a state are as follows.

First that governments should act to correct, supplement and, only if absolutely necessary, displace the market system of exchange. Governments' intention in acting in this way would be the promotion and development of greater equality, democracy and welfare, goals that Crosland believed were the shared property of the allies of welfare statism. Crosland's prescription for this sort of activity takes into account that welfarism, while the shared property of the policy elites of the two major parties, had not necessarily permeated the social and political structure of the system as a whole. The proposition lying behind this prescribed role for government can be expressed thus. In a liberal-democratic, mixed economy society there will exist, notwithstanding broad party political consensus, a plurality of power bases and different sites of economic control. Sometimes, when consensus at the top fails to trickle down, governments would need to be prepared to lay down ground-rules, especially in the industrial field, to ensure conformity with the government's own view of the national interest (Crosland, 1975). Or, as Crosland had put it during the period we are now considering:

to guide the private (and public) sector to forms of *collective* action to achieve collective goals which individuals cannot achieve with the same measure of success, by their isolated efforts (Crosland, 1956, p. 61 emphasis added).

Second, governments should use social expenditure and other means at their disposal to *modify* inequalities and injustices associated with a market system of distribution (Crosland, 1956). This prescription acknowledged the potential lack of fit between welfarism and a market system of economic distribution and proposed the solution that governments, when faced with aspirations in the private sector of the economy to maximise profit rather than to meet social and economic needs of citizens, should provide a countervailing system of need–satisfaction. Working through systems of social expenditure, governments should redistribute resources, through taxation, income maintenance or services in kind (George and Wilding, 1985; Sullivan, 1987).

In more concrete terms, Crosland's views on the role and nature of a welfare state, and its position in a mixed economy, provide interesting reading. They do so because they represented a social democratic manifesto and rationale for welfarism: a justification for maintaining a centrally funded universalist welfare state; a rationale for the extension of that welfare state to provide more equality through consumption-oriented social policies rather than production-oriented economic policies; a refutation of the right-wing prescription for less welfare; and a rebuttal of the aspirations of the Labour left for a marriage of economic and social policies intended to bring about equality of outcome rather than equality of opportunity.

As has been made clear above, Crosland, like the left of the Labour party, was unwilling to separate issues of social policy development from issues of economic development. In detail, this meant that full employment and economic growth were indispensable if Crosland's democratic socialism was to work. The lower the level of unemployment, the more economic power was shared with workers. If labour was in short supply, which would be the consequence of full employment plus economic growth, then a sort of equalisation would occur between unions and management in wage bargaining and negotiations over workers' terms and conditions of employment. Additionally, high levels of employment at reasonable rates of return meant that there would be less call on those areas of the welfare state most used during times of unemployment-related poverty: social assistance, social work and primary health care. Crosland's argument was that the welfare state had eradicated absolute poverty and that economic growth provided the resources to ameliorate relative poverty.

The welfare state *per se* was not to be about creating equality, nor even in many cases to be the major weapon in the attack against relative poverty. Nor was it, as we have seen above, to be seen as a battering ram to destroy remaining inequalities. In his own words, 'social equality cannot be held to be the ultimate purpose of the social services' (Crosland, 1956, p. 148). Rather:

The object of social services is to provide a cushion of security... Once that security has been provided further advances in the national income should normally go to citizens in the form of free income to be spent as they wish and not to be taxed away and then returned in the form of some free service determined by the fiat of the state. (Crosland, 1952, p. 63)

The welfare state in a post-capitalist society was to function to ameliorate the diswelfares created when the interaction between state regulation of the economy and the private industrial sector of the economy failed, without further help, to aid equality of opportunity.

In the political context in which it was made, Crosland's reformulation of the ends and means of democratic socialism not only clarified, and to some extent changed, the direction of the Labour Party's social politics. It also acted as a firm and important rebuttal of the ideas being floated by the Conservative right. It certainly had an effect on both strategy and policy in the Labour Party. From the mid-1950s until the untimely death of the Labour leader Gaitskell in 1962, the leadership of the party adopted a policy position which, while resisting the direction prescribed by the Labour left, appeared progressive and pro-active. It appeared progressive because it was concerned, albeit using a somewhat different definitional yardstick, with issues of equality, as were the policy positions of the left. It was pro-active because apparently egalitarian policies were developed from the centre rather than the centre reacting to developments from the left of the party, as had often been the case.

More than this, however, it was a direct rebuttal of the policy prescriptions of the Conservative right and the political principles which lay behind those prescriptions. The attack against the views and precepts of the right took the following form.

First, Crosland constructed, as we have seen, an argument for a universal welfare state which, while less extensive in its scope than some would have wished, was a counterbalance to the residualism of the right. Crosland's welfare state was to be universal in coverage, sufficiently resourced as to facilitate equality of opportunity for all citizens but was to stop well short of attempting to create equality of outcome. In other words all were to be catered for but the level of support was to be consistent with seeing the role of a welfare state as providing security rather than equality. This, of course was entirely consistent with the aspirations of Beveridge and Keynes and with the political centre of gravity in the postwar Labour party – Crosland had redefined rather than recreated Labour's social policy. However, and this is the crucial point, this approach to social politics attempted to neutralise the Conservative right's major attacks on the legitimacy and cost of state welfare. For Crosland was arguing loudly and clearly that the proper role of a state welfare system was not to bring about equality. The siren call of the political right was that its goal was to do precisely that. Crosland, in accepting that full equality was unattainable, and perhaps undesirable, appears to have taken the political rug from under his adversaries' feet. Welfare statism was legitimate because it was consistent with the values of a reformed capitalism, not inimical to them. The beauty of this reformulation of democratic socialism was that it sidelined the debate, raging at this time in the Labour Party, about state ownership of industry and argued instead that greater equality could be more effectively achieved in a market-oriented society by the twin mechanisms of progressive taxation and a redistributive welfare state.

His argument also took on board the apparently genuine view from the right that continued welfare state development was too costly for the British economy to bear, or imposed costs, both monetary and to freedom, on the individual which ought to be avoided. The response to this sort of argument is quintessentially Fabian. Welfare is to be financed out of economic growth. If growth falters then so should further welfare development. The welfare state should neither be financed excessively from direct taxation nor should it substantially affect the absolute material health of the rich. A 'growth premium' should be used to finance developments in welfare and those developments should be used to improve the social and economic position of the poorest while only marginally diminishing the wealth of the rich.

Social democratic views of the state and government are overt in Crosland's analysis. The consensus on rights has roots in a democratic tradition. It may, at times, have been forged out of struggle and conflict but once that consensus had emerged governments inevitably responded to an irresistible groundswell of opinion and the state machinery aided the expansion and implementation of social rights.

This, then, represented the democratic socialist approach to social policy and the welfare state in the postwar period. That approach was, however, to be significantly modified in the light of the election of four Conservative administrations in the 1980s and 90s that were, or appeared to be, committed to post-consensus, neo-liberal policies. These policies, or in some cases the rhetoric that surrounded them, challenged the very notions of a collectivist welfare state and citizen rights to welfare. Facing difficulties of attracting electoral support for labour economic and social policies, Labour in the 1990s appears once more to have redefined the essence of democratic socialism.

During the late 1980s and the early 1990s Labour's democratic socialism appears to have removed the language of equality from democratic socialism and to have moved closer, in social policy terms at least, to the Conservative hegemony of the preceding decade and a half.

It was the hope of many and the expectation of some that the election of a Labour government at the beginning of the 1990s would have marked the beginning of a reversion to the guiding hand of Keynes in economic policy and the principles of Beveridge in social policy. Moreover, there were certainly some elements of the old Labour in its 1991 document on the NHS. In a side-swipe at the Conservatives' emphasis on efficiency strategies in the NHS, the document asserts that 'most of what appears as inefficiency [in the NHS] is the product of underfunding'. The document also makes clear Labour's intention was to change the present balance of health authority membership: to replace the concentration on business interests, introduced by the Conservatives as part of the health service reforms, with a bias towards accountable community representatives in the first instance and by elected bodies in the longer term.

But even here there is also a substantial recognition of the durability and acceptability of some elements of the Conservatives' health service reforms. Of most significance, perhaps, was Labour's intention, despite earlier ambivalence, to retain the split between the purchaser and provider in the NHS, a crucial element in welfare pluralism in health. This is clearly an acknowledgement of the potential success of this mechanism in improving service. This, alongside another acknowledgement of Conservative social policy, might suggest that Labour, like the Conservatives, sees a degree of competition in welfare as likely to assist not only its commitment to peg direct taxation at its present level but also a commitment to meet patient need. These policy planks were substantially accepted in Labour's election manifesto and would have formed the framework of policy development had Labour been returned. Substantial refunding of the welfare state would, however, be dependent on significant economic growth.

Labour's move towards Conservative social policy aims is clear in other social policy areas as well. As we have seen a purchaser/provider split in personal social services, planned under the provisions of the National Health Service and Community Care Act (1990), has become common political property as has the elevation of the role of the voluntary organisations in both planning and providing care (Labour Party, 1990). One illustration of this is that Labour's revamped District Health Authorities would include substantial representation from this sector.

Of course large differences in approach to social policy remain between the major parties . The 'new' Labour party continues, for now at least, to reject opt-out schemes in education and health and therefore wish to draw a clear demarcation line between services regarded as public and those regarded as private. It is pledged to work to force the reversal of underfunding in the heartland services of the welfare state: health, education, and social security.

It had nonetheless moved a great distance, even before the watershed election of 1992. Its policy aspirations in the early 1990s appear to take account of the shifts in public opinion documented in recent commentaries on welfare provision. Labour may, in crude terms, have become more aware in the late 1980s of the complexities contained within public attitudes to welfare. Those complexities embrace not only the strong support for heartland welfare state services, which – or so it was argued in the last chapter – have acted as a brake on Conservative social policy plans, but also another set of attitudes.

The picture that emerges from a relatively recent and rigorous study of public attitudes to welfare can be summarised as follows.

1. Continued support for the heartland services of the welfare state (the NHS, state education and pensions) that exists not only at the level of principle but also at the more practical level of a willingness to pay more in taxes to protect the quality of services (Papadakis and Taylor-Gooby, 1987).
2. However, within this general support there appear to be extremely complex structures of opinion about welfare. This has led to much less significant levels of support for social policy areas in which social minorities are seen as the major beneficiaries and for some universal services, for example Child Benefit (Taylor-Gooby, 1986).
3. The coexistence, alongside support for the heartland services of the welfare state, of support for private provision in health, education and pensions and for fiscal subsidies to private services (Taylor-Gooby, 1986; Papadakis and Taylor-Gooby, 1987).

In other words, the strong support for the welfare state, which has acted as a bulwark against demolition, masks within it a public ambivalence – or did so in the late 1980s. The nub of the paradox is this. Public opinion appeared in favour of taking its welfare state neat while a significant minority appeared to favour a plurality of services where welfare state services represented one, possibly the main, option.

Shifts in Labour policy plans toward more toleration of a mixed economy of welfare appear, then, to shadow shifts in public opinion. That opinion, as well as signalling tolerance of a private welfare sector, also suggests that its presence is a key to the maintenance of quality services in the public sector. One interpreter of public opinion in this respect argues that the possibility of 'exit' from welfare state services is seen by consumers as increasing the influence of their 'voice' within them (Taylor-Gooby, 1986). The existence of a private sector is, therefore, seen as a guarantor of quality services in the public sector and of consumer responsiveness and accountability. If that opinion has influenced the political process of policy-making within the party, there have also been other less instrumental considerations that may have led it in the same direction.

Labour, in participating in such a change in the politics of welfare might well, of course, have sought to emphasise the continuity with, rather than the divergence from, previous policy positions on the welfare state. A Labour government might have argued that the party has always regarded the welfare state as an opportunity state. In this they would have been aided by the clear attempts of the party leadership over the last five or six years to make this very point.

I have drawn attention elsewhere to Labour's relatively recent attempts to defend the idea of fusion between a Beveridgian welfare state and a so-called 'opportunity state' (Sullivan, 1990). Both in a Fabian Society lecture in 1985 (Kinnock, 1985) and in a speech on the eve of the 1987 general election, the leader of the Labour Party tried to construct a defence for restructured Beveridgian democratic socialism in new political times. His argument was that a major function of the 'old' welfare state was that it had increased opportunity. In his 1987 speech he illustrated his point by a question addressed to his audience at the Welsh Labour Party Conference. 'Why', he asked, 'am I the first Kinnock to get to university and why is Glenys [Kinnock] the first woman from her family to have done the same?' (Kinnock, 1987). The answer was the welfare state and its widening of access to higher education. The speech was significant because it presented the welfare state as the 'opportunity state'. The argument being constructed was that it had only been possible to meet *individual aspirations* through *collective provision*. This appeal to the opportunity state is interesting because, while appearing to mine the rich seam of conventional postwar British democratic socialism and particularly the Crosland legacy, it also represents an acknowledgement of the changes wrought in United Kingdom social politics by the Thatcher experiment. In other words, there is an attempt to present, under the cloak of the old democratic socialism, a move from the old emphasis on the collectivity to a new emphasis on the individual. The welfare state is to be nurtured because it facilitates individual development. Taxation for collective provision is simply the investment to be paid for individual protection and progress.

This move has been reflected in many of Labour's policy documents in the late 1980s and the 90s. During this period, the party carried out policy reviews as part of the process of rehabilitating the party in the eyes of the electorate after a period in the early 1980s when it had appeared to be controlled by its left wing. Those documents that concentrate on welfare issues (Labour Party, 1989, 1990) are noteworthy because they stress the concern of the party with individual issues such as liberty, freedom of choice and consumerism that had been colonised through much of the 1980s by right-wing Conservatism in government. Labour's former deputy leader, Roy Hattersley, economically expressed the task addressed in these documents. In a short essay written at the end of the 1980s he argues that the responsibility of a future Labour government will be to 'provide and popularise an acceptable theory of distribution that is both consistent with egalitarian principles of socialism and with a modern economy' (Hattersley, 1989). Decoded, this amounts to an acceptance not only of much of the change wrought in methods of economic management in the 1980s but also of some of the directions in social policy followed during this decade.

Back to Labour – had it happened in 1992 – would not have meant back to a Beveridge-style welfare state. The extent to which improvements in services would have been affected under an incoming Labour government was dependent, however, on a notion that has always sat fairly comfortably with the idea of a Labourist/Beveridgian welfare state. That notion was that the good of the many should, in part be ensured, by the relative sacrifice of the few. Labour's mildly redistributive tax plans, which seem ultimately to have proved electorally unpopular, would have funded improvements in pensions and child benefit. The lifting of the ceiling on national insurance contributions would have funded increases in spending of £1 billion in health and £660 million in education. In the end, the so-called *Essex Man* phenomenon ensured a postponement, if not the cancellation, of a Labour administered post-Beveridgian welfare state (Aitken, 1992; Curtice, 1992; Gould, 1992).

In the period since 1992, however, even more significant changes have been afoot. Tony Blair's division of *socialism* into *social-ism* marked out new territory for democratic socialism. Although based on the tenets of the Labour leader's own ethical socialism, this approach replaces *old Labour*'s emphasis on the obligation of the state to encourage and, if necessary, pepper collective values with an individualistic appeal to citizen's altruism. In policy terms, this new communitarianism has led to the almost complete transmogrification of democratic socialism into support for an enabling state *pace* the Conservatism of the mid-1980s. Gone, it seems, is the idea of the state as the arbiter, regulator and sometimes provider of welfare. The democratic socialism of the late 1990s appears to have become an anti-statist set of ideas more reminiscent of the Liberalism of the end of the nineteenth century than of the democratic socialism of the postwar years. Readers may object that this reading of the recent past is unduly alarmist. However, this analysis draws further support, or so it seems to the author, from the policy aspirations of the *New Labour* government. Anticipated changes in the social security system – the welfare-to-work programme, the removal of the lone parent supplement and so on – augur ill for the idea of a revitalised, social democratic welfare state. Borrowing from the Clinton reforms in the USA, what appears more likely is a shift in the philosophy underlying social welfare. That shift is one from citizen entitlement towards citizen obligation with the state taking on an increasingly residualist role. This embryonic approach also appears to be mirrored in health policy. In relation to health, the present government seems likely to continue, and perhaps accelerate, the shift from universal entitlement towards individual responsibility that was a hallmark of the Thatcher and Major administrations. This is already clear in attempts to restructure services, in the shift from health education to health promotion strategies and in the shift in successive versions of *The Patient's Charter* towards stronger emphases on individual responsibility for health. Health policy then is moving slowly from a focus on 'need' to one on individual deserts. Indeed, these and other issues are encapsulated in the continuing debate over rationing and prioritisation of services in the NHS.

Given the newness of the government, the measured, academic response would be to regard the jury as still out but there appears at least *prima facie* evidence that the Labour Party, in moving away from social democracy, is also moving away from support for a social democratic welfare state. What an irony if the midwife of the welfare state also becomes one of its pall-bearers.

PART III

Welfare and the State

6

Education

Michael Sanderson

The State and Education

At the dawn of the century de Montmorency wrote the first historical study to examine the involvement of the state and education. He did so to criticise what he saw as the lack of a national education in the nineteenth century and to encourage 'the work of reconstruction and organisation (which) has been taken up by statesmen' in his own day (de Montmorency, 1902, p. vii). In truth the British, in contradistinction to the French and Germans, prefer to speak of 'government' rather than the 'state'. We also have a greater belief in the importance of civil society and civic culture – the world of business, work, family, leisure, religion – than in the power or desirability of the state to change things (Harris, 1990a). Accordingly the intervention of the state in education is a relatively late development. The turning of England into a literate society for the first time in the first two thirds of the eighteenth century was achieved by charitable and church activity. The first government grant of 1833 and Factory Act of the same year was partly in response to the fall back in literacy in the industrial north. Even then the creation of modern mass literacy by the mid-Victorians was a triple joint enterprise. First, there were annual state grants for building and running schools and state inspectors, second the private money and organisation of Church societies and third, working-class schools run by self-employed teachers paid for by working-class parents themselves (Mitch, 1992). After 1870 the state began to take a more positive role. The local government School Boards (1870–1902) raised rates to build schools and enforce attendance which became nationally compulsory for the ages 5–10 from 1880 assisted by free education from 1891. At a higher level local government built technical colleges from 1889 and in the same year central government began making grants to universities. The state was becoming more involved with education and Paul Johnson reminds us that in a society in which most people had no personal contact with the state around 1900, children – through their teachers – were very unusual in having regular contact with public sector employees (Johnson, 1994b, p. 479).

Various factors had drawn the state into education by the turn of the century. The increasing awareness of poverty and its possible actual increase in the late 1890s and 1900s increased the need for the state to appropriate responsibility for education from the poor parent by coercion and assistance. Poverty also diminished the likelihood that parents would forego child earnings for freely chosen schooling. The state also needed elites to provide leadership in government and Empire. Britain could not rely on the same narrow traditional class to produce leaders by heredity. In the views of public figures like Webb, Morant and Bryce elites must circulate and be replenished by outstanding ability from below, drawn up through the education system from the slum to the Oxbridge tutorial. Only the state could provide this capillary force. The state was also concerned about the competitiveness of the economy. The turn of the century was a period of anxiety about Britain's decline from former economic world primacy and a fear of trade competition from goods 'Made in Germany' and imported on the 'American Invasion'. Entrepreneurs assumed that the state would provide the educated labour force that industry needed, not that it was their job or that they could rely on the working man to pay for it himself. Compulsory state education also met other problems. It contributed to the decline of juvenile delinquency notable at the time. It also began to prepare the masses for war in South Africa and Europe by developing intellect, discipline and physique through schools. Overriding all these concerns was that of 'National Efficiency', to make the nation efficient to meet competition in peaceful trade and military conflict. Education from the elementary school to Imperial College was a key strand in these concerns. Our chief competitor, Germany, had a highly state controlled and financed educational system and by analogy it was thought that Britain had to move in this direction to match her. For such admirers of Germany like Haldane and many officials in the Board of Education, education was too important to leave to the free choice of parents and employers. The state had to coerce, enable and finance, to ensure the necessary service. Early forms of socialism from the 1880s also advocated state education as a right of the working classes, preparing them for jobs that would avoid poverty, enabling the ablest to rise and opening the minds of all to culturally richer lives.

The century opened with an act of destruction as a prelude to great creativity (Kazamias, 1966; Lowndes, 1969). In the later years of the nineteenth century higher grade schools had been established. These were elementary schools but in effect acting illegally as secondary schools largely for the working class. They had been justified as a way of giving working-class children unable to go to secondary schools a form of post-elementary education under the 1870 legislation intended only for elementary education. Unsanctioned by law they were declared illegal in 1900. This cleared the way for a sequence of measures which laid the foundation of British twentieth-century education. The 1902 Education Act created new Local Education Authorities

(LEAs) and required them to build new municipal rate-supported grammar schools. These now joined old endowed grammar schools and ensured that each town had at least one secondary school. Moreover, access to these grammar schools was facilitated by the provision of scholarships that enabled elementary schoolchildren to enter grammar schools by the 11+ examination and from 1907 grammar schools had to allocate a quarter of their places for such ex-elementary schoolchildren. What they learnt there would be useful since from 1904 they had to teach classics which were an entrance requirement to Oxford and Cambridge. LEA scholarships to university also began in 1902 and it was in this period 1900–09 that six major civic universities were granted charters as independent institutions. The expansion of higher education thus linked with expanding secondary education in the first decade of the century, both providing new opportunities for young people whose expectations had not hitherto included secondary and university education. The state had helped bring both about.

Beyond the academic other forms of education catered for other needs and abilities. Central schools were developed to provide a commercial education for future clerks and the women secretaries of the so-called 'white blouse revolution'. Junior technical schools (JTSs) with regulations in 1905/06 and 1913 provided technical training for 13+ year-olds in skilled crafts, engineering and construction. The creation of schools careers guidance in 1911 helped steer all these young people away from the 'dead-end job' which troubled the Edwardians as much as the 'decline of apprenticeship', while school meals (1906) and school medical inspection (1907) catered for their bodies as well as their minds. This strong intervention by the state in improving prospects for the young was the counterpart of the Edwardian legislation attacking the roots of the poverty of their parents. All these developments of state intervention in education (1902–11) were presided over by Sir Robert Morant, the Permanent Secretary of the Board of Education and avowed admirer of étatiste French and Germanic systems and quite the most influential shaper of the British structure in the twentieth century. Philip Gosden has observed 'thus in a decade or so following the Education Act of 1902 the central administrative agency for education was built up... largely under the direction of Robert Morant' (Gosden, 1966, p. 105). Shortly before the end of the First World War the state intervened again with Fisher's 1918 Education Act (Sherington, 1981). This raised the school-leaving age to 14 and enabled LEAs to provide day continuation schools from school-leaving to 16. They were to be counterparts of the JTSs in that together they replicated the purposes of the German Trade Continuation Schools (Fortbildungschulen). It was intended that they would ease the transition into work of the teenager by requiring part-time continued education at school and would provide an educational support for whatever trade training they were receiving. After the war a brief boom was followed by a slump starting in late 1920 and a cabinet decision to cut educational expenditure in December 1920 put into effect by

Circulars in January and August 1921. Sir Eric Geddes' committee on national expenditure reported in 1922 and called for further economies in spending on education. Capital expenditure on education accordingly fell from £2.7 million in 1920–21 to £1.2 million by 1922–23. This led to the abandoning of schemes for creating Continuation Schools and making them compulsory. The exception was Rugby where the school was especially valuable for the apprentices of local electrical works and railway workshops.

The state had a more lasting impact in the 1920s and 30s through its attempt to advance policies on the relationship of elementary and secondary education. Morant had left a system whereby all children attended elementary schools and a small proportion had the opportunity of moving on to grammar, central or junior technical schools. The vast majority stayed in elementary schools until they left at 13 with no pretence of secondary education. In the interwar years now that children stayed until 14 it was desirable to provide something more genuinely post elementary. Sir Henry Hadow, the Vice Chancellor of Sheffield University and Chairman of the Board of Education Consultative Committee was asked to consider this. In 1926 he proposed that after the age of 11 children should be selected by examination to go to secondary grammar schools or selective central schools. Those not selected could go to non-selective central schools (where available) and to senior schools. At 13 a few might transfer by selection to junior technical schools whose age of entry was later than that for other schools. These non-selective senior schools were the origins of the later secondary modern schools and were usually parts of the existing parent elementary school or even simply a marquee erected in the playground. The Hadow reorganisation, held up by the depression, was rather a feature of the 1930s than the 20s. In 1927 the number of pupils who had been reorganised in senior departments was 8 per cent, by 1938 it had risen to 48.3 per cent (Simon, 1974, p. 370). It was a stage in the evolution of 'secondary education for all' which became a popular slogan of the time. Raising the school-leaving age to 15, which would have provided even more years of post-primary education, was another unachieved goal of governments in 1924 and 1929–31 and a Conservative Act of 1936 which was never implemented.

The Butler Act of 1944 was the next major stage of state intervention. The importance of the Act tends to be exaggerated. It raised the school-leaving age to 15 but required little of LEAs beyond the provision of education appropriate to a child's 'aptitude, age and ability' without specifying what. The main achievement of the Act was the salvation of Church schools. Otherwise, Butler's arrangements perpetuated the selective tripartite structure created by Morant in the 1900s. The implementation of the Act proved a disappointment. Grave doubts were raised over the fairness of 11+ selection which seemed biased towards the middle classes, the increase in working class access to the grammar school was slight compared with the pre-war years, the LEAs failed to develop a genuinely tripartite system including technical schools. We shall see more of this later. Disillusion with the Butler Act prompted the shift in policy to comprehensive schools in 1965.

The idea of the comprehensive school went back into the interwar years. Sir Will Spens' Report in 1938 famously suggested that LEAs that had not yet completed the Hadow reorganisation might consider the multilateral school, as it was then called. Going to one large school where different capabilities could be catered for would obviate the social stigma of 'successes' and 'failures' attending different schools. The 1944 Act paid no attention to this through R.A. Butler in later life claimed to have been secretly attracted to comprehensives and had left the requirements of his Act deliberately vague to allow LEAs the leeway to adopt the form. Some did – Windermere in 1945, Anglesey in 1949 and Kidbrooke in London as the first purpose built comprehensive in 1954. The 1950s and 60s saw the important debate undermining the certainties of 11+ selection and the academic-social stratification it led to. In consequence, although most LEAs preferred to develop grammar and secondary modern schools, comprehensives were already growing under the Conservatives, from 13 in 1954 to 195 by 1964. Ideology apart they were regarded as most appropriate in housing estates or as focal points for thinly scattered rural populations. In 1965 Anthony Crosland become Secretary of State for Education. He brought a fierce hatred of grammar schools and a commitment to comprehensives as one of the key means of securing greater equality within society. His Circular 10/65 called for LEAs to present schemes for the abolition of the 11+ and move to some form of comprehensive organisation. Children in comprehensives soared from 128,835 in 1960 to over 3 million by 1980, overtaking those in grammar schools in 1969 and those in secondary modern schools in 1972. Margaret Thatcher's Circular 10/70 withdrawing Crosland's did not hinder the upward surge, further continued by Reg Prentice in 1974 with Labour's return to power.

The attempt to equalise opportunities through comprehensives was also accompanied by other measures both positive and negative to reinforce the quest for greater fairness. In 1967 the Plowden Committee on Children and their Primary Schools recommended the creation of Educational Priority Areas (EPAs). These were educationally deprived areas to which extra resources should be allocated to ensure that there were no classes over 30, provide extra pay to teachers and teachers' aides, buildings and more nursery education. In response the government allocated £16 million over two years for school building in EPAs and teachers in 572 primary schools of exceptional difficulty were selected for extra increments. However the belief in the EPA scheme dwindled in the mid-1970s. This was partly through a lack of money and partly through changes in ideas. Poverty came to be seen as chiefly the responsibility of, and eradicable through, the family and the individual rather than the school. There was a scepticism that individual disadvantage was clustered in a few areas and that dealing with areas and schools was better than targeting individuals in other ways (Smith, G., 1987).

On the negative side Labour was concerned to remove the privileges represented by the direct grant grammar schools. These were grammar schools which from 1926 were financed directly by the central government and were independent of the LEA. They charged fees even after the abolition of secondary school fees after the Butler Act and took a proportion of local (usually very bright) LEA scholarship children alongside the (much less bright) fee payers who were invariably 11+ failures either local or out of town. To socialists there was something deeply unfair about the state subsidising the academically weak offspring of well-to-do parents who were buying their way out of secondary modern and into grammar schools inappropriate for them. It diverted funds better spent elsewhere, perverted the supposed academic excellence of the grammar schools, impeded the creation of a meritocratic social structure by enabling academic failures to be decanted into middle-class professions. The direct grant grammar schools and their right to charge fees survived the 1944 Act and subsequent Labour government. But the firming of Labour policy in favour of the comprehensives threw the role of the direct grant schools into doubt. Hopes were expressed that they would participate in the comprehensive system. This polarised the Conservative positions as Edward Heath's government in November 1971 increased grants to the direct grant schools by £2 million. By 1975 it was clear that direct grants had either to be abolished by Labour or they would be further expanded by the Conservatives. Accordingly in 1975 the Labour government withdrew financial support from the remaining 151 schools, most of which went independent. It removed a privileged subsidised anomaly alongside the comprehensive system, forced the middle-class fee payers to bear the full costs of their children's schooling unsupported by the taxpayer, but likewise it removed from local parents who could not afford independent education an alternative to the comprehensive.

The next crucial intervention of the state was the expansion of higher education in the 1960s for various reasons (Stewart, 1989). Some were demographic. The increase in the birth rate at the end of the war created a 'bulge' moving through the educational system such that 18-year-olds would rise from 533,000 in 1959 to 812,000 by 1965. Other reasons arose logically from developments elsewhere in the education system as sixth formers rose from 32,000 in 1947 to 53,000 by 1958. The combination of 'bulge' and 'trend' to staying on would have entailed 25,000 students a year being excluded from university education were no expansion to take place. There were also strong motives of social justice. A third of children born in 1940 to higher professional parents went to university but only 1 per cent of children of semi and unskilled workers did so (Cmnd 2154, 1963, p. 50). It was hoped that university expansion would close this gap and grant changes in 1962 providing LEA finance for all students who gained a university place was intended to facilitate this. There were economic motives too. Britain's slow economic growth in comparison with her European competitors matched its low provision of higher education with only 4.5 per cent of 18-year-olds proceeding there. There was also too little attention to technology as opposed to science. While Robbins was cautious about specifying the precise contribution of higher education to the economy there was an optimistic belief that university expansion would generate economic growth. These unanswerable arguments inevitably forced the responsibility on the state. There had been claims for expansion at the end of the war and a good expansion had already taken place from 65,000 undergraduates in 1946 to 90,000 in 1960. But in the late 1950s the University Grants Committee (UGC) approved the creation of six new universities – Sussex, UEA in Norwich, York, Kent, Warwick and Lancaster – all agreed before the Robbins report, and Stirling the only one resulting from Robbins. This along with eight Colleges of Advanced Technology elevated to technological universities in 1965 entailed a massive increase in the role of the state. Students increased from 113,000 in 1961 to 200,000 by 1967 and the share of GNP rose from 0.3 per cent to 0.49 per cent. The UGC still remained as a buffer between the academically independent universities and an increasingly powerful paymaster state. But this intervention of the 1960s began the tilting of the terms of trade to the advantage of a mighty and interfering state and against an overextended, weakened and ultimately insupportable higher education system.

The last notable development to date is that of Kenneth Baker's 'Great Education Reform Bill' of 1988. This provided for the creation of City Technology Colleges (CTCs), secondary schools emphasising vocational technology independent of LEAs and, it was forlornly hoped, built by private industry rather than the state. A national curriculum was to be devised with the testing of the child at 7, 11 and 14. Most important, schools were to be enabled and encouraged to opt out of LEA control, receiving their financial support from central government. To date some 1,100 schools have opted out (*Financial Times,* 16 March 1996). The finance was in effect to be clawed back from local authorities by the centre. The main thrust of the Baker Act was greatly to increase central state power and control, imposing national curricula (subsequently extended to teacher training courses), taking over opted-out schools from LEAs, diminishing the role of the LEA over these and the CTCs. Yet it also decentralises through the creation of Local Management of Schools (LMS) whereby 85 per cent of funds for a school must be devolved to the school from the LEA. Open enrolment obliges schools to accept students to a calculated number allowing parental choice in the selection of schools. In all, power is given to the central state, to the schools and parents, the loser is local government.

The nature of state intervention has been varied as the foregoing outline indicates. Sometimes it has been through Acts of Parliament which appear as milestones through the century – 1902, 1918, 1944, 1988. Yet often quite as important have been various circulars and directives sent out by the Board of Education and its successors. Morant's circulars shaped the scholarship system and curricula of grammar schools in the 1900s and his changes in the Board regulations sanctioned the junior technical schools. One of the most important advances of the interwar years was Sir Charles Trevelyan's circular of 1924 requiring grammar schools to allocate 40 per cent of their places for ex-elementary scholars and it was Circular 1397 which enjoined the adoption of the Hadow reorganisation by LEAs. The first state proposals for comprehensive (then multilateral) schools came as a non-mandatory suggestion in Sir Will Spens Consultative Committee report in 1938 and the actual shift of policy to comprehensives was initiated by Circular 10/65, not by an Act of Parliament. The 1944 Act and the pamphlets explaining it were so vague and permissive in prescribing types and the balance of schools to be provided that individual LEA plans were approved (or not) by Ministers in subsequent years. At a higher and much rarer level the new universities of the 1900s and the 1960s were not created by legislation, but by Royal Charters from the Privy Council. In these various ways from Royal Charters through Acts of Parliament, Circulars and suggestions, pressures great and small, the state shaped the system in the twentieth century.

The Impact of the State on Education

In assessing the impact of the state on education we may consider three major questions – did it widen educational opportunities? did it help economic development? did it modify social attitudes? At the start of the century education was quite sharply stratified. The upper middle class went to independent public boarding schools, the middle class to day grammar schools mostly as fee payers, the working class to elementary schools. The last left school at 12 or 13 and expected nothing beyond the 'elements' although the ablest might proceed to higher grade schools. A small number might have won one of the 5,500 scholarships to local grammar schools provided charitably by the grammar schools themselves. The Cockerton Judgement by removing the higher grade schools and the 1902 Act by creating the municipal grammar schools opened up the way for widening opportunities for the working class. David Reeder emphasises that 'centralist intervention was the decisive factor in the reconstruction or reshaping of secondary education as carried through by the early twentieth century' (Reeder, 1987, p. 136). He is less clear on how far the grammar schools provided more opportunities than those they replaced, but some evidence suggests this was very likely so, even before 1914. First there were only 85 higher grade schools in 1902 but 736 new grammar schools by 1910. Second, whereas in 1897 the sons of skilled artisans and unskilled workers made up only 9.1 per cent of grammar school pupils they were 40 per cent of higher grade pupils. Yet by 1913 these groups made up 20.6 per cent of grammar school pupils. The average size of an old higher grade school would have to have been 4.45 times larger than a new grammar school (which is rather improbable) to yield equal capacities for the working class under the former system in 1897 and the latter in 1913. Gains must have been evident quantitatively and certainly qualitatively before 1914. Reeder is confident that this was certainly so in the 1920s.

The 1902 Act and Morant's subsequent policies in the 1900s, Trevelyan's raising of the proportion of grammar school places for ex-elementary school-children to 40 per cent and the Hadow reorganisation in conjunction with a low birth rate did lead to increasing opportunities before the Butler Act.

Table 6.1 Percentage of children attending grammar and independent schools *c.*1900–*c.*1940

	Born pre-1910	Born 1910–19	Born 1920–9
Lower middle class and skilled manual	7	13	16
Semi and unskilled manual	1	4	7
Status groups 5–7	4	9	

Source: Little and Westergaard (1964) and Floud (1954).

This had slight consequent effects on attending universities.

Table 6.2 Percentage of children attending universities

	Born pre-1910	Born 1920–9
Lower middle class and skilled manual	0.5	1
Semi and unskilled manual	nil	0.5

Source: Little and Westergaard (1964).

The 1944 Act did not have as much effect as was expected on widening opportunities. Floud, Halsey and Martin in their classic study of Middlesbor-ough and south-west Hertfordshire found that 'the likelihood that a working-class boy will reach a grammar school is not notably greater today, despite all the changes, than it was before 1945. Rather less than ten per cent of working-class boys reaching the age of 11 in the years 1931–41 entered selec-tive secondary schools. In 1953 in South West Hertfordshire the proportion was 15.5 per cent and in Middlesborough 12 per cent' (Floud *et al.*, 1956). State intervention from Morant to Hadow did have a greater effect on widening educational opportunities than the Butler Act had after 1945.

Widening opportunities in higher education came with the comprehensives and the 1960s university expansion.

Table 6.3   Percentage of children entering university 1930s–1970s

	Born 1920–29, entering university 1938–47	Born late 1930s, entering university mid 1950s	1972 Sample	
Professional and Managerial	6	14	20	
Non-manual and skilled manual	1	2.5	–	
Semi and unskilled working class	0.5	0.5	1.8	
		1961/62		1997
		3.2		5

Source: Little and Westergaard (1964).

However there is concern that although the aim is to get about a third of the population attending university by the end of the century yet there has been very little change in working-class participation between 1974 and the early 1990s (*The Independent,* 27 August 1992 on Halsey's Report for the National Commission on Education, 1992). The impact on widening opportunity has accordingly been patchy if creditable through the century. In school education there were undoubted advances between Morant and Butler, less so thereafter. In higher education there have been only modest improvements in the first half of the century but considerable gains since 1970 although disappointing in terms of the lowest social groups in the last two decades.

Has state intervention made education more fitting to serve the economy? This was motive in the 1900s, to resist German competition and it has been a cliché to justify almost all educational change since in these terms. If so it has not had much effect. Growth has been remarkably stable at around 2 per cent per year for periods 1873–1913, 1924–37, 1950–83 (Supple, 1994). On the other hand the stability of our own performance is underlain by our falling down various league tables from the richest country in the world to 15th in World Economic Forum ranking, 16th in GDP in the OECD, 19th in Institute of Management Development ratings. Of course it is beyond imagination that a small offshore island of limited resources could have remained the world economic leader throughout two centuries and there are many factors in our relative, not absolute, decline. But there are some areas where state intervention or the lack of it can be seen to have helped or hindered our economic position through the formation of a labour force.

The state deliberately set out to intervene in education to support the economy by its measures of the 1900s, notably through the creation of the junior technical schools. The policy was right but the impact only limited. Only 37 schools were created by 1913 and 324 by 1946, their peak. But they never educated more than 3 or 4 per cent of schoolchildren. Their impact was lessened by a variety of factors – they were more expensive to build, equip and run than grammar schools, their age of entry at 13 was at odds with other schools which admitted at 11, there was no agreement among psychologists that the skill aptitudes for which the schools catered were detectable, Socialists and trade unionists saw them as undermining apprenticeship, employers faced with depression and unemployed skilled labour in the interwar years saw no need to spend money producing even more (Sanderson, 1994). So small a part of the schooling system were they that if their entire output from their beginning had still been employed in 1961 they would have made up only 8.5 per cent of the labour force. Their successors, the Secondary Technical Schools (STSs) failed to develop after the 1944 Act. The Act did not require them (although the first draft had done so) and LEAs preferred to build grammar schools which voters, both Left and Right, saw as the gateway to middle-class professional careers. In 1955 Sir David Eccles, the Minister of Education, decided that there was no purpose in the STS, no more would be sanctioned and the future lay with putting technology into grammar schools. It was a disaster. Grammar schools were interested in teaching science, not technology and had neither the teachers, equipment or ethos for technology teaching. Nor was there any coherent policy as to what 'technology' in schools was to consist of. The Nuffield Foundation emphasised the scientific aspects and the Schools Council the crafts. Accordingly 'despite major efforts there has been no "technological revolution" in schools' (McCulloch *et al.*, 1985). Butler's deliberate removal of any reference to technical schools in his Act and Sir David Eccles total removal of them from any policy agenda from 1955 were two of the most fateful negative governmental decisions of the century. The *Financial Times* – the most acute observer of Britain's economy – concludes 'the absence of a tier of technical schools comparable with those found on the Continent and in Japan is the single biggest failure of postwar educational policy' (*Financial Times*, 9 May 1990).

The state embarked on a series of devices to fill in the gaps left by the collapse of the STS and the failure to introduce technology into schools successfully. These included the Youth Opportunities Programme (YOP) of 1978, followed by Youth Training Scheme (YTS) in 1983, followed by Youth Training (YT) in 1990 which were all criticised for offering training too unstructured and of too low a standard. For adults this was parallelled by the Training Opportunities Scheme (TOPS) of 1982 replaced by Employment Training (ET) in 1988. Training and Enterprise Councils (TECs) from 1990 were supposed to be the means by which employers assessed local training needs and assured that they were met. But in spite of this plethora of institutions and acronyms Derek Aldcroft finds 'no comprehensive and coherent programme of good quality emerged' (Aldcroft, 1992 p. 72).

Three initiatives might have been useful and some may still. The CTCs and GNVQ have proved doubtful and the third, 'specialist schools' have better prospects. The City Technology Colleges were announced in 1986 by Kenneth Baker and incorporated into the 1988 Act. They were to 'offer a curriculum with a strong emphasis on technological, scientific and practical work, business studies and design' (*The Independent*, 8 Oct. 1986). They were to be run not by LEAs but by trusts, they were not supposed to be selective but to take pupils from a wide ability range especially from the inner cities. To a large extent they were to be independent of the state but in practice since they failed to attract the expected business support government money supplied most of their funds. By 1993 £120 million of public funds and £35 million of private was spent on a mere 15 schools for 15,150 pupils. They were an excellent idea providing high quality education but of very limited impact and much more involved with the state than was intended.

With the failure of the CTCs, John Patten in September 1993 introduced yet another new initiative of 'specialist schools' in technology and languages partly financed by local business but with matching funds from the state. These are grant maintained or voluntary-aided schools already existing which change their status and so are easier to form than CTCs. There are now 151 of these schools in technology and 30 in languages (*Financial Times*, 21 May 1996) and Gillian Shepherd rightly wished to expand these schools which have attracted £18 million in private sponsorship. The schools are oversubscribed, frankly select by aptitude and are the most hopeful initiative to replace what was lost with the demise of the STSs.

The third initiative was the attempt to create technical qualifications, which have proved problematic. It was felt that A levels emphasise academic to the neglect of technological and applied concerns. To redress this the National Council for Vocational Qualifications was set up in 1986 by the Employment Department to devise more practical alternatives to A level. The General National Vocational Qualifications (GNVQs) were set up in 1992 but have been of only limited success. Although they include work-based assessment they have not found favour with employers (*Daily Telegraph*, 3 January 1996). They have been criticised for their lack of rigour in assessment especially in core skills and English in spite of a massively bureaucratic assessment system (*Times Education Supplement*, 14 June 1996). Sir Ron Dearing proposes retitling GNVQs as 'applied A levels' and £10 million has been allocated to improving assessment methods (*The Times*, 14 June 1996). State investment in examinations has not proved as successful as earlier forms like A levels (run by universities) or technical examinations run by the City and Guilds and the Royal Society of Arts.

At a higher level too state intervention, or the lack of it, in the shaping of higher education to support the economy has not been entirely happy.

When the new universities were created in the 1960s the UGC made it clear that they should not grow out of technical colleges or involve themselves with them. Moreover Planning Boards had to create liberal and scientific curricula, it was not expected that they devise programmes of study technically or vocationally orientated. The new universities were accordingly criticised for being too distant from industry, spatially on their green field sites in mediaeval cathedral cities and spiritually with their liberal curricula. At the same time the Robbins Report was pointing out England's backwardness in providing for technology in higher education. The new universities were planned long before the Robbins Report but the UGC and its Academic Planning Boards did not see the new universities as meeting those requirements. It is interesting, although hardly surprising, that the 1960s universities heavily supported by the state and planned by civil servants and academics had service to the economy much less prominent in their originating purposes than the Victorian civic universities created largely by businessmen a hundred years earlier.

This would not have mattered because alongside the 'new' universities were the nine Colleges of Advanced Technology (CATs) so designated in 1956 and elevated as technological universities in 1966 and 1967. Behind them 30 other leading technical colleges were elevated to polytechnics, undertaking degree work as universities in waiting. In many ways this was a proper recognition of the true status of the noble Victorian tradition of technical education these institutions embodied. However these institutions often dropped 'technology' from their titles and shifted their curricula in the direction of the liberal university model.

Table 6.4   Percentage of students in subject areas

	Technological Universities	Polytechnics
Arts and Social Studies	20 (1963)* 67.6 per cent (1974)	28.2 (1965) 50.5 (1978)
Sciences and Technology	80 (1963)* 32.4 per cent (1974)	57.9 (1965) 33.9 (1978)

*(proportions promised to the Robbins Committee)

Source: Pratt and Burgess (1977), p. 77. Venables, Sir Peter (1978), pp. 231–95. Matterson (1981), p. 67.

To an extent the technological universities and polytechnics were victims of the running down of the STSs and the failure of schools to produce potential technologists for higher education, and this 'policy drift' as it was called was the outcome (Sanderson, 1991). Here was a case for strong government intervention, even at the expense of academic freedom, for holding technological higher education firmly to a technological curriculum. Indeed this whole area at the school and higher levels is one that probably needed firmer state intervention on behalf of economic interests or a greater involvement of business in shaping the system even at the expense of the state. The contribution of education to growth in terms of the annual percentage growth rates of labour quality derived from improvements in education has been calculated by Matthews et al. (1982) who suggest that school education has played a slightly less, and technical and university education a slightly greater, role in a fairly constant situation. This beneficial impact has not been without an impact of cost as education has taken an increasing share of the national wealth from about 1 per cent of the national income in 1900 and 1920 to 4 per cent by the mid-1960s (Hicks, 1958; Vaizey and Sheenan, 1967) then from 4 per cent of GDP in the mid-1960s to 6 per cent by the late 1970s (Simon, 1991, p. 599). Education has been taking an increased proportion of the national wealth but without being able – amid all the other factors concerned – to deliver a rising rate of economic growth.

Table 6.5   Contribution of education to annual growth rates

	Formal Education	Technical Education	University Education	Total
1873–1937	0.4	0.1	0.00	0.50
1937–1964	0.4	0.2	0.05	0.65
1964–1973	0.3	0.2	0.05	0.55

Source: Matthews *et al.* (1982).

A third potential area of the impact of state education is that of the amelioration of social attitudes. Indeed this motive goes back to the first state interventions in education in the 1830s which chiefly were concerned with religion, social order and the reduction of crime. This was before the state became concerned with education for economic competitiveness (say 1870s) or social mobility (say 1890s). Here again the impact is dubious. In the 1900s state education certainly had an impact in reducing juvenile delinquency if only by keeping kids off the street (Gillis, 1975). One can hardly make the same claims for the rest of the century as male indictable offences rose from 50,253 in 1901 (1 in 314 of the population) to 126,584 by 1951 (1 in 166 of the population). The prison population had soared to a peak of 55,000 by 1996. Yet Gatrell points out that murder rates and violent crime were lower by the 1970s than they had been a century earlier and he enjoins 'very large doubts indeed' on any view as to whether crime is getting more or less in the twentieth century (Gatrell, 1990). Still less can we claim that education has been successful in reducing it.

Contentiously the 1944 Education Act endeavoured to bind children to the state religion by requiring each day's schooling to begin with a compulsory religious Christian assembly. Mass Observation noted in 1947 that most people wanted religion taught in state schools on the grounds that 'it makes you a better citizen even if you do not believe in it' (Obelkevich, 1990 p. 353). Yet membership of the Church of England fell from 3.39 million (8.2 per cent of the population) in 1939 which was not very dissimilar from 1900, down to 1.82 million by 1980 and 1.12 million (2.3 per cent of the population) by 1994 (the *Independent*, 26 November 1994). As an exercise in state education in support of the state religion it was a failure. Undeterred, the 1944 requirement was re-enacted in the Baker Act of 1988 and in 1996 Archbishop Carey still hoped to use state schooling to revive Christian observance.

Victorians would have been disappointed in the impact of state education. There is not much evidence and some negative that education has helped to sustain economic competitiveness or religious belief or a clear reduction of crime since 1900. It has had some effect on social mobility but not as much as expected. Of course education is a force for good and one can always argue that with no state education at all the economy, religion, crime and mobility would be even worse than they are. It is in any case quite impossible to isolate education's contribution in the complex of all these matters over a century. Indeed one of the clearest improvements in moral attitudes since the war has been a greater appreciation of animal welfare and rights and this is arguably more the result of television than state education. Certainly at the end of the century we would take a cooler view of the capacity of state education to ameliorate than a Victorian or Edwardian would have done in the 1830s or the 1900s.

State Intervention

Around the issue of state intervention have clustered various debates and we want to focus on three issues which are still live – the policies of Sir Robert Morant in the 1900s, the relations between the state and the private sector, and the superseding of the tripartite system by the comprehensive schools in 1960s and 70s.

Sir Robert Morant has come under criticism on two grounds; that his policies restricted opportunities for the working classes (Simon, 1965) and that he imposed anti-technical liberal education values on the system with long lasting adverse consequences for British culture (Barnett, 1986, pp. 223–5). The arrangements demolished by the Cockerton Judgement and the 1902 Act were those whereby able children from elementary schools proceeded not to proper secondary education but to the semi-secondary education of the higher grade schools. Sir George Kekewich, Morant's predecessor as the chief civil servant in the then Education Department positively approved of higher grade schools, in spite of their dubious legality, and did nothing to prevent their growth. He was a generous man by temperament and saw the higher grade schools as providing opportunities for poorer children that might otherwise be denied them. Indeed it could be argued that had this system been allowed to continue unchecked it might have led to a form of comprehensive schooling without passing through the tripartite phase. There is also no doubt that the higher grade schools were very fine buildings indeed (Nottingham and Norwich for example), flagships of School Board pride. Yet what replaced them – the grammar schools entered by scholarships through the 11+ provided for greater opportunities. It was probably so quantatively even before 1914, as we have seen, and certainly so thereafter. More important the grammar schools provided qualitative opportunities far in excess of those afforded by the higher grade schools. The scholarships both to grammar school and university, the academic curriculum including classics opened the doors to Oxford and Cambridge and the great professions. Here was the real ladder of opportunity not just a half way system producing shop assistants, clerks and craftsmen. When my father was at Blackpool Grammar School as a scholarship boy in the 1920s, his contemporaries included a future peer and governor of the Bahamas, a future senior civil servant in the legal department of the Treasury and, best known of all, Alistair Cooke the Anglo-American journalist – all from modest backgrounds. These were the true heirs of Morant, who was not a reactionary elitist unsympathetic to the lower orders but an educational policy-maker more than any other this century, concerned with devising structures which would facilitate social mobility.

The other criticism levelled at the policies of these years was that they battened old liberal education values on to secondary education to the denigration of scientific and technical education. Morant himself was a Winchester and Oxford man and a firm believer in the virtues of the classical education he himself had received. He wanted the new municipal grammar schools to make available something of the classical education already provided for a higher social class in the best public schools. This was partly the purpose of his 1904 Regulations laying down the arts curriculum including classics, for grammar schools. More controversially he put an end to some science-based grammar schools and adverse attention has been paid to this aspect of his policies (Vlaeminke, 1990). It also seems odd in the context of the fierce concern for scientific and technical education of the time. Yet Morant's policy was not due to any personal hostility to science. Some grammar schools had formed close relations with the Science and Art Department (SAD) in South Kensington which augmented the income of schools willing to bias their curriculum and take SAD examinations. Morant did not want grammar schools to become mini-technical colleges thereby warping that all-round education which was their purpose and, by neglect of the classics, denying that access to the ancient universities for those of modest origins. On the other hand Morant believed passionately in technical education, just how fervently is evident in the concluding page of his report on French technical education in 1897 (Sanderson, 1995). Far from being a classicist hostile to technical education he was an expert on continental systems of education and was determined to introduce something similar into England. Hence his creation of the junior technical school to be the equivalent of l'école primaire supérieure. Moreover Morant did not trust that these purposes of the circulation of elites and national efficiency could be brought about by leaving matters to free choice or even to the new local authorities. State direction through legislation (1902, 1906, 1907, 1911), circulars (1904, 1907) and Regulation changes (1905/6 as the prelude to 1913) was his style.

A second area of debate was whether the state should become involved with the private sector, the independent public boarding schools? The issue arose in the 1930s when a falling birth rate and the diminished prosperity of the middle classes constrained the market for public school places. As some schools feared not only loss of income but actually going out of business they were receptive to schemes to provide them with pupils paid for by the state. The government, in a most unusual initiative, set up Lord Fleming's Committee in 1942 (Board of Education, 1944) to look into this. This proposed various schemes whereby either local authorities or central government would pay for state sector pupils to attend public schools on an approved list. A few schools like Eton and Rugby and a few LEAs like Dorset and Hertforshire participated but the scheme largely failed. The central government would not provide finance and all the cost fell on the LEAs. Most LEAs, especially Labour ones, saw that the best way forward was to develop schools for all their children in their own LEA, not in supporting a small number of children and subsidising public schools elsewhere. As the public schools prospered again in the 1950s they had no need of socially dissonant local authority subsidised children and the LEAs put their pride and money into their own grammar schools.

The first initiative at a rapprochement between the state and the independent sector had come from the public schools themselves, through the Headmasters' Conference and the Governing Bodies Association. The next, more threatening, came from the Labour government of 1964 which wanted either to abolish the public schools as socially divisive or integrate them into the state system (Rae, 1981). A Public Schools Commission was appointed in 1965 to consider this and their solution was the provision of 45,000 assisted places to swamp the public schools with state children financed by central government. Nothing came of this. Paradoxically if assisted places had been seen by the Left as a means of absorbing public schools into the state system they were also seen by the Right as a ladder of opportunity for poor children of high intelligence into the middle class. The Education Act of 1980 created the Assisted Places Scheme in 1981, offering 55,000 places paid for by central government although only 4,000 were taken up. The debate between Labour and Conservatives over the relation of the state to the independent schools is clear cut. Labour has ruled out charging VAT on public school fees but may well abolish the charitable status of public schools which would lose them £42 million in tax relief and lead to the raising of fees by about 5 per cent (Rae, *The Independent*, 6 January 1995). Most certainly Labour would abolish assisted places. In short Labour would make the independent schools more truly independent, removing state subsides through tax relief and assisted places. It would thrust them more firmly into the free market of consumer choice and spending power, making them more reliant on parental fees which would probably result in the closure of a tail of the weakest schools. Conservatives, on the contrary, intend to increase assisted places by 4,000 (*Financial Times*, 1 March 1996) whereas Labour takes the traditional view that the money (£94 million in 1995) would be better spent in the state sector. Whether the private sector should be, made completely private or subsidised or integrated into the state system remains a live issue with, iron- ically, Labour taking a more free market and Conservatives a more state inter- ventionist position.

A third major policy debate was that over the implementation of the Butler Act. The Act required very little of LEAs other than they provide education appropriate for childrens' aptitude age and ability. The first draft of the Act had actually specified types of schools to be provided but subsequent modifi- cations left discretion to the LEAs. They developed grammar, secondary modern and technical schools not in a balanced tripartite manner but in the eccentric ratio 7:17:1. We have suggested that this limited the widening of educational opportunities and did not help the economy through the creation of a skilled labour force as much as it could have done. What concerns us here is the debate that led to the collapse of the LEA tripartite interpretation of the 1944 Act and its replacement by a more central state directed move to comprehensive schools.

Initial disappointment was caused by the awareness of what little advance the new system had made in raising the chances of the working classes in getting a grammar school education. Floud and Halsey, whose classic study of Middlesborough and south-west Hertfordshire showed this, were fairly content with the situation, thinking that about the right proportions of the working class were getting an academic education and making up about the right proportions of the pupils in grammar schools. However, various factors and findings began to undermine belief in the system.

First it became evident that chances of getting to grammar school were too dependent on regional variations in their provision (Douglas, 1964). Child- ren in the far south-west of England stood a 35 per cent chance of 'passing' the 11+, while those in the counties a little to the east in the central south coast stood only an 18.9 per cent chance. In one extreme case Nottingham provided only 447 places for 4,400 contestants in the 1950s. Second, the 11+ test was presented as being able to detect 'g' or general intelligence, the possession of which would qualify a child for the grammar school. Yet it began to dawn on parents that it was remarkable that in every grammar school in every town in every year there were just enough desks and chairs available in advance to receive those detected with the mysterious 'g' and there were always nearly twice as many children worthy of success in Devon and Cornwall as in Hampshire and Berkshire. It strained credibility and showed that reliance on local government had created a pattern of patchy inequitability, not a genuine national system. Third, the test itself was subject to criticism, in that while arithmetic and intelligence tests were relatively class free, the English examination tested language and vocabulary, fluency in which was more naturally acquired by children from cultured middle-class homes. Fourth, it was clear that middle-class children benefited even more in that upper middle-class mothers showed a greater interest in the education of their children than did lower working-class mothers. This interest (in desiring a grammar school place or staying on into the sixth form for example) trans-mitted itself to children between the ages of 8 and 11. This in turn could influence their intelligence so that children of different social classes but the same intelligence at the age of 8 could diverge in performance over the next two or three years. In this way the 11+ examination tested not only the intel-ligence of the child but indirectly the social class and aspirations of its mother which had helped to determine that intelligence. Fifth, some LEAs aggra-vated these tendencies by streaming children from the age of 7, building in self-fulfilling prophecies and zoning children to neighbourhood schools creating close connections between schools, the social class of their areas and the corresponding expectations of those parents. Sixth, and worst of all, most LEAs regarded those who did not achieve grammar school entry as 'failures' at the age of 11. The consequence was a considerable misallocation of ability. The Early Leaving Report of 1954 (Ministry of Education, 1954) found 14.5 per cent of boys in grammar schools leaving before the sixth form which suggested they were not using the schools to best effect and should not have been there in the first place. Conversely the Crowther Report (Ministry of Education, 1959) found that 29 per cent of RAF National Service recruits had been allocated at the age of 11 to types of schools lower than their acad-emic abilities warranted. Many of these deficiencies in the operation of the 1944 Act arose from the vagaries of a system which placed a greater premium on local discretion rather than on the uniformity and equity of a more state-directed system. Defenders of the grammar school continued to emphasise its high academic quality and its traditional role as the ladder for the intelligent working-class child. But Anthony Crosland whose *Future of Socialism* (1956) had already advocated the comprehensive school as one of the foundations of Socialism, became Secretary of State in 1965 and required LEAs to draw up plans to move to comprehensivisation.

The issue is far from resolved. It is Conservative policy to have a grammar school in every town. This can be brought about by allowing private enter-prise to build private grammar schools but run with government money even in areas with adequate schooling (*Daily Telegraph*, 11 March 1996). Another way to increase grammar schools will be to allow schools especially in Labour areas to apply for grammar school status where there is parental demand (*The

Times, 13 June 1996). This will entail rights to reintroduce selection of pupils. Labour abolished direct grant grammar schools (schools receiving direct grants from central government rather than their LEA) in 1975. Yet Labour, embarrassed by the choice of selective schools by Tony Blair and Harriet Harman is now distancing itself from opposition to selection and grammar schools. In 1996 there are still 160 grammar schools which were never converted to comprehensives, although they are a minority in England's 40,000 secondary schools which are mostly LEA comprehensives (*Financial Times*, 16 March 1996). But this debate is not over.

The Future

What of the future? There are various broad ways in which the role of the state in relation to education may change. We may categorise these as paying for education, the relation of central and local government, the concern for standards, the economic and social rationale for education.

First the state will shift some of the burden of paying for education from the taxpayer to the ultimate beneficiaries – parents, students and employers. It is an old argument. In Victorian times before 1891 the working classes funded their own elementary education in the expectation that the advantages of being literate would lead to better paid 'aristocracy of labour' jobs, which would enable them to recoup their investment. Such assumptions underlay English approaches to technical education in the nineteenth century when apprenticeship distributed the real costs between apprentices (in foregone wages) and employers (in costs of training) both expecting to gain in the near future in enhanced earnings skills and labour value. This English approach contrasted with continental assumptions of reliance on publicly funded colleges where both pupil and the interests of the employer were subsidised by the taxpayer. The continental approach was less self-evidently equitable than English *laissez-faire*. There is an increasing awareness of this and willingness to embrace pre-1890 logicalities. The contemporary manifestation of this lies in reducing state grants for university students and requiring them to provide for themselves an increasing proportion of their maintenance and tuition. This has several advantages. It makes students think of themselves as consumers and customers looking for value and gives them the higher motivation associated with the self-employed. Since the student has to think in terms not only of recouping costs but of making them yield a return it may make students think of degrees as investment rather than consumption goods and bring some market pressures to bear on the distribution of the curriculum. Not least it will remove some taxation burden from the 70 per cent of the population who do not go to university.

Charles Clotfelter has recently given an attractive analysis of American private universities largely independent of the state (Clotfelter, 1996) where they have the flexible capacity to adjust fees, income and salaries free of state interference. This enables them to respond to market demand and compete with each other in maintaining excellence. It is a salutary contrast with Britain where the state is a paymaster that cannot afford what it demands and saddles the universities with administrative trivia beyond belief in the attempt to secure 'quality assurance' it cannot trust the market to deliver. It cannot be long before leading universities take the American track to independence with top up fees as the first step. The Labour manifesto of 1997 has made it clear that higher education 'cannot be funded out of taxation' and that student maintenance will have to be repaid by graduates on a future income-related basis. Since for the state to finance all grants and maintenance at universities would cost an unthinkable extra 3p on income tax we must expect more fee paying, student loans, graduate taxes or industrial finance as the way forward.

But if the state is likely to shift more of the running costs on to students why not more of the capital costs on to employer end users? Recently Smith Kline Beecham (SKB) has complained that universities are so underfunded that chemistry departments no longer have the equipment to train graduates in the work SKB requires (George Poste of SKB in *Financial Times*, 7 June 1996). If this is so why does not SKB (and Glaxo and Zeneca and the rest) provide the equipment for a select number of chemistry departments to ensure the quality they require rather than rely on 'the government' which has failed them? Indeed British Aerospace has proposed a 'University of Industry' financed by leading firms and supplying what they require. Some universities are beginning to call the bluff both of private industry and the state. Cambridge – echoing SKB – has made it clear that its chemistry laboratories are insufficiently equipped to maintain the high international standards expected of it. Some universities have recently ceased teaching chemistry and physics and this trend will continue. The government is likely to maintain tight constraints on public expenditure and accordingly for industry to secure the well-qualified science graduate labour it requires, it will increasingly have to pay a larger proportion of the costs of producing it itself.

There are some who would see an even more radically diminished role for the state at the school level. James Tooley of the influential Institute of Economic Affairs has recently argued cogently that the state should have virtually no role in school education (Tooley, 1996). Entrepreneurs could provide schools just as they provide supermarkets, and parents will pay fees (with a safety net for the very poor) as they do even in poor countries. The school-leaving age could be reduced to 14, then all school leavers could be provided with a 'learning account' fund to be spent where and when at the discretion of the holder – on sixth form, technical or university training. This fund would be paid for by the reduction in the school-leaving age, and the abolition of assisted places. The reduction of taxes resulting from the shedding of state provision of education would increase the spending power of students and parents to pay for education and accordingly increase the market pressure they can bring to bear on the providers of education. Right-wing libertarians would even abolish the national curriculum and assisted places as no business of the state.

Another view is that in the future all schools should be independent and competitive. All parents would received educational vouchers which they could use to pay the full or part fees at any school of their choice according to its charges. The dichotomy of state independent schools would be removed and all schools would be partly financed by the state through vouchers in subsidy of fees. This is being tried with vouchers for nursery schools in an initiative started by Gillian Shephard in 1995. £700 million has been taken from LEAs to provide vouchers worth £1100 per 4-year-old which parents may choose to spend either in the private or LEA sectors for three terms of nursery education. Ironically in the pilot scheme in Norfolk the LEA is winning as parents spend the vouchers in the reception classes of LEA primary schools they expect to enter. The fear is that children who come from private nursery providers may be discriminated against when it comes to entry into the state primary school. In the meantime some schools are semi-privatising their finance, asking parents for extra voluntary sums (not quite charging fees), receiving money from well-wishing commercial organisations like Alton Towers, Warburgs Bank, sometimes in connection with advertising. Another way forward is represented by the company Nord Anglia plc, a company with shareholders which offer to take over schools, paying the teachers and running at a profit. It is within its horizons to take over a whole LEA. The reticence of the taxpayer to pay for schooling will lead to a combination of these various devices.

Second, if there is a case for central government devolving more of its educational responsibilities to consumers, employers and providers so paradoxically it has taken more power *vis-à-vis* local government. At the moment 85 per cent of local government funds come from central government and only 15 per cent from the community charge. Of all local government expenditure 45 per cent is spent on education. This leads to claims from centralisers that education might as well become an entirely centralised service – as prisons moved from being a local to a central service in the nineteenth century. There are various reasons for this. The national curriculum requires a national content with standards determined and monitored by Ofsted. The emphasis on quality audit and league tables makes it more anomalous that local authority delivery should permit variations in quality of service throughout the country. Concern for uniformity exceeds that for local democracy which permits variety of provision. Central control facilitates tight restraint of public expenditure where again education is a crucial big spender. It is much easier for a largely uncontrolled central executive to bear down on education in the remorseless concern to cut public expenditure. The cutting back of local government was an aim of the Thatcher administration as a means of eradicating a century of socialism deeply entrenched in local democracy. Were education to be removed from local government then there would be strong grounds for abolishing local government altogether, indeed this possibility was discussed in cabinet in 1990.

Moreover the assertion of centralised state control was regarded as necessary to break the power of a supposed 'educational establishment'. This establishment was held responsible for a decline in educational standards and a consequent failure of education to support an economy becoming less competitive in the context of relative decline. The devolved authority of so much of English education, once perceived as a distinctive liberal strength – in contrast to the étatisme of France and Germany – is regarded as having 'failed the nation'. The LEAs with their comprehensive schools; teacher training colleges and university education departments with questionable teaching methods producing 15,000 'unsatisfactory' teachers unchecked by HMIs; the UGC with its failure to prevent 'policy drift' and defence of the high cost low productivity universities of the 1950s and 60s; examining bodies providing a range of pick and mix exams but no prescriptive curriculum – all claiming independence or an arms length relation with the state have all been held culpable and curbed by central government in recent years. The role of the LEA has been diminished by opting out, the UGC replaced by the Higher Education Funding Council for England, 'the inspectorate' brought under Ofsted, a national curriculum imposed with regular testing. This downplaying of LEAs, the teaching profession and universities by a centralising government is at one with the attack of the Conservatives on other professional vested interest groups – the Church, doctors, barristers, the Stock Exchange – whose privileges, independence power or influence have been checked in the 1980s and 90s (Perkin, 1989).

It may seem paradoxical that a government devoted to 'rolling back the frontiers of the state' should have adopted so centralising and statist a stance. In truth Thatcherite Conservatism is closer to Benthamite Utilitarianism than old Toryism. For Bentham and his followers happiness was maximised usually by leaving the individual to pursue self-interest untrammelled by state interference. Yet in certain key areas – public health, the regulation of poverty and education – Benthamites saw the necessity of a strong coercive centralised state. In education Benthamites favoured a curriculum orientated to vocationalism and technology, a strong central government department, a strict system of inspection, audit and control over localities, a suspicion of institutions validated by custom and antiquity. No Secretary of State for Education or Prime Minister in the twentieth century has so reflected the Benthamite cast of mind as Margaret Thatcher.

Third, there is national unease with standards in education – nearly half of 11-year-olds failing to reach expected standards in English and maths, ten per cent of children leaving with no qualifications, a discontented teaching profession with, on the Director of Ofsted's admission, 15,000 inadequate teachers, complaints from employers and perceived deficiencies compared with our industrial competitors. Energetic attempts are being made to raise standards with complex systems of testing, appraisal and quality audits. At schools children are tested at 7, 11 and 14 and the results of the 11-year-olds published. The Conservatives proposed to publish all results and introduce them for 5-year-olds to provide an initial benchmark. At the higher education level elaborate systems of appraisal were introduced in the early/mid-1990s, whereby staff are subject to annual performance appraisal by supervisors, appraisal by students of units taught, reviews of student appraisals by panels, biennial reviews of units and quinquennial reviews of courses, Teaching Quality Assessment by HEFCE panels about every five years, Quality Audit procedures reviews over about the same time and the Research Assessment Exercise also quinquennially. Although the time and bureaucracy costs of these exercises are immense they are justifiable and will undoubtedly continue. The long-term stagnation of university salaries since 1981 and real decline in the last ten years have meant that university teaching has ceased to be a job attractive to people of calibre and acumen. Accordingly as university real incomes have sharply declined since 1986 it is during this time that these complex systems of appraisal and audit have been introduced to compensate by administrative control what can no longer be ensured through the market. An unsatisfactory feature of the present system is that state money is based upon research appraisal not upon the assessment of teaching. It is surprising that the NUS as representatives of the increasingly cash paying customers have not raised more objections to this. If fee paying is introduced students are rightly going to insist that the quality of the teaching they receive is formally taken into account in the assessment of universities for state grants.

Has this concern about standards had any effect? We love to dwell on our defects. In January 1997 only 20 per cent of Britons aged 16–60 could answer twelve simple arithmetic questions, bottom of a league led by Japan with 43 per cent (*The Times*, 17 January 1997). In the same month the Organisation for Economic Co-operation and Development found that nearly half British adults lacked the literacy skills needed to cope with modern life (*The Independent*, 9 January 1997). Yet this disguises the raising of standards over the years. In 1964/65 nearly two-thirds of school leavers left with no graded examination pass but this had fallen to 9.4 per cent by 1984/85. Continuing from then the proportion of pupils gaining five or more A–C grades at GCSE rose between 1988 and 1996 from 20 to 32 per cent in poor areas and from 30 to 48 per cent in more affluent ones (the *Independent*, 30 April 1997). A level entries have risen from about 100,000 in the 1950s to over 700,000 by the mid-1990s and pass rates from just under 70 per cent to over 85 per cent over the same time. Average points scores at A level have risen from 16 in 1993 to 18.3 by 1996 (*Financial Times*, 20 November 1996). Curmudgeons may claim that examinations are getting softer but there is no more evidence for this than that the ascent of Everest or 'four minute' mile have, likewise since the 1950s, become easier.

Fourth, the state has to retain a close involvement in education because of its implications for the economy and social structure. We have earlier suggested ways in which the neglect of certain areas of education may have contributed to our relative economic decline and have welcomed measures like the CTCs and specialist schools and Sir Ron Dearing's proposals to improve GNVQ which may improve the situation. For the future the new Labour government is clear that 'too little investment in education and skills' has underlain poor economic growth (Labour Manifesto, *The Times*, 4 April 1997). Mindful of the fact that nearly two-thirds of the workforce lack vocational qualifications, various measures are proposed for the near future to address the better relation of education to the economy. Public money will be invested in training through Individual Learning Accounts of £150 per person, kick started with £150 million taken from TECs. Through these Learning Accounts individuals will buy skill training. A University for Industry as a public/private partnership 'will bring government, industry and education together'. Moreover it is planned with agreement with British Telecom to wire up all educational institutions to create a National Grid for learning to generalise IT skills through the system. Above all Labour intends to increase spending on education moving money away from TECs and nursery vouchers and social security to redress the £3 billion drained from education by previous Conservative administrations.

The new government also sustains the traditional Socialist belief that the state should use the educational system to influence the social structure through the provision of opportunity. Grant maintained grammar schools will be retained. In primary schools classes will be reduced to 30 for 5-, 6- and 7-year-olds with £180 million taken from the assisted places scheme. The disadvantaged will be benefited by educational action zones (which sound like EPAs) where low standards will be attacked by good teachers and heads specially recruited to under-achieving schools. Even if educational disadvantage can be addressed and rectified at the lower end of society, it seems likely that special privilege will remain unassailable at the top. Although the abolition of assisted places will divert state funds from the public schools the abolition of the independent sector remains unthinkable. The Manifesto deplores that 'the educational apartheid created by the public/private divide diminishes the whole education system'. Yet it is highly unlikely that the Blair government 'will do more than readjust the knot of the old school tie' (*The Times*, 24 April 1997). The old criticisms remain. The over-production of graduates forces recruiting employers even more towards the public schools as purveyors of 'quality'. In no other European country 'do the moneyed and professional classes utterly reject the systems of education used by the majority'. This is not an area where state intervention in education is likely to interfere with the social structure at the higher end.

Historically, state involvement in education is a relatively recent development and is not an inevitable way of running an education system. The future, in spite of ideologues, is likely to remain a balance of state and other interests with a diminished role for local government, a shift of burdens from the taxpayer and central state to tax-relieved consumers and employers. Yet the central state will remain active in trying to use the state education system to inculcate in the people a greater sense of its British and Christian national culture and to stave off further relative economic decline, raise standards and extend opportunities.

Health

Helen Jones

Introduction

While the nature of state intervention in health care has changed out of all recognition during the course of the twentieth century, a number of recurrent themes can be identified at the key moments of change, before the First World War, at the end of the Second World War and toward the close of the century. All three periods were marked by major upheavals in social policies, in which health policies played an important part. Health reforms were, therefore, part of a wider political agenda, and generated enormous controversy most notably between political parties and between governments and the medical profession. Before the First World War the introduction in 1911 of National Health Insurance (NHI) for a limited section of the population was part of David Lloyd George's economic and foreign policies; under the postwar Labour government, the introduction of the National Health Service (NHS), funded largely from general taxation and available to the whole population, was part of a broad-based governmental strategy of gaining control of the economy and welfare provision; in the late 1980s health reform was part of a strategy to inject private enterprise methods into a state-run institution and to promote a mixed (private and public) economy of welfare into Britain. On all three occasions there was one individual, Lloyd George, Aneurin Bevan and Margaret Thatcher, who promoted the reforms. The early and late twentieth-century reforms were strongly influenced by developments abroad, whereas the ideas in the mid-century were largely home-grown. Throughout the century, whatever the pattern of health intervention devised and fought over by politicians, there has been an abiding assumption that women have a vital and usually informal role to play in health promotion, and that to a large extent individuals are in control of their own health. These assumptions, which academics failed to dislodge, influenced governments' agenda throughout the century. The Labour government elected in May 1997, however, has laid great emphasis – in ministers' rhetoric and government papers – on reducing inequalities in health. How far this will produce policies which reduce inequalities in health remains to be seen.

At the beginning of the twentieth century, a new-born baby girl had a life expectancy of 49 years, and a boy 45 years; by the end of the century they could reasonably expect to live to 79 and 74 respectively. This improvement is largely due to the decreased likelihood of dying from an infectious disease early on in life, rather than from a dramatic extension to life when elderly. While there has been a shift in common causes of death from infectious diseases to coronary heart disease and cancer, class inequalities in standards of health and life expectancy remain.

The Early Twentieth Century

In the early part of the century formal health care was patchy. Many working-class men belonged to friendly societies which covered them for hospital or general practitioner (GP) treatment, and payments in time of sickness, unless they suffered from a chronic illness which meant that they were too high a risk to insure. Green argued that friendly societies or Medical Institutes covered a surprisingly high proportion of working men and those not covered by private insurance could use Poor Law facilities (Green, 1985). Only a minority of the working class, however, could benefit from friendly societies as women and children were not normally covered. The bulk of the working class relied on free treatment at hospital out-patient departments or dispensaries. GPs, more numerous in prosperous areas, provided their services on a direct payment basis for the better-off.

Hospitals were a last resort, especially for the working class. Two types of hospitals ran alongside each other: voluntary hospitals, supported by voluntary contributions, which usually charged patients, so were used either by those who could afford to pay directly for their services or by those who belonged to a hospital insurance scheme, perhaps run by a friendly society; and workhouses (in 1913 renamed Poor Law Infirmaries), supported by local taxes which were free but usually of a low standard and, even after 1929 when they were taken over by local authorities and underwent a name change, carried the awful stigma of a Poor Law institution.

In the early years of the twentieth century this rudimentary health care system offered great scope for expansion at a time when the combination of domestic and foreign policies conspired together to make such expansion politically attractive. Wide-ranging political concerns relating to party politics, the demands of the labour market, international economic competition and defence policy placed social policies in general and health policy in particular high on the political agenda. Social policies were attractive to members of the 1905 to 1914 Liberal governments because they provided the Liberals with a distinctive and positive strategy, which had the bonus of offering an antidote to socialism. The immediate pressures of party politics also affected Lloyd George's calculations. Wrigley has cogently argued that the labour movement exerted growing pressure for social reform to which Lloyd George had to respond for two reasons. First, the Liberals perceived the Labour Party as a growing threat and Lloyd George frequently advocated social reforms as an alternative to socialism. Second, from the end of 1910 the Liberal government was in a minority and Lloyd George had to do a deal with Labour to get the Party's support in Parliament (Wrigley, 1971, pp. 26, 39).

Health policies offered the prospect of tackling the supposed decline in standards of health which it was feared was weakening Britain's ability to compete in international markets and to defend the empire. Britain, it was believed, needed to foster a nation more physically and economically efficient. The 1904 Inter-Departmental Committee on Physical Deterioration, set up in response to revelations during the Boer War of the poor health and therefore inability of so many young men to defend Britain and the empire, reported that standards of health and morals were not genetically inherited; environmental and behavioural changes could, therefore, improve standards of health. The committee did not believe that there was a progressive deterioration of the race taking place, and indeed a rapid improvement in standards of health was possible if there were changes in food, clothing, overcrowding, cleanliness, drunkenness and home management (Parliamentary Paper, 1904). A range of policy initiatives, such as infant welfare clinics, school meals and school medical inspection, already tentatively emerging, were thereby given a boost.

The first proposals for substantial changes to the hotch-potch of health services, and indeed the first call for a national state health service, came in Beatrice and Sidney Webb's 1909 Minority Report on the Poor Laws. Two years later Lloyd George introduced a major piece of health legislation, and although he claimed that one had inspired the other, the 1909 proposals and the 1911 legislation could not have been more different. Why the difference?

One point supporters and critics of Lloyd George's national health insurance proposals were agreed upon was that they at least had the merit of being opposed by Beatrice and Sidney Webb. These two Fabians were experts in the field of Poor Law analysis and more than anyone had thought through a replacement service for the existing Poor Law, and concomitantly a health system. In order to understand the reasons behind the united opposition to the health policy recommendations of the two most informed individuals on the Poor Law in the country, the personalities and principles involved in Poor Law reform need to be understood.

In 1905, not long before the fall of his Conservative administration, the Prime Minister, Arthur Balfour, set up a Royal Commission to review the deeply unpopular Poor Law, with Beatrice Webb as one of the Commissioners. She succeeded in making herself even more unpopular with her colleagues than the Poor Law itself. One of her biographers describes her as antagonising and irritating the other Commissioners by her over-hastiness, impatience and arrogance towards them (Radice, 1984, pp. 162–3). William

Braithwaite, a civil servant closely involved in drawing up national health insurance, makes clear in his memoirs that in policy-making circles the Webbs were figures of fun; their rudeness and socialism proved a lethal cocktail (Braithwaite, 1957, pp. 23, 116–17). As personal relationships went from bad to worse Beatrice, with her husband Sidney, shaped their own Minority Report. Their proposals for an integrated health system were part and parcel of their proposals for ending the Poor Law. They privately lobbied well-placed politicians and, when that failed, they launched an equally unsuccessful public campaign (Radice, 1984, pp. 169–75).

The Minority Report of the Poor Law Commission contains the first call for a unified national health system, a call which is shot through with a concern for national efficiency, a matter of perennial concern to the Webbs. Disease for the Webbs was the enemy of efficiency, and they deplored its effects on infants, schoolchildren and young people, the 'productive power of the future'. They criticised the absence of medical and midwifery services for women, because of their role as mothers and as industrial workers (National Committee to Promote the Break-up of the Poor Law, 1909, p. 286). For the Webbs one of the disadvantages of the medical branch of the Poor Law was that it was a deterrent to people seeking treatment which meant 'personal suffering and reduction in the wealth-producing power of the manual working class' (National Committee to Promote the Break-up of the Poor Law, 1909, p. 290).

The Webbs believed that national efficiency could be achieved by using a health care system to regulate the behaviour of the working class. On 17 July 1906 Beatrice Webb noted in her diary 'In listening to the evidence brought by the COS [Charity Organisation Society] members in favour of restricting medical relief to the technically destitute, it suddenly flashed across my mind that what we had to do was to adopt the exactly contrary attitude and make medical inspection and medical treatment compulsory on all sick persons – to treat illness, in fact, as a public nuisance to be suppressed, in the interests of the community' (Mackenzie and Mackenzie, 1984, p. 45). 'Domiciliary treatment should be withheld where proper treatment in the home is impracticable; where the patient persistently malingers or refuses the prescribed regimen; or where the patient is a source of danger to others' (National Committee to Promote the Break-up of the Poor Law, 1909, p. 290). The Minority Report argued that the primary aim of a health service should be the prevention of ill-health. The existing Poor Law service, with its gaps and overlaps, should be replaced by a merger of the Poor Law and Public Health authorities into a 'United Public Medical Service' (National Committee to Promote the Break-up of the Poor Law, 1909, p. 285).

Today one is struck more by the heartlessness of the tone of the proposals than by their socialism, although both aspects made the Report unattractive to contemporaries. In fact, as Radice has pointed out, whereas the Majority Report was favourably, and the Minority Report unfavourably, received, their proposals for an end to the general workhouse and the transfer of the Poor Law to local authorities, and a substantial extension of social services for the sick, aged, children and mentally defective were not dissimilar (Radice, 1984, p. 172).

Lloyd George asserted that his health reforms were a response to the Royal Commission on the Poor Laws. Not so, claimed Bentley Gilbert who has argued in great detail that national health insurance grew out of what everyone saw as an inevitable extension of the 1908 Old-Age Pensions Act to widows and orphans. Old-age pensions were non-contributory, but for the scheme to be extended only a contributory scheme was thought viable. So, Lloyd George went to Germany to see its contributory old-age and invalidity pension schemes. Lloyd George originally envisaged his scheme protecting the wage-earner or *his* survivors. He wanted to raise the standard of living so as to remove dependence on the Poor Law; pauperism, not sickness, was his main concern. Treatment only came on to the agenda later. As the aim was to support the breadwinner during illness, provision for dependants was almost entirely absent (Gilbert, 1966, pp. 291, 298, 314). It should be clear, however, from this brief summary of Gilbert's extensively detailed work that Lloyd George was indeed concerned to alter the way in which the Poor Law was used. He, like many of his contemporaries, operated, moreover, in a political culture which was preoccupied with national efficiency (a concept layered with assumptions about the way in which gender roles operated in, and interacted between, the labour market and the family). Numerous historians have already pointed out that Lloyd George's priority was to protect the incomes of workers who could not work because of illness. In order to allay fears that the distinction between the deserving and undeserving poor, inherent in the Poor Law, would be ditched, Lloyd George modified his proposals so that benefits could only be paid to those willing to follow doctor's orders (Fox, 1986, p. 6).

Bentley Gilbert argued that Lloyd George's aim was to prevent 'pauperism' caused by ill-health, not to promote good health. Cash benefits, not medical ones, were the key to the system because it was assumed that if the man, who brought in the family wage, could continue to have an income when off work through illness, he could maintain himself and his family. A range of evidence strongly pointed to women suffering worse health than men, but this was irrelevant as women were not perceived to be chief breadwinners. The fact that in many families the man did not provide a family wage was not taken on board, except insofar as single women were to be covered. Voluntary insurance for married women was really a footnote to the scheme.

Two linked assumptions about the needs of the labour market and the nature of the family lay behind health insurance. This link is well illustrated by the treatment of young workers and single women. Young workers between the ages of 14 and 16 were not covered even though they suffered the highest accident rate at work; presumably it was assumed that they lived at home and could therefore be kept by their father when out of work. Yet, many young people were in the labour market precisely because the family could no longer keep them. Although they were young, they still needed health insurance: young did not mean healthy in an age when young people worked long and unsocial hours in jobs which were often unregulated by law. Only 10 per cent of married women were part of the formal economy; the other 90 per cent were excluded from NHI. Ill-health was only perceived as a social problem when a failure to participate in the labour market affected a man's breadwinner role in the family. Government intervention to prop up a woman's role in the family was confined to advice on good mothering through infant welfare clinics. This never involved financial support, either for medical treatment or anything else, because a mother's contribution to family life was not thought to be a financial one. Only when married women were making a financial contribution to the family did the state step in to provide financial support. Yet, these may well have been the women best able to afford medicines as they were the ones in work.

The plans for national health insurance were very much the brain-child of a small group of individuals, none more important than Lloyd George. Braithwaite saw the NHI Act as Lloyd George's personal achievement: apart from the Treasury no government department was behind the measure, the Local Government Board under John Burns was hostile, and many of Lloyd George's other colleagues were lukewarm. Various interest groups were hostile along with Conservative backbenchers and the Northcliffe press (Braithwaite, 1957, pp. 17–18). Lloyd George threw himself into the research before plans were drawn up. In 1908 he visited Germany to find out about German social insurance (Braithwaite, 1957, p. 22). Lloyd George and the rest of the government were greatly concerned about developments abroad, in particular Germany, which acted as both a threat and a role model. While the German system had the most direct influence on Lloyd George, by 1911 a number of other European countries – Austria, Belgium, France, Denmark, Italy and Norway – also had some provision for sickness, accident and old age (Harris, 1946, p. 28). Hennock has shown how Lloyd George learnt from, and improved upon, the German scheme (Hennock, 1987, p. 177). Indeed, the public belief that Britain was apeing Germany may even have fuelled hostility to the scheme, although this was only one of many criticisms of it.

The National Health Insurance Bill prompted a range of opposition. The attitude of members of all the parties was important because after 1910 the Liberals were a minority government; horse-trading was crucial to the Bill's passage. The Labour Party divided over the issue with Philip Snowdon and Keir Hardie opposing the contributory principle as a tax on poverty (Gilbert, 1966, p. 441), and Lloyd George only secured Labour Party support when he agreed to introduce payment for MPs. Conservative backbenchers were hostile to health insurance and at one point Lloyd George was seriously pursuing the possibility of a coalition in order to remove the issue from party politics. More serious opposition, however, came from outside Parliament. A number of trade unions were suspicious, but their hostility was neutralised when they were allowed (along with friendly societies) to become approved societies through which the scheme would operate. The doctors were not so easily won over. At the end of 1912 a crisis blew up when the BMA threatened to boycott any doctor who took part in the scheme. The government made a new offer to the doctors of 9s instead of 8s 6d per insured person per year which was attractive to doctors in industrial areas earning less than half that amount, and finally the BMA released doctors from a pledge to boycott the scheme.

Under NHI all manual workers, aged over sixteen, earning below £160.00 a year were covered for medical, sickness, disablement, maternity and sanatorium benefits. Cash benefits were administered through Approved Societies and medical and sanatorium benefits through Local Insurance Committees.

For a contribution of 4d a week from men and 3d a week from women there were three types of NHI cover. First, there were cash payments of 10s a week for men, and 7s 6d for women. The disparity between men's and women's rates of benefit increased over the years. In 1915 and again in 1932 women's cash benefits were cut. Married women who were covered by NHI were subject to strict surveillance by health insurance visitors, on account of their unexpectedly high insurance claims. There were also 5s a week disablement benefits, and 30s maternity benefits although the latter were wiped out by the midwife's fees, leaving nothing for additional food and basic extras for the mother or baby. (Married women in paid work could, in addition, claim maternity benefit in their own right, which meant that they received £3.00 instead of 30s.) Much of the unexpected NHI costs were due to women's claims which were put down to malingering rather than ill-health, the former of course could be dealt with by tightening up the system; ill-health was a much bigger problem.

Second, there were medical benefits, such as GP consultations, drugs and appliances. Specialist treatment was not included. Third, there were additional benefits which the Approved Societies offered, but it was difficult to know before joining a scheme where the best deals were to be found. NHI did not cover either the better-off or large sections of the poorest in society, that is the dependants of the insured, or young workers between the ages of 14 and 16. The self-employed were not covered. Medical services were limited even for those covered by NHI; there was no cover for specialist advice and many could not get ophthalmic, dental or other treatment through NHI. Still others were not covered for convalescent homes (Political and Economic Planning, 1937a, pp. 13–15, 211). By the Second World War, NHI covered less than half the population, and the only specialist services for those in NHI were for VD and TB.

In its favour, Braithwaite claimed that NHI did at least bring relief to those destitute and suffering, and it raised the standard of medical practice in industrial areas (Braithwaite, 1957, pp. 40–1). Titmuss pointed out that it spelt the eventual end of less eligibility by introducing benefits as a right in return for contributions; it led to calls for insurance against more risks and, in fact, in 1925 the Conservatives added orphans' and widows' pensions to the scheme (Braithwaite, 1957, p. 44).

The compromises built into the system inevitably led to criticisms. The wide range of societies working under the Act meant that there was such a variety of benefits that a compulsory and supposedly uniform system provided very different benefits to those it covered. It left the health system uncoordinated and it left the bulk of the working class without adequate medical care (Braithwaite, 1957, pp. 40–1). It did nothing to stem the tide of financial crises for the voluntary hospitals so that by the end of the 1930s there was an urgent need for them to be put on a more secure financial footing (Webster, 1988b, p. 22).

Local authorities were responsible for environmental health which included clean food, milk, air and water, and refuse collection; they ran infant welfare clinics, TB clinics and sanatoria, and from 1929 they took over responsibility for the old Poor Law hospitals. Inevitably, services around the country varied enormously with poor areas usually receiving the poorest services. The wealth of an area was not the only determinant of services, however, as the political outlook of a local authority and the views of the local medical officer of health as to whether ill-health was primarily due to environmental factors or individual ones also played a part.

The piecemeal reforms of the interwar years belies the enormous amount of effort spent on trying to redefine and change the contours of health provision. In 1919 the newly founded Ministry of Health scooped up overall responsibility for local authority health services and the National Health Insurance Commission. In Whitehall it was assumed that this move would lead not only to greater coordination of health services but also to the development of a more comprehensive service. Such hopes were soon dashed. Lord Dawson, chair of the new Consultative Council on Medical and Allied Services, produced a report for the coordination of services (including private medical practitioners) and health centres across the country. This plan, and others for coordination and expansion of services, remained a dead letter.

Throughout the interwar years there were a number of women-dominated, interrelated campaigns for pain relief and hospitalisation at childbirth; better maternity care; birth control; better child and maternal welfare services, in particular for local authority infant and maternal welfare centres to offer women medical and financial support; family allowances; nursery schools, and a variety of measures to reduce the maternal mortality rate. Eleanor Rathbone spearheaded the call for family allowances, Marie Stopes demanded birth control information to be made widely and freely available, and

Margaret MacMillan advocated nursery schools in the inner cities. The National Birthday Trust Fund promoted the professionalisation of midwifery, pain relief for poor women in childbirth, and provided supplementary foods (controversially marmite rather than milk) for pregnant women in the depressed areas. If successful these campaigns would have improved the standard of living and the health of the poorest sections of society, in particular women and children. The majority of the campaigns called for greater intervention by the state; paradoxically, because of the failure to gain this objective, the campaigns generated more activity in the voluntary sector.

Thus, on the outbreak of war, NHI covered part of the working class, overwhelmingly men, for GP and some other services; some single women in employment were covered, but in 1932 the few married women who were in the scheme had their benefit levels cut. Two hospital systems ran alongside each other, the least well resourced under local authorities, and voluntary hospitals which normally required payment, either through insurance, or direct payment; by the outbreak of war the voluntary hospitals were suffering a severe financial crisis. Local authorities' services varied enormously, and most were far from adequate. The plethora of overlapping yet inadequate health care facilities had been roundly criticised for a number of years and were widely regarded as ripe for reform.

The Creation and Operation of the NHS

By the outbreak of the Second World War some kind of reform was inevitable; the war and postwar political situation influenced the shape of those reforms. Titmuss provided the first and most influential view of the creation of the welfare state and the NHS when he argued that the welfare measures of the war and immediate postwar years were the direct result of wartime circumstances: the evacuation of Dunkirk in 1940 and the air raids created a solidarity which cut across class lines; and evacuation brought home to the middle class and the more prosperous sections of society the extent of poverty and ill-health among the urban working class. The government, moreover, was aware of the importance of sustaining both morale and an efficient workforce, and therefore placed great stress on a healthy population with a better life to look forward to after the war. While Titmuss saw the wartime hospital service providing a blueprint for the future, he himself emphasised the shortcomings of wartime health care services for civilians (Titmuss, 1950).

A challenge to the once widely held view that social solidarity and political consensus led to the welfare state has been mounted (Macnicol, 1980; Jefferys, 1987, 1991). Jefferys has argued that there was controversy on party political lines both before and after the publication of the 1944 White Paper on the future of the health services (Cmd 6502, 1944), and Labour and Conservative

MPs endorsed the White Paper for very different reasons. The Labour Party attacked the secret agreements reached after the publication of the White Paper between Henry Willink, the Conservative Minister of Health from 1943 to 1945, and the BMA. When the parties endorsed a National Health Service in the 1945 general election they were envisaging two quite different services (Jefferys, 1987).

From the outset of war a national hospital scheme was under discussion although it was envisaged that national health insurance and the voluntary hospitals would remain. A serious reassessment of the health care services was not embarked upon until later on in the war.

In June 1941 the Beveridge Committee on Social Insurance and Allied Services was set up to review the whole question of unemployment and health insurance as well as workmen's compensation. When the Beveridge Report appeared at the end of 1942 it recommended a comprehensive social security system, based on subsistence rate benefits 'from the cradle to the grave'. A basic assumption of the Report was that there would be child benefit, full employment and a National Health Service for prevention and cure of disease and disability (Cmd 6404, 1942, pp. 153, 158). Almost immediately Conservative MPs secretly reported that in order to protect private medical practice they wanted national health insurance restricted to those with incomes under £420.00 a year. The next month, however, the government, following the popular reception of the Beveridge Report, publicly accepted it in principle. At no time during the war was there any question of the voluntary hospitals being 'nationalised'.

In February 1944 the Cabinet approved a White Paper on the *Future of Health Services* which was debated the following month in the House of Commons. As the White Paper was vague on all the contentious issues it allowed maximum agreement at the time of its publication while storing up controversy for the future. Labour ministers had ensured that the White Paper included the establishment of health centres, which would lead to a salaried health service and the Labour Party generally accepted the document although it would have liked it to have gone further.

The Conservatives, like Labour, were broadly in favour of the White Paper (far more so than they had been over the Beveridge Report), but there were rumblings of discontent which suggests that even in its cautious generalisations the government had gone too far for many of its supporters. A number of Conservative MPs feared that the voluntary hospitals might be under-funded in the future and that a salaried medical service would destroy the special doctor/patient relationship. Few attacked the White Paper's underlying principles (*Hansard*, 1944). The publication presaged a long and contentious series of negotiations between the Ministry of Health and the BMA. Willink was involved in discussions which led to proposals more acceptable to doctors and unacceptable to the Labour movement. It was agreed that the administrative role of local government would be weakened, new financial provisions would be made for the voluntary hospitals and doctors in health centres would not be the salaried employees of local government. By the time the coalition broke up the government was close to accepting a National Health Service in principle, but on Willink's own later admission it was different from the one created by the postwar Labour government. In particular, Willink did not believe that the Conservatives would have accepted the nationalisation of the voluntary hospitals, yet if two hospital systems had continued it would have been impossible to finance the voluntary hospitals or to have had a national hospital plan for the whole country. In retrospect Willink praised Bevan for the 'wise and important' change which introduced one unified hospital system (see Foot, 1997, pp. 360–1). At their 1945 annual conference the Conservatives welcomed, after brief criticism, a comprehensive service, available to all. In contrast, the Labour conference bitterly attacked the concessions it was rumoured the medical profession had prised out of Willink. If the Conservatives had won the 1945 general election they would have introduced a National Health Service in name but it would have been very different from either the one outlined in the coalition's White Paper or the service that was introduced by Labour after the war.

In 1945 the Labour Party was returned to office with a commitment to a universal, free and comprehensive health service. The proposals put forward by Aneurin Bevan, the new Minister of Health, differed from the 1944 White Paper in one important principle; the voluntary hospitals were to lose their charitable status and be taken over by the government: they were to be nationalised. Bevan's plan, which he put to the Cabinet in October 1945, included other changes too: it gave more control to the Ministry of Health and greater encouragement to health centres and group practices in areas where there was a shortage of GPs. There was to be a salaried element in GPs' pay along with a capitation fee. Hospitals were to be reorganised with the hospital governing system under regional boards, accountable to the Ministry of Health (Morgan, 1984a, p. 154).

Bevan faced opposition from within the Cabinet, from the medical profession and from the Conservative Party. A row broke out in Cabinet, between those, led by Herbert Morrison, Lord President of the Council between 1945 and 1951, who wanted voluntary and municipal hospitals to remain under local authority control, and the majority of the Cabinet, led by Bevan, who wanted to end the charitable status of the voluntary hospitals and bring all hospitals under central government control. Bevan won the battle in Cabinet and then took on the medical profession, in particular those wealthy doctors at the head of the BMA who resented greater state control and the salaried element in doctors' pay.

As the NHS Bill was passing through Parliament the Conservative Party maintained that it accepted the Bill in principle but opposed the clauses which differed from the 1944 White Paper, in particular the nationalisation of the voluntary hospitals (which was a matter of principle).

There are historians who still argue that the welfare state grew out of a political consensus. Their definition of consensus includes a framework of common assumptions about the role of the state and a commitment to collective provision of comprehensive welfare services (Kavanagh and Morris, 1989; Marquand, 1989; Dutton, 1991). These criteria did not exist either at the planning or implementation stages of the NHS. If one takes into account both the antipathy of much of the Conservative Party and medical profession during the war and in 1946 during the passage of the NHS Bill, it is hard to see the creation of the NHS as the outcome of political consensus. Between 1945 and 1951 disagreements within the Cabinet, between the government and the medical profession, and between the government and Conservative opposition all undermine the view that the NHS received an unanimously warm welcome. Webster, official historian of the NHS, rebuts the idea of a consensus over the creation of the NHS. Public opinion saw none of the consensus about which some historians have written. In the early 1950s a majority of the population saw the two parties as having distinct party differences; it was only in the later 1950s, when Conservative governments did not dismantle the welfare state, that political parties were popularly seen as having converging policies (Webster, 1988, pp. 389–93).

Morgan, pointing out the lack of continuity between wartime Conservative plans and postwar Labour ones, listed the main aspects of the 1946 National Health Service Act which became operational in July 1948: the nationalisation of the hospitals; new regional hospital boards; the creation of health centres; a better distribution of doctors around the country; and new salary provisions for doctors, including provisions for specialists to treat private patients in NHS hospitals (Morgan, 1984a, p. 157). Although there were fears that the doctors might refuse to work in the new system, at the last moment Bevan won them over with a conciliatory gesture, confirming that a whole-time salaried service would not be introduced, so the capitation element would continue, and doctors would be free to air their opinions publicly on the running of the NHS (*Hansard*, 1948). As a result of disagreements at the planning stage of the NHS compromises were reached which automatically built weaknesses into the system. The NHS was mainly a national *hospital* service with few resources for preventing ill-health.

Although divided at the planning stage over control of the NHS, the Labour Party was united in its commitment to a service free at the point of use. Within the Conservative Party there was no such agreement. Yet Labour, not Conservative, politicians fell out over payments for certain services while the Conservatives governed for 13 years without fundamental public disagreements over the financing of the NHS: Labour, faced with the realities of office, had already fought the Conservatives' battle. Disagreements over the funding of the NHS related almost entirely to the overall costs of the service. Little attention was paid to the distribution of resources between primary (non-hospital-based) and secondary (hospital-based) services, between teaching and non-teaching hospitals, or between regions (Webster, 1988b, p. 292).

As soon as the NHS came into operation its costs dominated discussion. In 1949 the government authorised prescription charges but never implemented them, and in 1951 the government introduced charges for spectacles and teeth. Aneurin Bevan, by now Minister of Labour and National Service, Harold Wilson, President of the Board of Trade, and John Freeman, Financial Under Secretary at the War Office, all resigned.

One long-term consequence of a Labour government accepting prescription charges was that the Labour Party was never able to criticise, with any moral authority, future Conservative governments for extending charges, and indeed Conservatives were quick to point to a precedent which had been set by Labour.

The Labour movement's fear that the Conservatives would dismantle the health service when returned to office proved unfounded. By the time the Labour government fell in 1951 the Conservatives' problem was to find a distinctive policy which would not be open to the criticism that the Tories were undoing Labour's achievement. The Guillebaud Committee was set up to report on how the NHS might be managed more efficiently with an eye to making savings. In 1956 its Report gave the Conservatives no ammunition for an attack on the NHS, rather the reverse, for the Report concluded that more, not less, should be spent on the NHS (Parliamentary Paper, 1955–56). Savings were made by implementing Labour's provision for prescription charges, and by increasing spectacle and dental charges. (In 1964 Labour abolished prescription charges, and in 1967 reintroduced them.)

Both supporters and critics of the NHS viewed it as the flagship of British socialism. Aneurin Bevan certainly believed that the creation of the NHS was a watershed in health service provision. After 1948 the financial worries associated with medical treatment vanished. The importance of a free service, especially for children, young workers, and the vast majority of married women who had not been covered by national health insurance, should not be underestimated.

This initial picture of a distinctive health service which sliced a clean break with the past needs modification. Most historians now point to significant continuities in health care provision. The creation of the NHS did not in itself lead to the building of any new hospitals, the training of extra doctors or the evolution of new drugs and treatment (Watkin, 1978, p. 1). The provision of health care improved dramatically, but inequalities in access and use, and class-related inequalities in standards of health persisted.

Bevan's compromises had sown the seeds of future problems and left in place many features of the old health care system. As a result of the compromises which he made with the medical profession, teaching hospitals were given a special status and a disproportionate allocation of resources, private practise and pay beds in NHS hospitals were permitted, doctors, but no other health workers, were allowed to sit on management bodies and the proposed health centres which would have played a major role in preventative work and coordination of services were shelved because of doctors' fears that they would become subject to local authority control. Regional inequalities were built into the system by allowing teaching hospitals to continue to hold a special status. The emphasis on a hospital service rather than on primary and preventative community care, coordinated through health centres, meant that the NHS was increasingly out of step with the changing health needs of the population.

The funding of the NHS remained an unresolved problem. The NHS had rapidly lodged itself in the hearts of the nation, and the Guillebaud Committee had found no scope for substantial savings or increased efficiency. In the 1960s a new hospital building programme, the development of new drugs and medical technology all reinforced the idea that the NHS was central to rising standards of health, and an essential part of the British way of life. Critical voices demanded more, not less, NHS provision. Academic criticisms of inequalities in standards of health related to the social and economic structure of society carried no weight in policy-making circles.

Late Twentieth-century Reforms

In the 1970s when it became clear that full employment was no longer inviolable, politicians of all shades continued to accept that the NHS remained sacrosanct. Mrs Thatcher recognised that it was the yardstick by which the population judged the government's commitment to the welfare state. (In effect, therefore, it was possible to erode other aspects of the welfare state so long as the NHS was not touched.) In her famous words 'The National Health Service is safe with us'. Yet, Mrs Thatcher's third and final administration did set in motion fundamental reforms of the NHS.

After 1979 the overarching thrust of policy was to encourage business enterprise, and to discourage individuals and families depending on state welfare. Reliance on the market and greater choice for individuals were the goals of a whole swathe of policies, to which the NHS, despite being one of the most prominent state institutions, remained largely immune. From 1979 governments encouraged private health care; from 1983 health authorities were required to contract out domestic, catering and laundry services. Much was made of these reforms in the early 1980s although now it is generally thought that the contracting out of ancillary services was not a fundamental change. Still, reforms were demanded: the NHS faced mounting problems, most of them common to the Western world: the costs of the NHS were skyrocketing as a result of rising expectations, ever more costly and feasible medical interventions, and an ageing population. Other clouds over the NHS, such as the balance between prevention and cure, the integration of services and management structures rumbled on.

It was not until Mrs Thatcher's government had been safely returned to power in a third successive general election victory that it felt secure enough to dislodge the jewel in the postwar socialist crown. By early 1987 Mrs Thatcher's patience with the NHS had run out. She recognised that much of the NHS's work was of a high quality, but the caveats were longer than the praises: the NHS was not sensitive enough to people's wishes or to costs, it was inefficient, and hospitals and local health authorities performed with inexplicable variations. Mrs Thatcher wanted, too, to see a flourishing private sector. Her own choice of private treatment personalised a public debate. The shape of the reforms was influenced by Professor Alain Enthoven of Stanford University who put forward the idea of an internal market within the NHS. Early in 1988 Mrs Thatcher set up a ministerial health review group which she chaired. When she feared that the Secretary of State for Health, John Moore, was not up to the task she replaced him with Kenneth Clarke who out-raced Mrs Thatcher in his charge towards change. His headlong rush to introduce changes, his refusal to take advice and experiment with pilot projects, the nature of the reforms and his bruising style combined to earn him the almost united hostility of the medical profession which mounted a highly personalised campaign against the proposed reforms. These reforms had emerged from the ministerial health reform group and appeared in a 1989 White Paper which was followed in 1990 by the National Health Service and Community Care Act.

The key aspects of reform were that an internal market would operate within the NHS, creating a clear distinction between 'purchasers' and 'providers' of health care. Mrs Thatcher claimed that the reforms aimed to introduce competition between NHS hospitals and between the NHS and the private sector in order to increase efficiency and to benefit patients, both rather vague goals. Hospitals were to be free to opt out of District Health Authority control and to become self-governing Trusts, able to sell their services in the public and private sectors. GPs could control their own budgets if they chose to opt out (Thatcher, 1995, pp. 571, 606–17). Social service departments also became purchasers of care for the elderly and disabled who were to come under the government's care in the community policy, roundly criticised for allegedly abandoning the vulnerable to the whims of the market and placing an intolerable burden on families, particularly women, as part of a governmental agenda of cutting back on state provision and assuming that women should and could play a more active and informal caring role.

The opposition criticised the government's reforms, in particular, internal markets, although at times this generated more heat than light, as for instance during the 1992 general election campaign when criticisms of the government were lost in a fog over the 'war of Jennifer's ear' as it was dubbed by the media. The Labour Party advertised its criticisms in *NHS: The Threefold Tory Threat. Underfunding, Commercialisation, Privatisation* (Harman, 1992). Academics and a chief executive of an NHS Trust publicly criticised the reforms for creating a two-tier health service, in effect a first-class and a second-class service; and for decentralising responsibilities without devolving power (Riddell, 1991, p. 141; Paton, 1993; Salter, 1994). Others were unsure whether firm conclusions could be drawn about the impact of the reforms (Glennerster, 1994).

While the jury was still out on many aspects of the changes, the push towards a mixed economy of health and welfare continued. The 1992 White Paper, *The Health of the Nation: A Strategy for Health in England*, set targets for reducing coronary heart disease and stroke; cancer; mental illness; HIV/AIDs and sexual ill-health; and accidents. The strategy adopted for meeting the targets involved creating 'healthy alliances' between various organisations and individuals. *The Health of the Nation* saw improvements in these areas of health coming through changes in the behaviour of individuals and groups; it made no reference to the structure or organisation of society (Department of Health, 1992). Yet, many attempts have been made over the years to draw attention to class (and later, gender and ethnic) inequalities in standards of health, most notably in the 1979 Black Report and in a 1988 report by the Health Education Council (Health Education Council, 1988; Jones, 1994, pp. 172–92). In the mid-1990s Richard Wilkinson made an important contribution to the debate when he argued that standards of health in affluent societies are influenced less by people's absolute standards of living than by people's standard of living relative to that of others in the society. Inequalities and hierarchies create psycho-social factors which undermine rather than improve standards of health. Improvements in health will not therefore come from tinkering with the health care system, but from reducing relative deprivation and promoting a more equitable distribution of resources (Wilkinson, 1994). Although in the early 1990s there were some stirrings of recognition in Whitehall that the issues which have engrossed academic debate over inequalities in health do need addressing by governments, messages from academics are awkward for governments of any hue because of their far-reaching implications (Department of Health, 1991, 1994). It is far safer to stick to rearranging health service delivery and squabbling over national or local pay bargaining agreements.

The Future

In the late 1990s public controversies revolve around money and financing health care; rationing within the NHS; the workings of the internal market: hospital trusts and GP fundholding; and community care. Calls have come from across the political spectrum for more private financing of state services.

In September 1995 Healthcare 2000, an inquiry team with members from both left and right, called for a more open debate on the possible future funding of health services, suggesting that a range of possibilities, such as raising taxes, introducing new taxes, charging for extra services and rationing services should all be considered in order to bridge the gap between demand on the health service and its resources. The suggestion that while general taxation should remain the basis of NHS funding, additional taxes were inevitable led to an outcry from two uneasy bedfellows, Stephen Dorrell, Secretary of State for Health, and UNISON, the biggest health service union. Dorrell claimed the report said nothing new, while UNISON accused the team, which was funded by drugs companies, of insidiously undermining the NHS.

Private finance is certainly set to play a larger role in the NHS, so blurring further the lines between state and private health care. Under the Private Finance Initiative (PFI) health care Trusts are required to seek private finance for development schemes before bidding for government money. It is envisaged that private consortia will build and run new hospitals, leasing them to Trusts. Criticisms that this was yet another example of creeping privatisation of the NHS led Dorrell to claim that no such scheme would apply to clinical services, only to health facilities. One of the Labour government's first moves was to strengthen and make operative PFI. Other evidence of increasingly entwined state and private health care came in the autumn of 1996 when it emerged that, as a result of the growth of pay beds in Trust hospitals, the NHS is now the chief provider of private health care. One of the first actions of the new Labour government was to try and kick-start the PFI which had never left the starting blocks under the Conservatives.

While both the Labour government and the Conservative opposition accept a role for private finance and companies in the provision of health care, not least because of the endless demand for health care while resources are finite, alternative proposals from beyond the party political spectrum suggest that there may be alternative ways of meeting health care needs. First, there is a move towards evidence-based medicine (EBM), which involves collating evidence on which treatments do, and do not, work. It has been estimated that between 3 per cent and 5 per cent of all hospital admissions are due to adverse reactions to prescribed drugs. The Audit Commission estimated that inappropriate drug prescriptions by GPs alone costs the NHS £420 million a year. Alternative and complementary medicines are booming, and this is seen as another potential means of saving the NHS money. While there are those who are offering a more optimistic picture of the future, the immediate need to ration services is undiminished.

Rationing became a particularly emotive issue in the tabloids when in January 1995 Cambridge and Huntingdon Health Authority took the decision not to treat 'Child B' (Jaymee Bowen) for leukaemia because it was argued the prognosis was so poor. She did in fact die after private treatment, but the image presented was of a health authority not treating her because of the expense when the prognosis was so poor, rather than a clinical decision free of financial concerns.

Roughly one in three health authorities explicitly ration treatments, not only those regarded as non-essential or of doubtful clinical value, but also preventative services such as routine ultrasound and urine tests in pregnancy, screening for brittle bone disease and screening for heart conditions and cancer. As well as rationing at the local level, there is evidence that the last Conservative government, despite its public pronouncements, set in motion discussions among senior clinicians and health officials over setting national priorities. The Labour government has tried to avoid getting publicly embroiled in the issue and instead has focused on switching resources from managers to direct patient care.

The role of health managers in rationing services is particularly controversial. While Stephen Dorrell, when Secretary of State for Health, publicly told health managers to seek the assistance of senior medical and nursing staff when making rationing decisions and justifying them to the public, the Labour Party claimed that it would not allow managers to stop doctors treating patients. At the beginning of 1996 the Labour Party claimed that since 1989 there had been a 400 per cent increase in managers while nurses and midwives suffered a 13 per cent cut. As well as sky-rocketing numbers of managers their costs vary enormously with some health service Trusts spending five times as much on managers as others.

The whole bureaucracy of health service Trusts is portrayed as wasteful, as for instance when it was claimed that each Trust spends an extra £1 million a year dealing with fundholding GPs. Evidence that GP fundholders did not provide a better service to their patients reinforces the picture that the internal market was inefficient. The internal market was blamed for mislaying £422 million, while a single hospital Trust allegedly lost £3.5 million in a business venture.

The Labour government is phasing out gradually GP fundholding and instead gathering practices together into 500 local commissioning groups, a move which is intended to cut bureaucracy and avoid patients with GP fundholders receiving preferential treatment. Saving money which the Conservatives spent on bureaucracy is meant to go to cutting waiting lists, in particular for cancer patients.

Community care is another area which has been under constant attack. Research which shows that roughly half the elderly who live alone receive no help from social services, and a constant stream of reports that services for the mentally ill are either lacking or totally inadequate have fuelled debate not only over the current provision, but also over future funding. Numerous suggestions have been put forward as to how the needs of the increasing number of elderly will be met in the future, but the problem remains unresolved. The Conservative government's plans for a 'partnership' between private insurance companies and the government whereby the state would match any private insurance cover for long-term care was dismissed in the summer of 1996 by the Conservative-dominated Commons Health Select Committee, primarily on the grounds that until the government provided costings it was just pie in the sky.

While the Labour Party in opposition attacked Conservative government policies as they unfolded over the years, in the run up to the general election differences between the two main parties became less distinct. Old Labour Party promises to scrap the internal market were modified, and an earlier commitment to reintroduce free eye tests and dental check-ups disappeared. The most radical claim in the Labour Party manifesto was that 'Labour will set new goals for improving the overall health of the nation which recognise the impact that poverty, poor housing, unemployment and a polluted environment have on health' (Labour Party, 1997 p. 21).

In the late 1990s all the parties display, superficially, strikingly similar priorities in their health policies. All profess a commitment to a 'modern' National Health Service that is not burdened by excessive bureaucracy. The parties claim to want greater public information, devolved powers and partnerships between public and private organisations. All emphasise prevention and rising standards of living (Jones, 1998). In the details of policy, however, the parties diverge. The Labour Party, although highly critical of the Conservatives when they introduced the internal market, has chosen to build on it, rather than demolish it. In December 1997 the Department of Health published a White Paper on *The Future of the NHS*. Individual fundholding by GPs negotiating annual contracts will end and instead all practices will be brought together with community nurses in primary care groups which will commission health services on a three-yearly cycle. This change is to reduce the amount of paper generated and to remove the inequalities which built up between fundholding and non-fundholding practices. Every three years health authorities will produce health improvement programmes which will provide the framework for health services within their area. The services will be provided by health authorities, local authorities, hospital Trusts and primary care groups. Health authorities will then allocate funds on the basis of these plans to primary health groups. So while the division between purchaser and provider will remain, the Labour government aims to change the rules of the competition and attack inequalities.

The reduction of inequalities is the centre-piece of the Labour government's rhetoric over health. While the Conservatives in office had emphasised the importance of individual responsibility for raising standards of health and had set specific, and largely unrealistic, targets for reducing illness, New Labour resurrected an old Labour concern with inequalities in health resulting from factors which are often beyond an individual's control. Echoing a manifesto commitment to reduce inequalities in standards of health, on 5 February 1998 Frank Dobson, Secretary of State for Health, told the House of Commons, 'This government recognises that poverty, poor housing, low wages, unemployment, air pollution, crime and disorder can all make people ill in both body and mind' (Department of Health, 98/051). Launching the Green Paper *Our Healthier Nation* (Department of Health, 98/050) he promised that the government would coordinate policies across departments, and it would encourage contracts between central government, local government, individuals and local agencies to improve health. The government was setting up ten Health Action Zones and would pour money – siphoned-off from the lottery – into healthy living centres. The government scrapped almost all the Conservatives' targets, presumably because it realised that they were only hostages to fortune, and instead Dobson claimed that the government would support local strategies with local targets. He linked the government's attack on health inequalities with other government policies for reducing inequality, such as the Social Exclusion Unit, the minimum wage, employment creation programmes under welfare-to-work, and the release of money from the past sale of council houses to be spent on new and improved housing. Fine words butter no parsnips and so far we have no more than the government documents and public statements on which to judge Labour's policies. Only time will tell whether the claim on 5 February 1998 of Tessa Jowell, Minister for Public Health 'Tackling inequality sits at the heart of this government's promise of a modern and fair Britain' is true (Department of Health, 98/050). The problem remains that while ensuring that money is well spent in terms of outcomes, and reducing health inequalities do not necessarily require extra funding for the NHS, continuing to provide existing NHS services requires substantially greater sums of money than are likely to be made available in the foreseeable future. At the beginning of the century and in the middle of the century politicians successfully shifted the health agenda; the challenge for the Labour government is to do the same again as the new century dawns.

Employment, Unemployment and the Labour Market

Sean Glynn

In modern Britain income from employment remains, overwhelmingly, the main source of material welfare, either directly, or through immediate personal dependency. In relation to this dependence on wages and salaries, state welfare benefits are relatively minor. The labour market is, therefore, much more important than the welfare state in determining welfare, although this relative importance has diminished over time. Since the earlier twentieth century the employed, and their direct dependants, have fallen as a proportion of total population. This trend reflects a number of influences including a general decline in labour force participation, a reduction in average family size, changes in age structure and earlier retirement (Halsey, 1972). Nevertheless, income in employment is still overwhelmingly important as the prime source of welfare, and this is unlikely to change.

Recognition of the importance of employment has been an important influence in welfare reform and the establishment of welfare systems. The Liberal reforms of pre-1914 gave particular attention to the labour market, encouraging the ability to participate and providing help for some of those who could not do so (Thane, 1982, Ch. 1). In the interwar period coping with unemployment became the main welfare concern and a new system of social security was established against the background of a persistent labour market crisis (Crowther, 1988). In the 1940s Beveridge, an expert of long standing on the British labour market, viewed labour market change as an integral part of his proposals for welfare reform. His stated view was that 'full employment' was a *sine qua non* of the welfare state (Beveridge, 1944; Harris, 1977). There is no doubt that exceptionally high levels of employment after the Second World War greatly assisted the establishment of the Beveridge system and helped to ensure its apparent early success (Lowe, 1994a, pp. 99–113). It was also no coincidence that the welfare state began to be questioned when full employment started to disappear in the 1970s. More recently, the welfare debate in Britain has been very directly related to the labour market with the use of political slogans such as 'welfare-to-work'. These debates seek to address the causes of poverty, rather than needs and measures of relief, and are realistic at least to the extent that they recognise the important links between labour market failure and welfare need (Barr and Coulter, 1990). Assumptions relating to the idea of a 'dependency culture' are more controversial but the view that macroeconomic policies can no longer be relied upon to solve unemployment and poverty problems is becoming axiomatic.

As a simplification, it may be said that there are two basic causes of poverty, both absolute and relative, and these are 'no pay' and 'low pay'. First, absence of income from employment may arise as the result of incapacity for work, by virtue of age or ill-health, or through unemployment from whatever cause. In all societies there are people who are either unable or unwilling to participate in remunerative employment and twentieth-century Britain is no exception. However, levels of participation have varied very widely over time and between different social groups and sexes. It is clear that the determining factors, economic and cultural, are extremely complex (Glynn, 1991). During the nineteenth century British society developed a pronounced 'work ethic' which has probably been enhanced in the twentieth. Work came to be seen as a means of personal fulfilment and identification as well as an economic necessity. The term 'unemployment' appears to have entered the political vocabulary in its modern sense only in the 1880s (Harris, 1972). Before that time it could be applied to upper-class males without abusive implications, despite the fact that many gentlemen of wealth were beginning to follow the egregious example of Prince Albert who was a busy man despite being both rich and 'unemployed' (Thompson, 1963).

Second, poverty may arise as a result of inadequacy of income in employment, a major cause of poverty in late nineteenth-century York, and wage inadequacy has remained an important if insufficiently recognised influence in creating welfare needs (Rowntree, 1941). Wages are not usually related directly to individual and family needs and there has been a persistent tendency for the British wage spectrum to extend below poverty lines as variously defined (Phelps Brown, 1981). Low pay arises from a range of demand and supply influences in the labour market and recent welfare debate has given it increased emphasis (Wilkinson, 1989). It is a matter of opinion which of the above two influences is the more important 'generator of poverty' *but*, in any event, there are important causal links between the two and both arise directly from the nature of the labour market.

Conventional economic theory links wages to productivity. Companies will continue to take on workers and expand output until individual output falls to the same level as the wage paid. Expansion of employment beyond this point will involve a loss for the employer. In an efficient labour market wages will, therefore, tend to approximate to marginal revenue product, that is the output of the last worker engaged (Hughes and Perlman, 1984). This simple theory is axiomatic to much of labour economics but it rests on a number of assumptions which rarely exist in the real world. Nevertheless, the *average wage equals marginal product* assumption underpins much of modern attitudes to employment and unemployment. It gives rise to the view that the essential cause of involuntary unemployment is 'high' wages and the notion that workers must 'price' themselves into employment. Such attitudes were widely held in the interwar period and were challenged by Keynes. More recently they have been re-asserted (Glynn, 1991, Ch. III). The labour market, including the level of employment, provides the means whereby the productive potential of labour is translated into reality, generating a welfare return. It has a fundamental role, therefore, in determining the material welfare of the majority and in setting what are acceptable welfare (non-poverty) standards. Beyond this the labour market has important non-material functions in relation to social and political cohesion as well as individual identification and psychological well-being. Income from employment also has a determining role in social redistribution. Britain, along with every other advanced industrial society, established a welfare state in the twentieth century based upon funds arising largely from the taxation or subvention of income earned in employment, either directly, at the point of receipt, or in the purchase of goods and services. There was rather less inclination and effectiveness in relation to taxes on property, profits and wealth (Atkinson, 1975). Also, much of British income redistribution was *inter vivos* and within rather than between social groups. The main function of the welfare state, as established in the 1940s, appears to have been to redistribute working-class income *within* the working class over the life-cycle. Those in work subsidised the young, the old, the sick and the unemployed, becoming, in due course, beneficiaries in their own right. Redistribution from rich to poor and between social groups did take place, but on a limited basis, because one of the basic principles was 'equal contributions for equal benefits'. Also, the system of direct taxation was less progressive than might have been the case. Before the Second World War manual workers paid very little in direct taxation. In the 1930s income tax commenced on incomes over £5.00 per week and the average weekly wage was about £3.00. From the 1940s income tax moved down the income scale and wage earners faced rising burdens of income tax and national insurance deductions from pay.

In short, it can be said that social welfare has been heavily influenced and largely determined by conditions in the labour market. It is this influence which sets the basic standards and helps to establish the economic, political and fiscal parameters for any system of redistribution between individuals and groups over time. Of course, there are many commentators who would not accept any simple model of economic fundamentalism or market determination, and there is no intention to suggest one here. All markets are social creations and this applies *a fortiori* to the labour market and perhaps to the British labour market in particular. Labour markets are heavily influenced by non-economic considerations, not least for the simple reason that they involve human beings rather than inanimate items. Politics, culture, tradition and psychology all have an important influence which may defy simple economic analysis. Reality is always much more complex than the world of economics textbooks. All modern industrial societies have developed welfare adjuncts, and not simply to deal with labour market casualties on humanitarian grounds. Social welfare systems have important roles in sustaining economic and political systems. At a basic level there is a need to supply increasingly healthy, educated and housed labour forces and, until recently at least, the necessity for state intervention at some level was perceived in order to alleviate these and other supply-side deficiencies in the voluntary sector. Labour force quality has been an important issue in British public debate since the late nineteenth century and remains so today. In recent years 'training' has been given particular emphasis, alongside debate about what is genuine training and what is not. On the demand side, also, welfare systems have been seen by some as a threat to the economic system and a feature in relative economic decline (Barnett, 1986). It is important, therefore, to avoid simple economic determinism. In what follows the main intention is to outline and examine those features of the historical record which seem most relevant, without commitments to any particular ideological or theoretical platform.

Pre-war Developments in the British Labour Market

In the late nineteenth and early twentieth centuries the British labour market appeared, ostensibly at least, to be functioning efficiently. The market 'cleared' in the sense that, on the official figures, unemployment was low and labour appeared to be efficiently allocated and deployed. Between 1855 and 1914 officially measured male unemployment fluctuated between 2 and 10 per cent of the (defined) male workforce over the trade cycle, averaging approximately 4–5 per cent (Beveridge, 1909). Most contemporary economists, not to mention politicians, would probably regard this as a very acceptable level which might be termed 'full' employment at the present time. The official figures, compiled by the Board of Trade, were based upon the returns of certain trade unions, many of which paid unemployment benefits in some form to members. This represented a biased sample, skewed towards skilled workers in 'staple' manufacturing industries (Garside, 1980). In Victorian and Edwardian Britain there was a persistent tendency for unskilled manual labour to be in excess supply and consequently weak in terms of bargaining power. The result was long hours, low wages, insecurity of employment and under-employment. Rowntree's survey of working-class incomes in York at the end of the century revealed that low wages (in relation to stringently assessed minimal needs) were by far the most important factor in causing poverty and there can be little doubt that this reflected the national picture (Treble, 1979). Rowntree also identified a 'life-cycle' with poverty being most likely to occur in childhood, old age, and during family formation. Most Victorian working-class children probably experienced poverty. Adult males and their dependants were likely to fall into poverty after marriage and family formation and poverty was also likely for those who survived beyond the ability to work. Excess supply of labour gave rise to a highly differentiated structure of employment, with persistent casualisation and under-employment, especially in less industrialised areas and notoriously in London (Stedman-Jones, 1984). This was the situation in the 'First Industrial Nation', the richest country in Europe in per capita terms, and the heart of the world's greatest empire. Over time the British workforce proved itself to be materialist and highly responsive to economic incentives. Work ethic was not the only influence in the gradual elimination of low income lifestyles and fatalistic attitudes. Materialism was also an influence on falling birth rates and family size from the 1880s onwards. Social mores gave rise to higher expectations than the economic system could deliver and worker expectations were to become a powerful influence in the twentieth century.

For females the situation in terms of employment was much worse than for males. Social attitudes combined with economic circumstances to place severe restrictions on female employment opportunities, placing a premium for women on marriage (Lewis, 1984). The clearly established norm was that married women did not seek paid work except in the most extreme necessity. Acceptable female work was severely limited by the fact that most jobs involved physical labour in work situations where women were vulnerable and at a physical disadvantage. Women workers, as a result, crowded into a relatively small number of 'acceptable' occupations which were relatively low paid. Female emancipation, and enhanced participation, depended very much on reductions in family size, but also on increased demand for labour and the emergence of 'acceptable' employment opportunities. This appears to have been more important in the long run than any relaxation of sexist attitudes. Female participation rose during both world wars but afterwards tended to fall back to pre-war levels (Smith, 1986a). Major long-run changes in female workforce participation came only after 1950 and this depended very largely on full employment and the emergence of new technologies and patterns of work organisation (Glynn and Booth, 1996, pp. 277–82).

Before 1914 British employers faced a 'buyer's market' for unskilled labour and there were few complaints in relation to supply or quality. While Britain has been criticised for failing to develop technical education, as in Germany and elsewhere, there is little evidence of skills shortages (Sanderson, 1988). Training was overwhelmingly in-service and *ad hoc*, with continued reliance on traditional apprenticeship for the more skilled. Apprenticeship and skilled status tended to decline gradually over time with changes in technology and work organisation, but this was partially offset by a rise in semi-skilled occupations. There has been a lengthy and unresolved debate about 'entrepreneurial failure' in Britain and this is part of a wider discussion (Kirby, 1981). Britain lagged behind competitors in the development of modern business organisation, in particular, large, effectively organised corporations (Chandler, 1990). Labour management was part of this. Gospel has shown how there was a comparative failure to manage and deploy labour effectively (Gospel, 1992). British employers failed to develop 'internal' labour markets and continued to rely on open market hiring and firing with adverse consequences in terms of training, quality and efficiency.

Despite apparent employer complacency in relation to most labour market issues, other than worker organisation, wider concerns did begin to arise before 1914 and 'national efficiency' became an important public concern. From the 1880s unemployment was an issue in British politics and the main agency of public welfare provision, the New Poor Law (1834), began increasingly to be seen as inadequate and unsatisfactory (Harris, 1972). In the 1880s unemployed demonstrators raised the demand for 'Work or Maintenance' (Stedman Jones, 1984). This symbolised a challenge to Victorian concepts of the 'undeserving' poor and the principles of the Poor Law, in particular, the 'Workhouse Test' (no outdoor relief) and the notion of 'less eligibility'. These principles were designed to ensure that public welfare did not influence the labour market in general and wages in particular, as the pre-1834 'Speenhamland' system had done. However, by the end of the Victorian era it had become clear that the British economic system experienced downturns every seven to eleven years which gave rise to serious unemployment. Respectable working men who became unemployed in these circumstances could not be labelled 'undeserving', and it was increasingly questionable as well as impractical that they should be forced to resort to Poor Law relief on the principles of 1834.

The Liberal reforms of 1906–14, which are usually seen as the beginning of the modern welfare system, were motivated by a range of influences, mainly political but aimed at changing the labour market (Thane, 1982). Questions of 'national efficiency' combined with an aim to remove certain 'deserving' groups from the stigma of Poor Law dependency. There may also have been a desire to emulate foreign examples and to forestall more radical alternatives including the newly created Labour Party (Peden, 1991). Behind the various political and social motivations it is possible to discern ideas about a more scientific approach to the supply and deployment for labour in, for example, reforms in health and education as well as the establishment of national insurance (1911) and Labour Exchanges (1908) and regulations relating to wages and 'sweated' labour. A variety of small and experimental changes tested the margins of political and administrative possibility, as perceived most importantly by Churchill and Lloyd George, and this provided scope for reformers such as Beveridge, Llewellyn-Smith and Webb (Thane, 1982). In any event, these reforms made little real difference to the labour market and the mass of poverty which influenced and constantly threatened the bulk of the population.

What did have a major impact was the First World War, not least because it transformed the labour market (Burke, 1982). War brought full employment, perhaps for the first time in history, and labour experienced a new status and bargaining potential in both economic and political terms (Winter, 1986). This carried over and intensified in the postwar boom which lasted until April 1920. The manifestations included a sharp rise in earnings, shorter working hours, a doubling in trade union membership, from 4 to 8 million, and a revitalised and much strengthened Labour Movement. Things were never quite the same again, despite the onset of mass unemployment in 1920 (Marwick, 1968). Subsequently, and throughout the entire interwar period, unemployment remained stubbornly high, never falling significantly below 10 per cent, on the official figures, even in the best years, and rising to 23 per cent in the trough of the 1930s depression (Glynn, 1991). These figures, based on registration of insured workers, are not comparable with those previously quoted, but there is no alternative series which is. The main impact of interwar unemployment seems to have been in preventing radical economic adjustment and social change as the result of an essentially political compromise. The trade unions defended the gains they had made before 1920, more or less successfully, in very difficult circumstances (Wrigley, 1987). Money wages were more or less held constant after 1923, despite heavy unemployment, and real wages rose as prices fell. In general, employers failed to capitalise on their bargaining advantages in relation to pay and organisation. Government opted to hold the ring, failing to tackle unemployment directly in effective ways, but also declining to support wage cuts after the General Strike of 1926 (Glynn and Shaw, 1981). Of course, changes did occur, but the economy and labour market tended to remain embedded in a nineteenth-century setting with a continued dependence on the ailing staple industries (Crafts and Thomas, 1986). The social welfare which did eventuate came on an *ad hoc* and piecemeal basis (Crowther, 1988). Nevertheless, by the end of the 1920s there had been what amounted to a major transition in social welfare provision. Government had learned, in a hard way, that there was no going back to the pre-1914 *laissez-faire* version and, in terms of welfare, the notion of 'work or maintenance' had been more or less accepted, on a national scale (Digby, 1989). National insurance had been extended to cover two-thirds of the workforce and the Poor Law had effectively been replaced by a social security system (Glynn, 1991, pp. 80–91). There had also been an, albeit reluctant and unacknowledged, acceptance by central government of responsibility for running the economy and this included attempts to raise the level of employment (Garside, 1990). These changes were dictated by economic and political realities rather than idealogy.

Economic and social theory, as well as administration, struggled to keep pace with circumstances (Glynn and Booth, 1987). In the longer run it was external circumstances which proved to be the most important influence for change with the drift to war in the later 1930s. The de-radicalizing and stulti-fying influences resulting from mass unemployment in the interwar years produced, in the longer run, a desire for radical change. This was manifested in the 1940s with the catalyst of war. Inevitably the interwar period invites comparison with the years since the mid-1970s. Both were periods of mass unemployment but reactions were different in each period. In interwar Britain there was government inactivity and social compromise. In the later period mass unemployment enabled a determined prime minister to pursue radical changes on the basis of old ideas in new and more sophisticated forms.

Post-1945 Developments in the British Labour Market

After an interval, the Second World War transformed the labour market even more completely than during 1914–18 (Glynn and Booth, 1987, pp. 175–95). The 'full employment' which came in 1940 was to last for three decades, and arguably longer. In wartime circumstances government intervention and control achieved previously undreamed of dimensions and the parameters of political and administrative potential were enormously extended. However, in recent years historians have begun to question the extent to which British social and economic attitudes were radicalised and changed by the Second World War (Smith, 1986a). Claims made by Titmuss, Marwick and others that the war was a fundamental turning point have given way to a greater emphasis on the continuity of social attitudes and ideas (Titmuss, 1958; Marwick, 1988). Also, the social reforms of the 1940s are seen as being less radical and less far reaching in their effects than was previously supposed. In the longer historical view the welfare state appears to be shrinking retrospectively in terms of its impact and the origi-nality of its conception.

Nevertheless, postwar full employment was undoubtedly a major influence for change, not least in its impact on social and welfare development. In the view of Beveridge, full employment made the welfare state possible and was an essential ingredient in the system. In the view of Peter Townsend, full employment did more to relieve poverty in Britain than the welfare state *per se* (Townsend, 1979). These views have a particular relevance to the welfare debate at the present time. It is surely no accident that the welfare state was successfully established during circumstances of full employment and that it first began to be seriously questioned in fundamental terms when heavy unemployment began to reappear.

In retrospect the period of postwar full employment may seem to social historians to assume some of the characteristics of a golden age. Growth was higher and the benefits more evenly distributed than ever before or since (Feinstein, 1994). Yet inflation remained modest and the balance of payments was stronger than in recent years. Social cohesion was better, crime was lower, there were dramatic improvements in education and personal fulfilment as well as very perceptible improvements in material standards. While all these observations are demonstrably true, the reality was not quite so golden. Economic crisis never seemed to be very far away and was a frequent reality against a background of relative economic decline.

Economic *angst* focused increasingly on the labour market and from the mid-1960s the trade unions began to assume the ascribed role of villain in the mind of the political elite. It was argued that the unions were exploiting 'monopoly bargaining power' with adverse consequences for public finance and the national economy. Inflation was assumed to be largely of the 'cost push' variety and the direct result of wages rising faster than productivity. In turn, this was seen as the main reason for Britain's persistent balance of payments problems and relative decline. The full employment commitment accepted by British postwar governments obliged them to expand the economy through fiscal and monetary means so that general unemployment failed to curb wage demands. In 1968 the 'In place of strife' episode suggested that these views had influenced a Labour government (Glynn and Booth, 1996, pp. 293–8). In fact, most of the above assumptions were questionable if not erroneous. Nevertheless, the trade unions lost the battle for public, expert and political opinion.

It is not entirely clear why Britain experienced full employment during this period but the accepted view is that it was not *directly* the result of government economic intervention (Matthews, 1968). However, the stated commitment to employment at a 'high and stable level' seems to have been an important influence. Government also acted as a 'sweeper' in the labour market and, to some extent, as an employer of last resort. As a result of the substantial increase in government activity, at all levels, and greatly increased expenditure, there was massive job creation by the public sector. This supplemented an investment boom in the private economy to produce exceptional levels of employment. On the official figures, based on insured registration, unemployment was usually below 2 per cent. This resulted in worker 'choice' on an unprecedented scale and, in a 'seller's' market for labour, individual and collective bargaining power was greater than ever before. Differentials tended to narrow, women and immigrants were able to enter the labour market much more readily and groups hitherto regarded as 'unemployable' were able to undertake productive and remunerative employment. In welfare terms the benefits were enormous and far reaching. With involuntary unemployment virtually abolished, except in some of the old and declining industrial areas, there was a dramatic reduction in social inequality, and poverty was said to be eliminated before being rediscovered in the later 1960s (Townsend, 1979).

Behind this apparent success there were many problems, particularly on a regional basis (McCrone, 1969). In the immediate postwar period British manufacturing did remarkably well only to succumb gradually as other industrial economies recovered and became more competitive and industrialisation progressed in traditional markets (Cairncross, 1992). The new welfare system made important contributions to postwar economic success. Workforce improvements flowed from reforms and increased activity in education, health and housing and skilled workers were exported on a substantial scale to Australia, Canada and elsewhere. On the whole, therefore, a virtuous circle operated between the welfare system and the labour market, with each helping to sustain and enhance the other.

The Return of Unemployment

There is no clear agreement about when and why the period of postwar full employment came to an end, but economic crisis was certainly the agent of change and the oil crisis of 1973 was undoubtedly a crucial event. However, well before 1973 the labour market had become an area of constant conflict and public concern (Cmnd 3623, 1968). By the 1970s both full employment and the welfare system were being criticised on both pragmatic and intellectual grounds in an atmosphere of ongoing crisis (Brittan, 1975; Bacon and Eltis, 1976). The first OPEC oil shock in 1973 came on top of a political conflict involving industrial relations. The Heath government in 1970 had obtained a mandate to 'reform' industrial relations through legal changes. The attempts to implement these changes were strenuously resisted by the trade unions with a fair degree of success and the resultant crisis included the 'three-day-week' of 1973. The lesson which was eventually taken on board by the Thatcher government was that Heath attempted too much, too quickly, and that full employment enabled the unions to resist successfully. Unemployment did rise sharply under Heath to levels previously considered intolerable in postwar political circumstances (Glynn, 1991). In 1972 the Heath government did a policy 'U-turn' as unemployment approached the politically unthinkable level of one million.

The oil crisis of 1973 represented a massive shift in the terms of trade against Britain, not then an oil producer, and this imposed a need for real income adjustments. In the circumstances which prevailed, wages and public spending were more or less maintained. As a result, the necessary and inevitable adjustment fell with devastating impact on the private and corporate sector (Artis and Cobham, 1991). The resulting squeeze on profits and collapse in asset values had a major impact on opinion. Inflation was the principal mechanism of change and the view developed that the primary causes of inflation were government spending and trade union power which depended on full employment (King, 1976). This view prevailed despite the Labour government's efforts to trade on fraternal relations with the trade union movement and the apparent success of the 'social contract' in the mid- and later 1970s. For a time wages were held and actually fell in real terms. There was also some government success in the deployment of a 'social wage' concept which implied direct links between the labour market and the welfare system. These strategies were eventually blown apart politically by the failure of the government's incomes strategy in 1978–79. Against a background of anticipated inflation of 10 per cent the government attempted to impose a 5 per cent pay norm. The subsequent 'winter of discontent' may have sealed the fate of the Callaghan government.

In the 1970s the welfare state came under attack from both the left and right in an atmosphere of economic and financial crisis and growing pressures on state finance. The virtuous circle between full employment and welfare which Beveridge had perceived was beginning to be broken and replaced by a vicious circle running from unemployment to crisis in public spending. While the left argued that the system had failed to eliminate poverty and to make substantial inroads into social and economic inequality, the right identified welfare and full employment as the essential causes of Britain's relative economic decline. In the event, it was the latter view which was to prevail politically (Keegan, 1984).

The Thatcher Years

In 1979 the Thatcher government inherited an economy which had recovered remarkably well from the first oil shock of 1973 (Artis and Cobham, 1991). However, there was a second oil crisis in 1979 with the Iran–Iraq war and further need for adjustment despite Britain's emergence as a major oil producer. The decision to embark upon a monetarist experiment was conditioned in part by Conservative inability to influence the labour market in traditional ways through incomes policies which had been used, in one form or another, by all postwar governments (Jones, 1987). Implicitly, this meant a final and formal rejection of the 'postwar consensus' and adherence to full employment policies. The latter had already been substantially relaxed by previous administrations, but the perception remained that employment levels were a crucial influence on the re-electability of British governments. Indeed, the Conservatives had campaigned on the employment issue in 1979 with the slogan 'Britain isn't working'.

The monetarist episode of the early 1980s led Britain into mass unemployment which has persisted to the present time. Tight fiscal and monetary policies coincided with the emergence of sterling as a petro-currency. The result was massive job losses and the elimination of approximately 20 per cent of national manufacturing capacity in the space of one or two years, This was not the result of inefficiency in British manufacturing industry, nor was it the influence of 'globalisation'. The essential cause was a massively over-valued currency resulting from inappropriate economic policies (Keegan, 1984). As a result, export markets were lost to British producers and, more important, there was massive import penetration, notably from EEC sources. Unemployment rose from about one million in 1979 to more than three million by 1983, and the official figures, albeit substantially revised, continued to rise until 1985 (Johnson, 1991). The government was able to survive this thanks to the political luck and skill of a remarkable prime minister and the popularity which followed the recapture of the Falklands. Opposition tactics and divisions were also helpful (Young, 1991). Short-run failure in economic policy was actually turned to advantage: in a context of mass unemployment Thatcherite 'reforms' were much easier to implement than might otherwise have been the case. In particular, unemployment weakened the unions and made restrictive legislation easier to implement, albeit on a gradual basis (Gospel, 1992). Breaking the political mould in the 1980s owed a great deal to changes in the labour market and to unemployment in particular.

There was one important area of policy failure. The commitment to reduce public spending was not fulfilled despite draconian approaches to the public sector, and this was largely due to unemployment (Glynn, 1991, p. 135). In the early 1980s there were widespread cuts in public spending, welfare bene-fits were eroded and restricted generally, but rising unemployment had the effect of pushing the public spending total upwards (Dilnot and Walker, 1989; Humphries and Rubery, 1992). Rising unemployment affected public spending across a broad front, far beyond unemployment benefits and social security, and it became increasingly clear that there were links between changes in the labour market and crime, family break up, invalidity, ill-health, child abuse, drug addiction and other social problems, although the existence and exact nature of these was keenly debated (George and Miller, 1994).

Clearly there were major changes in the labour market after 1979 but these are still not fully analysed and understood. It is not clear to what extent change has been simply a reaction to mass unemployment rather than due to secular socioeconomic developments which came for other reasons. For example, the growth in part-time employment is the result of both choice and necessity. Many prefer part-time employment, but for others it is a forced choice because full-time work is not available. New insecurities in employment, changed managerial attitudes, loss of rights in employment, declining worker represen-tation and other important changes are very largely the direct consequence of raised levels of unemployment. More recent explanations in terms of 'glob-alism' lack empirical conviction despite the rise in unemployment levels throughout the OECD economies. Lower growth and changes in the macro-economic climate offer more relevant explanations of international trends.

In spite of widespread criticism and perceived crisis, the British welfare system has coped remarkably well with circumstances which it was never designed or intended to confront. Since the 1970s heavy unemployment and the consequent increase in poverty and inequality has been mitigated to an extent which might not have been politically possible in the interwar period. There have been additional problems. In particular, changes in family composition resulting in a rise in single parenthood and demographic changes have given rise to increased old-age dependency on pensions, social security, health and long-term care. These problems are influenced by, and may in part be the consequence of, unemployment. Welfare reform, so far, has largely taken the form of gradual erosion and piecemeal change rather than drastic restructuring. Welfare spending has remained roughly constant at about 25 per cent of GNP since the mid-1970s and the burden of taxation has fallen, nevertheless, the cost of welfare is a matter for public debate. Politically pragmatic perceptions remain that financial relief for the unemployed and other indigent groups and individuals must be socially afforded and that cash payments, albeit increasingly contingent, are the cheapest and most effective means of granting relief (Glynn and Howells, 1980). So far, at least, work creation, 'workfare' systems and wage subsidisation have been largely avoided on practical and cost grounds, despite discussion, ideological searching and some marginal experimentation with particular groups of unemployed. The main change affecting adult male, mainstream unemployed was the introduction of the Job Seeker's Allowance (JSA) in 1996. There was little opposition and, as intended, the number of claimants fell. This was followed in 1997 by a continued rise to 1.8 million people out of work and receiving benefits as a result of ill-health. This exceeded the JSA total. Workfare models from abroad range from the 'benign' Swedish system, which involves genuine efforts to place the long-term unemployed, to the more punitive versions adopted in some parts of the USA which are clearly intended to deter applicants for relief. In 1997 the Blair government introduced a scheme for young workers based on the Swedish model and making use of a 'windfall' tax on the privatised utilities.

In the 1990s there has been a growing awareness of the important consequences of conditions in the labour market for other areas of social and economic activity and in conditioning attitudes (Hutton, 1995). Heavy unemployment does not simply affect the unemployed but acts as a conditioning influence on the entire labour market, influencing wages and work attitudes as well as employer approaches. In turn, this has important effects on social and political perceptions. At the present time British institutions and attitudes still largely reflect the implicit assumption that a return to something like full employment will be possible eventually. Policy debate and formulation, however, has begun to accommodate the alternative possibility that full employment as seen in the years between 1940 and 1970 may never return.

Assessing the Impact of State Intervention

There is a long history of state and other institutional intervention in the labour market and this has been well documented by historians. Notable examples of intervention include the medieval guilds and the Elizabethan Statute of Artificers, but these are far from isolated and simply represent more formal manifestations of a persistent tendency. There is an equally long history of unemployment relief in a variety of forms (Garraty, 1978). In the classical view intervention reached an historic low point in the nineteenth century and the New Poor Law of 1834 was designed to ensure a complete separation between welfare provision and a free market for labour. In the Victorian tradition, adult male labour was regarded as being largely beyond the scope of intervention, although there was legislation relating to children, women and other disadvantaged groups. In the early twentieth century changing attitudes followed democratisation, union growth, the emergence of the Labour Party and the growing acceptance of widening state responsibilities. Before 1914 government had gradually increased its regulatory powers and had begun to intervene in industrial disputes (Wrigley, 1987). This was rapidly enhanced by the First World War when there was widespread government intervention in the labour market, including allocation of labour, as well as the commencement of rent controls and a no-strike agreement with the trade unions (Burke, 1982). Since that time British governments have continued to accept extensive responsibilities towards the labour market, although these have varied greatly in nature and extent. In general, it can be said that the principle of not interfering directly with the market for adult male labour has tended to survive, largely intact. In the mid-1990s Britain was one of few industrial countries without minimum wage legislation.

Assessing the economic impact of state intervention is both an impossible and highly controversial task. Clearly there was an accretion of micro-level intervention and regulation of employment which undoubtedly had an impact. On top of this, it is also the case that macroeconomic policies have been important, but to what extent? One of the most daunting realities in relation to any assessment is the remarkable tendency towards conformity and convergence in the world's industrial economies. Over time broadly similar patterns of employment, at least in the developed countries, have tended to emerge. This suggests not that governments have had no impact but that in the free enterprise economies, at least, governments have tended to do similar things (Baumol, 1986). There are two possible explanations for this. Economic conditions may be similar, or tend to become so as markets become more global. Alternatively, in an increasingly competitive world, there is emulation of success. Non-conformist systems tend to fail or to be taken as models when they succeed (Jones, 1994). In the 1980s British government increasingly took the view that the labour market was overregulated and inflexible and that the welfare state had created 'dependency'. It also ceased to accept responsibility for the level of employment or to set employment targets. This represented a revival of pre-war government attitudes. Historically, therefore, the postwar era of full employment stands out as a highly exceptional period (Glynn, 1991, Ch. 2). In the early 1990s the Major government presented the view that it was following the 'virtuous' American example of deregulated labour markets in contrast to the more regulated and 'failing' European model (Hutton, 1995). Even allowing for political rhetoric there can be little doubt that policies have had an important impact, but how can this be assessed?

In viewing labour markets the main attention must be given to wage levels and distribution. Wages reflect and determine market conditions, bargaining power and welfare outcomes. In the late Victorian era, there is evidence that wages adjusted to the economic cycle and variations in employment levels, albeit in a 'sticky' and incomplete manner. Wages also tended to fall in sympathy with prices after the 1920 downturn (Broadberry, 1986, 1990). However, from 1923 until the late 1930s money wages, on average, appear to have remained more or less constant against a background of price decline (Dimsdale, 1984). Real wages were, therefore, tending to rise despite heavy unemployment. In the 1980s and 90s this experience has been repeated in that, despite heavy unemployment, money wages rose faster than prices, for those in employment (Johnson, 1991). This 'inflexibility' of the wage system from 1923 coincided with the establishment of the modern unemployment benefit system through national insurance and social security under a variety of names. The implication is that the welfare system influenced the labour market by preventing wage collapse in the face of mass unemployment. In turn, it can be argued that the benefits were, at least in part, responsible for unemployment (Benjamin and Kochin, 1979). Such arguments, of course, ignore the implications for demand implied by reduced or zero benefits and involve an implicit faith in the ability of a more 'flexible' system to adjust on the basis of lower wages.

Whatever the counter factual arguments, the reality seems to be that relief for the unemployed is a political necessity in modern democratic circumstances. This was perceived in the interwar years and attitudes have not changed fundamentally in recent years despite extensive debate about benefit levels and conditions, including talk of 'workfare' and other alternatives. To a degree, therefore, modern political circumstances and realities dictate that a free market for labour cannot be allowed to operate fully to the point where desperation promotes radical wage adjustments. In recent years, however, this assumption has begun to be tested at the margins and for particular, heavily disadvantaged socioeconomic groups. The manifestations include falling real pay at the bottom end of the wage spectrum and changing conditions of work, the erosion of rights in employment and changed employer attitudes.

The Key Policy Debates

There have been two key policy debates in the twentieth century affecting employment and the labour market. Command versus free market systems and Keynesian versus classical, and new classical views. The former debate is now generally regarded as resolved, since the collapse of the Soviet Union, but its importance earlier in the century is difficult to exaggerate.

By the late 1930s in Britain domestic and international circumstances had come near to creating an intellectual consensus that the state must assume a greatly enhanced role (Booth and Pack, 1985). There were differing views about the Soviet Union, Fascist Italy and Nazi Germany, but even moderate British opinion favoured increased intervention. These views were shared across the political spectrum from the Labour left to Liberal reformers such as Keynes and Beveridge and radical Conservatives such as Harold Macmillan. The emergencies of the Second World War brought many interventionist ideas into reality and Labour victory in 1945 ensured the continuation of an enhanced state role (Morgan, 1984a). However, in the postwar period wartime controls were largely dismantled and Britain failed to develop a planning regime, opting not only for an essentially free market economy but also for free collective bargaining in the labour market (Tomlinson, 1987, 1990). The reasons for this development are complex but it is clear that trade union attitudes were an important influence which a Labour government, even if it had been inclined to do so, could not deny (Tiratsoo and Tomlinson, 1993). The unions desired a restoration of their traditional bargaining role and were opposed to any suggestion of wage control or regulation. Employers also favoured an end to controls and a free market outcome. In the 1970s there was a strong revival of dirigiste attitudes on the Labour left, articulated in particular by Tony Benn, but these failed to capture the Labour Movement or to win widespread public support (Godley, 1978).

In British industry both workers and employers have tended to oppose state control, in general, except in cases where there were clear and immediate partisan advantages. While the coal miners demanded, welcomed and gained from nationalisation, workers in general agreed with employers in resisting wage controls. This is scarcely surprising in view of the fact that British governments have been involved actively in trying to restrain wages for most of the twentieth century (Jones, 1987). These attitudes help to explain the failure to develop a planning regime. Britain also failed to develop a successful corporate economy (Middlemas, 1986; Gospel, 1992). While the unions were widely blamed for 'cost push' inflation in the postwar period there is ample evidence to suggest that union leaders were mainly concerned with urging 'restraint' on their members and unions were, more often than not, led from behind. In short, the evidence suggests that the British polity produced little support for a collectivise and planned approach and this was perhaps most clearly seen in labour market attitudes.

In the present century British economic policy can be said to have come full circle progressing from classical, through Keynesian and back to a revived or new classical view (Bleaney, 1985; Tomlinson, 1990). The reality, of course, is much more complex and cannot be examined here, but it can be noted that the major points of difference relate specifically to the labour market. In the classical view full employment would result as a matter of course in a freely functioning labour market where wages could adjust (Winch, 1969). This was clearly not the case in the interwar period and Keynes developed his alternative approach largely because of concern about unemployment (Stewart, 1967; Peden, 1984). In the Keynesian view unemployment resulted from 'demand deficiency' and the appropriate remedy was government intervention through fiscal and monetary policies. There is some debate about to what extent and when 'Keynesianism' was actually accepted by British policy makers and also how Keynesian it was when accepted (Booth, 1989). Beveridge appears to have fully realised the potential of Keynesian economics between writing his famous report on social services in 1942 and producing *Full Employment in a Free Society* in 1944. The latter part of his title is significant. It implied that full employment could be delivered without the need for a command economy. Indeed, the view was that under a Keynesian system it would be possible to have a liberal or free market economy with a minimum of state intervention at the macroeconomic level (Beveridge, 1944; Harris, 1977).

Keynesian techniques were adopted by the Treasury in the 1950s but were used mainly to restrain levels of economic activity in order to control inflation (Matthews, 1968). Full employment resulted mainly from real world circumstances rather than direct government intervention to raise aggregate demand. In conditions of full employment economic policy focused increasingly on the problems of inflation and the balance of payments and the need for wage restraint in the face of these. Behind this was an emphasis on economic growth and concern about British relative decline. In these circumstances, established economic opinion was on a collision course with the trade unions.

The classical revival in economic and political theory developed in the USA and had little influence on British policy before 1979. Three important elements can be discerned: first, new attitudes towards and methods of analysing government decision making and activity (Buchanan and Tulloch, 1962); second, new views about the importance of monetary aggregates (Friedman and Schwartz, 1963); third, new views about the role and effectiveness of markets and the role of government. These views began to influence policy debate in the 1970s but achieved very little acceptance outside financial and fringe political circles. They were pursued in an evangelical way by the Thatcher government in the 1980s and came to have a major impact on policy which continued into the 1990s (Keegan, 1984; Young, 1991). This provides an example of the fact that major new policy departures may not be the result of prior consensus, intellectual or otherwise. By the late 1980s, after a third Conservative electoral victory, the policy debate in Britain had been shifted substantially and Margaret Thatcher had played an important personal role in this. In the 1990s full employment commitments were conspicuously absent from political agendas and the policy debate on labour market issues focused mainly on the 'supply side, with particular attention being given to training' (Commission on Social Justice, 1994). The European Social Chapter and the idea of a minimum wage were also matters for debate. It was by no means clear that any of these would, if imple- mented, have much impact on the mainstream labour market and it was clear that the debate had become ideological and highly politicised. The Major government tended to take the view that any intervention in the labour market, other than deregulation, was counterproductive and would destroy jobs. On the part of the Labour Party there was a clear reluctance to make traditional commitments in terms of full employment and incomes policies and some lack of confidence in relation to proposals such as a minimum wage. In welfare policy there was a new and shared emphasis on using the welfare system to get recipients into the labour market, rather than on how to deal with social needs as such (Field, 1995). These developments reflected economic and political circumstances rather than intellectual attitudes, and there was a large measure of agreement about the desirable direction of policy. The Blair government certainly sought to make changes in the labour market but these were far from fundamental.

Prospective Developments

Full employment is no longer on the British political agenda and this reflects an intellectual and expert postwar consensus that macroeconomic policies, at least on a unilateral basis, cannot deliver. This view is supported by arguments based on the concept of 'globalisation', the need to control inflation in an increasingly open and competitive world, and underpinned by new concepts in economic theory (Grieve Smith, 1997). Mass unemployment can be ratio- nalised, as it was in the interwar period on a not dissimilar basis, and this in turn can affect political perceptions (Glynn, 1991).

Unemployment will continue to fluctuate over the economic cycle but, in the foreseeable future, it will remain very high by postwar standards. Unof- ficial estimates put 'true' current levels at 4–5 million although the much criticised official figures are well below half of this. Much depends on defi- nitions and methods of measurement but the main point is that a much smaller proportion of the male population is economically active than was the case 30 years ago and this seems likely to continue, with important socioeconomic consequences (Commission on Wealth Creation and Social Cohesion, 1995). Welfare policy will have to continue to adjust to continued high unemployment, labour market 'flexibility' and consequential insecurities. This will mean increasing inequality and poverty, both relative and absolute. Welfare needs will inevitably increase, but this will not be matched by ability or willingness to pay unless political attitudes are radically altered. This seems unlikely and it is therefore inevitable that there will be continuing attempts to reduce welfare costs and to pursue 'welfare-to-work' options. The move away from social insurance ideas and systems will continue, giving way to increasing integration of the welfare system with the labour market. Welfare will increasingly take the form of employer subsidy through the wage system and the employed will be encouraged to make private insurance provision against unemployment and other contingencies. The Job Seeker's Allowance, introduced in 1996, was an important step in this direction. However, 'workfare' options involving genuine work creation are likely to prove too costly and the main emphasis will be on subsidisation of low paid jobs in the small firm service sector.

Unemployment will continue to place a heavy burden on the welfare system in addition to the cost of unemployment relief. Insecurity in the labour market will have important consequences for other markets such as that for housing. Insecurity will mean that many will be unable to make adequate pension, housing and other provisions and this will create welfare needs. In turn, this will mean increasing pressure on basic benefits with continued emphasis on selectivity and contingency at the expense of universal and optimal provision. There will be less concern with need and more with status: implicit revival of the Victorian idea of 'deserving'. The labour market will become more differentiated with increasing variation between social groups and for individuals over time. These developments will inevitably lead to greater social divisions, the possible creation of an 'underclass', and a variety of social exclusions which could have important political consequences (Marris, 1997). Historically labour market failure has been linked with the emergence of political extremes in some countries, but not in Britain. A despairing, apathetic, but potentially fickle electorate is more likely, at least in the medium term.

In future the labour market will punish and reward with greater emphasis and intensity, lavishly at the top and viciously at the bottom. Inevitably the virtue of 'self-help' will be extolled in some twenty-first-century form and this will have consequences for the education system. Greater demands will be met by self-funding rather than state provision and the system will become increasingly competitive, hierarchical and vocationally orientated. These likely developments are no more the result of blind market forces than they represent a deliberate and conscious substitution of economic efficiency for social justice. Economic forces are not blind and economic efficiencies are not necessarily the obverse of a just and cohesive society. A society which is richer in *per capita* terms than ever before, but which feels that it can no longer afford to eliminate poverty clearly has organisational and attitudinal problems. Social and economic theorists will address these problems in the future just as they have attempted to deal with even more serious problems in the past. In doing so it appears that there will be a change in the usual order of priorities. In the past there have been attempts to construct welfare systems which were designed to deal with deficiencies in the labour market. In future, the labour market will be expected to deal with perceived deficiencies in the welfare system.

Poverty and Social Security

Pete Alcock

The Policy Context

Social policies are the product of history and not of logic. This is a simple message. But it is an important one to remember especially in the field of poverty and social security, for it makes the complexities and contradictions that have surrounded the development and implementation of policy throughout the last century easier to understand – and also perhaps easier to sympathise with. If one were to begin planning social security policy anew in the 1990s, one would not end up with the complicated system we have today; but that is a luxury which policy planners do not enjoy. Policy planning must build on the legacy of the past; and as we shall see that legacy provides a policy context in which the successes and failures of the past continue to dominate the prospects for the future.

Certainly there can be no doubt that the policy context of social security and anti-poverty policy in Britain is both complex and contradictory. Policy is informed by different, and conflicting, views:

- about both the nature and scale of the problem of poverty
- about the proper role of the state in responding to this
- about the principles upon which such state policy should operate
- about the people upon whom such policies should be targeted.

Different policy goals have been pursued at different times and new principles have been grafted on to old structures and practices. There is thus overlap of provision, and yet there are also gaps. Some people within the social security system are likely to be receiving support from several different departments of both central and local government, under different benefit schemes, paying out different amounts of money, under different criteria for entitlement – for the same basic needs. Others may be poor and in need, and yet receive nothing.

This is in large part because the different governments who have presided over the development of policy over the century have operated with different policy goals, informed by very different visions of the proper role of state action in securing social change (see Hill, 1990; Ditch, 1999), as discussed in the chapters in Part II of this book. That no one of these visions has dominated over the others is a good thing in political terms – in a democracy supporters of conflicting perspectives have every right to argue for, and win, support for their vision – but in policy terms the consequence of this is the likelihood that no one vision is ever fully realised.

However, the complexities of social security and anti-poverty policy are not only the product of political and policy disagreement. They are also the result of the impact of massive social and economic changes which have been taking place outside of, and largely independent of, the direct policy context. In the twentieth century these include major changes:

- in demographic trends – fewer births, smaller families and longer lives
- in family and community patterns – later marriages, more divorces and increased social and geographical mobility
- in economic forces – falls and rises in unemployment, changing patterns of work and dramatic growth of living standards.

These changes, and many more, have significantly influenced patterns and risk of poverty, and the need for and impact of social security. And, given such change, perhaps the most surprising revelation is not the diversity of policy change and achievement but its consistency. For overall social security provision through the state and outside it has continued to grow both in scale and in scope throughout the century, and yet levels of poverty have remained widespread and persistent.

The Development of Policy

The nineteenth-century legacy

All social change takes place within the legacy of past change. At the beginning of the twentieth century the ideas and the actions of the Victorian era exercised a strong and enduring influence over future policy development; and in many respects this influence has remained throughout the rest of the century too. Victorian poverty and social security policy had been dominated by the philosophy and practice of the Poor Law (Rose, 1972; Thane, 1982, Ch. 2; Jones, 1991, Ch. 2). In simple terms the Poor Law had two aims:

- the relief of poverty, or pauperism – so that only those in proven destitution would be supported
- the operation of a punitive regime, less eligibility (see Novak, 1988, p. 46) – so that those covered would be encouraged to seek self-support.

These goals of selective provision and discouragement of dependency are still very much with us today.

However, even in the nineteenth cnetury the Poor Law was not the only form of support. There was also a developing collection of privately organised and financed protection provided through the trade unions and the friendly societies, which operated insurance-based cover for significant sections of the working class; and there was support through voluntary action from middle-class philanthropic activity, largely coordinated by the Charity Organisation Society (COS) (Jones, 1991, Ch. 4). This mixture of state, private and voluntary activity has also characterised twentieth-century social security provision, as we shall return to discuss later.

Nevertheless at the end of the last century there was pressure for change to the Victorian model of social protection. The first major surveys of the extent of poverty in Britain carried out at the end of the century by Booth (1889a) and Rowntree (1901) revealed that the problem was much more serious and widespread than complacent official opinion had assumed, and that it was the product of complex social forces not just the idleness of a reprobate residuum. Clearly, this research implied, the Poor Law was not relieving poverty.

At the same time the growth of insurance protection through the friendly societies, allied to the growing power of the trades unions and the emergence of the Labour Party, provided a model of an alternative vision of social security, which had potentially widespread political support. By this time too, this insurance model of protection had been used to provide public social security support in other industrial countries, most notably in Germany where it had been introduced by Bismarck to meet the pressure of working-class demand.

At the beginning of the twentieth century therefore the efficacy of the Poor Law was under question and the potential for alternatives was under examination. In 1905 the government appointed a Royal Commission to review the operation of the Poor Laws in the expectation that major change was likely to ensue. In fact the constitution of the Royal Commission included members with very different views about policy reform reflecting the dominant debate at the time between the philanthropic tradition of the COS, with its emphasis on discretionary support for individuals linked to strong moral guidance to encourage self-protection and self-improvement, and the socialist ideals of the Fabian Society, with its belief in collective support for all based on guaranteed rights to state support. As a result their deliberations were a contested and long drawn-out process, and when they reported in 1909 (Cd 4499) the Commissioners produced two reports because all the members could not agree (see Jones, 1991, Ch. 7).

The *Majority Report* (Cd 4498, 1909) was dominated by the views of the COS, in particular Helen Bosanquet, and it favoured the development of protection through philanthropic action bolstered by strong moral guidance for the poor. The smaller *Minority Report* (Cd 4499, 1909) was dominated by the views of the Fabian Society, in particular Beatrice Webb, and it favoured the introduction of collective benefits and services financed out of taxation and provided by the state to all citizens in need. Although the Minority Report had no official status, it was widely promoted by the Fabian Society; and in effect the debate between the different perspectives was continued after the Commission was wound up, notably within the newly formed London School of Economics (LSE) which was established by the Webbs to promote academic research and debate but included elements of the social work training developed by the COS (see Harris, 1989).

Despite their disagreements, however, all members of the Royal Commission were united in their view that the Poor Law should be radically reformed. And in the first two decades of the twentieth century such reform was introduced, although it did not draw directly on either the philanthropic or the Fabian perspectives of the Commissioners. Policy reform is of course predominantly the result of political pressure not academic argument; and the political pressure on the governments of the early twentieth century came not from the arguments of philanthropy or Fabianism, but rather from the demands of a more powerful and well-organised labour movement with a growing tradition of self-protection through insurance.

Replacing the Poor Law

The first new measure for social security and the prevention of poverty was the old-age pension introduced by the new Liberal government in 1908. Pensioners had been identified by Booth's research in London as a significant group among the poor (Booth, 1894), and for them the rigours of the Poor Law were a particularly cruel imposition. They have also remained a major element of the poor throughout this century and have been the focus of a range of specific social security protections. The 1908 old-age pension was not generous, it was only paid to the over-70s and was subject to a test of means – 'five shillings a week for cheating death', as one popular song put it. But, as the same song also celebrated, it took people 'out o' workhouse' and thus removed them from dependence upon the Poor Law. This was a model that was to be followed with varying degrees of success by later reforms to social security in the rest of the century.

The old-age pension was in most respects a universal payment, a point to which we shall return later, but the later reforms to social security in the first quarter of the twentieth century followed the insurance model developed by the friendly societies and implemented in Germany under Bismarck. Insurance protection was based on benefits paid, notionally at least, in return for contributions made into a protection scheme, hence the link with self-help. In 1911 such protection was introduced for sickness and unemployment experienced by workers, although protection was limited initially to certain areas of the labour market. The insurance scheme was based on contributions from employees, employers and the exchequer – popularly described as 'ninepence for fourpence' when the workers contribution was 4d and the other two made up a further 5d.

In the years immediately following the First World War, at a time when employment was growing, the scheme was relatively successful in providing protection. It was extended to more and more workers and the pension payment too was put on to an insurance basis. However, by the 1920s and 30s economic growth had turned to economic depression, the numbers of unemployed workers grew rapidly and the Unemployment Insurance Scheme came under increasing pressure. The governments of the 1920s sought in various ways to respond to the pressure of demand on the Unemployment Insurance Scheme. First attempts were made to discourage dependency by seeking to ensure that claimants were 'genuinely seeking work' (Deacon, 1976), but this did not prevent the scheme moving into deficit by the end of the decade. Unemployment insurance had been developed as an alternative to the Poor Law, and, as with pensions, it had lifted some people off dependency on this now widely discredited form of state support. However, despite the criticisms of both sections of the Royal Commission, the Poor Law had remained in place and dependence upon it had begun to grow again during the depression. Any wholesale withdrawal of insurance protection would throw the unemployed once again on to the Poor Law, and this Labour government of the late 1920s was determined to avoid. But by 1931 the situation had reached crisis point and so what was proposed instead was a cut in insurance benefit levels together with an increase in contributions (to help balance the books) and the imposition of a means test on claimants who had been on insurance benefit for over 26 weeks (Deacon and Bradshaw, 1983, Ch. 2). This was opposed by some Labour MPs and led to the resignation of the Prime Minister, Ramsey MacDonald, in 1931. However, he was returned to power that year as the head of a new National Government and led the implementation the changes.

At the same time the Poor Law was also subject to reform. It was retitled Public Assistance and control was passed from the old Guardians to local authority Public Assistance Committees, who also adminstered the new means test for the unemployed. In 1935 this was converted into a separate scheme called Unemployment Assistance. Despite these changes, however, the new assistance schemes were less generous and more punitive than insurance protection. They continued to carry the stigma of the Poor Law, and they included what was called the 'household means test', under which no benefit would be paid to claimants while there was another adult member of the household (such as a grown-up son or daughter) in employment or on benefit. Assistance was therefore much less popular than insurance. Both were also ineffective in preventing poverty. In 1935 Rowntree (1941) repeated his survey of poverty in York and found continuing high levels, especially now among the unemployed. And this was again accompanied by political action, including the 'hunger marches' organised by the Unemployed Worker's Movement.

With the beginning of the Second World War, unemployment began to decline, the separate treatment of unemployed and other assistance claimants was brought together under one Assistance Board and the household means-test relaxed. These temporary wartime expedients, however, were not sufficient to tackle the many problems which were now felt to exist within the pre-war provisions for social protection. In 1941 Beveridge, a former Director of the LSE, was appointed by the government to review the provision for social insurance and other allied services with a view to recommending reforms which could be introduced after the war.

Beveridge took his brief somewhat beyond the narrow scope which some senior politicians and civil servants had expected of him. When his report was published in December 1942 it contained a thoroughgoing blueprint for a complete revamping of social security protection, and placed this within the context of other state welfare measures aimed at removing the social evils which he argued had stalked prewar Britain during the depression. The Beveridge Report (Cmnd 6404, 1942) remains the only comprehensive review and reform programme for social security produced in the twentieth century. It became a bestseller in the bookshops and, coming as it did after the crucial military victory at El Alamein, it marked the beginning of a new phase of optimistic restructuring of social policy within the country.

Beveridge and the welfare state

In more general social policy terms the most important aspect of Beveridge's report was the context in which he set his proposals for benefit reform and the combating of poverty. Beveridge predicated his plans for social security upon a wholesale restructuring of the role of the state within capitalist society, and in this way his proposals shared common ground with some of the wider economic policies being developed at the time by his Liberal colleague Keynes. Both Keynes and Beveridge believed that state intervention should be utilised to create employment through stimulation of the economy and that beyond this public services should be established by the state to provide for all major social needs (Beveridge, 1944). In particular Beveridge spelt out the need for family allowances (as a financial support for the parents of children) and a National Health Service; and he assumed, or hoped, that these and other reforms would accompany his proposals for dealing with poverty and social security. Indeed to a large extent the viability of his plans depended upon them. At first it was far from clear that such a radical programme of welfare reform would be countenanced by the government after the war (see Sullivan, 1996, Ch. 2); but with the election in 1945 of a Labour government openly committed to the development of state welfare most of his expectations were realised.

The Labour Prime Minister Attlee had, like Beveridge, worked at the LSE. Beveridge's report presented academic arguments for a welfare state. Attlee's leadership represented the political realisation of these. As the other chapters in this book have discussed, the welfare reforms of 1945–51 were the most far reaching and comprehensive in the century, and they could rightly be said to have established a welfare state within the country. However, the reforms took place within existing social and political institutions and left the basic economic structure of British society more or less intact – a 'British revolution'. In many respects they also built on the strengths of provisions which had been developed in the earlier half of the century, and Beveridge's social security reforms were a definite example of this.

Beveridge has been described as a 'liberal collectivist' (Cutler *et al.*, 1986). He believed in public provision through the state and he was strongly opposed to the divisiveness and stigma associated with the means tests of the Poor Law and Public Assistance schemes. However, he also believed in principles of self-protection through insurance developed by the friendly societies and he claimed that, 'The capacity and desire of British people to contribute for security are among the most certain and impressive social facts' (Cmnd 6404, 1942, p. 119). Beveridge's principle recommendation therefore was for a plan for social insurance.

The pre-war insurance protection had been modelled in part on the self-help developed by the friendly societies, and to maintain this tradition they had been retained to a limited extent as administrative agents within the state scheme. Alongside the public provision there was also a plethora of private insurance companies offering a range of schemes for protection (see Silburn, 1995b). Beveridge wanted to replace all this with a single and comprehensive scheme, administered and financed through the state, but based on the principle of insurance. This was a similar ideal to that once held by Bismarck, but Beveridge's vision differed from the continental social insurance model in that it was based on flat-rate contributions (all would pay the same) and flat-rate benefits (all would get the same). It meant that contributions could be fixed at a level that all could afford and that benefits could be fixed at a level sufficient to prevent poverty – but no more. Continental insurance provision paid earnings-related benefits designed to protect the standard of living during periods of labour market absence. Beveridge saw this as a role for private protection outside of the state and he feared that if benefits were set at too high a level they would interfere with the incentive to work for wages in the market.

Although earnings-related provision was introduced later into the British social security system, the National Insurance (NI) Scheme established by the postwar government in 1946 was based on Beveridge's flat-rate principle, and benefits were set at a presumed subsistence level, based on figures derived from Rowntree's pre-war research into poverty. The NI ideal, however, depended upon claimants having built up an entitlement to benefits through contributions made while participating in the labour market. When the scheme was introduced no-one could possibly meet such contribution criteria, and this would mean in particular that all retired older people would be excluded from the new pension protection. For Beveridge this was an essential feature of the insurance plan – benefits should be seen as 'paid for' by past contributions. However, it was politically unacceptable to the government and so all pensioners were given immediate entitlement to benefit. The consequence of this of course was that, since there were no accumulated reserves to draw on, the contributions collected in the first year of the scheme had to be used to pay these new beneficiaries. This meant that the scheme, desite its nominal insurance basis, in practice worked on a pay-as-you-go principle with current contributions being used to meet current benefit needs.

The pay-as-you-go principle is in practice that used by most state social insurance schemes. Social insurance does not operate like private insurance by investing contributions to build up a fund for future beneficiaries. This is probably sensible both in principle and in practice, although of course it is not really insurance but rather a form of hypothecated taxation. The taxation through contribution for employees was supplemented in the postwar scheme by contributions from employers and from the Treasury – as with the pre-war schemes NI was seen as a partnership between workers, industry and the state, although the terms of this partnership have been altered over time.

Beveridge's expectation was that NI would provide comprehensive social security cover by paying benefits to those categories of people – the unemployed, sick or retired – most at risk of it. It was a scheme for protection for those outside the labour market. For those in work (and Beveridge's anticipation was that all able to work would be expected to do so) wages would prevent poverty, and low pay was not expected to be the problem that it had been at the beginning of the century. For those with dependent families, however, wages would be supplemented by Family Allowances introduced in 1945 which contributed towards the costs of childcare – although not for the first child of the family.

For those out of employment, however, NI protection did not prove to be as comprehensive as Beveridge had hoped. Insurance benefits were only paid to those who had paid the requisite number of contributions into the scheme – in theory, if not in practice, contributions bought benefit entitlement; and thus there were some poor people, such as unemployed school leavers, who could not claim. For those who were so excluded, support was to be provided by a reformed public assistance scheme, retitled National Assistance.

National Assistance was introduced in 1948 and paid benefits to those not protected in any other way and thus it operated through a means test, although the test was applied to families (couples and dependent children) rather than households as in the pre-war scheme. Assistance remained a secondary, and more stigmatised, benefit, but this was not seen as a serious problem as it was only to be a minor – and declining – form of provision for those outside NI. However assistance benefits included full payment for the cost of rent, whereas the subsistence levels fixed in the NI scheme only included a notional element for rent. This meant that for many NI claimants with high rent costs assistance payments could also be claimed.

There were thus two elements of overlap between the NI and assistance schemes – some were excluded from NI and had to claim assistance instead and some of those included in NI also needed assistance support in addition to insurance benefits. These were not identified as serious problems by politicians or academics in the euphoria surrounding the establishment of the 'comprehensive' postwar social security scheme – although they have become much more serious problems since. Postwar euphoria was bolstered by the apparent success of the Beveridge plan in combating poverty too when a repeat of Rowntree's poverty research in York in 1951 showed a sharp decline in the numbers of poor (Rowntree and Lavers, 1951) – but this too proved to be a premature judgement.

The rediscovery of poverty

Beveridge's expectation that assistance would play a minor role in the postwar social security scheme was never realised. By the end of the 1950s there were over one million people dependent on it, many of them pensioners whose NI pensions were not sufficient for their needs. However, there were also many pensioners who were not claiming the assistance support to which they might be entitled – quite possibly because of the stigma of Poor Law which they still associated with it. In a seminal piece of research carried out in the early 1960s, again at the LSE, Abel Smith and Townsend (1965) examined the government's own statistics and found large numbers of people living below the assistance benefit level. Many of these were pensioners, most others were families with children.

The academics claimed that poverty had thus been 'rediscovered' within the affluent welfare state society of the 1960s, and that this meant that the postwar welfare reforms were not operating effectively and should be changed. In fact the issue was more complex than a simple rediscovery, as Townsend's work involved a redefnition of the problem of poverty to adjust this to the new social conditions of affluent postwar Britain and the development of new methods of analysis utilising government statistics on living standards (see Alcock, 1997, Ch. 5). Nevertheless the message was a clear one, and it was taken into the political arena by a new pressure group founded by Townsend and Abel Smith to popularise their research: the Child Poverty Action Group (CPAG).

The message was also translated into concrete proposals for reform of pensions and family allowances which were received with some sympathy by the Labour government which came to power in 1964. However, the Labour government of the 1960s did not display the reforming zeal of the postwar

Attlee regime, nor did they enjoy the economic prosperity of the Conservative regimes of the 1950s. Radical social security reform therefore was no longer at the top of the policy agenda.

In the 1960s pensioners were the largest group among the rediscovered poor. Proposals were considered to move pensioners off possible dependence on assistance benefits by extending NI cover to include an additional earnings-related payment, as was the case in most continental social insurance schemes. However, the plans to implement this were delayed and deferred, and it was only eventually in 1978 when the State Earnings-Related Pensions Scheme (SERPS), as this change came to be called, finally came into operation. In 1966, however, earnings-related payments, in return for earnings-related contributions, were introduced for unemployment and sickness benefits within the NI scheme, aimed at lifting them above assistance benefit level. But these were only paid for six months and by 1969, at their height, only 20 per cent of the unemployed were receiving them (Atkinson, 1972).

The introduction of the earnings-related principle significantly altered the NI scheme envisaged by Beveridge. However, this did not mitigate its continuing overlap with dependence upon assistance support, which in the 1960s and 70s continued to grow in scale (Deacon and Bradshaw, 1983, Ch. 6). The assistance scheme was revamped in 1966 and renamed Supplementary Benefit, under the control of a new body: the Supplementary Benefit Commission (SBC). It remained, however, a means-tested scheme for those excluded from full NI protection. It thus retained its secondary and stigmatised status – it was popularly referred to as 'the social'; and it retained the problems of low take-up of benefit as many of those entitled were either ignorant or fearful of claiming (Deacon and Bradshaw, 1983, Ch. 7; Hill, 1990, Ch. 7).

Despite the problems of low take-up, however, by the end of the 1970s the numbers dependent upon the SB assistance scheme had grown to around four million, with the increasing numbers of unemployed comprising a larger and larger proportion. The impact of means-testing was thus becoming more and more extensive. This trend was accentuated furthermore by the development at the same time of new means-tested social security benefits covering wider and wider sections of the population (Deacon and Bradshaw, 1983, Ch. 5).

The most important of these new benefits were Rent and Rate Rebates (later called Housing Benefit), providing a contribution to the cost of rents for NI claimants and those on low wages, and Family Income Supplement (later called Family Credit, FC), providing a state supplement to low wages for families with children. Both of these were introduced on a national scale by the Conservative government of the early 1970s as part of a deliberate attempt to target new benefit support at particular groups not adequately covered by past social security protection. They were also accompanied by the expansion of means-tested support for a range of other needs such as school meals and clothing and health prescriptions and charges; and in 1976 the

National Consumer Council counted 45 different means-tested schemes operating in Britain affecting a wide range of the population (National Consumer Council, 1976). This was significant evidence of a 'drift towards selectivity' within social security.

It is tempting to conclude from this that the rediscovery of poverty within the British welfare state resulted not so much in consolidation of the postwar Beveridge plan for poverty prevention through insurance, but rather in a return to the poverty relief measures of pre-war public assistance, suitably redesigned for a post-welfare state public. This is almost certainly not what the academic campaigners, such as Townsend (1979, 1984), had in mind in their exposure of the continuing problem of poverty within affluence, however; and it ignores some significant improvements in social security protection that did follow from the pressures put on government over this period.

Perhaps most significant of all improvements was the general rise in the level of social security payments and benefit levels. Public expenditure on social security increased both absolutely and relatively throughout the 1960s and 70s, and not entirely as a result of the growing numbers of people claiming support (Barr and Coulter, 1990). Benefit levels were increased, in particular in the mid-1970s under Labour when they rose in line with rises in both prices and earnings, although as a proportion of average earnings their relative position did not in practice improve (Bradshaw and Lynes, 1995). The introduction of earnings-related payments for NI claimants also operated in practice to improve protection for those who were within the scheme.

Perhaps the most important success for the poverty campaigners, however, was the transformation of Family Allowances into a new universal Child Benefit. The postwar Family Allowance scheme had paid a limited flat-rate benefit to families, but only for second and subsequent children. It was supplemented for those in work and paying taxes, however, by a child-related tax rebate. In the 1950s and 60s the level of the allowance payment had fallen in value in relative terms, at the same time as levels of poverty among families had begun to rise. A rise in the allowance was therefore a major feature of the political campaigning by academics in the 1960s – hence the establishment of the CPAG.

In the 1960s after a long and difficult campaign some increase was eventually secured, with the value of this being 'clawed-back' from the better-off via a reduction in the child tax rebate (see Banting, 1979). In the 1970s the clawback principle was taken much further with the tax rebate being removed altogether in return for the introduction of a new universal payment for all children, now called Child Benefit. This was an important step in social security reform for the Child Benefit payment was a genuine universal benefit – parents of all children receive it and levels of take-up are very high. It remained only a contribution to the costs of child care, but as a universal payment it helped to lift families out of poverty without the contradictory poverty trap problems of targeted provision, which we discuss later.

However, its birth was a protracted and conflictual affair, with the Labour Cabinet split on the merits of the scheme (see Field, 1982).

The 1970s also saw the introduction of some other new universal benefits, although the scope of these was rather more limited as they only applied to those experiencing additional costs associated with disability. Mobility and Attendance Allowance (later amalgamated into Disability Living Allowance) were benefits paid as a contribution towards the extra costs associated with disability in the two areas of mobility and personal care. They were universal in that payment depended neither on NI contributions nor test of means, and they extended both the scope of benefit cover and its scale. Benefits now met some of the costs of *care* through *cash* support within social security; and by being paid in addition to other provision they raised the incomes of many disabled people. But they were only available to those with proven medical needs, and the medical tests associated with these proved to be stringent and to deter some potential claimants from receiving their benefits (Walker and Walker, 1991).

What both these new universal forms of benefit also did, however, was to complicate even further the benefit maze which characterised British social security protection at the end of the 1970s. Despite the comprehensive, and simplistic, ideals of the Beveridge plan benefit provision had grown to cover a wider and wider portion of the population and to incorporate an ever more disparate range of payment schemes. This picture remains in the 1990s, but it has been subject to rigorous challenge in between.

A return to assistance

During the 1980s and early 1990s Britain experienced a form of government which was, ostensibly at least, openly critical of the social policies which had dominated welfare provision after the Second World War. Commentators had argued that postwar policy had been the product of a consensus between the major political parties over the role of the state in the provison of welfare (Addison, 1975). After 1979 this consensus was shattered by the Conservative governments under Margaret Thatcher, who saw the welfare state not as the solution to the problem of poverty but rather, in part at least, as its cause – extensive state support discouraged private protection and investment and seduced claimants into a 'benefit dependency culture'. Thatcherites also saw social security not as a means for redistributing resources to even out inequalities, but as a burden on state expenditure to be reduced as far as possible and replaced with private protection through the market.

In the 1980s and early 1990s, therefore, the predominant theme in welfare policy was one of 'rolling back' the boundaries of the welfare state rather than extending them (see Johnson, 1990; Deakin, 1994), with the challenge to poverty coming not from redistribution towards the poor, but rather from increased economic growth for all. This link between an alternative conception of poverty and social security policy was an important feature of the Thatcherite policy agenda. In the 1980s government spokespersons, such as Moore (1989), argued that absolute poverty no longer existed in Britain because of welfare reforms and that the living standards for those at the bottom should rise as part of a general growth in economic performance and not as a result of redistribution from the 'wealth creators' above them. This was sometimes referred to as the policy of 'trickle-down', and it was neatly encapsulated by another minister, Joseph (Joseph and Sumption, 1979, p. 22), in his claim that, 'You cannot make the poor richer by making the rich poorer'.

From this vision flowed a belief in the need to restrict welfare dependency and to target relief on those really in need, while encouraging those who could to support themselves through employment and self-help – a return to some extent to the values of the nineteenth-century Poor Law. In particular it was hoped that tackling over-generous social security through more accurate targeting would help to reduce the overall cost of public spending in this area; but in practice this strategy failed lamentably. Social security expenditure grew inexorably throughout the 1980s and 90s and the policy of greater targeting proved to have quite contradictory effects on the so-called dependency culture. At the same time both government statistics and independent research suggested that the problem of poverty was growing in scale and in depth.

In the early 1980s the Conservative governments attempted a series of piecemeal reductions in benefit levels and entitlement criteria. In 1980 NI benefit levels were cut when set against inflation and the earnings-related payments for the unemployed and sick withdrawn. These were the first direct cuts in benefit levels in Britain since 1930, and yet they were accompanied by an increase in contribution levels. This was because the cost of NI benefits was growing due to increasing unemployment and because the government was seeking to alter the balance of funding for the scheme by reducing the Treasury contribution to it. In effect, however, it constituted a direct assault on the scope of the supposedly central role played by NI in social security protection. This was taken further later in the decade by the removal of protection for short-term sickness and maternity from NI and the transfer of these to the private sector as employment (rather than benefit) rights, and by the tightening of the entitlement criteria for receipt of NI benefits which operated to exclude increasing numbers of particularly unemployed people from insurance protection (see Alcock, 1995).

The effect of these reductions in NI protection was to increase dependency upon means-tested assistance benefits, especially in a climate of rising unemployment, rising rent costs and more widespread low pay. By the early 1990s over eight million people were dependent upon the major means-tested benefit (now Income Support) and around a third of the population were in receipt of some form of means-tested benefit (Field, 1995). The drift towards means-testing had become a headlong gallop.

In the mid-1980s the government responded to the increasing pressure on the social security system by instituting a major review of benefits. Norman Fowler, the Secretary of State, called it 'the most substantial examination... since the Beveridge Report forty years ago'. In fact the examination which was carried out was far from substantial – NI benefits were largely excluded from consideration, initial proposals on pensions were rapidly withdrawn, and the main focus was on a restructuring of means-tested benefits.

The reforms which followed the 'Fowler Reviews' were actually implemented in 1988, after the Conservatives' third election victory in 1987 and at a time of far-reaching and radical reforms in other areas of welfare. By these standards the changes made to social security were relatively small. Supplementary Benefit was retitled Income Support and Family Income Supplement became Family Credit, Housing Benefit having replaced Rent Rebates a few years earlier. And entitlement to all these benefits was brought within one scale to make administration easier and to remove some of the worst effects of the 'poverty trap', discussed below. Technically speaking the reforms were sensible although limited, but they affirmed the displacement of insurance by assistance at the centre of state protection, and they did nothing to transfer additional resources to those dependent on this (Evans *et al.*, 1994).

The replacement of insurance benefits with means-tested provision was taken further in the 1990s by additional cuts to NI benefits – most notably by the replacement of Unemployment Benefit with the Jobseekers' Allowance in 1996, under which NI entitlement was restricted to the first six months of unemployment. Other changes encouraged greater dependency within families, with reduced rates of benefit being introduced for under-25s and 16- to 18-year-olds being excluded from state protection altogether. In the late 1980s Child Benefit levels were also cut against inflation, because of fears of the high cost of such universal protection, but some restoration of this was made in the early 1990s.

Despite all the changes to benefit entitlement made in the 1980s and 90s, however, the overall cost of social security protection continued to grow inexorably, reaching over £85 billion a year in the mid-1990s, and remained far and away the largest item of government expenditure. In fact of course social security should more accurately be seen as a redistribution than a consumption of resources – money paid in benefits is a transfer from tax or NI payers to benefit claimants. Claimants can then spend this money on goods or services and may do so in ways which boost their local economy – albeit at the expense of some other spending elsewhere. Benefit expenditure was growing, however, because the demand for protection was growing; and over this the government seemed largely unable, or unwilling, to exercise real control. The exception to this was the growth in pensions.

In the Fowler Reviews separate attention had been paid by one review group to the issue of state pension provision. In Britain, as in all industrialised societies, towards the end of the twentieth century the numbers of older people relative to the rest of the population were growing, and most of these older people were living longer. The government was becoming concerned therefore about the potential cost of future pension commitments, in particular because the pay-as-you-go nature of the NI scheme meant that these would have to be financed out of future contribution payments. As a result they wanted to cut pension expenditure and encourage private provision for retirement.

The initial response to the pensions dilemma was a proposal in the 1985 Green Paper on social security reform to withdraw SERPS. This would have been a dramatic change, especially as it had been understood that the scheme had cross-party support when it was introduced in the 1970s and was still only slowly moving towards maturity. The government's belief was that SERPS could be abolished because additional earnings-related pension protection was now available to a broad section of the population through private and occupational pension schemes, thus obviating the need for comprehensive state protection. Certainly occupational pensions in particular had been growing rapidly throughout the postwar period, and those covered by such schemes had been permitted to opt out of SERPS in 1978, and so pay lower NI contributions. However, occupational pensions did not cover all and generally benefited most the better-off. The government's hope was that they could be expanded and accompanied by free-standing private pension schemes for those not able to join occupational protection; but this was not a hope shared by the major providers of private and occupational pensions, who did not relish taking on responsibility for pension protection for a wider range of poorer workers and non-workers. The pensions industry and employers' representatives thus joined with the Labour opposition in opposing the proposals to scrap SERPS, and these were withdrawn in the White Paper which preceded the eventual reforms.

What happened in 1988 therefore was that future entitlement to SERPS was cut back, to reduce the future cost of the scheme, but the scheme itself was retained. Nevertheless private pension protection was openly encouraged and supported – in particular through reductions in NI contributions for new members of private schemes; and the scope of private pension cover expanded rapidly. Much of this new protection was less secure than that which could be provided by the state, however, as was revealed most graphically in the collapse of the Mirror Group pension scheme in the early 1990s; and, despite the state support, private pensions also failed to provide adequate cover for the low paid (Waine, 1995).

The problem of the potential burden of future pension expenditure was the major question concerning both politicians and academics who looked at the British social security system in the 1990s. It was spelt out in general terms in a pessimistic paper from the Department of Social Security (DSS, 1993), and was the subject of a number of independent reviews and proposals for reform (Falkingham and Johnson, 1993; Commission on Social Justice, 1994; Field, 1995). It is quite likely that the cuts in entitlement to SERPS and the tightening of regulation over private pensions will not be the only changes to be made to pension provision at the end of the twentieth century, and in 1997 the government once again announced plans to replace SERPS with private provision for future pensioners – although traditional supporters of state protection have continued to call for revitalisation of the Beveridge-based social insurance plan (Townsend and Walker, 1995).

The policy dilemma to be faced at end of the century, however, is not just one of a perceived crisis in the cost of social security protection. New research conducted by the Joseph Rowntree Foundation – one hundred years after Seebohm Rowntree's seminal surveys – has revealed the problem of poverty once more to be widespread and growing. The Rowntree research of the 1990s consisted of a range of different projects examining different aspects of the distribution of income and wealth in Britain; but the work was a coordinated programme and the findings have been collected together and summarised by Hills (1995, 1996). Their conclusions bear out the picture emerging also from government statistics (Department of Social Security, 1995a), that despite a general rise in living standards the incomes of those at the bottom have been stagnating or even declining in real terms while those at the top have risen dramatically, returning income inequality in the country to the levels experienced before the postwar welfare reforms (Hills, 1996, Ch. 1) – the process of 'trickle-down' has not worked in practice.

At the end of the twentieth century therefore the future development of policy on social security and poverty faces a series of curious, and seemingly irresolvable, dilemmas.

The comprehensive insurance protection envisaged at the height of welfare reform has not materialised and has been displaced by selective means-tested support which penalises those dependent on it, or seeking to escape from it.

- Although there have been cuts in benefit levels and benefit entitlement, and the encouragement of private protection, dependency upon state protection continues to grow and the cost of benefit payments is increasing in both relative and absolute terms.
- Despite a century of economic growth and unparalleled affluence there are a wider range of more diverse and overlapping social security measures affecting a wider range of the population than ever before.
- Both government figures and independent research reveal that in the 1990s poverty is still endemic in the country and levels of inequality are as wide as they were at the beginning of the century.

These conclusion suggest that behind the relatively simple story of policy development lie some difficult and contradictory problems of principle in the use of social security to prevent poverty. If these cannot be addressed then the development of policy in the next century will be unlikely to escape the conflicts which have dominated this one.

The Impact of State Policy

The impact of state social security policy on the extent and the experience of poverty in Britain in the twentieth century has been dramatic. However, it has also been complex – for it is not only state security policy which has affected the problem of poverty, and it is not only the problem of poverty at which social security policy has been aimed.

Combating poverty

For the early researchers on poverty, such as Booth and Rowntree, and their Fabian colleagues in academia and politics the case for the development of new policies for social security was seen as predicated on the aim of preventing poverty. This culminated in the middle of the century in the Beveridge Report (Cmnd 6404, 1942) and the use of social insurance to remove 'want' (his term for poverty); and the research carried out again by Rowntree in 1951 (Rowntree and Lavers, 1951) suggested that this had been a successful strategy. This success, of course, has been questioned by the rediscovery of poverty within the welfare state in the 1960s (Abel Smith and Townsend, 1965) and the evidence of increased inequality in the 1990s (Hills, 1995, 1996).

However, these continuing problems should not deflect attention from the real achievements made by social security policy in redistributing resources towards the poor. Overall those at the lower end of the income scale benefit from the redistributive effects of state taxation and social security policies (Falkingham and Hills, 1995). This evens out the inequalities which undoubtedly would otherwise exist within society, and perhaps more importantly it provides vital sources of income for many millions of people who would otherwise have little or nothing to live on. Social security may not have removed poverty; but it has certainly reduced its extent and depth.

Social security has goals other than the elimination of poverty, however, to which we will return below; and conversely poverty has been the focus of state initiatives other than social security. The experiences of poverty which are linked to housing, health and education for instance have also been tackled through state policies to improve the quality of houses, tackle ill-health and extend education opportunity to all. Furthermore in the latter quarter of the century in particular a range of specific local regeneration initiatives aimed at working with poor people within particular geographical areas have been grafted on top of these basic state services. These include central government initiatives to target additional regeneration resources into poor areas and to support community-based projects to help people to challenge their experience of poverty, and local government strategies to tackle disadvantage through the development of new policies such as welfare rights advice and assistance for local claimants (see Berthoud *et al.*, 1981; Alcock, 1997, Ch. 15).

However, both these targeted initiatives and the wider provision of social security and social services can only operate to ameliorate the consequences of inequality and deprivation which flow from the broader economic forces shaping the distribution of resources within society. Social security and social services aim only to *re*distribute resources, not to control their initial production or spread.

Social security and redistribution

Social security policy is thus a mechanism for this redistribution. Money (or its equivalent) is collected in the form of taxes and contributions and is given out in the form of benefit payments. At any particular time there are some people who are contributing and some people who are benefiting – although there may also be some who are doing both – and, if those who are benefiting are (or would otherwise be) poor, then social security will reduce poverty.

Redistribution from rich to poor is called *vertical redistribution* and it is the form of support which characterised nineteenth-century Poor Law provision, and has been continued in the twentieth century in social assistance. Vertical redistribution directs resources to the poor and it generally involves means-testing, to ensure that resources go only to the poorest. This may divide those who receive from those who pay for benefits, leading to stigmatisation of dependents and to other problems discussed below.

Social security does not just redistribute from rich to poor, however, it also redistributes to all classes of people across their life cycle. Social security benefits such as Child Benefit and retirement pension provide support for children (and parents) and retired people. This is called *horizontal redistribution*. It is in part a response to Rowntree's identification of risk of poverty with certain stages of the life-cycle and it is the basis upon which most twentieth-century social insurance protection is provided. Horizontal redistribution aims to prevent poverty by predicting times at which people are likely to need support; but it also acts more generally as a means of evening out resources across the life-cycle. This is particularly true of private social security protection, such as private pensions, which can be seen as a form of individual savings or deferred earnings; but it also true of some state benefits, such as earnings-related benefit supplements, which use public resources to provide some protection for individual living standards.

State social security policy in Britain in the twentieth century has used different policy measures to engage in both vertical and horizontal redistribution – at the same time, and often affecting the same individuals under each different system. Falkingham *et al.* (1993) have concluded that in practice horizontal redistribution has been of more overall importance than vertical redistribution, although both overlap. Social security does not just aim at targeting resources on to the poor therefore. It is also not the only mechanism for the redistribution of such resources.

Social security outside the state

At over £85 billion a year in the mid-1990s state social security protection is certainly a massive exercise in the transfer of resources within society. Most such transfers take place through the state – and rightly so. The state within a democracy represents the only agency with the political legitimacy to use compulsion to take resources from some citizens and give them to others. And, because of the economies of scale involved, the state can also carry out such redistribution much more efficiently and effectively than any other agencies could do. Nevertheless there are many other agencies which do redistribute resources within society and do this in effect to provide social security, and perhaps to combat poverty.

At the end of the twentieth century in particular there has been a major growth in the use of private and commercial agencies to provide social security. These include employers, who are now required to provide sick pay and maternity pay protection for (some of) their workers, and who also may provide pension protection through payments into occupational pension schemes (Mann and Anstee, 1989). They also include private schemes for pension protection, or for sickness cover or support with housing costs (such as mortgage repayments) run by insurance companies and operating on a strict actuarial insurance basis.

At the beginning of the century voluntary action to redistribute resources was widespread and was seen by the Majority Report of the Royal Commission on the Poor Law as a desirable alternative to state benefit protection. In practice such a dominant role for voluntary support has never been achieved; but voluntary agencies have continued to play a significant role in the transfer of resources and the relief of poverty. This can be seen in the local 'Help the Aged' community shop, in national organisations like the Women's Royal Voluntary Service and in international agencies like Oxfam.

Finally, and perhaps most importantly, protection and redistribution are provided informally by citizens for themselves, their families and their neighbours. Social policy commentators generally regard the informal sector as in practice the largest arena of welfare activity (see Alcock, 1996, Ch. 6), and this is particularly true in the field of personal care, despite the limited cash benefits now available to people with chronic sickness or disability. But it is quite probably true too of direct cash provision. If we include private savings, family and household sharing, and inter-generational transfers (such as inheritance) then the scale of informal social security protection is massive, and it is probably one of the most effective means of preventing poverty.

Limitations in state protection

One of the reasons for the development and maintenance of private, voluntary and informal measures for social security protection is the limitations which exist within state provision, especially as an effective means of preventing poverty. As we have seen, not all state benefits are aimed at combating poverty. However, many are and yet they often fail in achieving this.

One of the most obvious limitations in state benefit policy is the failure of the benefits agencies to deliver the benefits to all of those who might be entitled to them. It is now widely recognised within social policy that the access to social services is as important as the provision of them (see Alcock, 1996, Ch. 13). In social security there is much evidence that the delivery of benefits is far from effective and that there are many people who do not in practice take up the benefits to which they might be entitled (see Hill, 1990, Ch. 7). According to the government's own figures the take up of the major means-tested benefits, such as Income Support and Family Credit is somewhere between 75 and 90 per cent of total benefit resources (Department of Social Security, 1995b). There is evidence that higher levels of non-take up are associated in particular with means-tested benefits (Deacon and Bradshaw, 1983, Ch. 7) – and means-tested provision has become much more widespread within the state system in the later quarter of the twentieth century.

The other major limitation within state benefit protection is also associated with means-testing, and thus has been growing in significance at the end of the century. This is the problem of the 'poverty trap'. The targeting of benefits on those who are poor requires the use of tests of means and needs and the tailoring of benefit entitlement to the household size and living costs. It also means, obviously, that, if the circumstances of households improve, then benefit payment must, progressively, be withdrawn.

This means that for those who are out of work in receipt of targeted benefits which cover the cost of childcare and rent or mortgage payments, the wages that could be received in available employment may not in practice be sufficient to substitute for these benefits – the *unemployment trap*. For those in work on low pay and in receipt of means-tested support it means that any increase in wages will be offset by a loss of benefit entitlement thus leaving households little better off – the *poverty trap*. And for those relying on income from savings or investments it means that the capital sums providing this income will disqualify recipients from entitlement to means-tested support – the *savings trap*.

These traps have always accompanied the use of means-testing, even though their impact has changed as benefit rules have altered (Deacon and Bradshaw, 1983, Ch. 8); and the effect of them all is to provide perverse incentives for those in receipt of means-tested benefits to continue to rely on these, rather than seeking to provide for themselves through employment, promotion or investment. This is the very problem which governments in the late twentieth century have disparagingly referred to as the 'benefit dependency culture', and yet it is a direct – and predictable – consequence of the use of state resources to relieve poverty through targeting on the poor. Social security may therefore be reinforcing the problem of poverty rather than relieving it; and state provision may be undermining the market economy rather than supporting it. This suggests that some key dilemmas lie at the heart of the state social security strategy.

Key Policy Debates

What is to be done about poverty?

Social security provision has done much to alleviate the problem of poverty in Britain. However, as we have seen, it cannot alone remove poverty from the country. This is in part because there is disagreement both about how to define and measure poverty and about the extent of the role the state should play in combating it, and we do not have the space to review these disagreements here (see Alcock, 1997). But it is also because there is disagreement about what form social security intervention should take in the combating of poverty – in particular about whether the aim of the state should be to prevent poverty or to relieve it.

- Poverty *prevention* requires state policy to be proactive in identifying the circumstances which lead to poverty and in intervening to ensure that support is available to all those who might be at risk. This means intervention in the economy to support jobs and wages and the use of universal or insurance benefits to provide support for those outside of the labour market. If this works successfully then no-one becomes poor and all in society have an investment in the use of resource transfers to secure this. If it works unsuccessfully then intervention in the economy leads to market failure and unemployment and the cost of providing universal benefits means that these cannot be kept at a level high enough to prevent some becoming poor.
- Poverty *relief* requires state policy to respond reactively to poverty by targeting resources upon those in need, both inside the labour market and without, through the use of means-tested support. This has been referred to as a 'casualty approach' to welfare (Townsend, 1984) because it deals

with the consequences of deprivation rather than its causes. If it works successfully then all those who are poor receive targeted support to lift them above the poverty line and limited resources are concentrated on those most in need. If it works unsuccessfully then targeted benefits fail to reach many of those who might be entitled to them and those receiving state support are trapped into dependency upon it.

In twentieth-century Britain both poverty prevention and poverty relief have been prominent, if contradictory, elements of social security policy. Both have succeeded to some extent, but both have also experienced significant failures.

How should resources be redistributed?

Linked to the debates about the role that the state should play in combating social policy is the debate about how resources should be redistributed in order to achieve this. The issues surrounding the redistribution of resources are many and complex. There are the questions of whether support should be provided to individuals or households, whether support should take the form of cash or services, whether support should seek to preserve past living standards or merely provide for subsistence, and whether entitlement should be based on rights or subject to discretionary judgement. These are issues which we cannot explore here (see Spicker, 1993). However, there is one fundamental issue which has divided debate throughout the twentieth century – the question of whether redistribution should be horizontal or vertical.

- *Horizontal* redistribution, as we have seen above, is based upon Rowntree's notion of life-cycle needs. Its aim is to use public agencies to transfer resources across generations within the population – in particular by moving resources from those in employment to those with caring responsibilities or in retirement. Horizontal distribution is not the same as private insurance, it does not save people's resources for use at another time; but it does encompass a collective notion of insurance in that all might expect to contribute to and benefit from it at different points in their life course. Horizontal redistribution is thus based on enlightened self-interest. If it works successfully then it provides for all. If it works unsuccessfully then it interferes by providing money for some who do not need it and failing to support adequately some who do.
- *Vertical* redistribution is based on the transfer of resources from rich to poor. Its aim is to combat poverty by targeting resources on those in need and to even out the inequalities between classes of people. Vertical redistribution does not seek to benefit all, but rather to shift support from those that have enough to those that do not. It is thus based on altruism, albeit altruism which is often limited by a concern not to give too much. If it

works successfully then vertical redistribution operates on the 'Robin Hood' principle to equalise social differences. If it works unsuccessfully then it leads to social divisions between those who pay and those who receive – characterised by the phenomenon of 'scroungermania' (Golding and Middleton, 1982).

In twentieth-century Britain both horizontal and vertical redistribution have been pursued through social security, and together have resulted in massive transfers of resources between people throughout society. However, not all have been adequately protected by this and at the end of the century, despite the highest levels of transfer, divisions between people have been growing.

Looking to the Future

There is no doubt that considerable change, and some real progress, has been made in poverty and social security policy throughout the course of the twentieth century. At the end of the century more people are protected and a wider range of forms of support are available. At the same time, however, poverty and inequality are growing and it is tempting to conclude that policy development has almost completed a circle of departing from reliance on Poor Law and assistance only to return to it once more. When we add to this the growing concerns in political circles with the supposedly escalating costs of social security, the prospects for policy development in the twenty-first century do not look likely to lead to a positive revitalisation of state support.

In practice looking to the future can take the form of either prediction (gazing into the crystal ball) or prescription (setting the agenda for desired reform), although both frequently overlap. There is no shortage of prescriptive models for future benefit reform, and indeed lively debate is conducted about the merits and problems within different approaches (Alcock, 1987, Ch. 11; Hill, 1990, Ch. 9). They include:

- Negative Income Tax – replacing all benefits with tax reliefs which could be paid as 'negative taxes' to the poor (see Dilnot *et al.*, 1984)
- Basic Income – providing all people with a standard benefit which could be topped up by wages or by benefits for those out of work (see Atkinson, 1995)
- Social Insurance – extending social insurance cover to include all benefit claimants and withdrawing means-tested support (see Lister, 1987).

Prediction is more difficult, and less often attempted.

In the immediate future, moving towards the turn of the century, it is difficult to see social security escaping its current complex and contradictory structure. As we said at the beginning current provision is the product of history. This history cannot be forgotten or abandoned overnight. This is particularly the case because many millions of people – indeed indirectly at least the whole of British society – have expectations and investments which are tied to current benefit support. Realistic policy change is inevitably likely to result in 'losers' and 'winners' from any process of reform. Significant changes will lead to significant numbers of losers, and this is a price which cannot be born either politically or morally.

Change in whatever direction is likely to be gradual therefore and, if the past is anything to go by, faltering. Overall perhaps gradual change is no bad thing – and so it is the direction of change rather than its pace which is perhaps the most important issue to be determined. In the early part of the twentieth century social security policy moved away from assistance and towards insurance, culminating in the Beveridge reforms of the 1940s, and poverty and inequality were gradually reduced. In the latter part of the century policy has moved away from insurance and back towards assistance, albeit in new and more generous forms, and poverty and inequality have gradually increased.

At the end of the century it is probably fair to say that the problems of poverty and inequality have once again become matters of significant political importance, and that the future direction of social security policy is once again facing a potentially important turning point. In such a context the protagonists of social insurance are once again raising the debate against selectivity (Silburn, 1995b).

However, the challenge to state protection provided by the growing levels of private and voluntary provision now confuse this picture considerably. The private sector is claiming that it too can provide insurance protection against poverty needs, and voluntary action is supported by those on the left (Field, 1995) and the right (Green, 1996). Furthermore within the public sector the pressure to reduce expenditure commitments and to target resources has secured significant support across the political spectrum. In this climate it seems likely that, despite its delivery failings and perverse contradictions, the targeting approach will remain the dominant theme within state support at the opening of the twenty-first century – and only when these failings and contradictions have become manifest as political problems, as well as practical ones, is this direction likely to change. For those who are poor in the 1990s, unfortunately, this may turn out to be a long time to have to wait.

10

Housing

Norman Ginsburg

Comparing the housing situation in Britain today with that at the turn of the century there are obviously huge differences, but there are also features which remain relatively unchanged and even a sense in which the situation has turned full circle. Features of the late 1990s which contrast sharply with the situation in 1900 include the enormous improvement in the quality of housing, government housing policies costing around £20 billion or 3 per cent of GNP each year, and the growth of owner occupation to include two-thirds of households. In 1900 overcrowded, insanitary and insecure housing conditions were experienced by a substantial minority of the population. Beyond legislation governing the closure of the worst slums and the rehousing of those housed therein, there was nothing that could be described as housing policy. In 1900 around 10 per cent of housing was owner occupied and 90 per cent was rented from private landlords, who, in England and Wales, were middle class or petit bourgeois with modest investments. Throughout the century housing has continued being consumed predominantly in the private sectors, albeit regulated and subsidised in various ways. Hence in 1995, 77 per cent of dwellings in Britain were either owner occupied or rented from private landlords (excluding housing associations, 82 per cent if these are included). This is a very significant contrast with other fields of social welfare such as health care and education where consumption has been predominantly in the public sector since the Second World War. As at the turn of the last century, today there is considerable uncertainty about the future of housing consumption and housing policy, with a strong emphasis in governing circles on individual households meeting their housing needs on their own in markets kept as free as possible from state intervention. For fifty or sixty years in the middle of the century, from the 1920s to the 1970s, governments developed interventionist approaches to housing. Since the mid-1970s, or arguably even earlier, governments have sought to disengage from housing, although by no means successfully. This aim has been pursued much more vigorously since 1979. Hence there is a sense of turning if not a full circle, then certainly some way back towards Victorian values in housing.

Such a periodisation of housing consumption and policy is used by Daunton (1987) and Harloe (1995). Daunton argues that there have been two 'fundamental shifts' or 'tenurial revolutions' in British housing this century. At the end of the First World War private landlordism was pushed into apparently terminal decline with council housing and owner occupation becoming the officially sponsored tenures of choice. Then in 1979 with the election of the Thatcher government or possibly even a little earlier, the intensified drive for owner occupation as the only officially sponsored tenure of choice ushered in the second revolution. As Harloe shows, these shifts in housing policy can be set firmly in the context of twentieth-century economic history. The period up to the First World War saw the last throes of liberal capitalism with housing produced by small entrepreneurs, financed by small investors and consumed in a relatively free market. The period from the 1920s to the 1970s witnessed the rise of welfare capitalism, mass production and mass consumption, sometimes known as Fordism. In this period housing was increasingly produced by large firms, financed through major building societies and public loans, and consumed in a subsidised, mixed economy of housing provision. The most recent period has been one of welfare retrenchment, recessions and increased welfare risks including homelessness, repossession and eviction in which the mixed economy has to some extent been reprivatised with the sale of council houses and withdrawal of subsidies to all tenures. Production and consumption of housing are dominated more than ever by increasingly deregulated national or multinational corporations and banks.

Such an account may suggest that housing consumption and housing policy have been shaped entirely by economic and financial processes allied with dominant political ideology and public administration in each era. But housing has of course also been shaped by popular pressures 'from below' which have taken many different forms – consumer pressures from mortgage borrowers and house buyers, tenants' movements, squatting and other pressures exerted by and on behalf of homeless people, resistance to Rachmanite landlordism and so on. A full understanding of the origins and implementation of housing policy should encompass sociological pressures as well as the conventional political and economic forces creating change. Policy-making and implementation in housing has not been a smooth and rational process; there are abrupt moments of change and unpredicted outcomes.

The Period up to 1914

At the turn of the century private rented housing was already in something of a crisis, from which it has never really recovered. The immediate factors facing landlords were falling demand with slowing population growth and stagnation of wages, and increasing costs due to tighter sanitary and building regulations, rising interest rates and sharply increasing local property taxes (the rates, levied by local authorities). Landlords also believed that the balance of power between landlord and tenant was too much in the tenants' favour in terms of both legislation and the ability of tenants on the ground to mobilize community support against evictions (Daunton, 1990, p. 228). Englander (1983), however, suggests that the balance of power generally favoured the landlord. By the turn of the century people of modest means had many more alternative avenues for secure investment which were likely be less troublesome, less taxed and more lucrative, such as municipal bonds and building society savings. Daunton (1983, 1987), Englander (1983), Offer (1981) and Hamnett and Rudolph (1988) among others have debated the relative importance of such factors in precipitating the decline of private landlordism and the extent to which terminal decline had set in before the First World War. A key factor was the political impotence of the landlords in opposing the serious effects of rising rates, in reforming landlord–tenant legislation in their favour and in trying to get financial support from local and national government. Landlord organisations concentrated on negative campaigns against property taxation and collectivism in general. As Daunton (1990, p. 225) shows 'the landlords lacked a distinctive political voice and their claims were ignored by political parties with other interests to serve'. The Conservatives already emphasised support for the growth of owner occupation as well as protection of big landed interests rather than small landlords. The Liberals, representing industrial and finance capital, were keen to increase taxation of landed property to support the development of local government and infrastructure. The emerging Labour Party was hardly likely to support the private landlord who was identified with so much of the housing miseries of working people in the nineteenth century.

While New Liberalism triumphed in other areas of social policy between 1906 and 1914, there were few significant policy developments in the housing field with the possible exception of the Housing and Town Planning Act 1909. This Act modestly facilitated local authorities' growing efforts to provide housing, although not to the extent of subsidising them, and, for the first time, gave local authorities powers to control some developments. Wilding (1972) has shown that by 1914 the Liberal government was ready to give local authorities powers to acquire land for housing development by themselves and by private enterprise, and a statutory duty to oversee adequate housing provision. These gradual shifts in stance in governing circles were partly a response to the effective and vocal campaigning by local trades councils, tenants organisations and local Labour parties (Wohl, 1977). In 1898 the Workmen's National Housing Council was formed by three socialist trade unionists and developed a national campaign for 'municipalisation of housing' and 'fair rent courts' in the years up to 1914 (Englander, 1983). In general however, housing conditions and pressures in 1914 were little different from the late nineteenth century.

From 1915 to the 1970s: Liberal Collectivist Housing Policy

In the years from 1915 to 1930, four planks of liberal collectivist housing policy in Britain were developed, only a few vestiges of which survive today. The four planks were:

1. Rent control/regulation for private rented housing without significant fiscal incentives or cash support for landlords or tenants.
2. Nationally regulated and subsidised provision of local authority rented housing for the 'respectable' working class.
3. Programmes of Victorian slum clearance with replacement council housing for poor people.
4. Fiscal and general government support for owner occupiers.

The development of New Liberal policy in the housing field was delayed in effect until after 1914, but thereafter policy change was accelerated compared to other areas of social policy. In understanding how this momentum developed, each plank needs analysis in its immediate context. There was no long-term strategic thinking behind these developments, they were largely pragmatic responses to short-term political pressures. One factor which lay behind them all was the fear of communism and a sharp realisation in governing circles that Dickensian housing conditions and high rents contributed substantially to working-class unrest. Housing policy provided a relatively 'quick fix' which generated economic activity and long-term investment, particularly when compared to the very short-term impact of costly social security payments and the much longer-term impact of expenditure on health care and education. Hence the policy story for most of the century has been a stop–go rollercoaster of increasing subsidy to stimulate economic activity and withdrawal of subsidy to prevent hyperactivity. Equally the effects of wider economic policy have sometimes had much more drastic consequences on the housing market than anticipated. Hence in the 1980s fiscal policy and the deregulation of credit fuelled the house price boom, which then turned to a slump. The slump in the housing market then helped to nourish the recession with the government searching for non-inflationary means of encouraging economic recovery by stimulating the housing market. Housing has always been particularly sensitive to shifts in economic policy and vice versa.

Regulation and disinvestment in private rented housing

The period opens with arguably the single most significant piece of housing legislation this century, the Rent and Mortgage Interest (War Restrictions)

Act 1915 which introduced rent control to the private rented sector. After the war decontrol on vacant possession was permitted but in 1931 69 per cent of housing in England and Wales still had controlled rents. Nevertheless controlled rents were between 15 and 40 per cent higher than pre-war levels and according to Nevitt (1966, p. 115) were controlled 'at about their market level' between 1923 and 1933. The Protection from Eviction Act 1924 was passed by the first Labour government giving some security of tenure to tenants in the face of landlords seeking vacant possession. Given the unwillingness of governments to give financial assistance to landlords and tenants, these measures, alongside the factors from the Edwardian period discussed above, contributed substantially to the slow decline of the tenure through to the 1980s. In the interwar period, however, the decline was very modest with almost a million new privately rented homes coming onto the market and 1.4 million lost to owner occupation and slum clearance. The 1915 Rent Act not only controlled rents, it also controlled landlords' mortgage costs, so that much of the burden of control fell on the lenders (Hamnett and Rudolph, 1988, p. 55). In effect the Act cut landlords off from mortgage finance. The legislation of 1915 and further legislation in the 1920s regulating the landlord–tenant relationship established a legal regulatory regime governing the housing of the great majority which had not existed before the war. This was a very significant extension of the state's involvement in private housing.

The 1915 Rent Act was introduced in some haste after months of rent strikes and popular agitation across the country as landlords raised rents to exploit wartime shortages and the wages paid to munitions workers. The greatest agitation took place in Glasgow, Red Clydeside as Britain's foremost industrial city was known. Most of the working-class districts were on rent strike by the summer of 1915 and workers also took industrial action in support (see Damer, 1980; Melling, 1983). The rent strikes were led by women such as Mary Barbour of the Independent Labour Party with the support of Red Clydesiders like John Maclean. The 1915 Act is an unusually clear example of working-class and women's struggle bringing about social policy reform. It was certainly a great victory for women, the labour movement and for tenants. The Clydeside movement to protect tenants from decontrol, eviction and rises in controlled rents continued throughout the interwar period (Melling, 1980; Englander, 1983), which deterred governments from introducing full decontrol and deregulation. The outcome of the struggle was that the burden of rents on working-class households was much easier than it had been before the war, something which continued on into the 1950s for many. The downside is that low rents inevitably meant low levels of investment in repairs and maintenance by landlords so that the sector stagnated and Victorian slum conditions continued to be experienced well into the second half of the century. The failure of governments to take positive action to improve conditions in the private rented sector, beyond the selective sledgehammer of slum clearance, is perhaps the most outstanding blot on housing policy this century.

The policy cycle was repeated in mid-century. Rent control was reimposed on all private rented housing at the beginning of the Second World War and decontrol on vacant possession was allowed under the 1957 Rent Act, an early example of deregulatory social policy in the postwar period. The tenants' movement was now much weaker and the sector was much smaller than in the 1920s. The Conservative government of the day apparently hoped that gradual decontrol would reinvigorate the private rented market as market rents were restored. In fact it accelerated the decline of the sector as landlords sold out to owner occupation or property developers. Without the tax breaks and subsidies available to the other tenures, there was little prospect of a competitive return on investment in the private rented sector despite the prospect of market rents.

The impact of the 1957 Rent Act was particularly significant in inner London which had the highest proportion of private rented housing in England, often situated on prime development land. Rachmanism, after the notorious Peter Rachman (Green, 1979), became a byword for landlords who harassed their tenants in order to gain vacant possession. By the early 1960s growing homelessness, insecurity of tenure and Rachmanite intimidation was being linked to what Labour called 'the infamous Tory Rent Act' and was damaging the Conservatives' image. A few months before the 1964 election the government commissioned the Milner Holland (1965) report on *Housing in Greater London*, (Cmnd 2605) far and away the most searching and critical government report on any aspect of housing this century. The report advocated more investment in social rented housing, stronger legal protection for tenants, and financial and fiscal assistance to private landlords. The first two were taken up by the incoming Labour government, but not the latter. The 1965 Rent Act established the 'fair rent' system (see Ginsburg, 1979, pp. 122–3) which regulated private rents until the full deregulation of rents for new tenancies introduced in 1989.

Council housing for the 'respectable' working class

Although some local authorities had developed council houses before 1919, provision on a mass scale with subsidies from central government started after the First World War in fulfilment of Lloyd George's promise in the 1918 election campaign of 'homes fit for heroes to live in'. In 1917 a Commission of Inquiry into Industrial Unrest reported that housing conditions were a major factor creating unrest and called for mass provision of cheap housing (Wilding, 1973, p. 321). The Housing and Town Planning Act 1919, which was the last significant piece of Liberal social legislation, introduced quite generous government subsidies for council house building. This was the first in a series of acts continuing through to the 1970s which enabled local authorities to build modest houses, to a standard often higher than the speculative builders, for respectable working-class families. Standards for council house building were inspired by the pre-war Garden Cities movement and were established nationally by the Tudor Walters report of 1918 (Swenarton, 1981, Ch. 5). The provision of municipal housing on such a scale is unique in Western capitalist nations. It originated as a short-term response to the postwar political crisis and the threat, both real and imagined, of Bolshevism. Its origins must also be traced to the pre-war pressures from the left for municipal housing, the failure of private landlords to get government financial support, the continuing agitations of private tenants and the success of council housing schemes produced before the war by the London County Council and others (Swenarton, 1981, pp. 27–44).

The housing pressures on government waned somewhat by the early 1920s as demobilisation was completed and the threat of Bolshevism receded. Yet it was clear that little investment in the private rented market was forthcoming partly because of the new regulatory regime. In 1923 a Conservative government introduced modest capital subsidies for house building in all tenures including local authorities where they could show that their activity would not interfere with private enterprise. The legislation that secured a permanent future for council housing was Labour's Housing Act 1924, the 'first substantial measure of legislative socialism' (Middlemas, 1965, p. 151), the minister responsible being John Wheatley, a former Red Clydesider. Although the Conservatives soon returned to power, in 1925 they implemented Wheatley's Act without amendment, which as Holmans (1987, p. 308) says, marked the acceptance of council housing as a major feature of the welfare state for the subsequent fifty years. The Act gave local authorities the leading role in the provision of rented housing with reasonable subsidy from central government. It produced over half a million council dwellings by the mid-1930s, mostly small houses with gardens, for 'respectable working-class families' in which the male breadwinners had secure employment and a steady income. Council rents were considerably higher than controlled private sector rents, although of course the quality of the accommodation was much better. According to Bowley (1945, p. 129) 'the market for local authority homes was largely confined to a limited range of income groups, that is, in practice, the better-off families, the small clerks, the artisans, the better-off semi-skilled workers with small families and fairly safe jobs'. Bowley (1945, p. 130) noted that 'the working-class families who benefited most directly from the subsidies... were among the best off... who were least in need of financial aid of any sort' while the subsidies were financed in part through the taxes and rates paid by poorer households. Yet these measures, by establishing council housing as a collective provision for the working class as a whole, meant that the sector could not be marginalised as just housing for poor people. This aspiration of council housing 'for all' housing the widest possible mix of people inspired Aneurin Bevan's housing policies in the 1940s and continued to shape progressive attitudes to council housing into the 1970s.

Thus if access to Wheatley's council housing was somewhat limited in practice, the socialist notion that council housing should be of good quality and accessible to all was taken up with enthusiasm by Aneurin Bevan, the left-wing minister responsible for housing in the post-1945 Labour government. Bevan was faced with huge logistical problems in tackling housing production, not least the acute shortage of building materials. He had to fight a series of battles with the construction industry and government bureaucracy, and particularly with Treasury colleagues both for more spacious council houses with more built-in amenities and for the public borrowing required to finance development. In 1947 the latter battle was lost as expenditure cuts were made in fulfilment of conditions attached to loans from the US government (Marshall Aid). As Cole and Furbey (1994, pp. 63–9) suggest, this moment marked out the limits of the Labourist welfare state in which, despite Bevan's hopes, there was not going to be quality council housing for all. There are strong parallels with the Liberals' retreat from the universalist 'homes fit for heroes' commitment after the First World War. The decline in output of council homes in the context of the acute postwar shortage contributed significantly to Labour's defeat in the 1951 election. The Conservative government then implemented a big programme of council house building for general needs, achieving cost reduction by using non-traditional building methods and by diminishing quality and amenity standards. The Macmillan boom, after the minister responsible, produced all-time record numbers of new council houses in the early 1950s which contributed to their re-election in 1955. Thereafter council housing became more explicitly targeted on meeting the needs of slum dwellers and other low income households, while the skilled and semi-skilled working class transferred increasingly into owner occupation.

Slum clearance: council housing for poor people

Apart from the maintenance of rent control, the measures of the 1920s had not touched most of those living in the worst housing conditions, concentrated in the poorest wards of the big cities and in towns hit by industrial decline particularly in the north-east (Stevenson, 1977, Ch. 3). Overcrowding in the 1930s was at much the same level as before the war affecting over a million households; around half the homes of the 1930s had either no fixed bath or no hot water supply to a sink. During the 1930s some attempts were made to address these problems in the form of 'slum clearance', a focusing of local authority activity on the demolition of unfit housing with the residents rehoused in council housing. Slum clearance is an example of the 'targeting' of welfare policy on the poor, as distinct from the more universalist philosophy behind the Wheatley Act which sought to meet housing needs generally, not specifically the needs of poor people. Initially in the early 1930s the slum clearance programme was run alongside the Wheatley programme, but the latter was then phased out. Government in the 1930s was dominated by the Conservatives, after the fall of the second Labour government in 1931, who presided over a boom in home ownership, facilitated by cheap money and deflationary policies (see below). Slum clearance proceeded at a modest pace, producing just over a quarter of a million dwellings in the 1930s, leaving most slum dwellers untouched. This compared with little more than a year's production by the private sector in the 1930s boom (Harloe, 1995, p. 186). The policy represented a switch back to nineteenth-century 'sanitary policy' which limited public responsibility to clearing housing which represented a threat to public health. The council housing built to replace the slums was of significantly lower quality than the Wheatley houses. It generally took the form of flats built at high density in inner areas or estates isolated on the periphery of towns with little or no amenities (Merrett, 1979, p. 57). Two health inspectors (M'Gonigle and Kirby, 1936) examined a slum clearance scheme in Stockton-on-Tees in which half of a socially homogeneous area had been rehoused on a new estate, with the other half left behind in slums. The rehoused families were paradoxically much less healthy, because the council rents were much higher and they experienced more unemployment due to the distance of the new estate from the centre. Policy implementation was clearly well intentioned but inappropriate to the social and economic realities of poor people's lives, as shown also by Damer (1974).

The policy cycle was repeated after the Second World War. From the mid-1950s the Conservative government once again abandoned the idea of quality council housing for general needs in favour of a much more meagre and targeted slum clearance programme. From the mid-1950s to the early 1970s government used the subsidy system to encourage local authorities to build at high densities, often high-rise flats, using 'cost-effective' non-traditional methods. This produced housing which was, once again, in many respects inappropriate to the needs of working-class families and which in many cases soon exhibited fundamental structural faults such as chronic condensation. Looking back over the century, it is clear that council housing never established itself securely as a 'universalist' provision for all who needed it; modest attempts to develop it as such were made in each decade immediately after the two world wars, but for most of the century council housing has been residualised as a provision for people with low or very low incomes. Council housing has existed in the shadow of the growth of working-class home ownership since the 1920s.

Policies in support of owner occupation

It is often considered axiomatic that governments, including Labour governments, have supported and encouraged the growth of home ownership in Britain through explicit housing policies and housing-related aspects of economic policy. This is demonstrably true of the period since the late 1960s, but it is more difficult to demonstrate for prior decades. Indeed the implication of Saunders (1990) is that by focusing housing policy on council house building for general needs and for the replacement of cleared slums with little financial assistance to the lower income owner occupier, governments in effect held back the growth of home ownership. One does not necessarily have to go that far to observe that there were indeed few explicit policy measures in support of home ownership in the period up to the late 1960s. Politicians, particularly Conservative politicians, were apt to make enthusiastic endorsements of the ideological and social benefits of home ownership since the First World War, but this was rarely translated into explicit policy. It is undoubtedly true that explicit encouragement of owner occupation was not particularly needed perhaps, since the long-term attractions of building up equity savings through owner occupation were readily apparent to almost everyone. Encouragement of the growth of home ownership has nevertheless been a central plank of government policy since at least 1919 (excepting the period 1939–51), but it was until quite recently largely implicit or implemented by default. In other words it emerged through the effects of policy on the other tenures, which made rented housing unattractive to many people on middle incomes, and also through sustaining economic conditions in which the owner occupier housing market could thrive. More explicit policies in support of owner occupation emerged in the 1960s and 70s as it became clear that owner occupation was apparently affordable and preferred by a clear majority of the electorate.

The first great boom in owner occupied housing in Britain took place in the interwar period. Between 1914 and 1938, as a proportion of the housing stock, owner occupation rose from 10 per cent to 32 per cent and the actual number of owner occupied homes more than quadrupled. The contribution of government policies to this phenomenon is difficult to assess. As early as 1920 Neville Chamberlain, at that time a Conservative opposition front bencher, was writing in *The Times* championing the cause of the owner occupier whose 'every spadeful of manure dug in, every fruit tree planted converted a potential revolutionary into a citizen' (cited by Merrett, 1982, p. 6). This was translated into policy by Chamberlain's Housing Act 1923 which gave a lump sum subsidy to builders completing modest houses for owner occupation. The Act also encouraged local authorities to provide mortgages, to guarantee building society mortgages and to lend money to builders for new building. Ball (1983, p. 40) has suggested that these measures were just 'a response to Conservative aversion to council housing rather than specifically to support the growth of owner occupation'. The government apparently expected the subsidies to be taken up by private landlords. Nevertheless the Housing Act 1923 made a significant contribution to the growth of home ownership in the 1920s, subsidising at its peak perhaps as much as 18 per cent of completions for owner occupation in 1926–27 (Merrett, 1982, p. 7). The beneficiaries of these subsidies were generally households with average or above average incomes.

The steady development of new owner occupied housing in the 1920s was followed by a dramatic boom in the 1930s with a sharp peak in the middle of the decade. A host of 'market' factors contributed to the boom including the rise in real incomes for white-collar workers and workers in the new industries, cheap building labour due to mass unemployment, the entrepreneurial zeal of the building societies and speculative house builders, and the availability of cheap housing land on the edge of towns unrestricted by planning controls (Ball, 1983, pp. 29–36). There was a huge inflow of funds into the building societies and banks from the late 1920s onward as the world economy slumped. Economic policy contributed directly to the housing boom in the form of the National government's policy of low interest rates, the so-called 'cheap money policy', which emerged in 1932 (Pollard, 1969, pp. 236–8). Mortgage interest rates in fact fell only very slowly and modestly in the 1930s because the building societies established an interest rate cartel in the early 1930s to protect themselves from cut-throat competition. The relatively high rates to investors increased the inflow of funds to the societies, so the effect of cheap money here was indirect, although the building contractors benefited more directly from cheap bank loans.

Both the governments of the time and subsequent economic historians expressed uncertainty about the macroeconomic effects of the house building boom (Daunton, 1987, pp. 104–7). On the one hand there is the view that the boom, supported by cheap money, took Britain out of the slump, generating a multiplier effect on the whole domestic economy. On the other hand there is the view, apparently taken by the Treasury at the time, that the boom created instability and distortion in the domestic economy by channelling investment into housing exchange and over-indebted home owners rather than into capital investment in manufacturing and other export-orientated activities. There are of course strong echoes here of some of the issues surrounding the 1980s home ownership boom.

By the late 1930s certain aspects of the unregulated development of the housing boom created national political concern. In order to keep the boom going, building societies were taking more risks in their lending policies. The length of mortgage loans was increased to an unprecedented 25 years and loans were extended to cover up to 95 per cent of the purchase price in a market where the price of houses was falling slowly. Lenders had much greater confidence in the security of borrowers and in the quality of speculative building. In some cases the builder and building society colluded to produce inflated selling prices and poor quality houses (Daunton, 1987, pp. 83–5). The illegality of the latter practice was exposed in 1939 leading to the Building Societies Act 1939 which introduced much stricter regulation of the societies' financial involvement in property development. The environmental effect of the housing boom was another matter which created pressure for government intervention. The boom contributed to what was then called suburban 'sprawl', the largely uncontrolled development of cities along radial, arterial roads, so-called 'ribbon development' (Hall, 1974, p. 40). An environmental lobby, led by town planners and conservationists, succeeded in getting regulatory legislation on ribbon development passed in 1935, though effective planning control of housing development was not secured until after the Second World War.

The importance of the interwar period is that it saw the establishment of the infrastructure of the owner occupied housing market which remains much the same today, a market shaped predominantly by the building societies and the speculative house builders as described by Ball (1983). During this period explicit government intervention was modest, the role of government being more like that of a 'guardian angel' (Ball, 1983, p. 40) over market-led developments.

The 1940s saw two policy innovations affecting the long-term development of owner occupied housing. First, there was the creation of local development control principally through the Town and Country Planning Act 1947 in order to facilitate and regulate housing development and to avoid the offensive, haphazard sprawl of the interwar years. The extent to which the system has operated in the interests of developers or of local communities remains a subject of keen debate (Ball, 1983, Chs. 7 and 8). A second, more modest innovation was the introduction of housing improvement grants for owner occupiers and private landlords under the Housing Act 1949. This is the first example of a 'welfarist' policy in respect of owner occupiers, since the grants were to be targeted by local authorities on bringing properties up to a minimum sixteen point standard. The period from the early 1950s to the late 1960s has much in common with the first boom, but with one huge difference, namely house price inflation developing more or less in line with wage inflation over the period as a whole. The number of owner occupied dwellings in Britain as a proportion of the total rose from 29 per cent in 1951 to 50 per cent in 1970. The period opens with the removal of the fetters on the house builders by the end of 1952 and the ending of all the licensing controls by the end of 1954. The early 1950s saw a strong restatement of Conservative commitment to creating 'a property owning democracy', a phrase first coined by the future Prime Minister, Antony Eden at the 1946 Party conference. This was spelt out for the first time in a government policy document in a 1953 White Paper:

One object of future housing policy will be to continue to promote, by all possible means, the building of new houses for owner-occupation... Of all forms of owner-ship this is one of the most satisfying to the individual and the most beneficial to the nation. (Ministry of Housing and Local Government, 1953, pp. 3–4)

Analysts have differed in their views of the extent to which this ideology was translated into policy. Cullingworth (1979, p. 100) suggests that few positive measures were actually taken to implement such statements which therefore 'had a hollow ring'. Merrett (1982, p. 28), in complete contrast, sees the 1951–61 period as one in which the government enthusiastically supported private housing development for owner occupation, a 'grand design' already becoming the centrepiece of British housing policy. Although there were no really extravagant and explicit policy measures in support of owner occupation, there was a series of discrete policy moves stretching over the period as a whole, which nurtured the steady expansion of the tenure including: the 1957 Rent Act which hastened the decline of private landlordism; the move away from general needs council housing provision; the taxation of development values in 1953 which encouraged land sales for housing development in the suburbs; government schemes which underwrote building society advances of more than 90 per cent of the valuation of a property in certain circumstances (Merrett, 1982, pp. 29–30), designed to encourage lower income owner occu-pation, particularly of cheaper, older property.

Really significant forms of financial assistance to owner occupiers emerged in the 1960s out of general tax reforms by both Conservative and Labour governments. It was not until the mid-1970s that government conceded that these are forms of 'assistance' to owner occupiers but nonetheless they were certainly conceived as such. The reforms (see Boddy, 1980, Ch. 9) installed mortgage interest tax relief as the explicit form of assistance, and also exempted home owners from capital gains tax and from taxation on their imputed rental income (that is, the rental income they would have if they rented out their home and lived elsewhere). It is extremely difficult to compute the overall net cost of these fiscal measures but Hills (1991, p. 208) estimated that in 1988/89 the net cost of these 'tax expenditures' was £10.7 billion. Funding and eligibility for home improvement grants to owner occu-piers was also extended during the 1960s (Balchin, 1995, Ch. 4). Alongside the general increase in household earnings in the 1960s and 70s, these measures contributed to strong growth of working-class and lower-middle-class home ownership in the 1960s and 1970s accompanied by big house price booms in the 1970s. Indeed government financial assistance to home owners was contributing to inflation by supporting demand, as observed by Ball (1983, p. 341). Throughout the century up to the 1980s as demonstrated by Boddy (1980) the building societies received favourable tax treatment and crisis support from governments.

The 1970s: a Watershed for Housing Policy

The 1970s are often identified as a turning point for the welfare state in Britain, and the key event is usually seen as May 1979, the election of the first Thatcher government. While 1979 was a very significant turning point for housing policy as we shall see, the 1970s saw the emergence of policies which prepared the ground for Thatcherism, but also significant popular pressures and resistances which shaped policy in progressive directions which survived into the 1990s. The decade opened with attempts by a Conservative government to raise council house rents by instituting the 'fair rent' system used in the private rented sector. This provoked enormous resistance among tenants and some Labour councils, and was finally abandoned when Labour returned to power nationally in 1974 (Ginsburg, 1979, pp. 152–6). The campaign contributed to the eventual introduction of housing benefit in 1980 (see Malpass, 1990, Chs 6, 7), which cushioned low income tenants from rent increases though it symbolised the final demise of the principle of universal low rents for all to which tenants' movements had subscribed since the start of the century. A second important struggle resulted in the Housing (Homeless Persons) Act 1977 which instituted the right of homeless families to a permanent local authority tenancy (Wates, 1980; Raynsford, 1986). Despite its numerous loopholes and deficiencies, this Act symbolised official recognition of homelessness and is the only piece of legislation ever to establish a right to shelter. It was the culmination of over a decade of pressure from squatters, pressure groups, charities and churches. A third significant advance was the rising challenge to institutional racism in housing, particularly in the allocation of council housing, which was facilitated by the Race Relations Act 1976. This eventually led to significant changes in local authority practice in the mid-1980s (Ginsburg, 1992).

In part reflecting these popular movements, a struggle was going on inside the Labour Party during the early 1970s. Party policy sought radical reform of regressive mortgage tax relief (Ginsburg, 1983, p. 45) as well as renewed support for council housing. When re-elected in 1974, however, these issues were referred to an expert committee whose Green Paper report finally appeared in 1977. Meanwhile the government's efforts to expand construction of social rented housing foundered on the rocks of the public expenditure restraints introduced in the wake of the IMF crisis in 1976. The Green Paper envisaged no major policy changes and looked forward to the continued expansion of owner occupation, acknowledging the undoubted popularity of the tenure without recognising the inflationary consequences of its fiscal support. Thus:

> More and more people would like to become homeowners... we should not let our concern for those who are badly housed lead us to overlook the reasonable housing ambitions of the community in general... public sector housing investment must be directed selectively. (Cmnd 6851, 1977, p. 8)

The reform of mortgage tax relief was dismissed as 'unfair' (p. 39) and, in the preface by Peter Shore (p. iv) (the then Secretary of State), as overturning household budgets 'in the pursuit of some theoretical or academic dogma'. This proved to be no problem at all for John Major when reform finally came in 1991. The Green Paper encapsulated a certain amount of complacency about the success of postwar housing policy in finally eradicating the Victorian slums, suggesting that in future its role would be confined to assisting marginal groups. The Green Paper does represent something of a watershed in the development of Labour housing policy in government. It represented the final abandonment of universalist notions of council house provision and the unambiguous adoption of support for owner occupation as the preferred tenure for government sponsorship. This provided almost a consensual starting point for the unleashing of market forces under Mrs Thatcher.

Housing Policy Since 1979

The two main planks of housing policy since 1979 have been, first, the drive to extend owner occupation as far as possible and, second, to retrench severely expenditure on council housing by raising rents, privatisation and cuts in bricks and mortar subsidies and investment. Housing policy has thus played a direct role in the growth of both homelessness and tenure polarisation by marginalising tenants and limiting the supply of social rented housing. The fall in house prices and hence of confidence in owner occupation in the early 1990s produced a short-term policy reverse with increased investment in housing association provision and in refurbishment of council estates, but the fundamental principles of Conservative policy remain unchanged. The government has toyed with the possibility of engineering a serious revival of private landlordism, but the cost implications in terms of housing benefit to tenants and possible tax incentives and capital subsidies for landlords make this unattractive to the Treasury.

The extension of home ownership

Since 1979, particularly in the early years of the Thatcher administration, the drive to extend home ownership has been enthusiastically pursued. Hence between 1979 and 1989 the number of owner occupied dwellings in Britain increased by over 4.5 million, almost half a million a year on average. From 1989 to 1995, however, owner occupation has only increased by 1.1 million, around 180,000 a year on average, one-third the rate of increase in the 1980s. The two key policy elements were, first, the introduction of the right to buy with considerable discounts for tenants of social rented housing in the Housing Act 1980. By the end of 1995, almost 1.7 million dwellings had been sold to local authority and housing association tenants in Britain generating receipts of over £26 billion with discounts of a further £24 billion (Wilcox, 1996, pp. 48–9), making it far and away the biggest of the privatisation programmes. Given that access to, and allocation of, council housing in the postwar decades favoured white households, inevitably this privatisation was particularly disadvantageous to minority ethnic communities. However, where Afro-Caribbean families have had the opportunity to buy quality council housing they have been more keen to do so than whites according to Peach and Byron (1994).

The second policy element was the deregulation of mortgage finance achieved by a number of financial policy changes culminating in the Building Societies Act 1986 (Boddy, 1989). These measures allowed building societies to increase their borrowing and opened up the mortgage market to more competition. Mortgage rationing disappeared and lenders were willing to lend increasing proportions of properties' value, exposing themselves and the borrowers to greater risks. In the run up to the 1983 election the government even increased the ceiling on mortgage interest tax relief from £25,000 to £30,000. The cost of mortgage interest tax relief, the most significant 'subsidy' to owner occupiers, jumped from £2.2 billion in 1980/81 to £4.8 billion in 1985/86. In retrospect the first half of the 1980s was the zenith of pro-home ownership policy. Thereafter the government gradually accepted that the encouragement of home ownership was fuelling inflation as the increased demand for owner occupied housing and mortgage finance pushed up house prices and interest rates. These arguments began to take greater precedence over ideological commitment to home ownership, despite Mrs Thatcher's tenacious personal commitment to the drive for owner occupation (Lawson, 1992, pp. 819–21).

Withdrawing support for home owners

A series of policy changes since 1986 has retrenched a considerable amount of financial support to owner occupiers, particularly the payment of mortgage interest to new income support claimants (ISMI – income support for mortgage interest) and mortgage interest tax relief (MIRAS). Up to 1986 all claimants of income support (supplementary benefit) had their mortgage interest costs met in full, though the number of such claims was very small until the 1980s. From 1986 ISMI was cut to half mortgage interest costs for the first 16 weeks of a claim and from October 1995 ISMI was withdrawn completely for the first nine months of a claim. The cost of ISMI had quadrupled between 1988/89 and 1993/94 to a peak of over £1.2 billion. The 1995 ISMI cut is a particularly harsh blow against families on low incomes at the margins of owner occupation and will inevitably increase mortgage arrears and repossessions. The Conservatives believe that the withdrawal of ISMI will encourage lenders and borrowers to bear the burden of insuring mortgage costs through private insurance policies. However, as Williams (1995, p. 19) suggests, at least 2.5 million borrowers will struggle to get adequate cover due to their employment situation (temporary or flexible contracts), health, age or reason for leaving employment (for example to care for a dependant). The Conservative government has conceded that some of these groups should get 80 per cent ISMI after two months and 100 per cent after 6 months. Of ISMI claimants, 43 per cent are unemployed and in some cases might in the future be able to be covered by private insurance. However, most ISMI claimants are over 60 or lone parents or disabled and are therefore very unlikely to get adequate private cover. On top of that Ford *et al.* (1995) have demonstrated that private cover often does not offer adequate protection for unemployed home owners falling into arrears and that two-thirds of mortgage protection policy claims were unsuccessful.

The retrenchment of mortgage tax relief began in 1988 with its confinement to one allowance per dwelling for new loans, ending the 'double relief' enjoyed by couples which was worth over £200 a month to households at peak interest rates. In an act of remarkable folly, borrowers were given five months notice of this change, which stoked up house prices fiercely in the summer of 1988. This was followed in 1991 by withdrawal of relief at the higher tax rate; it had always seemed particularly unjust that higher rate tax payers benefited from greater relief. Finally in 1994 MIRAS was cut to 20p in the pound and in 1995 to 15p in the pound. With these measures and the fall in interest rates since 1992, the cost of MIRAS fell to well under £3 billion in 1995/96, compared with a peak of £7.7 billion in 1991/92.

The crisis of home ownership

This series of measures, particularly the withdrawal of double tax relief in 1988, contributed to the fall in house prices and the stumbling drive for owner occupation in the 1990s. Of course other factors have stifled demand for home ownership, particularly the growing insecurity of income and employment in the flexible labour market. House prices fell most dramatically on estates and in areas of low cost owner occupation. The consequences have therefore been felt most drastically by households on modest or low incomes on the margins of owner occupation in the forms of negative equity, mortgage arrears and repossessions. In 1993, 26 per cent of households who bought homes between 1988 and 1991 held negative equity (Dorling, 1995, Tables 4.27, 4.28). These households were concentrated in the south of England and were mostly young buyers of cheaper property. Any notion that negative equity differentially affected more affluent households in more expensive property is completely wrong, because such households usually have considerable equity and house price falls have been generally far less significant on more expensive property. At the peak in 1992 over 1.75 million households, over 10 per cent of home owners, had negative equity, but this has fallen away significantly with the recent modest recovery in house prices. Nevertheless there remain serious pockets of long-term negative equity, particularly smaller homes 'where demand has been affected by the trend for younger households to rent rather than to buy' (Wilcox, 1996, p. 55). By the mid-1990s negative equity was no longer concentrated in the south of England with high levels recorded in East Anglia and the East Midlands (Wilcox, 1996, Table 45).

The recession of the 1990s produced an explosion in mortgage arrears; at the peak in 1992 there were over 300,000 cases of arrears in excess of six months. In 1995 this had fallen back to around 200,000, compared to only 33,000 in 1982. The impact of such arrears on individual households is vividly portrayed in five case studies presented by Ford (1995). These households live in the shadow of regular court proceedings threatening repossession and frequently have to forgo basic necessities in order to keep up payments. In 1995 49,410 homes were repossessed for mortgage arrears which was an increase on 1994 though certainly less than the peak of 75,540 in 1991, while back in 1980 there were only 3,480 repossessions. During the 1990s this most traumatic experience for home owners has become a permanent feature and a mass phenomenon. Between 1990 and 1995 almost 350,000 owner occupier households lost their homes through repossession, on average about 230 every working day, a brutal consequence in part of pro-home ownership policy.

Given the data on the differential impact of negative equity, unemployment and job insecurity, it is reasonable to suggest that arrears and repossession are more likely to be experienced by low income households and therefore by households headed by independent women and by minority ethnic households. The deregulation of mortgage finance in the first half of the 1980s swept away much of the institutionalised conservatism of the lenders which had differentially affected independent women and low income minority ethnic groups. Hence in the 1980s the growth of mortgaged owner occupation was particularly strong among single women, divorced/separated women and Afrio-Caribbean and Bangladeshi households (see Wilcox, 1996, Tables 28b, 29a). It is therefore likely that these groups have suffered particularly badly in the downturn of the 1990s. There is also some evidence of a return to institutionalised conservatism among the lenders which differentially affects such groups (Jones, 1995).

Social rented housing

Since 1979, the most consistent aspect of government policy has been a panoply of measures to wind down the role of local authorities as managers and providers of rented housing. This has been driven by the government's broad attack on the principle of public service provision, and local government power in particular, by the constant pressure to reduce public spending, by the belief that council estates delivered votes for the Labour Party and by the drive for home ownership. The outcome is that the proportion of local authority dwellings in the stock has fallen from 31.4 per cent in 1979 to 18.9 per cent in 1995. The most significant measures which have contributed to this decline are council house sales (discussed above) and the virtual ending of investment in new council house building. In 1994 1,623 new council homes were completed in Britain compared with 76,997 in 1980. Also since 1988 almost a quarter of a million council dwellings have been transferred to housing association ownership.

The commitment of Conservative governments to housing associations as the alternative form of social rented housing has never been wholehearted. Throughout the 1980s the number of housing association starts averaged around 14,000 a year, by no means making up for the decline in new council house building. In the period 1979–94 there was also a 62 per cent decline in the number of house renovations by housing associations, which had been their predominant area of activity before 1979. In response to the crisis in owner occupation and rising public concern about homelessness, the number of housing association starts in the 1990s up to 1995 averaged around 30,000 a year. The finance for this increased investment was facilitated by the 1988 Housing Act which deregulated housing association rents and pushed housing associations into seeking private capital finance. Also as a one-off initiative in 1992/93 known as 'the housing market package' the government financed the purchase by housing associations of 20,000 new houses from private developers to help out the house builders at a cost of around £600 million. However, since that year gross investment by housing associations (including private finance) has fallen consistently. Following a further big cut in the November 1996 budget, public capital investment in housing associations in 1997/98 will be about one-third of its 1991/92 level. All this indicates that government concern about homelessness in the early 1990s was a temporary expedient.

Housing benefit and rising social rents

Since the election of the third term Thatcher government in 1987, government policy for all sectors of rented housing has arguably been dominated by one principle above all – raising rents. The rationale is that driving rents towards market levels will generate more private investment in rented housing, facilitating the withdrawal of public funding to the social rented tenures as well as improving quality and supply in the private and housing association sectors, while low income tenants are protected by housing benefit. Thus between 1988/89 and 1995/96 the cost of housing benefit in cash terms tripled to almost £12 billion.

This regime alongside the deregulation of private sector rents in 1989 has inflated private rents, possibly beyond 'market' levels subsidised through housing benefit (Ginsburg, 1995, pp. 6–7). Hence over the seven years to 1995/96 the cost of housing benefit for private tenants increased almost threefold (Wilcox, 1996, p. 76). In attempting to limit these costs, the government has tried to cap housing benefit for private tenants, thereby pushing some households below the poverty line and even making some households homeless (Bramley, 1995). In January 1996 much tighter limits on private rent eligible for housing benefit were introduced, and from January 1997 all private tenants will be limited to housing benefit equivalent to the average local rent for a 'suitable size' home. Restrictions on housing benefit for single people under 25 introduced in October 1996 will be extended in October 1997 to all people living under 60 living alone. They will only be eligible for housing benefit equivalent to the average rent of a room in a *shared* home.

Local authority rents rose in real terms by 36 per cent between 1988/89 and 1993/94, having remained fairly steady through the mid-1980s after the 51 per cent real rise between 1979/80 and 1982/83. Under the subsidy regime constructed during the 1980s, the government was able to control closely the level of local authority rents (Ginsburg, 1996, p. 142). The rise in housing association rents is also a direct consequence of rent deregulation and the higher cost of private finance. Hence, housing association fair rents (for pre-1989 tenancies) rose 27 per cent in real terms between 1989/90 and 1993/94, while housing association assured rents (for post-1988 tenancies) rose by 43 per cent in the same period (Newton, 1994, Table 125). In effect the capital subsidies being withdrawn from the social rented sectors are being partially replaced by a revenue subsidy in the form of housing benefit accompanying the greatly increased rents. About 65 per cent of council tenants and 61 per cent of housing association tenants were receiving housing benefit in 1994. So in respect of the social rented sectors, the rise in housing benefit costs is largely a reflection of the reduction of other subsidies.

Increasing numbers of households with incomes just beyond eligibility for housing benefit have found their incomes (net of rent) considerably reduced by rising rents. The rising rent regime has also obviously exacerbated the housing benefit poverty trap. For example a two-parent family with two children and a rent of £50 a week in 1994 was only £12 a week better off earning £230 than earning £60, without taking into account the cost of school meals and travel to work (Ford and Wilcox, 1994, p. 70). In this way the rising rent regime keeps more people on the dole, thereby sustaining public expenditure on the benefits system.

The Conservatives began to recognise the problems created by its rent raising policy in the 1995 White Paper, which announced that in future guideline rent increases for local authorities will be brought in line with inflation with the aim of maintaining affordability by establishing 'a stable and sustainable level of guideline rents in real terms' (Department of the Environment, 1995, p. 27). Councils who raise rents beyond the guideline to finance more repairs and maintenance will be penalised by loss of housing benefit subsidy. Having relinquished regulation of housing association rents in 1989, the government does not have any direct means of holding down rents should it want to do so. Nevertheless recent policy suggests greater hesitancy in government about the wisdom of moving towards market or capital value rents in the social rented sector.

Single women, divorced/separated women and their children, Afro-Caribbean, African and Bangladeshi households are much more likely to live in social rented housing than other groups (Mason, 1995, Table 7.3; Wilcox, 1996, Table 28b). This is so despite the growth of owner occupation among these groups discussed above. Hence the rise in rents, the worsening of the housing benefit poverty trap and the overall decline in investment in the social rented sector since 1979 have differentially affected these groups. In this way, as within owner occupation, policy has contributed to reinforcing gender and ethnic divisions.

Homelessness and Tenure Change Since 1979

Since 1979 the number of households accepted as homeless by local authorities under the homelessness legislation has been taken as the 'headline figure' for homelessness. This figure increased steadily every year from 57,200 in England in 1979 to a peak of 151,720 in 1991 since when it has fallen slowly, down to 125,500 in 1995. The recent fall seems to be accounted for by the increased availability of privately rented accommodation and a substantial increase in the amount of new social housing provision since 1992 (Holmans, 1996, p. 10). This situation has generated some complacency within the Department of the Environment as to future needs for social rented housing, so that it is quite likely that the number of homeless acceptances will start rising again in the late 1990s. The Housing Act 1996 has withdrawn the right of homeless families to a tenancy in the social rented sector, with the intention of pushing even more homeless families into the private rented sector. There is considerable evidence that for homeless families this sector compared to social rented housing provides lower quality accommodation, at greater cost to the taxpayer (through housing benefit) and with less security of tenure (Bramley, 1995; Holmans, 1996).

The annual homelessness acceptance figures are of course just a measurement of the local authority response over a year, based on a fairly restrictive definition of homelessness. A snapshot picture comes from 1991 census data analysed by Holmans (1995, Table 4) suggesting that on census day there were approximately 110,000 concealed families (such as families having to live with parents), 50,000 would-be couples living apart, 140,000 sharing households, 100,000 single homeless people in hostels and so on and 10,000 squatters and rough sleepers, as well as the 22,000 families accepted as homeless and living in hostels and bed and breakfast. This gives a total of 430,000 households who could legitimately be described as homeless.

With the increase in homelessness, the 1980s also witnessed a dreadful rise in the number of households in temporary accommodation. Families accepted as homeless usually have to endure a period of weeks, months or even years in temporary accommodation before getting a secure tenancy. At the end of 1980 in England 4,710 households were in temporary accommodation, but by the end of 1992 this had risen to an appalling peak of 63,070 (Wilcox, 1996, Table 84). This accommodation is often entirely incompatible with normal family life, particularly hostels and bed and breakfast. At the end of 1991 over 12,000 families were in bed and breakfast at enormous cost to the taxpayer. In 1990 the government at last made a positive response to the situation by funding local authorities to lease private sector properties on a two- or three-year basis (Edwards, 1995). This accommodation is more appropriate to the needs of homeless families and is generally less expensive than bed and breakfast. The numbers in bed and breakfast had fallen by 1994 to two-thirds of the 1991 level, but they started to rise again in 1995 as the private sector leasing 'experiment' has withered (Wilcox, 1996, Table 84).

Tenure has been a significant social division in Britain since the First World War, but it has become even more so since the mid-1970s. One of the simplest ways of indicating this is that in 1994 only 8 per cent of owner occupied homes in Britain were flats compared with 38 per cent of council homes and 58 per cent of housing association homes. Between 1980 and 1993 the average income of household heads in council housing fell from 48 to 35 per cent of the average income of household heads in mortgaged owner occupation, and from 84 to 59 per cent of the average income of household heads in outright owner occupation (Wilcox, 1996, Table 33). Between 1980 and 1991 the proportion of owner occupiers in the bottom decile of the income distribution fell from 21 to 11 per cent (Malpass and Murie, 1994, Table 6.1). In 1994/95 the average gross weekly household income in council housing was £172.69, compared with £448.64 for owner occupiers; 46.7 per cent of council tenant household income came from social security compared with only 9.3 per cent for owner occupier households (Wilcox, 1996, Table 34). Given the widening of income inequalities generally since 1979, all these statistics demonstrate a rapidly increasing polarisation between households in owner occupied and in social rented housing in terms of incomes and labour market status. It may be argued that social rented housing is now more effectively targeted on households with the lowest incomes, but this is at the expense of physical as well as social exclusion on council estates. The process also reinforces the image of social rented housing as a residual and stigmatised provision for poor people, who have little political clout in bidding for adequate housing management and maintenance.

Conclusion – Agendas for the Future

In general Conservative housing policy has became more rational in the 1990s. The 1995 White Paper talked of the development of 'sustainable home ownership' and of social rented housing continuing to have 'an important role' for people on low incomes as 'the most cost effective way to ensure that they have access to a decent home' (Department of the Environment, 1995, p. 26). Positive measures from the Conservatives to further these aims have, however, been somewhat lacking. In relation to owner occupation, the phasing out of MIRAS and its replacement with a mortgage benefit to help low income owner occupiers would concentrate assistance on those most likely to be threatened by arrears and repossession. The Liberal Democrats are the only major party to advocate this change. Both Labour and the Liberal Democrats advocate the phased release of capital receipts from council house sales to increase investment in social rented housing. At least £5 billion is said to be available, but there is serious doubt as to whether a future Labour Chancellor would agree to this. Labour's housing spokesperson has admitted that this measure on its own would not be sufficient to bring investment in social rented housing up to adequate levels (Birch, 1996, pp. 18–19). The Liberal Democrats and many housing professionals have suggested that more capital investment could be facilitating by changing restrictive rules on what constitutes public sector borrowing, thus giving local authorities the same borrowing powers as their counterparts in other EU countries (Hawksworth and Wilcox, 1995). Labour have promised to restore the rights of homeless households removed under the 1996 Housing Act, while the Liberal Democrats go much further with the notion of a legal 'right to shelter' (Birch, 1996, p. 44). Finally both Labour and the Liberal Democrats are committed to reform of housing benefit to ease the poverty trap.

Recent housing policy has been dominated by the dream of setting housing markets free with adverse and sometimes disastrous consequences for inadequately protected consumers and those for whom the market cannot provide. The social and economic costs of the pressures and insecurities created by inadequate or unaffordable housing and homelessness are enormous. The inefficiency of contemporary policy is that it relies on inadequate short-term remedies such as private renting for homeless families and expensively subsidised rents while avoiding sufficient long-term investment in bricks and mortar including in the private sectors. The measures discussed above would go some way towards mitigating the increasing housing pressures on low income households, but more wide-ranging and positive measures are needed to achieve social justice in housing such as those advocated in Goodlad and Gibb (1994). Tougher regulation of mortgage lenders and private landlords to protect consumers, empowerment of tenants in social rented housing and the development of social rented housing as a positive public service would establish a long-term basis for tackling social injustice in housing.

The Blair government will be faced with a rising demand for housing into the next century which, as discussed above, cannot be met by the supply of housing envisaged by the outgoing administration. It is more than possible that official homelessness will start to increase once again. The Blair government commitment to tight control of public expenditure offers little room for manoeuvre in tackling these problems, although certainly capital receipts, local housing companies and the restoration of the rights of homeless families will make a positive contribution. There seems little likelihood of a radical change in the direction of housing policy, which will remain confined to a market regulatory role supported by selective assistance to many, but by no means all, low income households.

PART IV

Welfare Outside the State

11

Voluntary and Informal Welfare

Jane Lewis

The historiography of the British welfare state has tended to focus almost exclusively on the role of the state and to stress the eventual triumph of collectivism over individualism, with Britain emerging from the darkness of the Poor Law into the light of the Beveridge Plan of 1942 and the postwar welfare state. This is a story of linear development and progress. However, it is a story that was thrown into question by the apparent reversal of the late 1970s, which began with James Callaghan's (the Labour Prime Minister) speech of 1976 in which he told the Labour Party conference that governments could no longer expect to spend their way out of recessions, and continued with Margaret Thatcher, who sought to diminish the role of the state in terms of both public expenditure and size of bureaucracy, and to promote instead the market, the voluntary sector and the family as providers of welfare.

However, rather than seeing the story of the modern welfare state as a simple movement from individualism to collectivism and ever-increasing amounts of (benevolent) state intervention, it is more accurate to see Britain as always having had a mixed economy of welfare, in which the state, the voluntary sector, the family, and the market have played different parts at different points in time. This might have been more obvious earlier had British historians and social policy analysts engaged in more European comparative research. For example, many European countries have had long experience of the kind of separation of (state) finance from (private and voluntary) provision in the realm of social services, something that has become an explicit policy goal in respect of British social services only since 1988. In a majority of continental European countries a mixed economy, or welfare pluralism, has been the norm. In Britain, Richard Titmuss' (1963) innovative postwar classification of social provision in terms of occupational and fiscal welfare in addition to that provided by the state nevertheless omitted analysis of provision by the voluntary sector and the family, both vital providers of welfare and both historically dominated by women.

The story of the family has been characterised by continuity. As Ann Oakley (1986) has remarked, the family has always been the main provider of welfare. Late nineteenth- and early twentieth-century social theorists saw the family as the seat of altruistic feeling and the place where the weak would be protected (Spencer, 1876; Bosanquet, 1906). The family (and in particular female family members) as the locus of informal care was rediscovered during the 1980s, when women's unpaid work as carers for elderly and other depen-dent adults, as well as for children, was subjected to analysis (see especially Finch and Groves, 1983).

The story of the voluntary sector has been characterised more by change. Turn of the century voluntary action encompassed a wide variety of forms: charity in the sense of the better-off assisting those who were less well off; mutual aid, most importantly in the form of trade unions and friendly soci-eties; and the informal help that the poor rendered the poor. A French study of the 1870s calculated that a large majority of British adults belonged to an average of between five or six voluntary organisations, which included trade unions and friendly societies, both of which played a major role in securing for their members financial protection against sickness and unemployment; savings societies of various kinds; and literary and scientific institutes (Harris, 1993). Frank Prochaska (1988) has also emphasised the extent to which the poor relied on the generosity of the poor in times of need, most of it organ-ised informally. However, it is difficult to calculate the amount of money given by charities in poor relief. Humphreys (1991) has suggested that the medical charities and philanthropic public works accounted for a substantial part of late Victorian voluntary endeavour and has argued that any claim that charity provided considerably more in poor relief than the Poor Law must be treated with suspicion. Still, the early twentieth-century voluntary sector bulked exceedingly large in terms of social provision. The relationship between the voluntary and statutory sector changed significantly during the century as the balance within the mixed economy shifted in favour of the state. In the late twentieth century, the issue is whether that relationship is changing yet again and whether the voluntary sector is once again assuming a more prominent role.

The extent and nature of family and voluntary provision are crucial for our understanding of modern welfare states. Recent influential typologies of welfare states have tended to deal only with the state provision of welfare. For example, Esping-Andersen's (1990) categorisation of welfare regimes into the social democratic (Scandinavian), catholic/conservative (continental) and liberal (Anglo-Saxon) collapses when either the voluntary or family provision is considered. Kuhnle and Selle (1992) have observed that Denmark, Norway and Sweden have had very different patterns of voluntary organisation, and Leira (1992) has pointed out that while the Swedish state took increasing responsibility for childcare during the post-Second World War period, this was not the case in Norway. Informal and voluntary provision have been and are integral to the fabric of modern welfare states, but have been conceptualised differently over time and between different countries. In Britain, apart from the early and late twentieth century, when there has been a debate, informal provision has been assumed by government and Britain has never had the kind of explicit family policy, designed to bolster the family, as has France. There has nevertheless been an implicit family policy (Land and Parker, 1978) based on the assumption that 'the family' will care. In contrast, the role of the voluntary sector has always been the subject of debate, and in both Britain and the United States has been conceptualised as part of the fabric not just of social provision, but of modern liberal democracies.

Early Twentieth-century Voluntary Provision

There is a growing, mainly American literature, which seeks to explain the existence of voluntary organisations and the role they play in social provision. Economists argue that they are the result of state or market failure. For example, Hansmann (1987) has suggested that where information asymmetries exist, contract failure occurs. Contract mechanisms may fail to provide consumers with the adequate means to police producers, and where consumers cannot evaluate services and need protection by providers, non-profit organisations will appear more trustworthy. Weisbrod (1988) has stressed the extent to which the market or the state may fail to meet minority demands, which will then be met by voluntary organisations, but as the demand expands it will likely be met by the state. This kind of explanation tends to put the state, the market and the voluntary sector in separate boxes, such that the relationship between the state and the voluntary sector in particular becomes at best complementary and often conflictual. There is little room for the kind of conceptualisation of voluntary organisations as part and parcel of the fabric of the state that was the hallmark of turn of the century Britain and also seems to have characterised the Norwegian experience (Kuhnle and Selle, 1992). Harris (1990a, p. 67) has described the aim of Victorian governments as being 'to provide a framework of rules and guidelines designed to enable society very largely to run itself'. This did not amount to rank atomistic individualism: 'the corporate life of society was seen as expressed through voluntary associations and the local community, rather than through the persona of the state' (ibid.). Voluntary organisations were not, as Thane (1993, p. 358) has remarked, 'the fortuitous corollary of the limited state but (were) integral to the conceptualization of that state by its leaders'.

Salamon's (1987, 1990) theory of voluntary sector failure is more broadly in tune with the historical evidence. He has argued that voluntary organisations were perceived in most Western countries as the first line of defence, but their weaknesses – insufficiency, particularism, paternalism and amateurism –

rendered increasing cooperation with the state inevitable. The voluntary sector is so diverse and differs so greatly in its historical development between countries that it is highly unlikely that such single-discipline theories using a relatively small range of variables could be successfully applied to all cases. Salamon is right in stressing the error of compartmentalising voluntary, statutory and market provision. He prefers to look for the degree to which the boundaries between the sectors were in fact blurred. This is useful for the British case from the end of the nineteenth century, when the strict division between state provision, in the form of the Poor Law, and the market was significantly diminished, and when new forms of cooperation between the state and the voluntary sector, particularly in relation to government funding of voluntary organisations, became more common. But even this does not quite capture the complexity of the historical relationships, as Ware (1989) has recognised. Late nineteenth-century charity leaders advocated close cooperation with the Poor Law while at the same time insisting on a separate sphere for charity. The point is that both the conceptualisation and the nature of the early twentieth-century state were quite different from those of the late twentieth. Thus the meaning of a call for greater reliance on voluntary provision in the 1980s and 90s will be different from a similar set of convictions in the 1880s and 90s.

Social provision at the turn of the century was administered and financed at the local level. This meant that in many ways it was easier for a measure of welfare pluralism to exist. Certainly charity was exceedingly diverse. There were city missions; district visiting societies; mothers' meetings; a huge variety of provident clubs allowing working people to save for items such as the Christmas goose and boots, an expenditure which always posed a threat to the fragile family economy; and organisations to meet almost any conceivable human (and animal) need, whether medical, financial or for leisure. Mutual aid societies were extremely important in the years before the First World War. Friendly societies and trade unions, for example, employed 'club doctors' to attend to their members. Beveridge (1948) calculated that about 4.75 million were members of registered societies offering medical benefits in 1910. Green (1985) has suggested that as many again were members of unregistered societies and that 9 of the 12 million originally included in the National Health Insurance Scheme introduced in 1911 were thus already members of societies offering medical care. Older interpretations of the medical benefits offered by friendly societies tended to suggest that the societies protected their own funds first and their members' health and welfare second (for example Gilbert, 1966; Klein, 1973), but more detailed investigation has revealed the extensive rules governing the clubs' contracts with the doctors they employed and the power of lay committees to enforce them (Yeo, 1979; Green, 1985). It is not clear that the introduction of state health insurance in 1911 either greatly improved access to medical care – women and children were the largest group left unprovided for – or improved the quality of care.

In one crucial area of voluntary provision, that of 'personal social service', the voluntary sector was strongly linked to the family. This part of the voluntary sector was staffed predominantly by women and the work of personal social service was closely allied to their role as informal providers of welfare in the family. A substantial amount of charitable endeavour in the early part of the century centred on making sure that family members played their proper part in securing each other's welfare. Indeed, much of our knowledge of family provision during this early period is filtered through the writings of voluntary workers.

Personal Social Service[1] and the Family before the First World War

There was considerable concern about the willingness and capacity of the working-class family to provide for its members at the beginning of the century. Anxiety centred most strongly on the working-class husband and father's capacity to support his wife and children. In 1906, Helen Bosanquet, a leading member of the Charity Organisation Society (COS), clearly described the characteristics of the stable family. It required the firm authority of the father and the cooperative industry of all its members, the wife working at home and the husband wage-earning. Bosanquet made the connection between the stable family and the national importance of maintaining male work incentives particularly forcefully:

> Nothing but the combined rights and responsibilities for family life will ever rouse the average man to his full degree of efficiency and induce him to continue working after he has earned sufficient to meet his own personal needs.... The Family, in short, is from this point of view the only known way of ensuring with any approach to success that one generation will exert itself in the interests and for the sake of another. (Bosanquet, 1906, p. 222)

Concern about working-class mothers centred less on a fear of their unwillingness to perform their duties and more on their ignorance of them. Bosanquet believed that the stable family sheltered young and old in one strong bond of mutual helpfulness (making old-age pensions, then under discussion, superfluous), and rendered the development of 'a residuum' (an underclass) impossible, by training its young in the habits of labour and obedience. She made the point that families at both ends of the social scale failed to conform to this model of family life. However, much more concern was generally expressed about the working-class family, because it stood to become a public charge.

Major theorists of the place of charity at the turn of the century, including Loch, the general secretary of the COS; Bosanquet, academic philosopher and member of the COS; and Urwick, head of the COS's School of Sociology from 1903 and of the LSE's Department of Social Administration from 1912, as well as Bosanquet herself were anxious above all to promote the family as a provider of welfare and believed that state intervention could only undermine family, and in particular parental, responsibilities. The work of those involved in the huge number of voluntary organisations engaged in the practice of personal social service centred on eliciting the family's contribution to welfare.

Evidence of family failure was twofold: first, the physical welfare of children measured by indices such as the incidence of child neglect and the infant mortality rate, and second, the number of families seeking relief under the Poor Law. Men were suspected of laziness and unwillingness to shoulder the responsibility for providing for women and children. The economist Edgeworth quoted approvingly the comment that a social worker made in 1908 to the effect that 'if the husband got out of work, the only thing the wife should do is sit down and cry, because if she did anything else he would remain out of work' (Edgeworth, 1922, p. 453). Women were held responsible for the management of households and the welfare of children. Commentators at the turn of the century tended to show more sympathy for working-class wives, regarding them for the most part as well-meaning but ignorant and often oppressed by selfish husbands. In 1870 the first Married Women's Property Act was passed primarily in order to give working-class women control over any earnings they might make. It was felt that they merited this protection as 'the great educators of the working classes', and as chancellors of the domestic exchequer (Cmnd 441, Q. 1154). The fatalism of working-class mothers in respect of the health and welfare of their children was generally deplored by contemporary reformers and has been interpreted by some historians as indicating that women in the past did not love their children (for example Shorter, 1977). However, as Ross (1993, p. 167) has commented, working women's devotion to their children's health and welfare was at odds with their 'linguistic frugality'. The idea that babies did not necessarily 'come to stay' can be interpreted as part of the necessary process of distancing in a period of high infant mortality.

Voluntary Visiting

Personal social service was carried out by large numbers of charity organisation societies, and parish visitors, as well by more specialised workers, such as Octavia Hill's rent collectors. The major theorists of charity insisted that charity was not philanthropy; it was not merely a matter of the rich giving money to the poor. The goal of charity was rather the promotion of a sense of membership in society and the practice of charity was centred on the nature of the obligations attaching to that membership and the ways in which a particular individual could be enabled to participate as a citizen. The basic conditions of membership were that an individual must become socially efficient, that is self-sustaining, and morally competent. For Bernard Bosanquet, the behaviour of people within their families – whether they were capable of caring for and supporting each other – was the test of citizenship and an ethical state (Bosanquet, 1899). Furthermore, the fulfilment of citizenship obligations in an ethical state had to be voluntary, which was why charity and not the statutory authorities was accorded such importance. In the view of the COS, it was the task of charity to work alongside the Poor Law, with charity playing the leading role. Applicants for help that proved 'unhelpable' would be passed to the Poor Law authorities. Charity was thus conceptualised as a social principle. Its purpose was to create self-maintaining and participative citizens and the locus for its work was the family.

The practice of personal social work was believed to be the means of achieving the kind of social progress envisaged by the leaders of the charity organisation movement. Lasting reform could only be achieved by changing people. Social workers would work with individuals and their families to change their habits, build up their characters and give new purpose to their lives. Individual social work was above all a form of education and had the additional advantage that it sprang from the self-development of middle-class people to the point where they responded voluntarily to the noble impulse of fulfilling their obligations to their fellow citizens. The test of charity was the successful promotion of economically independent and fully participative citizens (Loch, 1923). Social work with individuals and families was the means of achieving this; no social advance was possible without individual improvement.

Personal social service was usually called 'friendly visiting' at the turn of the century. The term social work began to be used in the 1890s and tended to be used interchangeably with 'casework', indicating that personal social service had come to mean, in theory at least, the careful and sympathetic investigation of the applicant's case and the formulation of a plan of treatment. Friendly visitors were assigned families and told 'to befriend, aid and elevate' the people they visited (Charity Organisation Society, 1870). Hill, Bosanquet and later the Edwardian Guilds of Help did most to develop the idea of friendly visiting. Visitors were invariably female, reflecting a gendered division of labour within charity; committees were male dominated.

Volunteer visitors and early infant welfare clinics – 'schools for mothers' – focused on educating mothers rather than on providing treatment, which would have undermined the father's responsibility to provide for his family. Mothers were often also encouraged to participate in cookery demonstrations and become members of savings clubs. Women visitors were often untrained, something that Octavia Hill deplored, arguing that volunteer did not have to be synonymous with lack of training. It is likely that many rode roughshod over the cultural practices of poor families. In 1907, visitors were being advised that they should knock before entering a working-class home (Kanthack, 1907). Somerset Maugham's portrayal of home visiting in *Of Human Bondage*, published in 1915, might have been somewhat exaggerated, but it nevertheless captured the element of control that accompanied so much personal social service:

> the district visitor excited their bitter hatred. She went in without so much as a 'by your leave' or a 'with your leave'... she pushed her nose into corners, and if she didn't say the place was dirty you could see what she thought right enough. (Maugham, 1915, p. 560)

The first lesson for friendly visitors according to Octavia Hill was to befriend the poor, rather than to approach them as people in need of assistance. This immediately called the practice of mixing cash relief with visiting into question, because as Hill put it, 'doles darkened friendship' (Hill, 1877, p. 60). She warned that it was never easy to help a member of one's own family and that the difficulties would be greater still when dealing with strangers, but that it would help the visitor if she tried to deal with the poor as she would a family member. Too much help and the person needing assistance would become dependent, too little and he would lose hope. At the end of the day, the aim of the visitor was to bring about change in the households she visited. As Hill put it: 'my only notion of reform is that of living side by side with people, till all that one believes becomes clear to them' (Maurice, 1928, p. 211). This kind of voluntary social action was 'detailed' (American reformers called it the 'retail' method of social reform, as opposed to a 'wholesale' legislative approach) (Richmond, 1899), and it consisted of infinitesimally small actions designed to change the way in which the poor behaved. Hill insisted that good personal social service was not paternalistic; all people, rich and poor had to come to their own decisions as to what constituted right action. It could not be imposed from above. The visitor could not learn the true cause of a family's difficulty until she was prepared to care for that family, no easy task in the noisy, smelly courts of early twentieth-century London. With friendship came trust and then the visitor could be sure that the family was ready to listen. In her work of housing management, Hill believed that trust grew not just out of friendship, but out of the fulfilment of the mutual obligations of landlord and tenant, out of the business relationship. In friendly visiting, the visitor was supposed to gain the household's trust and then lead by example. But in the end the visitor was expected to try and get poor families to see the virtues of middle-class ways, values and culture. In Geoffrey Best's judgement, the poor were helped if they would submit (Best, 1964).

While it is unclear how far visitors followed Hill's instruction to treat poor families with the same courtesy and respect that they would show personal friends, the leaders of the charitable world of personal visiting did have a considerable sympathy with, and understanding of, the life styles of poor families, and particularly of the women in those families. Helen Bosanquet recognised the difficulty of budgeting on an irregular income and of avoiding the temptation of credit. She demonstrated a thorough knowledge of the options of borrowing, pawning and delaying payment and her estimate of the rates of interest involved – 24 per cent for pawnbrokers and up to 400 per cent of private money lenders – has been confirmed by historians (Tebbut, 1983). She understood how a housewife might use the pawnbroker as a way of equalizing income, and she appreciated the problems of cooking on an open fire, condemning the typical ignorance of the well-meaning philan-thropist of the limitations that this imposed on the choice of menus. There was in fact little to differentiate her understanding of working-class family life from that of the group of Fabian women who undertook an investigation of family life in Lambeth before the First World War (Pember Reeves, 1915); their differences lay in their interpretation of the proper role of the state, not in their diagnosis of working-class family life. Bosanquet was also sensitive to the difficulty of communication between middle-class social workers and the poor and the difficulty social workers would experience in knowing how their advice was being received and interpreted (McKibbin, 1978).

Helen and Bernard Bosanquet were convinced that the key to social change was character. Successful personal social service meant changing matters such that the poor were able to make more of their lives than they did before, in other words, so that their characters would be able to master their circum-stances (Bosanquet, 1901). The apparent inability of the poor to think ahead, to save for periods of sickness or unemployment, for example, was regularly cited as evidence of moral and intellectual disorganization and failing of char-acter. Helen Bosanquet compared five families she observed across the back garden of her East London house in the early 1890s (when she was serving as a district secretary of the COS before her marriage to Bernard Bosanquet). She noted that the children of number 4 lived in the same surroundings and had the opportunity to go to the same school and yet were in a much more distressed condition than their neighbours. she concluded that it was 'whole-some home atmosphere' that was wanting, clearly a case where the inculca-tion of good habits rather than money was what was needed (Dendy, 1895).

Bernard Bosanquet stressed that the focus on character did not mean attributing all blame for a person's position to that person and leaving him to his fate. That would have been the attitude of *laissez-faire* individualists, but those advocating the principle of 'true charity' were eager to provide the means to help those in need by strengthening their characters, which according to their analysis was where any problems lay, rather than in poverty or ill health *per se*. Helen Bosanquet felt that the 'poverty lines' set by social investigators like Booth and Seebhohm Rowntree had a 'false air of definiteness' about them (Bosanquet, 1903, p. 1). She could not accept Rowntree's conclusion that there was evidence of structural poverty in York due to low wages alone and quite independent of character. Bosanquet believed that the family was the primary institution in which character was developed and in which cooperative individuals and rational citizens were produced. In her last major book, *The Family* (1906), she argued that the Family (always capitalised) was the fundamental social unit. Its importance lay in the part it played in stimulating the interests of the individual. 'Natural' affection between husband and wife, and between parent and child ensured that homes became 'nurseries of citizenship' (Bosanquet, 1895, p. 10). In a manner remarkably like the structural functionalist theory of the 1950s, the family was seen as playing the crucial role in socializing the individual (Parsons and Bales, 1955).

Bosanquet anticipated the need for large numbers of volunteer social workers to help their fellow citizens who found themselves in distress: 'There is as it were, an army of social healers to be trained and organised' (Bosanquet, 1909, p. 115). The problem was that the army was not forthcoming, nor was the practice of social casework quite in line with the ideal. Hodson, a young woman settlement worker at the turn of the century, recorded her experiences visiting for the COS. She found the dirt and noise of the neighbourhood trying. She did not like visiting after dark and she also found it difficult to follow the principles she had been taught: 'The unfortunate part of it is, that I find it so very difficult to apply the theories of relief, as taught by the COS, to any of the practical cases I come across.' She agreed that most of her cases exhibited failures of character and that money was therefore not the answer. However, she was unsure as to how then to proceed, finding COS ideas 'interesting, generally convincing, but a little paralysing' (Hodson, 1909, p. 22).

Family and State

Leading opinion within the world of charity believed that there was little material aid that could be offered the family that would not damage family responsibility and subvert character. The most likely agent to intervene – by offering old-age pensions, or national insurance against sickness and unemployment – was the state. State intervention was condemned as likely to undermine character, whereas volunteers offering personal social service, suitably trained, would serve to strengthen character and deepen the ties of voluntary obligation within the community. Achieving social change by changing habits was acknowledged to be an inordinately slow business, but it was felt to be the only sure route to permanent improvement.

The COS took a particularly strong stand against one of the early measures of the reforming Liberal government of 1906–14, the 1906 Education

(Provision of Meals) Act. In a lecture delivered to the London COS in 1901, Bernard Bosanquet summarised the reasons why the Society felt it had to oppose free school meals:

> By a law of social development, then, the individual and the family under normal conditions have to maintain themselves by the exercise of personal energy and mutual aid; and only on these terms are they competent to render the best service to the community. It should therefore be the chief aim of social effort to help the individual to maintain himself throughout life, and to strengthen the sense of obligation and affection which is inherent in the family. All legislation or voluntary action that has a social purpose should be judged by this standard. It is right or wrong as it promotes or frustrates this aim. (Bosanquet, 1901)

Another COS member, Joseph Lee, described the Society's opposition to school meals as a crucial last stand: 'outlying territory we can abandon, but here our citadel is reached. If we cannot defend this wall we might as well surrender' (Lee, undated).

The COS was the most influential voluntary organisation offering personal social service at the beginning of the century. One of its members, Helen Bosanquet, was responsible for drafting the 1909 Majority Report of the Royal Commission on the Poor Laws (McBriar, 1987). However, by the second decade of the century its strongly held views as to first, the need to preserve separate spheres of action between the state and the voluntary sector, and second, its firm opposition to state intervention and commitment to voluntary action designed to bolster the family, were coming under attack from new personal service organisations (the guilds of help and councils of social welfare) and from a wide variety of social activists and academics. Urwick, who played a major part in developing the idea of charity as a social principle, was not disturbed by the idea of the state giving material aid to families in the form of school meals and medical inspection, or national insurance cover. He believed that this would enable the family to carry out its obligations regarding the proper socialization of children better. A substantial number of politicians were perturbed by the idea that the state might subvert family responsibility, but were convinced by arguments put forward from all points on the political spectrum that, in the words of Markham, a New Liberal and prominent anti-suffragist and social activist, it was 'increasingly difficult to accept the view that the great forces of the state are only to be at the service of the pauper, the lunatic, and the criminal' (Markham, 1911). Invoking the contemporary concern with national efficiency in the wake of the Boer War, Markham went on to voice a common concern: 'some of us feel that the State cannot for the sake of its own future tolerate a hungry child'. Barnett, the founder of the Toynbee Hall Settlement, also came to accept that there was a greater role for the state in meeting men's needs, which he defined as things that are 'good', but which men did not necessarily recognise to be such (for example education) (Barnett and Barnett, 1894), while Alfred Marshall, the neoclassical economist looked forward to the time when the Poor Law would be abolished and 'higher forms' of aid for the working classes would be introduced (Marshall, 1892).

The politicians were nonetheless cautious. In the case of school meals, parents were expected to contribute to the costs and the school attendance officer was usually given the task of assessing means. When school medical inspection was introduced in 1907, parents (usually mothers) were advised as to what was wrong with their children, but were not provided with access to treatment. National Health Insurance, introduced in 1911, covered only wage earners, not dependants, which meant that parents (fathers) were expected to exercise their obligation to maintain.

There was in fact no convincing evidence that parents were unwilling to shoulder their responsibilities, but as the social surveys of London and York by Booth and Rowntree showed, irregular income, low wages, unemployment and large families conspired to make it difficult for some 33 per cent of families to make ends meet. It is notable that the experience of mass unemployment followed by the disappearance of both un- and under-employment during the Second World War served significantly to moderate concern about the role of the working-class father. Considerable attention was given to the problem of 'rebuilding' the family by doctors and policy-makers during the late 1940s (for example Marchant, 1946), but the focus was on social dislocation as the primary cause of family failure rather than on the economic responsibility to maintain, and hence on the role of the mother rather than that of the father. In the main, commentators were more optimistic about the capacity and willingness of fathers to provide. The vast majority, it was believed, would cooperate with the new state welfare apparatus legislated by the Labour government of 1945–49 and designed to secure the health and welfare of the nation. A minority of 'problem families' were expected to need help to take advantage of the new services.

This analysis represented a significant shift in the diagnosis and treatment of social problems. First, the ideas of state intervention as 'enabling' rather than subverting family responsibility had triumphed. Second, while the best form of treatment of problem families was still believed to be by social casework performed by volunteers, the rationale had undergone subtle change. At the beginning of the century, influential leaders in the world of charity and government officials were concerned that the state should play only a residual role in the relief of poverty and the effort of charity was directed primarily towards making families self-sufficient by encouraging good work habits, good household management and childcare, and saving for periods of misfortune. By the late 1940s, the role of the state as the primary provider of welfare had been established and the main focus of attention was on the need for families to respond to the fabric of social provision erected for their support.

The Changing Role of the Voluntary Sector in Mid-century

There is little evidence that the early twentieth-century state deliberately set out to erode voluntarism. Nevertheless, as Beveridge (1948) recognised, compulsory social insurance sounded the death knell for mutual aid friendly societies, and Prochaska (1988) has suggested that the growth of government responsibility for welfare contributed to the devitalisation of Christian charity. Against these pessimistic views of the effect of state intervention on charity must be set the argument that it was not so much government activity as the development of market society that served to erode altruism (Ware, 1990). Insofar as the market expanded social relations beyond local communities and thus threatened the web of charitable relationships and autonomous organisations that had characterised the late Victorian state, this argument carries weight. And in an increasingly secular society, the moral imperative to altruistic behaviour retreated before the market's demand that individuals be self-interested.

Government intervention measured by public expenditure continued to grow rapidly during the interwar years and the relationship between the state and voluntary sector also changed. Prochaska (1988) has emphasised the extent to which voluntary agencies retained their autonomy during the inter-war years, but contemporaries stressed the financial difficulties of many voluntary organisations (not least the well-known problems of the voluntary hospitals) and state subsidy to the voluntary sector increased. It was part of the re-thinking of the relationship between the sectors that many people no longer viewed financial dependence on the state as problematic. Relations between the state and voluntarism became more blurred during the inter-war years. Llewellyn Smith, statistician and civil servant, spoke in 1937 of a 'borderland' rather than a borderline existing between them. Constance Braithwaite, who owned that she was trying to reconcile her faith in philanthropy with her commitment to socialism, came out in favour of a national minimum: 'my conclusion is that the relief of poverty should be the responsibility of the State and not of charity, but that charitable relief will and should continue as long as poverty exists which is not adequately relieved by the state' (Braithwaite, 1938, p. 16). This left voluntary organisations, in her view, with a supplementary, experimental or pioneering role.

Elizabeth Macadam took a similar view in her influential analysis of the 'new philanthropy' published in 1934, in which she called for closer cooperation between the state and voluntary organisations. She welcomed the Webbs' idea of the 'extension ladder' as a prescription for voluntary/statutory relations, which they first put forward as part of the political campaign to break up the Poor Law, following the 1909 Royal Commission Report. In other words, voluntary organisations would influence and supplement public services, but no longer aim to be the first line of defence for social service as the Bosanquets and Loch had wanted. Simey, a lecturer in public administration at Liverpool University, followed Macadam's lead in seeing nothing beyond a supplementary role for the voluntary sector. But these were only prescriptions for voluntary action. They were not accurate descriptions of the pattern of voluntary activity, which was rather unpredictable. For example, Fox (1993) has shown how the voluntary sector retained monopoly control of district nursing until as late as 1948, and Thomson (1992) has shown how voluntary organisations ceded control of mental institutions in 1913, but kept hold of care in the community.

Beveridge was a firm believer in voluntary action and harked back strongly to the turn of the century insistence on the importance of the 'spirit of service'; the good society could only be built on people's sense of duty and willingness to serve (Beveridge, 1948, p. 151). He intended state provision as a national minimum, which left plenty of room for social provision above that minimum. In particular, he believed that many things could not be accomplished simply by the redistribution of resources. Money was not everything and there was a need for services 'which often cannot be bought with money, but may be rendered from a sense of duty' (ibid., p. 320). Beveridge had a clear picture of voluntary organisations as autonomous and driven by social conscience. Indeed, Beveridge saw voluntary action as an important counterweight to the business motive and, like many others, as a fundamental ingredient of modern democracy. Voluntary organisations provided the opportunity for free association and participation, as well as variety and spontaneity (Lindsay, 1945). Later still, Crossman (1976) came to the view that voluntary action was to be valued for its idealism and had a role to play in humanising state bureaucracies.

However, voluntary organisations were still perceived as supplementary, or at best complementary, to the state and the desirability of direct provision by the state was not questioned. Indeed, during the period of the classic welfare state in the three decades following the Second World War, the relationship between economic growth and state social provision was believed to be positive. An organisation like the COS accepted the postwar welfare legislation; in 1946 it changed its name to the Family Welfare Association. In 1941 it sponsored a conference in Oxford to discuss social reconstruction. Participants made it clear that they saw a major role for voluntary organisations in the postwar world in helping 'misfits'. If the 'welfare state' would look after the 'ordinarily unfortunate', then voluntary action would help those who fell through the welfare net. Beveridge certainly approved of this kind of thinking. When he addressed the COS's general meeting in 1943, he told his audience that what the state provided had to be the same for all citizens, but there would always be scope for providing individual care for those who needed something more or different.

Thus by mid-century the relationship between the voluntary and the statutory sectors had changed significantly from a partnership that was conceptualised in terms of separate spheres of interest, to one in which the voluntary sector took note of what the state provided and undertook to supplement and complement it, often in return for state financing.

The Discovery of Carers

The tendency of functional sociology in the 1950s was to stress the way in which the family had ceded 'functions', such as educating children and caring for elderly people, to the state. However, Anderson (1977) showed that about the same percentage of elderly people were in institutional care at the beginning of the century as at the end. Nevertheless, the 1981 census showed almost one-third of elderly people to be living alone, 45 per cent of elderly women and 17 per cent of elderly men. But, as Willmott (1986) pointed out, when the proportion of elderly people with children living nearby and providing informal care was considered, as many were probably in receipt of informal care, usually at the hands of a female relative, as a generation earlier.

The discovery of carers and the unpaid work of caring for young and old was in large part the product of feminist research during the late 1970s and early 1980s. Oakley's (1974) pioneering research on housework as a form of unpaid work was followed by extensive analysis of caring. In 1982 the Equal Opportunities Commission (EOC) estimated that there were 1.25 million female carers in Britain, while the 1984 Women and Employment Survey found that 13 per cent of all women and more than 20 per cent of women aged 40 or over had caring responsibilities for sick or elderly dependants (Martin and Roberts, 1984). It was not until the late 1980s that analysis of the General Household Survey revealed the importance of spousal care and the fact that a significant minority of carers were husbands (Arber *et al.*, 1986). Of the large majority of female carers, some 45 per cent were shown to be spouses and 35 per cent daughters. Qureshi and Walker's (1988) research showed the existence of a perceived hierarchy of preferred carers, with a daughter the firm favourite in the absence of a spouse. The publicity accorded demographic change, whereby the number of people aged over 75 – the age group commonly agreed to be in need of most care – was shown to have increased by 20 per cent between 1971 and 1981 and was projected to rise by 30 per cent by the year 2001 (Ermisch, 1983), also drew attention to the issue of social care. In addition, during the 1980s, the National Council for Carers and their Elderly Dependants and the Association of Carers worked successfully to put caring on the political agenda.

Caring by women in families was not new to the last quarter of the twentieth century. It merely achieved new visibility in respect of both children and elderly people. In the years following the Second World War, doctors and psychologists (especially Bowlby, 1951) stressed the importance of the mother/child relationship as the key to the healthy development of the child, with maternal 'adequacy' as the most important variable. The main focus of anxiety thus switched from the working-class husband to the working-class wife and mother. Married women's work outside the home was strongly condemned. Winnicott told his radio listeners that 'talk about women not wanting to be housewives seems to me just nonsense because nowhere else but in her own home is a woman in such command' (Winnicott, 1957, p. 88). Natural motherhood meant full-time motherhood. Anything less was believed to risk adding to the population of juvenile delinquents. Childcare was thus assumed to be the private responsibility of women within the family and as such remained invisible. However as much larger numbers of married women entered the labour market, albeit usually in part-time jobs, childcare provision became a policy issue. It has remained a matter for public debate during the last quarter of a century, but government has maintained a position of 'neutrality', meaning that whether or not women go out to work and how they solve their childcare problems if they do so is a matter for them alone. This contrasts with the policies in some other European countries, such as France, where government sees it as a state responsibility to try and reconcile family and working life. The result of British policy is one of the lowest levels of public childcare provision in Europe.

Caring for elderly people also became a more visible social issue in the last 25 years. Most of the daughters caring for elderly relatives before the 1970s had been single women living at home; it was very difficult for such women to obtain mortgages in their own names until the late 1970s. These women were assumed to be the 'natural' carers of elderly parents and again, their work remained largely invisible. In their study of the slow development of home care services, Means and Smith (1985) cited examples of geriatricians and politicians in the 1950s who expressed the belief that it was part of women's normal role and duty to care for the elderly. Similarly, in acclaiming the family bonds revealed by his study of family in London's East End, Townsend (1957) concluded that people with families, especially daughters, made few claims on the state and that it would therefore be counterproductive 'if the state, through housing and other policies, separated individuals from their kin and thus made more professional services necessary'. But in 1976, Moroney drew attention to the high rate of marriage and the dwindling number of single women (Moroney, 1976). The ratio of single middle-aged women declined from 160 per 1000 elderly people in 1911 to 50 per 1000 in 1971. In addition, given women's much higher labour market participation rate, caring often entailed considerable financial sacrifice (Nissel and Bonnerjea, 1982). The invalid care allowance was introduced in 1975 as a benefit designed to compensate carers who gave up paid employment to care. Feminists drew attention to the nature of caring: to the fact that it involved more than tending, amounting to both labour and love (Graham, 1983). As Land and Rose (1985) observed, the injunction for women to care is so strong that it is very hard to know where the love ends and the compulsory altruism begins. The attention drawn to the numbers of women caring, to the fact that this was largely unpaid work, to the amount of money such work saved the state, and to the increasing numbers of elderly people needing informal care made the women's work of caring for elderly dependants a policy issue.

However, it was a strong plank of Conservative policy beginning in the early 1980s that the family should play a larger role in social provision. Ferdinand Mount, Mrs Thatcher's family policy adviser in the early 1980s wrote of the family's 'permanent revolution against the state' (Mount, 1983). He condemned the erosion of parental responsibility in terms not unlike those of early twentieth-century commentators and argued that the social workers, health visitors and similar officials employed by the state were guilty of unwarranted interference; the family would do best if left alone. The 1981 Government White Paper, *Growing Older*, clearly stated government's increasing concern to limit the obligations of the state in respect of the elderly:

> Whatever level of public expenditure proves practicable, and however it is distrib-
> uted, the primary sources of support and care for elderly people are informal and
> voluntary. These spring from the personal ties of kinship, friendship and neigh-
> bourhood. They are irreplaceable. It is the role of public authorities to sustain and,
> where necessary, develop – but never to displace - such support and care. Care *in*
> the community must increasingly mean care *by* the community. (Cmnd 8173, 1981)

The document argued that families were best placed to understand and meet the wide variety of personal needs of the elderly person and admitted that this 'may often involve considerable personal sacrifice, particularly where the 'family' is one person, often a single woman caring for an elderly relative'. Unlike the literature of the 1950s and 60s, the burden falling on women was recognised, but women were also effectively being told that they had no alternative but to shoulder it. Such a strategy rested in large part on the idea that there were untapped sources of informal care which can be called into play to attend to the needs of an increasing population of old and very old people (Walker, 1986). However, the typical woman carer is married and middle-aged, someone Brody (1981) has called the 'woman in the middle'. From 1950 through to the early 1970s such a woman was likely to have left the workforce to care for children and was also available to care for elderly dependants, however in the late twentieth century such a woman is most likely to be in the workforce. Nevertheless, a 1980s study of community-based services showed that family care was likely to be treated as an alternative to state provision; where there was a daughter available to care the level of services, such as home helps and meals on wheels, was lowest (Arber *et al.*, 1986).

From Supplementary and Complementary to Alternative Provider: the Voluntary Sector in the Late Twentieth Century

Beginning in the 1960s, the voluntary sector underwent rapid transformation with a new generation of volunteers setting up self-help and new campaigning bodies, such as Gingerbread, Child Poverty Action Group (CPAG) and Shelter, as well as feeding a massive expansion of organisations such as Oxfam (Deakin, 1995). The Seebohm Committee's report on the personal social services recognised the importance of the pioneer and 'watchdog' role of voluntary organisations and encouraged local authorities to include volunteers in their plans, albeit in a supplementary role. During the 1970s the sector became increasingly confident with the setting up of the Volunteer Centre (as a result of a recommendation by the Aves Committee set up to review the role of the volunteer in the social services) and the new coordinating body, the Voluntary Services Unit within the Home Office. Standards of training also rose significantly within voluntary organisations. By the end of the 1970s some commentators were prepared to argue for 'welfare pluralism', lauding the merits of the voluntary sector in comparison to the rigid bureaucracy of state welfare (Gladstone, 1979; Hadley and Hatch, 1981). These writers envisaged welfare pluralism more as self-help and community development, building welfare provision from the bottom up with greater community participation. It had little in common with the 1979 Conservative government's determination to treat the family and the voluntary sector (and the market) as alternative providers to the state, something which represented a major change in the nature of the voluntary/statutory partnership.

During the 1980s, government sought to promote the voluntary sector by giving tax concessions and introducing payroll giving in 1987. However the financial results for the sector were disappointing. Expansion of the sector was largely due to the massive use by voluntary organisations of the Manpower Services Commission's community programme, whereby the unemployed were offered work (Addy and Scott, 1988). The closure of the programme in 1988 struck a severe blow to the finances of many voluntary agencies. At the end of the 1980s, government took steps actively to promote the new mixed economy of care by introducing market principles into social care services. The new policy of community care sought to turn local authorities into 'enablers', who would purchase more than they provided and so promote a more mixed economy of care, which in turn was seen as central to achieving greater choice for users as well as services that are of higher quality and more cost effective. Both the Association of Metropolitan Authorities (1990) and the National Council for Voluntary Organisations (1990) resisted any move toward contracting to provide services on the basis of price-based competition, and in 1991 the government guidance acknowledged that one of the chief strengths of the statutory/voluntary relationship was the closeness of contact between them and concluded that the new relationship was best conceived of as 'being a contract culture involving close ongoing relationships with providers, rather than being based upon anonymous short-term price competition' (DoH and Price Waterhouse, 1991, p. 11).

However, the idea that voluntary organisations will agree a plan of service provision and also agree to become providers under service agreements or contracts represents a major shift in the understanding of the voluntary/statutory partnership. First there is the question as to how far voluntary organisations are prepared to see themselves as primarily service providers. Second, even for those with a long history of service provision, albeit often as only one element of their work, partnership has previously been understood in terms of complementarity or supplementarity (Kramer, 1990). As Saxon Harrold (1990) has pointed out, recent trends mean that voluntary organisations are being asked to fill the gaps left by the withdrawal of state provision, which is tending to transform voluntary organisations into alternative providers. Contracting also represents a major change in funding patterns. The grant aid that so many voluntary agencies came substantially to depend on during the twentieth century was never unconditional, but the profiles of many organisations were mixed in terms of service provision, information and advice activities, and campaigning. Grants often supported all these as well as core administrative work. In contrast, contracts are for specific services and the campaigning and administrative work of organisations may not be covered by them.

Running a contract has proved significantly different from administering a grant. The process of formalisation that is involved may encourage greater clarity, but also serves to increase the bureaucratic aspects of the organisation, which may in turn militate against flexibility and responsiveness, the commonly agreed strengths of the voluntary sector. Working to a contract may provide more stability of funding for voluntary organisations, but also may raise difficulties in regard to (i) the relationship between paid and unpaid staff as 'professional' standards of assessment, management and evaluation are imposed by contracts, (ii) governance, as the pace of change increases and executive members become more remote from the kinds of changes that officers perceive as necessary, and (iii) goals, as more of the organisation's efforts are directed towards the kind of services that the purchaser wishes to buy (Lewis, 1993, 1994).

Futures

Both the informal and the voluntary sectors have been lauded by government in the policy documents of the last 15 years for the more flexible and responsive care that they can provide for vulnerable people. In the case of informal carers of elderly dependants in particular, their work has achieved much greater visibility. The 1989 White Paper, *Caring for People* (Cm 849, 1989), which preceded the 1990 NHS and Community Care Act, listed support for informal carers as its second priority. However, in a climate where the pressure on resources continues to grow alongside an expanding needs, there is little evidence in the 1990s of more help being offered to carers. Many local authorities have made genuine attempts to assess the needs of carers as well as those of the people cared for, but it is not uncommon for there to be conflict between the two groups. The flexibility of informal care means in practice the way in which it is responsive to the needs of the dependant. But in everyday terms, such responsiveness often translates into a number of caring routines that are remarkably inflexible for the carer. Different carers want different kinds and combinations of help: some want institutionally provided respite care every few weeks or every few months, while some want domiciliary care overnight or for a couple of hours each day. Meeting these requirements has been shown to be crucial in preventing carer stress and breakdown (Levin *et al.*, 1983). However, first, dependants are not always sympathetic to help for carers and, for example, resist going into respite care, and second, such individually negotiated packages of care can prove very expensive, as local authorities are beginning to find. With limited resources, local authorities have had to draw the eligibility criteria for services tighter and tighter, with the result that need has come to be defined in terms of high risk and high dependency. Dependants who have a carer present are less likely to be so defined and therefore less likely to receive service. This has always been the case and despite promises in the 1989 White Paper to the contrary, is likely to remain so for the foreseeable future. In the case of childcare, government has only in 1998 taken responsibility for formulating a national childcare strategy.

The family has always been the major provider of welfare and there is no prospect of this changing, although the effects of profound family change in terms of high divorce rates and the increasing number of lone parent families are as yet unknown. If the family and primarily women within it are to continue to care, how to value caring is likely to become a bigger issue. Two ways of valuing care have emerged in the last two decades: payment by the state for care, and individual rights under the social security system to caring benefits. Pay rates in the case of the former tend to be extremely low and employment conditions poor or non-existent (Glendinning and McLaughlin, 1993; Evers *et al.*, 1994). The latter are potentially radical, involving as they do, the recognition of claims based on caring. However, the basis of such benefits may not in fact be so clear cut. For example, the British invalid care allowance was introduced in recognition of the impact of caring on paid work, it was therefore conceived of as a compensation for income foregone rather than as a wage for caring. The eligibility criteria for the benefit are also linked to the receipt or non-receipt of other benefits by the person being cared for, which, as Lister (1995) has pointed out, also means that it is not an independent citizenship benefit. Substantial numbers of women want to care and the issue of valuing their work is a major factor in allowing them to make this choice. But it is equally true that substantial numbers would want to choose not to care, in which case good quality domiciliary and institutional care must be available. The tendency on the part of government and the firm conviction on the part of some academics (for example Booth, 1985) to condemn institutional provision has increased the pressures on women to care.

The invitation extended by the Conservative governments of the 1980s and 90s to voluntary organisations to play a larger role seemed initially more auspicious. The American literature stressed that the move to contracting offered voluntary agencies the opportunity to become partners rather than supplicants (for example Kramer, 1993). To some it seemed as though voluntary organisations might emerge once more as the provider of first resort. However, the nature of the voluntary/statutory partnership in the late twentieth century is quite different from that at the beginning of the century, and for agencies that are funded largely by government, it is difficult to see how the balance of power can ever rest with the voluntary organisation. In addition, in the new world of enabling, voluntary organisations can expect to face increased competition from private agencies. Contracts tend to assume that the contractor is the same form of organisation as the purchaser and do not make allowance for different forms of management. Taylor and Hoggett (1993) have considered the potential for remaking contractors in the image of the purchaser. If indeed the historical role of the voluntary sector is to undergo profound change, such that it ceases to be either complementary or supplementary to the statutory sector and becomes instead an alternative provider, then the implications for mission, management and governance are huge. Salamon (1987) suggested that the voluntary and statutory sectors are complementary in terms of their strengths and weaknesses, making collaboration sensible, but quasi-market relationships are not inherently sympathetic to a collaborative form of partnership.

Billis (1993) has warned of the dangers of an instrumental use of the voluntary sector which emphasises only those attributes that are of direct use to government. The process of contracting, which carries with it the idea of formalising arrangements between the parties and of producing a uniform, high-quality service, highlights both the tensions inherent in the relationship between the statutory and voluntary sectors and the ambiguities inherent in the nature of voluntary organisations. Billis (1989) has argued that, while voluntary organisations are primarily associational, they overlap both the personal and bureaucratic worlds. The management of the ambiguity requires an understanding of the ground rules of both the associational and bureaucratic worlds, an appreciation of membership, mission, informality and democracy, on the one hand, and managerial authority and accountability, levels of decision making, career progression, staff development, conditions of service and explicitly policy-making, on the other. Voluntary organisations balance the demands of bureaucracy and association. It may be suggested that contracting will tend to shift the balance towards the former. Certainly, Knight's (1993) report on voluntary action, in which he pushed enabling to its logical conclusion and advocated dividing voluntary organisations into autonomous campaigners, on the one hand, and a 'third sector' of contracting, not-for-profit services providers, on the other, rode roughshod over the participatory and associational nature of voluntary agencies, the very attributes that made postwar commentators see them as crucial to the fabric of a liberal democratic society. The new basis for partnership may be firmer insofar as voluntary organisations may come to adopt more bureaucratic features, but this also implies a significant change in the nature of voluntary organisations, which may not be cost free.

12

Commercial and Occupational Welfare

Margaret May and Edward Brunsdon

Private Welfare: A Kaleidoscope of Traded Care

As previous chapters show, the restructuring of state welfare in recent decades has inspired an extensive reappraisal of traditional accounts of British welfare provision. While, however, there has been renewed interest in informal and voluntary care, the production and consumption of private welfare has attracted little historical interest and is still framed by the concerns of postwar analysts. Whether in the hands of its neo-liberal advocates or their Fabian and Marxist critics it has been presented as an undifferentiated entity, conceived in terms of either the assumed economic calculations of providers (the so-called 'for-profit' sector) or price-theory mechanisms (as a representation of 'the market' or 'market welfare'). While rhetorically effective this essentialism has tended to mask the disparate arrangements and processes that constitute the trading of welfare (Hindess, 1987; Papadakis and Taylor-Gooby, 1987). It has also led to a skewed focus on services displaced by the state and the neglect of those that continued to be privately purchased and produced.

To avoid such distortions, it is imperative that private welfare markets are recognised in their multifarious forms, effectively as a kaleidoscope of traded care. They vary not only in the products sold, but in size, structure, consumers, producers, suppliers, degrees of competition, modes of regulation and forms of state intervention (Brunsdon, 1997). Some markets deal in financial products designed to provide 'cover' against life-cycle 'risks', others involve the direct sale of services and benefits. Trading may be highly localised, national or supranational; it can involve small firms or be dominated by large conglomerates. It may involve different mixes of proprietary and provident businesses and a range of intermediary agencies. Consumption too can vary within and across different welfare markets. It may involve individuals buying for their own immediate or future use, or 'proxy' purchasers

271

such as relatives, unions, professional associations and, most significantly, employers procuring services for other current or potential 'end-users'.[1]

The sheer diversity of these trading arrangements presents considerable difficulties in generating a comprehensive picture. Nonetheless, it is the case that commercial and employer-sponsored provision have been significant features of people's lives for much of this century and without an understanding of these forms of traded care it is difficult to comprehend either past or current welfare arrangements. Our aim in this chapter is to explore the changing nature of private welfare over the century and the factors influencing its varied developments. While some markets experienced continuous growth, others fluctuated or declined. To capture their uneven fortunes, we have necessarily adopted a general approach in which we adumbrate the main shifts in commercial welfare before focusing on a central feature of many markets – employer-sponsored provision.[2] We conclude with an overview of the changing pattern of private welfare and possible future trends.

Commercial Welfare Markets *circa* 1900–14

At the beginning of the century, few of the embryonic state services were free, let alone universal. Self-provisioning against life-cycle contingencies and the insecurities of a still-industrialising society formed a significant element of consumer spending and, for many Edwardians an unquestioned social fundament. A plethora of organisations had emerged to meet these needs; some operated nationally, but most functioned on a small-scale, local, basis. The nature and extent of commercial activity is consequently not easy to map. It is clear however that a wide range of options geared to different risks and incomes was available.

For consumers the most visible and crucial welfare markets were in housing. Construction, subject only to minimum regulation, was dominated by small firms building on land secured mainly from aristocratic or wealthy middle-class owners. Though some 10 per cent of UK tenures were owner occupied, most accommodation was privately rented (Balchin, 1995). Landlords typically owned only a few properties, purchased on mortgages with a view to securing immediate income and funding for their retirement and survivors (Stevenson, 1984). Rents, whether for suburban dwellings, inner-city tenements or lodgings, were governed by local conditions and, for consumers, constituted the major and unavoidable form of welfare expenditure.

While housing was predominantly commercial, the education markets functioned with a greater mix of suppliers. Elementary schooling had been free since 1891, but a network of fee-charging establishments still catered for upper- and middle-class children. State secondary education, established in 1902, was fee based. Despite the 1907 free place scheme, it remained the preserve of the middle and upper classes, whose status sensitivities were also catered for by local proprietary establishments, grammar schools and the nationally recognised public schools. Post-school provision also had to be bought and the charges for university and college tuition, professional traineeships and apprenticeships again made for a narrow range of purchasers.

For the majority of families, purchasing health care took precedence over education. Primary health care services – general practice, dental, ophthalmic and home nursing services (including midwifery) – were organised on a fee-for-service-basis. Hospital-based care, supplied primarily by the Poor Law infirmaries and voluntary hospitals, was also subject to charges. Given the stigma and low standards associated with the former, patient preferences lay with the voluntary providers, leaving elder care, chronic illness and mental health problems to the workhouse hospitals. Despite their charitable origins financial difficulties meant that many voluntary institutions by the 1900s operated means-tested charging schemes which excluded only the poorest (Abel-Smith, 1964). Patients could in addition purchase services directly from the consultants who, while working under honorary arrangements for the voluntary hospitals, ran parallel private practices. Poor Law care too was conditional on a test of destitution; the authorities had an obligation to charge for treatment, with husbands liable for wives and parents for children.

Prevailing morbidity rates meant that few households avoided medical costs. These were either met directly or through an array of insurance, loan and instalment schemes.[3] The most extensive cover was offered by friendly societies. Regulated under the Friendly Society Acts of 1876 and 1896, they insured contributing members for various 'non-trade benefits', most commonly: sick pay, medical expenses (including 'lying-in benefits' for members' wives), funeral costs and bereavement. Many also hired medical officers or GPs to check claims, assess the health status of prospective members and dispense treatment. Of the various types of society, the accumulating societies potentially offered the fullest protection, building up contributions in interest-earning reserve funds to cover both sick pay and medical costs. The largest ran nationwide postal schemes, attracting in the case of the Hearts of Oak some 303,000 members by 1910. The premiums levied by accumulating societies, however, confined membership, and the claimant risk, to the most secure occupational groups – primarily males in clerical and skilled manual work.

A second tier of friendly society schemes offered less extensive coverage for the lower waged in the form of specified medical services without sick pay. Many were highly localised, often unregistered, and operated as 'dividing societies', returning any end of year surpluses. Contributions and benefits varied with local conditions, but like the friendly society movement generally, membership was primarily male, occupationally based and involved extensive social commitments. While serving many purposes (Gosden, 1961; Yeo,

1979; Hopkins, 1995) this fraternalism also provided a safeguard against the risks inherent in insurance schemes.

The complexity of provision combined with the limitations of contemporary data make accurate estimates of the numbers protected (or claiming) problematic. Johnson (1985, 1996) provides an indicative figure when he suggests that by 1911 societies providing sick pay and a full range of medical benefits covered some 40 per cent of adult males in England and Wales. By then however many of the societies were in financial difficulties. While actuarial and administrative problems and irregular employment patterns were contributory factors, the main cause seems to have been the cost of supporting an ageing membership claiming extended sick pay. These factors go some way to explaining the reluctance of proprietary insurance carriers to enter the permanent health and medical insurance market. Similar concerns also influenced their decision not to enter the unemployment insurance market which was largely left to the better placed craft unions who developed schemes for some 10 per cent of the workforce (Harris, 1972). Short-term insurance for medical attendance or specified expenses presented less of a problem and advertisements in the local press of the time testify to the popularity of this form of commercial protection. There were some national carriers supplying this service (such as the National Medical Aid Company), but the majority of enterprises were local medical aid organisations, often run by doctors themselves. While the scale and financial stability of such undertakings remains unclear, it is apparent that they, along with the friendly societies, catered for a wide-ranging demand. By 1913 about half of Britain's twenty thousand GPs were engaged in contract practice (Honigsbaum, 1979), while upwards of 60 per cent of the British population were buying some form of medical cover and often also paying direct charges (Johnson, 1996).

Whether operating locally or nationally, suppliers of health and medical insurance competed for trade with those selling other products. Of these, the most critical for consumers were benefits for old age and survivors.

Although often seen exclusively in terms of pensions (Judge, 1984), protection against loss of earnings or the death of the main breadwinner was more frequently sought in other ways, most notably through life insurance. This was one of the first welfare products to gain tax relief and, by the 1900s, was a well-established form of social security offering both a type of survivor's benefit and, through endowment and investment arrangements, provision for old age.[4] It was also more concentrated and subject to a greater degree of state and self-regulation than other welfare products. The grounds for greater regulation have typically been explained in terms of the 'nature of life insurance itself' (Supple, 1984). Unlike other transactions, payment was (and is) prospective, long term, and dependent on the investment skills of the seller. While sales practices were the industry's responsibility, a series of measures stemming from the 1870 Life Assurances Companies Act gave policy holders and investors some protection against insolvency by requiring Life offices to retain minimum deposits and make returns to the Board of Trade.

Two types of cover were traded: 'ordinary life insurance' and 'industrial assurance'. The first was targeted at the industrial and professional middle classes and offered a lump sum on death to cover the needs of dependants. Consumers could also purchase endowment and with-profits policies. These became particularly attractive to the small but growing number of taxpayers following the budgets of 1889, 1907 and 1909. Sales of with-profits policies, for example, rose from 20 per cent to 38 per cent of the life market between 1900 and 1916 (Butt, 1984). For those on lower incomes, industrial assurance provided cheaper, albeit more limited, protection. Originally devised to meet the immediate expenses of bereavement, it was typically collected by commission-paid agents on a house-to-house basis. Both 'direct' and 'indirect' cover could be purchased to pay for the funeral and the costs of mourning. Given the status-driven ceremonies associated with bereavement, the costs could be considerable, particularly for lower income groups who faced the highest mortality rates. But with the ignominy of a pauper's funeral as the only alternative, private provision was a necessity (Rowntree, 1901). By 1911 some 42 million policies were in force offering near universal coverage (*Hansard*, May, 1911, XXV c. 609).

Both proprietary companies and the collecting friendly societies competed for this market. Despite their mutual status, the latter were not bound by the associative governance of less centralised societies and operated along the same lines as their proprietary rivals. The acknowledged market leader, with over half the industrial assurance policies in force was the Prudential. As the largest holder of Bank of England, railway and local government stocks and a key player in property and overseas development, it was also well placed politically, combining with other assurers, to sponsor a highly effective parliamentary lobby. Its power was clearly demonstrated when the Liberal government attempted to tighten sales practices and the operation of the agent system.

Given the unpredictability of working-class life, the agent system was seen as essential to maintaining payment and by 1911 over 100,000 agents were engaged in collecting the weekly premiums (Gilbert, 1966). With high returns dependent on multiple purchases and sales of new policies rather than renewals or extensions, it had, however, also aroused considerable criticism. This focused particularly on the prevalence of multiple purchases. Unlike life insurance, which was confined to an individual or spouse, burial insurance had long been offered for other close kin, especially children, enabling several family members to take out policies on a particular relative. To prevent potential abuse, the categories of 'acceptable' relatives were restricted by the 1909 Assurance Companies Act. Influenced by the industry, however, the government allowed some 10 million pre-existing policies to be given retrospective validation.

Burial-related insurance remained the core business of both mutual and proprietary assurers. With falling mortality rates however (especially among children), assurers had by 1914 expanded their business remit to encompass protection through endowments and bonus payments for old age and other needs. This growth occurred in tandem with contractual savings for other life-cycle risks to a point where it became accepted practice for working-class as well as middle-class people (Johnson, 1985). Coverage, though extensive, varied however and depended on actuarially based assessments. Constructed around the responsibilities of male wage earners, it was calibrated to accommodate income and status differentials between the two main social classes and within the working class. Like housing, health, social care and education it was also heavily stratified by gender. Life and industrial assurance premiums varied with age, health status and predicted mortality rates to the benefit of upper social groups, who also gained most from tax relief. Ill-health protection was similarly governed by risk-management and actuarial considerations. As previously indicated, underwriting sick pay was left to the friendly societies and largely confined to clerical and skilled workers. Medical attendance, the cheapest to insure, and most prevalent, was based on localised provider enterprises. Some schemes offered additional benefits or medical care for dependants, but few offered protection for non-workers. Working women generally were poorly covered (Thane, 1984). Regional differences added to these disparities as did the ephemeral life of the many small insurance businesses trading in the poorest areas.

With less than half the workforce adequately protected against the effects of illness and only 10 per cent insured against unemployment, the gaps in social protection as in housing, education and health care were all too visible to Edwardian social reformers. Yet for many contemporaries the foundations of effective commercial welfare had been laid, offering purchasers of different means a range of services from proprietary and mutual agencies. Between them, these vendors met the needs of substantial numbers of the population and were a vital economic resource, helping to sustain overseas investment and the City's role in world capital markets. They had come to share similar operating considerations and to uphold corresponding values. Pre-eminent among these were a commitment to voluntarism, thrift and familial responsibilities, in sum to the self-reliance widely accepted as the basis of social order in Edwardian society. In this context, the Liberal reforms of 1906–1911 can be seen as plugging gaps in market provision and securing the City's private insurance base. With state welfare designed as a 'lifeboat' for specific sections of the population, self-provisioning remained essential for those excluded from its ambit as did 'topping up' for those within it.

Commercial Welfare 1911–45

For most households the Liberals parallel expansion of statutory and private welfare was clearest in the health insurance and health care markets. Although the 1911 National Insurance Act introduced sickness/incapacity benefit and free GP services (under the 'panel system'), this was confined to workers earning less than £160.[5] Apart from a lump-sum maternity payment to an insuree's wife, dependants were not included. Moreover dental, optical and hospital treatment remained an individual responsibility. Public hospitals, under local authority control from 1929, still operated means-tested charges as did the voluntary hospitals. The latter's continuing financial problems also led them to introduce pay beds and encourage private practice. By the late 1930s the majority of their patients were fee paying and patients' payments accounted for over half of voluntary hospital income (Pinker, 1966; Cherry 1996). Patient fees also accounted for over half of GPs income (Chandra and Kakabadse, 1985).

With only 42 per cent of the population covered by the state scheme (Ministry of Health, 1939) and non-GP care for the majority, including women and children, remaining fee based, private provision continued to grow and the interwar years saw a number of new insurance-based initiatives. For higher income groups wide-ranging protection packages like those of the British Provident Association and The Bristol Contributory Welfare Association were developed. Cheaper forms of medical cover were also introduced for other income groups, many by the hospitals themselves. These included workplace 'clubs', Saturday Funds and the Hospital Savings Association (Cherry, 1992). Such schemes did not provide an automatic right to treatment, but there was an implicit assumption that patients diagnosed needs would be treated. Other schemes gave access to GP, ophthalmic, dental and home nursing services (Fox, 1996). By 1938 the majority of those eligible for National Insurance were also purchasing medical and hospital insurance (Herbert, 1939).[6]

The expansion of private medical insurance was furthered by the arrangements for administering the 1911 insurance scheme. In an attempt to ease the friendly societies' financial difficulties and boost self-provision, the Act's architects proposed to contract them as 'approved societies' to administer state health insurance, thus avoiding the need for a centralised bureaucracy. What was not anticipated however were the protests from proprietary carriers who foresaw sales being curtailed by the Bill's proposal for widows and orphans benefits and their rivals' potential access to a 'captive market'. In another demonstration of their political muscle, they persuaded the government to extend approved society status to include them and to drop its proposals for widows and orphans benefits.[7]

The insured population distributed itself almost equally between the large commercially managed friendly societies and the industrial assurance companies, giving both an unrivalled base for selling other financial services (Sinclair, 1932; Wilson and Levy, 1937). Despite high unemployment, the growing affluence of those in work combined with a pervasive sense of insecurity contributed to a further growth in industrial assurance and a significant upsurge in life insurance sales. Coverage of the former rose steadily, with the social surveys of the 1930s suggesting most working-class households, including the unemployed were purchasing policies (Massey, 1937; Pilgrim Trust, 1938; Rowntree, 1941). By the 1940s, over 103 million policies were in force, averaging more than £2.25 for each adult and child in Britain (Cmd 6404, 1942). Significantly, much of this growth was in endowment insurance, providing a lump-sum payment in old age or for dependants (Morah, 1955). Aided by a steady rise in the sums covered, industrial assurers' premium income rose by 236 per cent from £25.3 million in 1919 to £59.8 million in 1939 (Butt, 1984). The highest gains went to the proprietary companies, who by 1939 accounted for 80 per cent of the market, with the Prudential alone receiving a third of the premiums paid (Cmd 6404, 1942).

Sales of ordinary life insurance also surged, again led by the Prudential. The two million policies in force in 1900 rose to over six million by 1937, the majority being endowment or 'with-profits' based, giving suppliers a 220 per cent increase in premium income between 1919 and 1939 (Butt, 1984). By the late 1930s, life insurance comprised four per cent of consumer spending (compared to two per cent at the turn of the century), while voluntary savings through insurance exceeded the value of compulsory contributions by employees and employers to the National Insurance Scheme (Hannah, 1986). Escalating sales partly reflected the inadequacies of the 1909 and 1925 state pension schemes in the face of increased life expectancy and rising real incomes. But growth was also powered by fiscal changes and providers' market-making techniques. To counter wartime concerns that the rich were gaining disproportionate tax relief, the 1915 and 1916 Finance Acts limited life insurance premium relief to one half of the standard rate of income tax and seven per cent of the sum assured. The industry's lobbying however ensured this was offset by concessions allowing carriers to write off general management expenses against their investment income. They were thus able to claim relief for developing cheaper policies, while advertising them as tax efficient for consumers.

Market making involved the introduction of new products and the intensification of sales techniques differentially targeted at middle- and working-class consumers. New promotions included additions to existing forms of life insurance notably disability benefits and family protection policies, policies for women, and a stream of with-profits and endowment schemes. Selling generally involved an appeal to family obligations, the value of a prudential life course and the presentation of the insurance contract as a moral rather than a commercial transaction (Morgan and Knights, 1992). Deftly promoted through the expanding popular press and billboard campaigns, these tactics were reinforced by the sales pitch of commission-paid intermediaries. In the case of working-class households this relied on a more aggressive use of the agent system. The 'Insurance Mail', for instance, encouraged agents' use of 'befriending' techniques backed by 'horror' stories about the non-insured to sway reluctant payers and gain the local knowledge necessary to expand their customer base. Sales to the middle class were secured through a network of local solicitors, brokers, accountants and bank managers, whose advice, though tied to particular companies, added to the industry's carefully cultivated reputation for social responsibility.

From the mid-1920s, the major life offices' appeal to the obligations of middle-class breadwinners expanded further with the promotion of policies designed to pay for children's education. By 1938 some 10 per cent of those of school age attended fee-charging private schools. State secondary schools continued to operate means-tested charges and Treasury restrictions on free places meant that throughout the period over half the pupils in England and Wales were fee paying (Graves, 1943) Higher education remained fee based, as did much post-compulsory training. For aspiring parents, however, the priority lay with funding secondary education, the gateway to secure clerical work. The majority met this cost through a combination of direct payments and various forms of short-term savings, most notably building society accounts.

Like the friendly societies, building societies were rooted in nineteenth-century working-class mutuality. By the 1920s however they had become major savings institutions for all social groups and a primary means of funding private welfare. This was partly due to a favourable tax regime reinforced in the 1930s by the Treasury's 'cheap money' policies that encouraged high interest rates. It was also a function of the restructuring of what was still the most important form of commercial welfare, housing. Here the period saw the beginning of a switch from private renting to home ownership, which grew to 26 per cent of tenures by 1945; private renting fell over the same period to 62 per cent. Though well-paid manual workers were among the mortgagees, the majority came from upper social groups. The drift to home ownership partly reflected the flow of funds into the building societies and the rising prosperity which made borrowing and lending more attractive and private landlordism less appealing as an income earner. Rent control, slum clearance and increased local property taxes hastened this process, as did government subventions to private builders in the 1920s. But it was also encouraged by a powerful alliance of developers, transport and utility suppliers, all of whom promoted the familial and status-conferring benefits of private ownership (Weightman and Humphries, 1984).

In spite of the recession, then, by the outbreak of the Second World War, a constellation of different factors had powered the expansion of private welfare consumption alongside state provision. Indeed as Beveridge recognised the scale of personal welfare savings and expenditure was itself a measure of the potential for universal compulsory insurance and tax-funded public services (Cmd 6404, 1942). Growth, however, was uneven and varied between product markets and the protection offered to different social groups. Schooling and housing remained highly stratified and income rather than need governed entitlement to many forms of social protection. The late 1920s and 30s confirmed insurance carriers' concerns over the viability of unemployment insurance, which was left to the unions and the state. Medical cover too was left to other ventures. Different hospital contributory schemes bought variable standards of treatment, while voluntary hospitals' consultants increasingly treated fee-paying patients in private wards and outpatients in separate clinics. GPs too often appeared to focus more on their fee-paying than 'panel' patients, even cloistering them in separate waiting rooms (Glennerster, 1992). Despite the spread of municipal services many working-class mothers continued to rely on the domiciliary care of fee-charging midwives, while middle-class families contracted with the GP or private maternity units within the voluntary hospitals or small nursing homes. Dentistry remained a fee-charging business as did optical care, where small local traders by the 1930s faced competition from chains like Woolworth which offered 'do-it-yourself' tests and spectacles.

For much of this period notions of personal responsibility and self-reliance remained pivotal to public discussions of welfare. By the late 1930s however the limitations rather than the benefits of trading in welfare markets were attracting increasing attention. Although providers mobilised to defend their operations, concerted action was impeded by the disparate interests of vendors trading in different markets and a defence based less on consumer sovereignty than suppliers' rights to manage their businesses as they saw fit. Countering such arguments were both concerns over the vagaries of different welfare markets and criticism of commercial management practices, epitomised in the administration of state health insurance. This centred particularly on the ways in which industrial assurers appeared to exploit their approved society status to sell other products, the variability in the extra benefits they supplied and the collapse of the small democratic societies.[8] Presaging recent anxieties over personal pensions, the 1920 Parmoor and 1932 Cohen Committees revealed excessive administrative charges and a high lapse rate, both of which were attributed to the agent system. Consumers gained some protection in 1923 when industrial life companies were obliged to guarantee surrender values, but lapses and charges remained persistently high (the latter absorbing over a third of premium income by the 1930s). Some critics pressed for tighter regulation, others favoured not only abolition of the approved society system but state management of industrial assurance which the Labour Party had long advocated (Labour Party, 1923; Levy, 1937; Wilson and Levy, 1938).

These proposals were taken up by Beveridge who recommended the dissolution of the approved society system, the introduction of a statutory death grant and the nationalisation of industrial assurance.[9] Commercial practices had, he concluded, fostered inequities in health care and pressurised consumers into purchasing inappropriate, over-priced, and poor quality private insurance. Only a universal state-funded death benefit could ensure a service fit for the needs of the bereaved. Drawing a distinction between life insurance and industrial assurance, he advised the government to consider converting the latter from a 'competitive sellers' business to a 'monopoly consumers' service' by establishing an Industrial Assurance Board to take over responsibility for those assured for sums up to £300. This was justified partly by its close association with other forms of state insurance, but primarily by its 'special character' which 'made it so different from most other commodities that it [could not] safely be treated as an article of commerce'. Unlike other purchasers, customers of industrial assurance were peculiarly reliant on the seller. Its value was difficult for them to judge; once bought it could not be exchanged or returned without loss and it involved a substantial outlay over time. Independent advice was thus crucial, but generally limited to 'those of larger means'. In addition with 'all the money to speak of coming from policy holders', it involved little capital investment. Dividends to shareholders were thus an unnecessary charge on contributors, not a justifiable return for risk-taking (Cmd 6404, 1942).

Beveridge's depiction of the non-commodity characteristics of industrial assurance and the need for public protection were widely endorsed (Hilton, 1944). The insurance companies mobilised to protect themselves and the 'freedom' of their customers (Industrial Life Offices, 1944). While the collecting friendly societies focused on retaining their approved society status and funeral insurance, the major carriers concentrated on protecting their wider business interests. By the 1940s their sales were shifting closer to ordinary life insurance products and many were also moving into occupational pensions. Ceding their costly involvement in health administration and the popular death grant were a small loss compared to safeguarding these lucrative markets. Intense canvassing secured their position, the government announcing in February 1943 that 'with the other proposals of the [Beveridge] Report they had quite enough on hand' (Lafitte, 1945).

Commercial Welfare since 1945

In the debates leading up to the 1945 election, many thought that a Labour victory would herald the general demise of commercial welfare. Beveridge had continued to campaign for a state scheme for industrial assurance, while a number of Labour Party supporters held that the life insurance industry as a whole should be nationalised (Mikardo, 1948). There were calls for the collective ownership of land and housing, and state-only provision in education and health care. Once Labour came to power, however, a different welfare scenario emerged. While the Party had received strong electoral support, it met substantial resistance from commercial providers as well as a Conservative Party espousing the virtues of non-state provision. This opposition, in conjunction with the practical difficulties of implementing the more radical welfare proposals and securing the government's wider economic programme, led to a series of compromises which effectively built commercial provision into the new welfare edifice.

In the case of health care, while the voluntary hospitals and provident sickness schemes were mostly dissolved by the 1948 NHS Act, powerful lobbying by the medical profession secured the retention of private practice and the private business status of dentists, opticians, pharmacists and GPs. Interest groups also saw that postwar education did not preclude private schooling. With life insurance, the industry's lobbying (Industrial Life Offices, 1949) was sealed by the government's awareness of the difficulties of disaggregating this from other forms of insurance and its concern to avoid destabilising Britain's financial markets. The radical line was thus transmuted into stricter regulation, the tightening of life assurance sales practices and the vague promise of creating a public service through mutualisation (Labour Party, 1950).

If the survival of some forms of commercial welfare was the product of bitter negotiation, its promotion was specifically a feature of Conservative thinking. Contrary to much received opinion, the Conservatives never fully endorsed the universalist assumptions of the 1940s reforms (Glennerster, 1995). They opposed the fulcrum of state welfare provision – the 1946 NHS Bill – and from the 1950s advanced policies supportive of private production and consumption. The reassertion of individualistic values within the party was reinforced by the emergence of new justifications for commercial welfare. Rather than arguments based simply on the inadequacies of the state, private provision was increasingly presented in more positive terms as fuelling economic growth and securing the values of freedom, choice and individual autonomy (Hayek, 1944; Jewkes, 1952; Seldon, 1961).

Beyond these ideological shifts, Conservative policies combined with postwar affluence encouraged a change in consumer calculations. The state safety net meant many consumers could buy for reasons other than necessity, while the establishment of a national insurance and tax-funded risk-pool paradoxically increased their disposable incomes. The consequences were most evident in housing. While the private rental market continued to decline, home ownership expanded dramatically from 29 per cent of tenures in 1951 to 43 per cent in 1961. In the following decade, aided by favourable tax regimes under both Labour and Conservative governments, it expanded to 53 per cent. Slower growth in the 1970s gave way to further expansion in the 1980s, stimulated by discounted council house sales, the relaxation of planning regulations and other subventions aimed at fostering the Conservative vision of a property-owning democracy. By 1996, two-thirds of Britain's homes were owner occupied (Leather and Morrison, 1997).

Factors other than government policy also contributed to the development of this market. Forceful canvassing by the construction industry and their corporate financiers, both of whom had close links with the Conservative Party, ensured continuing pressure for 'new builds'. The distinctive characteristics of the commodity itself were also crucial. Owner occupied housing not only had an immediate use-value, but offered potential investment and status gains and, as a tangible product, enabled consumers to spread the cost of purchase over time. Traditionally the major suppliers of loans and mortgages were the building societies who collectively set borrowing and saving rates and whose 'balance sheet' approach in some ways held down demand in the immediate postwar years (Hamnett, 1994). From 1980, however, lending was opened up to the banks who, given the faltering returns of other investments, found it an attractive venture. Their entry, followed by the further deregulation of mortgage finance through the 1986 Building Societies and Financial Services Acts stimulated a surge in borrowing and a restructuring of the home loan market.

Building society lending for house purchases fell from 80 per cent of the total in 1980 to 51 per cent in 1993; the banks' share rose from 6 to 49 per cent; and a number of other lenders also entered the market (Whitehead, 1994). Heightened competition brought with it less stringent loan criteria, a new range of mortgage products and a wider customer base (Ball, 1990). The resultant consumer boom however was short lived and with the recession of the early 1990s, some two million householders were left in negative equity. A turbulent market brought further product innovation and provider restructuring. Several major societies shed their mutual status and home lending generally was transformed by a wave of mergers and the internationalisation of mortgage finance.

Similar processes characterised the postwar life insurance market. With the introduction of the state death benefit, industrial assurance became a form of life insurance sold on a direct collecting basis. Rising real incomes and the industry's success in securing a supportive fiscal and regulatory framework contributed to buoyant sales. Continued growth was also fuelled by large-scale advertising, the successive re-engineering of bonus, with-profits and other investment-linked policies and the expectation that the rising number of mortgagees had life cover. It was also boosted by tax-efficient sales to employers and budgetary changes which widened its appeal to non-taxpayers (Field, 1987). By the 1960s over half of UK households held life insurance policies. Despite the removal of personal tax relief on new premiums in 1984 and the imposition of insurance premium tax in 1994, sales continued to grow. By the mid-1990s, two-thirds of households in the UK were buying life insurance and the industry had experienced a seventeen-fold increase in real terms in the volume of life and pension premiums since

1950 (Boleat, 1994). As in the past sales were dominated by a few large companies. The Prudential remained pre-eminent (Pawley *et al.*, 1991), though new entrants such as Abbey Life using direct-sales strategies built up a strong presence. As with mortgage finance however, the liberalisation of the 1980s brought new competition from the banks and in the 1990s from high-street chainstores and supermarkets. With competition intensified by EU membership and concerns over globalisation, many life offices attempted to retain their market share and spread risks through mergers and entering other welfare insurance markets. For consumers, the emergence of composite providers brought 'one-stop' financial emporia cross-selling a range of once specialised products. It also brought new anxieties about inappropriate selling. Voiced less by working-class organisations than new middle-class-based consumer groups, this remained a contentious issue throughout the period. As in the past, however, successive attempts to tighten consumer protection were diluted by the industry's claim to self-regulation endorsed by the 1986 Financial Services Act.

That concerns about mis-selling were not misplaced was demonstrated by the promotion of a new form of commercial welfare – personal pensions. The 1986 Social Security Act provided substantial incentives for individuals to opt out of SERPS or occupational schemes into Appropriate Personal Pensions (APPs) and by early 1993 some five million people had either switched to or taken out APPs. The surge in pension sales partly reflected high-pressure marketing as the life offices, banks, building societies, chain stores and others competed for a share in a lucrative tax-subsidised market. Selling, however, was often undertaken by poorly trained sales staff working on commission. Members of occupational schemes were wrongly advised to opt out and women and others on low incomes persuaded to buy poorly designed products with high transaction costs and minimal returns (May and Brunsdon, 1996).

As the scale of malpractice became clear, both the industry and the government attempted to restore consumer confidence. LAUTRO (Life Assurance and Unit Trusts Regulatory Organization) and FIMBRA (Financial Intermediarists, Managers and Brokers Regulatory Association) tightened their procedures and from January 1995 the government required those selling pensions and other financial products to reveal their charges. Compensation procedures were also instigated (under the aegis of the Securities and Investment Board) but implemented remarkably slowly. The malversation did not however affect long-run sales. As the Major government wound down the state pension scheme, a further range of products were promoted and new vendors entered the market, many selling by phone or over the counter in retail stores or special 'pension centres' in Britain's shopping malls. Despite the many drawbacks of money-purchase and execution-only schemes (Waine, 1995), by the mid-1990s 20 per cent of UK households were contributing to personal pensions plans (Association of British Insurers, 1995).

In other welfare markets the postwar settlement led to very different patterns of development. In health and medical insurance, for instance, the advent of the NHS forced suppliers into a small niche market concentrating on a narrow range of surgical procedures. Three major formations emerged, the London Association for Hospital Services (renamed Private Patients Plan (PPA) in 1962), the British United Provident Association (BUPA) covering the majority of the provincial schemes, and the Western Provident Association (WPA). Demand for their products like those of the smaller surviving providents and proprietories grew slowly and unevenly, from 1.2 per cent of the population in 1955 to 5 per cent in 1971. Sales then fell off, but picked up in the late 1970s, reaching 7.5 per cent by 1981, primarily due to increased employer purchasing. Despite the government's predictions that over a quarter of the population would be insured by the end of the decade, growth in the 1980s proved volatile, peaking at 12.2. per cent in 1991 (Laing, 1992).

The prospect of long-term returns enticed new suppliers and from the late 1980s the market saw substantial restructuring as an influx of banks, building societies and insurance companies extended their welfare portfolios into this hitherto discrete market. Of these, Norwich Union invested heavily to gain 10 per cent of the market, while the longstanding market leaders saw their share fall – BUPA to 46 per cent and PPP to 27 per cent in 1996 (Laing, 1996a). Legal and General signalled a further threat to the established providents with its entry into the market in 1996. To raise the capital necessary to stave off increasing competition, PPP decided to demutualise while other organisations formed partnerships (for example BUPA teamed up with the Halifax to market health insurance to the latter's customers).

Restructuring, however, masked low profit margins and the continued volatility of sales. The economic recession of the early 1990s stalled corporate demand. Individual purchasing, apparently stimulated by concerns over NHS waiting lists and care standards, partially compensated for this, leaving cover at approximately 11 per cent of the population (Laing, 1996a). With stagnant demand but rising claims and medical costs and the taxation of insurance premiums carriers in the late 1990s were forced to increase charges.[10] To stem costs and rejuvenate demand, they tried to control health suppliers' through new contractual specifications. Some limited the range of hospitals from which customers could choose; where it was competitively priced, others bought services from NHS Trusts. Insurers also attempted to widen their customer base. Traditionally consumers were drawn mainly from managerial and professional groups (Higgins, 1992; Calnan *et al.*, 1993) and offered a narrow choice of policies. But with over 30 companies vying for custom, a new tranche of health insurance products were developed, ranging from six-week, budget and 'comprehensive' schemes, to policies targeted at families or particular sub-groups of the population. Hospital cash schemes were also revived (notably by the Hospital Savings Association), as was outpatient cover.

By 1996, over 400 different types of policy were on sale, even if some were very much minority interests. Critical illness insurance, for example, was purchased by only 4 per cent of the population. Nonetheless, with changes to statutory sick pay, incapacity benefits and primary care provision, health insurers were given several incentives to expand and, as their advertising indicated, they geared up for a long campaign to convince consumers of the need for cover. With the disintegration of NHS dentistry for adults, for instance, they launched a new range of dental care policies. These were schemes promoted not only by the established provident health insurers, but also by life offices, building societies, banks and retail outlets.

The Major government's attempt to shift responsibility for ill-health combined with the financial deregulation of the 1980s also prompted other developments. Mortgage protection schemes were encouraged, funeral insurance schemes resurfaced and several leading insurance carriers also piloted another new product, long-term care insurance. Long-term care insurance sales, however were constrained by low public awareness of the need for cover and political uncertainties over compulsory insurance. By 1995 there were only some 10,000 subscribers, mostly among those approaching or in retirement (Burchardt and Hills, 1997).

With their heavy dependence on private funding, developments in the hospital and primary care markets were similarly uneven. As previously indicated, private practice and beds were retained within the NHS, while outside it some 300 small hospitals continued to operate independently. From the late 1950s, BUPA established medical centres, nursing and pathology services and, to safeguard its insurance market, sponsored the Nuffield Nursing Home Trust. By 1979 Nuffield was the major provider of hospital provision, albeit within a declining market in which some 150 hospitals supplied 6,671 beds. Most of the hospitals focused on acute provision and, more particularly, on elective surgical procedures (Higgins 1992).

Ironically it was the Labour Party's attempts to phase out the remaining NHS pay beds in the mid-1970s which triggered a revival of private hospital provision. This was boosted in the 1980s by Conservative changes to planning regulations and consultants' contracts and the upsurge in private health insurance prompted by fears over the state of the NHS (Mohan, 1991). Between 1979 and 1989 private hospital numbers increased by 39 per cent (to 209), and capacity by 58 per cent (to 10,546 beds). Expansion was primarily funded by new proprietary providers, led by BUPA Hospitals Ltd and by American corporations conscious of both a downturn in their home market and the prospects of a supportive Conservative regime. By 1989, proprietary providers had captured 56 per cent of the market.

Their anticipated increase in demand however failed to materialise and the economic recession of the early 1990s brought further regrouping as American investors withdrew and European conglomerates entered the market. By the late 1990s the overcapacity brought further instability, particularly in

London, where overseas demand fell and provider competition increased as cash-strapped NHS Trusts expanded their private provision. By 1995 the NHS had become the third largest provider with 16.5 per cent of the acute private health market (Fitzhugh, 1996). Private health insurers seized on this development, devising policies to cover 'private' treatment in NHS hospitals. Having unsuccessfully pressed the government for a 'level playing field', providers responded by diversifying into day and cosmetic surgery, 'wellness' services and 'partnership' arrangements with NHS Trusts.

The last two decades of this century also saw significant changes in primary health care markets. From the late 1940s up to the 1970s, provision was predominantly state funded, GP private practice was minimal and the services offered by dentists and opticians conceived as supplementing mainstream statutory provision (Lee, 1971). Government policy was a key contributory factor in the stimulation of commercial production and consumption in the 1980s and 90s, although this occurred unevenly. While GPs remained within the NHS, those who became fundholders gained powers to purchase non-statutory services. The abolition of free dental checks and changes to dentists' contracts led to a growth in the market for adult dental care. Restrictions on the state funding of primary optical care for adults, combined with new technologies, brought a similar recommodification and a shift from its small-business base to chainstores selling optical goods and services, some on a self-selection basis.

The most fundamental changes, however, occurred in continuing care, traditionally an insignificant service market. The four-fold expansion of residential and nursing care for the elderly between 1970 and 1994 involved a major shift away from state provision. Whereas 69 per cent of long-term care was provided by the state in the 1970s, by the mid-1990s 76 per cent was supplied by independent agencies (Laing, 1995). Social security payments were partly responsible for the emergence of this new market. But growth was also funded by users and their families, a process furthered by the increasing numbers of owner occupiers entering care (Hamnett, 1995) and the transfer of financial responsibility to local government.

The new community care regime also forged significant changes in the structure of the market. Much of the initial impetus came from small entrepreneurs moving out of other businesses, particularly in holiday areas, and care professionals dissatisfied with the practices and opportunity structures of public providers (May and Brunsdon, 1996). During the 1990s, however, this family-run, 'cottage' industry, experienced a spate of mergers and an upsurge in corporate provision. By 1996 firms running three or more homes had captured 36 per cent of the market. With local authorities obliged to spend 85 per cent of their care budget on independent providers and the run down of NHS continuing care, commercial provision for other user groups also increased. Proprietaries and mutuals providing acute and long-term psychiatric care services began to emerge, and there was a significant expansion of services for children as well as day, respite and domiciliary care for adults (Laing, 1996b). By 1995, 29 per cent of local authority home care, for example, was purchased from independent suppliers (Department of Health, 1996). For much of the postwar era, the domiciliary care market had functioned as a less formalised version of the pre-war domestic service industry, with users buying help from a mainly female workforce trading individually on a 'cash-in-hand' basis. As in other service areas, the advent of state purchasing, however, encouraged corporate activity, though direct buying by users remained a matter of negotiation on the fringe of the formal economy.

In education too the 1980s and 90s were marked by considerable changes in consumption and production. Although secured by the settlement of the 1940s, those schools that remained fee based faced new registration requirements and strong competition from a free, upgraded state secondary system. Some 3,000 schools closed between 1951 and 1976 and the percentage of children educated independently fell from 10.2 per cent to 5.7 per cent. Thereafter intakes revived, particularly in non-boarding schools and especially in sixth-form provision, reaching 6.6 per cent overall in 1991 (Glennerster and Wilson, 1970; Kendall and Knapp, 1996). By the mid-1980s, although accounting for only a twentieth of all pupils, private schools taught 17 per cent of all sixth formers, 25 per cent of university entrants and 50 per cent of 'Oxbridge' acceptances (Papadakis and Taylor-Gooby, 1987).

Fears that Labour might abolish private schools' privileged tax status were partly responsible for this revival, stimulating a 'public school revolution' as providers updated their facilities and teaching, and marketed themselves as selling a superior product to that provided by the state (Rae, 1981). Recruitment also benefited from the falling taxation of upper income groups under successive Conservative governments, the continued exemption of school fees from VAT, government criticism of state school standards (preceding the 1988 Education Act) and the introduction of the Assisted Places Scheme in 1980.

From the early 1990s, however, as state schooling appeared to improve, access to higher education widened and the future of the Assisted Places Scheme became less certain, the private schooling market began to level off. In contrast other private educational provision saw continued growth. The steady rise in the numbers of working mothers and an increasing awareness of the importance of 'early years' education led to increased demand for pre-school provision. Those supplying services were predominantly single-trading childminders, although the 1990s also saw the emergence of small business provision and the entry of multinational providers such as Kindercare.

Supplementary and extra-curricular schooling for those of school age and post-compulsory provision saw a more marked and varied expansion. For most adults the discretionary grant system ensured that many forms of professional, vocational and adult training remained a matter for individual or employer funding, even when delivered in public institutions. With accreditation left to a wealth of autonomous bodies, and occupational progression increasingly linked to qualifications, the postwar decades saw a proliferation of training agencies selling courses of varying lengths and levels on both distance learning and an attendance basis. Initially secretarial, clerical and accountancy training, along with English language studies, were the most popular offerings, to which were added an ever-widening array of computing and business skills. By the 1990s, over 3,000 private institutions with some 700,000 paying students offered such training and many had also moved into GCSE, A level, GNVQ, NVQ and work-based tuition.

The upsurge in post-compulsory provision was the product of several factors. The uncertain labour markets of the 1980s and 90s fuelled consumer demand. This was reinforced by government attempts to reduce unemployment and improve the skill base of the workforce. Equally significantly, employer purchasing grew as many companies expanded provision and bought in training. By the late 1990s further education colleges alone collected some £300 million in fees, half from individuals, half from employers who also funded much of the training provided by commercial organisations (Layard, 1997). This form of proxy purchasing was but one of the many ways that employers' influenced welfare trading. As has been indicated by the review of the last fifty years of commercial welfare, they were major purchasers of life, health and medical insurance and their presence had a marked influence on trading in other markets. Moreover, by providing 'in-house' services employers also affected direct consumption and the role of state services. To fully understand the dynamics of different welfare markets, it is therefore necessary to consider changes in employer-sponsored welfare and its place in management practice.

Occupational Welfare 1900–14

At the beginning of the century the overwhelming majority of the workforce was employed in small family-owned, single-plant enterprises, operating in highly differentiated markets (Gospel, 1992). Ties between workers and their employers varied markedly. At one extreme, many industries relied on spot labour with employers' responsibilities limited to wage payments. At the other, Britain's emerging large firms were beginning to develop systematic welfare programmes designed to secure and retain a reliable workforce. In between a mass of small firms operated discretionary, paternalistic forms of labour management akin to those long practised on Britain's landed estates and by some leading Victorian industrialists (Child, 1969; Joyce, 1980).

Although the scale is difficult to estimate, many employers gave extensive bonuses or *ex gratia* payments to their workers both to reward loyalty and tide them over periods of ill-health and incapacity (Hannah, 1986). These were often complemented by home visits undertaken by the owners' female relatives. Many firms also sponsored 'sick clubs' offering medical and/or health insurance. Some functioned as voluntary provident schemes subsidised by employer donations, but most were compulsory, operating on either a 'dividing-out' or more permanent basis (Fitzgerald, 1988). Housing constituted a third type of provision although, in this era, it was most commonly provided by firms operating in remote or single-industry areas (Melling, 1981, 1992a). Beyond these individual benefits, there were a range of collective perquisites which included works outings, related recreational activities and various forms of 'civic benevolence' such as endowing hospitals, libraries and parks (Abercrombie and Hill, 1976; Warde, 1992). All were designed to promote commitment and identification with the firm within a general 'theatre of paternalism' (Morris and Smyth, 1994).

Welfare along these lines remained a feature of UK industry throughout the century (Bradley, 1990; Wray, 1996). Its counterpoint in the first two decades were the more formalised schemes in Britain's few large firms. The prime movers (Melling, 1992a, 1992b) were the railway companies, whose size and complex operations demanded a reliable workforce. To cultivate fidelity, they sponsored housing, recreation, education, care schemes, medical and health insurance and, above all, old-age pensions. Coverage, however, was stratified according to the status and responsibilities of employees, with pensions in particular being reserved for clerical and supervisory staff. Similar patterns of differentiated welfare were adopted by several other large firms, most notably those in branded consumer goods, in gas and other heavy industries where new continuous process technologies demanded a stable workforce (Melling, 1979; Fitzgerald, 1988).

Although the religiously inspired benevolence of employers such as Cadburys, Colmans, Crossfield and Rowntrees should not be underestimated, the role of welfare in enhancing a company's competitive edge was clearly recognised. As the evidence presented to the Army and post-Boer War inquiries showed, many were conscious of the productivity gap between Britain and her overseas competitors and of the ways in which 'national efficiency' could be secured through company as well as state welfare. Workplace services promised to enhance morale and with it productivity. Conterminously, they were also seen as a means of pre-empting unionisation. This was particularly clear in industries like railways and gas where occupational benefits, especially pensions, formed part of an anti-union offensive (Melling 1991, 1992a).

Notwithstanding such calculations, however, formalised workplace welfare remained a minority experience. Only 5 per cent of the workforce, for instance, were covered by recognised pension schemes before 1914 (Hannah, 1986). Moreover, employer-driven schemes were widely criticised by working-class organisations as a threat to wage levels and self-provisioning through the unions and friendly societies. Liberal policy-makers were more ambivalent (Hay, 1975, 1978) but concerned to preserve the work ethic and minimise the tax burden on employers. In the many negotiations over their reform proposals employers, although often divided, were committed to limiting the possible costs, safeguarding their own schemes and maintaining control over labour recruitment and retention. In this climate while instituting state provision the Liberal settlement also secured the expansion of occupational provision on the stratified lines pioneered by the larger firms.

Occupational Welfare 1914–39

This became apparent during the First World War when, to boost output and limit labour turnover, the government encouraged the establishment of a new range of work-based welfare. Health and safety regulations were tightened and employers exhorted to improve canteens, rest rooms and other facilities and engage specialist welfare staff. By 1918 over 1,000 specialist personnel staff had been appointed, giving company welfare a new credence and conceptual base (Niven, 1967). This was facilitated by the formation in 1913 of a professional body – the Workers Welfare Association (WWA) – whose dual aims were to disseminate good practice and the business importance of the personnel task.

In promoting the professional standing of its members the WWA (renamed the Institute of Labour Management in 1931) was supported by a growing literature and an increasing number of management-linked agencies. Some, like the Industrial Fatigue Research Board and the National Institute of Industrial Psychology were concerned with particular modes of labour management; others pursued a broader role. The Industrial Welfare Society, for example, ran an advisory service for employers and issued a stream of publications promoting company welfare and systematic personnel policies. Both were seen as necessary for the functional effectiveness of the increasing number of large firms whose industrial stability, it was held, could only be guaranteed by replicating the unitary ethos of family firms. As importantly, company welfare was seen to counter both state welfare and pressures for increased worker control (Industrial Welfare Society, 1934; Hyde, 1968).

The company welfare movement did little however to allay the markedly hostile relations in many industries which culminated in the General Strike of 1926. The experiences of national conflict led to renewed attempts to promote 'industrial disarmament' (Baldwin, 1937), signalled by the high-profile Mond–Turner talks and a further proliferation of welfarist literature. While the effects of the talks are still disputed, the 1930s saw a considerable expansion of occupational welfare. The numbers of full-time personnel staff increased (to 2,000 by 1939), as did the quantity and range of provision. Occupational pensions grew steadily, covering 13 per cent of the population by 1936 (Hannah, 1986). Sick-pay schemes, especially for those outside NHI, also proliferated as did 'top-up' provision for those within it. By the 1940s half of national insurance claimants were also covered by employer schemes (Titmuss,

1958). New benefits, notably, life insurance, secondary school fees, on-site health care, welfare advice and help with mortgages were also introduced, some provided 'in-house', others bought from commercial providers.

Employer action was stimulated by a combination of industry and firm-specific calculations, tax changes and the promotional strategies of external suppliers. Occupational pensions and life insurance, for example, were promoted by the introduction of tax relief for trust fund schemes in 1921, and, more significantly by the development of group schemes, first introduced for American firms operating in Britain by Metropolitan Life of New York in 1927. Heavily marketed as cheaper than traditional schemes, these group policies accounted for much of the 1930s growth in occupational pension and life insurance coverage. In some industries, notably retailing, company welfare was still contingent on non-unionisation. But for most large employers in the 1930s it formed part of the wider drive to develop more systematic employment policies and internal labour markets. Income enhancement and replacement benefits were typically limited to supervisory, clerical and managerial staff. Where people dined, played sport or sought advice depended on their position in the firm. It also depended on their gender. Company policy statements and the broader personnel literature endorsed the 'marriage bar' and, though considerable effort was expended on women's welfare, provision was predicated on their 'special needs'. Particular emphasis was placed, for example, on separate on-site health and welfare facilities and the use of female supervisors to ensure appropriate 'behaviour'.

Occupational Welfare since 1939

By the late 1930s, although still confined to a minority of employees, both the rationale and contours of company welfare were clearly set. War brought a more concerted movement to expand coverage. In 1940, the Factory Inspectorate were empowered to compel the appointment of welfare officers in factories with over 250 workers, with the Ministry of Labour providing the necessary training. They were also to make canteens compulsory and, more generally, press the value of works-based welfare, a conception endorsed by Bevin's joint production committees. By 1945, the numbers of specialist personnel staff had risen to over 5,000 (Niven, 1967); there were over 8,000 industrial nurses, and welfare units and recreational services had been established in many small plants (Pollard, 1962). New benefits were also introduced, most notably, transport subsidies and luncheon vouchers. The numbers covered by occupational sick pay and pensions grew and some firms extended protection to manual staff at minimal cost due to wartime taxation (Digby, 1989). The war also inspired a further surge of personnel writing and the reconstruction of the ILM as the Institute of Personnel Management in 1946.

The enhanced significance of company welfare was recognised in the protracted bargaining which led to the postwar welfare pact. Like its union supporters, the Labour government was equivocal. It attempted to tighten state regulation, particularly of pensions (under the 1947 Finance Act), but, in line with the Beveridge blueprint, many of its welfare innovations opened the way for more systematic employer-sponsored protection. Conservatives, however, saw it as both an alternative to state welfare and an expression of 'real' business interests (Conservative Party, 1947), and from 1951 did much to encourage employer provision, especially through fiscal policies. As Titmuss famously observed (1958, 1962), employee welfare expanded alongside state provision. By the mid-1960s occupational benefits of various kinds accounted for 11.1 per cent of the pre-tax costs of manufacturing firms. By the late 1970s this had risen to 19.4 per cent, and was even higher in service industries. Much of this was absorbed by life insurance and pension provision, which encompassed over half of full-time employees, and sick pay which covered a higher 70 per cent (Green *et al.*, 1984; Hart, 1984). But it also reflected the introduction of new benefits such as relocation and housing subsidies, company cars and medical insurance bought from commercial suppliers.

The growth and diversification of company welfare can be attributed to a fusion of different factors. The pre-war shift to large firms and new industries continued, necessitating more formal personnel strategies, a process hastened by the entry of overseas companies who often imported their own welfare practices. With British firms employing over 50,000 personnel managers by 1979, the profession's influence also grew (Gospel, 1992). More critically, low postwar unemployment and tight labour markets placed a new value on employee retention. Most studies suggest that, in this environment, company welfarism was employer driven (Green *et al.*, 1984; Hannah, 1986), buying allegiance and easing technological change. It was also prompted, however, by fiscal subsidies and, from the 1970s, by attempts to reward key employees without infringing income policies. This was particularly apparent in the supply of company cars and medical insurance, where employers' bulk purchasing did much to sustain commercial providers. With pensions and sick pay excluded from various wages policies, employers also came under union pressure to enhance non-wage benefits (Russell, 1991), while maintaining differentials (Mann, 1992).

By the late 1970s, however, the tax-assisted expansion of occupational welfare was beginning to attract criticism. Following Titmuss, a succession of commentators highlighted the extent to which provision was based not on need but occupational status with the most generous packages accruing to the mainly white males who staffed the upper echelons of Britain's major employing organisations (Sinfield, 1978; Reddin, 1982; Field 1987). Coverage remained concentrated in the public services and large firms, predominantly capital-intensive and consumer goods industries, financial services and high-street retailing. Entitlement varied within and across industries and between categories of worker. Most schemes were confined to full-time employees and, despite efforts at 'harmonisation', many distinguished between manual, non-manual and managerial staff.

Concerns about the inequities of occupational welfare were reinforced by growing awareness of the extent to which it was heavily subsidised by the tax system – with the highest relief again going to the most privileged (Sinfield, 1978). The undemocratic governance of many company schemes also drew criticism. Union representatives highlighted the potential for employer abuse of occupational pensions, while, more generally, Titmuss' strictures over the lack of employee control over pension fund managers were widely reasserted (James 1984). These two aspects of company welfare were also castigated by neo-liberal writers. While better known for their condemnation of state welfare, many were equally critical of the 'middle-class welfare state' of tax-subsidised company benefits. They were particularly opposed to occupational pensions which constrained free choice and, like company welfare generally, distorted normal market mechanisms (Chappell, 1988; Vinson, 1994).

Such censure undoubtedly influenced Conservative governments' attempts in the 1980s and 90s to promote self-provisioning as an alternative to both state and occupational welfare. Successive budgets abolished or reduced the relief on many key forms of company welfare, most notably company cars. The 1986 Social Security Act, as has been seen, empowered individuals to opt out of company schemes and buy their own personal pensions, although it also enabled companies to provide cheaper money-purchase schemes. As the 1985 Social Security Green Paper showed, however, these innovations were also conditioned by wider concerns over social security spending and the fact that occupational pension coverage seemed to have stabilised, leaving over half the workforce potentially dependent on the state (Nesbitt, 1992).

As in other areas, government policy was far from consistent and subject to contradictory pressures. The Maxwell scandal unleashed longstanding concerns over the governance of occupational pensions which, contrary to the government's deregulatory commitments, forced tighter control under the 1996 Pensions Act. Meanwhile other government policies contributed directly and indirectly to an expansion of employer's welfare responsibilities. Despite protests, they became responsible for managing and funding short-term sick and maternity pay, while a series of training initiatives aimed to increase their responsibility for staff development. Less directly, the government's commitment to containing public expenditure added to other pressures on employers to expand provision (May and Brunsdon, 1994; Income Data Services, 1995).

This was reinforced by a further transformation of personnel ideology. Influenced by Japanese and American thinking, the profession was recast in the new guise of human resource management and vested with a strategic significance in corporate planning. A stream of publications revalued employees as key commercial assets and proclaimed the role of inclusive welfare policies in securing the committed workforce necessary for an 'enterprise economy'. Combined with company-specific concerns, such tensions, endorsed by the high-profile advertising of commercial welfare providers, underpinned a number of key developments in the 1980s and 90s. First, a number of companies extended protection to the whole or significant proportions of the workforce. More commonly, many organisations, while retaining existing stratified schemes, introduced a new range of benefits aimed at the whole workforce, most notably counselling and wellness services. Third, there was considerable investment in what had been the least developed form of company welfare in Britain, staff training, although this appears to have disproportionately benefited managerial groups (Gospel, 1992; Smith, E., 1996). Finally, the two decades saw growing business involvement in community projects and 'partnerships' with voluntary agencies.

As in the past these initiatives were primarily launched by large employers. Provision in small organisations remained either minimal or, as throughout the century, highly informal and subject to the owner/manager's discretion. Tight profit margins meant many small enterprises could not afford occupational provision. Most offered only minimal money-purchase pension schemes and few supplied sick pay or other benefits. Yet by the 1990s small companies had once more become the major employers of labour in the UK, while the drive for 'flexibility' and the continued expansion of part-time and temporary work pointed to other limits on the proportion of the workforce eligible for employer-sponsored welfare. Moreover, though the 1990s recession did not stall large company's interest in employee welfare, it prompted a search for less expensive programmes. In pensions, for instance, there was a pronounced shift to cheaper money-purchase schemes and in sick pay, a closer surveillance of claimants. As significantly the HRM literature placed increasing emphasis on a new, 'enabling' role for corporate welfare with employers facilitating 'employability' rather than guaranteeing secure employment. Refashioned company welfarism on these lines was thus less a cure for declining state provision than an instrument for cushioning the move to 'leaner' organisations.

Into the Twenty-first Century

Viewing the position at the end of the century it is tempting to suggest Britain's welfare arrangements are at the point of turning full circle. Political discussion increasingly hinges on stimulating self- rather than collective funding; employer welfare too is refocusing on 'self-development' rather than long-service packages. Some commercial markets, particularly dental, optical care and funeral insurance, which in the immediate postwar years seemed doomed, have revived; new markets, notably in social care and post-compulsory education appear set to grow. Much, however, depends on the pattern of state intervention.

Like the longer-term growth of life insurance and owner occupation, the buoyancy of the continuing care and post-compulsory education markets partly reflects a supportive fiscal and regulatory environment and restricted state provision. In contrast extensive statutory services confined private medical insurance, health care and schooling to niche markets, highly dependent on consumer perceptions of the quality of statutory provision.

Differential development was also, however, a product of other factors. In some markets employer purchasing was particularly significant and, although influenced by changes in fiscal and social policy, primarily determined by labour management calculations. Individual purchasing too reflected an amalgam of concerns. In the absence of public provision, purchasing of some products remained a necessity, while state social security assumed a tier of personal savings whereby individuals safeguarded their living standards and those of their dependants. But welfare spending also brought other benefits. Buying rather than renting accommodation, for instance, conferred, like life insurance, greater 'ontological security' (Saunders, 1990). It also offered enhanced status and material gains, including the credit worthiness to buy other welfare goods. Similar advantages accrued from investing in post-compulsory training or private schooling, with its longstanding links to Britain's elite universities and professions. Providers did much to promote these expectations and their market-making activities proved crucial in maintaining trade and creating the power base for limiting state intervention. Some products lent themselves more to this process than others, particularly those which could be financed on a long-term basis with lenders covered by various warranties, where risks were predictable and benefits tangible and where consumers appeared to possess an information base.

In various combinations, these factors contributed to the overall resilience of private welfare and the dynamics of different markets. Far from being displaced by an expanding state in the second half of the century, private production and consumption grew along with it and continued its upward momentum as state spending slowed under the Thatcher and Major governments. By the 1990s human services absorbed around a half of Britain's income; 40 per cent of that sum was spent in private welfare markets. As throughout the century, housing claimed the bulk of personal expenditure, with 60 per cent of housing costs being met privately. Eleven per cent of schooling and 11 per cent of health care costs were also privately funded (Hills, cited in Glennerster, 1997). With the devaluing of the state pension, support in retirement became a personal responsibility once again.

The markets in which welfare was traded, however, bore little resemblance to those of the first part of the century or the consumer-driven model advanced in neo-liberal writing. In many instances what began as highly localised small-scale trading gave way to markets dominated by a narrowing number of national suppliers.[11] Equally significantly, many once discrete markets had converged. Pensions, income protection, mortgage finance, life and medical insurance had merged with conventional banking into one 'financial services' market. Closer links between insurers and service providers were also emerging, especially in health care.

From a consumer's perspective, composite traders operating by phone, on the Internet or in the high street eased purchasing. But a market comprising insurers, banks, building societies, supermarkets and other retailers increased the difficulties of making an informed choice. Independent financial advisors, and increased media coverage only partly met this dilemma which rekindled criticisms of sales practices and the ways in which self-regulation diluted consumer protection. By the end of the century a vocal alliance of consumer watchdogs, led by the Office for Fair Trading, were pressing for tighter controls. From very different starting points, the strengthening of consumer sovereignty through the resurrection of community or works-based welfare associations was also being advocated (Green, 1985; Field, 1996a; Mulgan, 1996).

As Britain moves into a new century, commercial and occupational welfare providers thus face both new opportunities and a requestioning of their role. They also face the challenges posed by increasing work flexibility, longer retirements and changing family patterns. Past trends suggest that in these circumstances purveyors and employers are unlikely to overcome the recognised barriers to private insurance or provide adequate protection for women and other low waged or irregular earners (Barr, 1990; Burchardt and Hills, 1997). Yet vendors are already experimenting with 'flexible' packages geared to funding mortgages, pensions and other welfare payments in less stable labour markets, while canvassing the need for more extensive personal savings.

The Major government's commitment to a 'shrinking' welfare state endorsed these developments; paradoxically Labour's proposed 'third way' points in a similar direction. On the surface this may appear unlikely. For example Frank Field, who served briefly as a Minister for Social Reform in the Blair government, favoured new organisational vehicles which bypassed current commercial welfare suppliers. New Labour is also likely to remove many of the tax privileges which underpinned the postwar growth of commercial and occupational welfare and has already signalled its antipathy to private education with the abolition of the assisted places scheme and nursery school vouchers. These initiatives, however, have to be set against other aspects of Labour's welfare agenda.

As the 1997 election campaign made clear, Labour is as committed as the Conservatives to low taxation and containing public spending to boost Britain's economic performance. Rather than an expanded welfare state displacing private provision, more complex changes are likely, with differing implications for different product markets. To begin with, given its fiscal rectitude, Labour is unlikely to substitute state for private provision. Those areas which were not incorporated fully by the state in the 1940s or have developed since seem set to remain. It also appears to be reprioritising within and between different state services. While the heartlands of the British welfare state are likely to remain intact, financial pressures may lead to greater concentration on 'core' provision, as is already happening in health care and pensions, leaving 'topping-up' to individuals. More generally, Labour seems to be moving towards a new conception of public services. Encapsulated in the notion of an 'investment welfare state', this implies a new covenant between state and citizen, based on 'thrift-for-all' through subsidised self-provisioning.

Greater self-funding of pensions and post-compulsory education, 'partnerships' with non-statutory agencies, including a revamped private finance initiative all point in this direction and new state-sanctioned forms of occupational welfare would certainly complement this agenda.[12] What is equally clear, however, is that Labour's 'third way' while encouraging commercial and occupational welfare also heralds tighter regulation of financial services and enhanced consumer protection in welfare markets generally. Far from dwindling, private welfare is thus set to remain central to Britain's welfare arrangements. But, as in the past, regulatory changes are likely to vary from market to market, contributing to the continued variability in the production and consumption of different services.

PART V

The Future

13

The Prospects for British Social Welfare

Robert M. Page

The contributors to this volume have explored various developments in British social welfare throughout the twentieth century. In this concluding chapter consideration will be given to the prospects for British welfarism at the turn of the century.

Despite a number of spirited attempts (see Page, 1996; Francis, 1997; Tiratsoo, 1997) to rebut some of the more 'jaundiced' overviews (Barnett, 1986, 1995; Marsland, 1996) of collectivism since the Second World War, it would be misleading to suggest that the 'classic' welfare state retains the degree of popularity which marked its inception in the 1940s. Before considering some of the reasons for this decline in popularity it is useful, first, to reflect on the reasons for the postwar 'euphoria' surrounding the establishment of the welfare state. According to Titmuss (1950) the emergence of more positive attitudes towards state welfarism owed much to the wartime experiences of both the civilian and service population. Although the validity of this assessment continues to be disputed (Harris, 1986; Smith, 1986; Fielding, 1992), it is difficult to refute the central thrust of Titmuss' thesis (Addison, 1975; Harrison, 1978; Mason and Thompson, 1991):

> The mood of the people changed, and in sympathetic response, values changed as well. If dangers were to be shared, then resources should also be shared... dramatic events on the home front served only to reinforce the war-warmed impulse of people for a more generous society. (Titmuss, 1950, p. 508)

Unquestionably the postwar welfare reforms of the Attlee governments were inspired by the desire to create a fairer, more egalitarian society (Francis, 1997) – a goal which was the more commendable given the parlous state of the national economy (Brooke, 1995; Tomlinson, 1998). The 1946 National Insurance Act represented a shift towards the more progressive principle of universality rather than selectivity while the establishment of a 'decommodified' health care system in 1948, which owed much to the tenacity of Aneurin Bevan, remains the greatest formal welfare achievement of the century (Morgan, 1984b; Webster, 1998). Progress was less remarkable in the case of education where the main success was the raising of the school-leaving age to 15 in 1947. Labour's housing policy also came in for criticism not least because of Bevan's laudable refusal to sacrifice quality for quantity. Although the level of completions (1 million by 1951) fell well short of earlier projections (4 to 5 million) this was no mean achievement given the depletion of the available stock as a result of enemy bombing, the high level of public expectation and severe resource constraints. As Jefferys (1992) notes, 'Bevan's house-building programme meant that affordable, decent accommodation was, as never before, within the reach of thousands of lower-income families' (p. 61).

For the public these various developments were indicative of a shift away from the moralistic judgementalism associated with the Poor Law towards a citizenship model of welfarism. As Harris (1996) points out:

> The rhetorical hallmarks of the early years of the welfare state were the replacement of 'charity', 'dependency', 'moralism', and bureaucratic surveillance of private lives by a new ethic of social 'citizenship'... [this new approach] stressed the virtues of 'universality' as opposed to 'selectivity', of social insurance as opposed to Poor Law and public assistance, of 'impersonal' entitlement rather than 'moralistic' discretion, and of benefits paid not on the basis of means-tests and proof of need but as an automatic right of citizenship. (p. 122)

The new citizenship which Labour hoped would take root in postwar British society was not to be equated solely with 'welfare' advances. The ultimate goal was the establishment of a socialist commonwealth (Fielding (1992). It was hoped that the more active forms of citizenship which had emerged during wartime would, with proactive government support, extend into the postwar period. It was envisaged that the establishment of new communities with good leisure and other facilities would create a genuine sense of neighbourliness and foster increased participation at the local level (Fielding, *et al.*, 1995). This more ambitious citizenship objective did not, however, resonate with the British public. As Fielding *et al.* (1995) note:

> many people were not really in sympathy with what Labour was trying to achieve. Britain might have come together to a certain extent during the war, but in the later 1940s had reverted to being a very divided society. Class and gender differences were pronounced, as were those based on occupation, place of residence and notions of respectability. In these circumstances, the impulse to community remained weak. (p. 128)

Although the public appeared less than enthusiastic about the prospect of a socialist commonwealth, they appeared to be more steadfast in their support for the welfare state and full employment. Such was the popularity of these measures that subsequent Conservative governments were reluctant to curb the forward march of state welfarism. Indeed, the fact that leading figures such as Butler and Macmillan were so supportive of state welfare measures has led a number of commentators to suggest that a consensus emerged in the period from 1945 to the mid-1970s (Kavanagh and Morris, 1989; Lowe, 1990; Dutton, 1991; Timmins, 1995). During this period it is contended that both main parties accepted the case for a mixed economy; the need for proactive government intervention to generate economic growth and secure high levels of employment and the desirability of comprehensive social service provision.

Those who reject the consensus thesis (Fraser, 1987; Pimlott, 1989; Glennerster, 1995) in whole or in part argue that the key differences between Labour and the Conservatives have been too readily overlooked. As Pimlott (1989) states,

> It is easy to take for granted hard-won reforms, and to forget how bitterly they were contested at the time. When one policy triumphs over another, it is tempting to regard the change as inevitable, and as part of a progressive, consensual evolution. Yet the reality of a radical reform is that it has seldom come without a fight. (p. 13)

Moreover, within both the Conservative and Labour parties one can detect evidence of division. In Conservative circles concerns were expressed about the adverse consequences of state welfare monopolies (Hailsham, 1959; Lees, 1961; Howe, 1965), the adoption of universalist principles (One Nation Group, 1959) and penal rates of personal taxation (Lewis and Maude, 1949). In the case of the Labour Party discussions about the pace of change (the consolidation/fundamentalist debate) and subsequently about the overall direction of policy (Crosland's 1956 revisionism) served to highlight the differences between democratic socialist and social democratic economic and social strategies (Jones, T. 1996).

Although there were undoubtedly some similarities in the post-1945 welfare policies of both the major parties it is questionable whether this can accurately be described as a fully fledged consensus (Deakin, 1994). There was cross-party support for a mixed economy, high levels of employment and a mature welfare state. Equally, though, more fundamental policy differences over such issues as equality, redistribution and universalism were not far beneath the surface. In short, the consensus was of a shallow rather than a deep kind.

The 'breakdown' of this shallow welfare consensus, which most commentators identify as having occurred in the second half of the 1970s (Lowe, 1993; Powell and Hewitt, 1998), signalled the start of wide-ranging reappraisals of the role and purpose of the welfare state. The most sustained attack on the welfare state has come from neo-Liberal or New-Right commentators. The theoretical insights of writers such as Hayek (1944, 1960) and Friedman (1962) formed the basis for both an economic and social critique of state welfare.

In terms of economic factors it was argued that growing state welfare activity had led to a decline in investment, activity and profitability in the 'productive' (manufacturing) sector of the economy (Bacon and Eltis, 1976). Indeed, by the early 1990s the Conservative government were issuing grim warnings about the exponential rise in social spending – particularly in the area of social security – which they contended was unaffordable (Department of Social Security, 1993).

New Right commentators also argued that the provision of 'free' services at time of need had encouraged consumers to make excessive demands for services while the absence of controlling profit and loss mechanisms had led to a lack of producer (doctors, teachers, social workers) interest in the price or opportunity costs of the services dispensed. Moreover, the welfare state was also indicted for undermining the incentive to work by the imposition of punitive tax rates and over-generous social security payments.

In the case of negative social consequences the welfare state has been criticised for undermining more traditional ways of satisfying human need such as family support, philanthropy and the market (Seldon, 1981; Green, 1993, 1996). Moreover the welfare state is seen as providing incentives for anti-social behaviour (Murray, 1984, 1990; Mead, 1986; Willetts, 1992). Murray (1994) has argued, for instance, that the increasing number of families which are headed by lone mothers (households which he believes provide a breeding ground for the development of an underclass) is linked in part to the fact that illegitimacy no longer carries any form of economic or social diswelfare for those concerned.

Crucially, the postwar performance of the welfare state also drew fire from its traditional supporters on the left who highlighted the rather modest achievements of post-1945 collectivism. In particular commentators such as Townsend (1958), Abel-Smith (1958) and Titmuss (1963) expressed disappointment about the failure of state welfarism to banish inequality – an outcome which was linked in part to middle-class capture of collective provision and the regressive nature of occupational and fiscal welfare.

The persistence of relative poverty as well as health and educational inequalities (Goldthorpe *et al.*, 1980; Halsey *et al.*, 1980; Le Grand, 1982; Townsend and Davidson, 1982; Whitehead, 1988; Oppenheim, 1993) has led to a noticeable loss of confidence in the reforming potential of the welfare state. Doubts have also been expressed about the quality of public sector administration (Piachaud, 1991; Meadows, 1996). As Tony Wright (1996) contends:

> it might be expected that those who are most committed to the public provision of services would also be those who display a restless ingenuity in ensuring that such provision is effective in terms of performance and outcome; yet, this has often not been the case. (p. 140)

This 'failing' has led not only to calls for more responsive forms of administration but also for a more participative form of social policy (Beresford and Croft, 1995).

As we approach the turn of the century it seems clear that there is to be a concerted attempt to 'reform' social welfare in Britain. Indeed The 'New' Labour government, which was elected in May 1997, has made it clear that its unwillingness to embrace neoclassical economic thinking should not be interpreted as a signal that it will return to an 'outmoded' classical social democratic strategy let alone a democratic socialist approach (see Gray, 1997a, Ch. 2). Instead it favours an ideology which has come to be known as a third way 'beyond left and right' (Giddens, 1994, 1996, 1998). According to Tony Wright (1996) – one of New Labour's key theorists – this 'liberal socialism' will be:

> diverse, pluralistic, and variegated, both politically and economically. It will be egalitarian enough to be socially inclusive, so that all its citizens are within reach of each other, but this will not be confused with identity of treatment or uniformity of provision. It will combine a commitment to a dynamic economy with a commitment to a decent society... It will know that its economic task is to make capitalism work more successfully, but it will also know that there are different kinds of capitalism. It will understand the virtues of markets, but also the vices. It will know that states can do too much, but also too little. It will recognise that decent societies pay decent taxes, but that spending more on one thing usually means spending less on something else. it will celebrate diversity, but also seek to nourish social unity. In rejecting a whole range of false opposites, the space is opened for a new politics of liberal socialism to be endlessly inventive in exploring how a clever state can operate. Old collectivists and new marketeers will not like it, but that is another argument in its favour. (pp. 143–4)

Crucially, New Labour believes that a 'modern' welfare state must adapt to contemporary economic conditions rather than seek to coset its citizens from the winds of change. It is accepted that the scale and pace of global economic developments (especially the deregulation of financial markets and the shift from manufacturing to service sector employment) has made it extremely difficult for any nation state to pursue social policies which the international financial community adjudge to be a fetter on capital accumulation (see Giddens, 1994, 1996; Held, 1995; Hirst and Thompson, 1996).

Accordingly, New Labour has become avowedly pro-market rather than merely market tolerant. As two key New Labour strategists – Peter Mandelson and Roger Liddle (1996) – make clear:

> New Labour welcomes the rigour of competitive markets as the most efficient means of anticipating and supplying consumers' wants, offering choice and stimulating innovation. Competition is the only effective force that prevents capitalists opting for a quiet life and managers spending their afternoons on the golf-course. (p. 22)

Although it is accepted that markets need to be judiciously regulated in order to ensure that they do not 'reinforce inequalities' or 'entrench privilege' (ibid., p. 22) this is not deemed to require a shift towards the interventionist, neo-Keynesianism, 'continental' stakeholding advocated by commentators such as Will Hutton (1995, 1997). While New Labour is willing to provide some protection for workers (as demonstrated by its willingness to sign up to the social chapter and to introduce a 'competitive' minimum wage), it is keen to retain a flexible labour market, which it believes will be essential for future prosperity. In essence New Labour will pursue what Thompson (1996, Ch. 18) and others have described as supply-side socialism – that is, a microeconomic strategy which aims to enhance the 'quality' and improve the use of 'factor inputs' to ensure higher productivity levels, lower labour costs and increased competitiveness. The promotion of full employment by means of deficit financing or the resurrection of corporatist policy agreements is no longer on the agenda (Anderson and Mann, 1997).

New Labour and the Welfare State

New Labour's social strategy is intended to dovetail with its economic philosophy.

New Labour accepts that the classic welfare state (see Lowe, 1994b) has become structurally deficient and outmoded, producer dominated, economically and socially disadvantageous and ineffective as an instrument for egalitarianism. In terms of structural deficiency, New Labour echoes the plea of the Commission on Social Justice (1994) for the development of an 'intelligent' welfare state:

> Instead of a welfare state designed for old risks, old industries and old family structures, there is a need for an intelligent welfare state that will be active throughout our lives, helping people to negotiate unpredictable change at work and home. Instead of a safety net to relieve poverty, we need a social security system that can help to prevent poverty. Instead of a health service designed primarily to treat illness, we need a health policy whose priority is to promote better health. In other words, the welfare state must not only look after people when they cannot look after themselves, it must also enable them to achieve self-improvement and self-support. The welfare state must offer a hand-up rather than a handout. (pp. 223–4)

For New Labour an intelligent welfare state strategy must reject the postwar 'revisionist' view that annual increases in public spending can be equated with social progress given that high levels of public spending can undermine economic prosperity. Accordingly, there is a reluctance to permit government expenditure to creep much above 40 per cent of national income (see Layard, 1997).

The principle of universalism must also, according to New Labour, be subjected to scrutiny. Although it can be a force for social cohesion it can also prevent scarce resources from reaching those in the most need:

> New Labour recognises that what is important is not just how much the public sector spends but how it is spent. Cutting waste and improving efficiency should be a priority, as should ensuring that public spending reaches the groups it is intending to benefit. (Mandelson and Liddle, 1996, p. 27)

Furthermore a shift away from 'municipal socialism and centralised nationalisation' (Mandleson and Liddle, 1996, p. 27) is seen as necessary to curb producer interests. Although New Labour are committed to combating social exclusion they are retreating from a traditional egalitarian strategy.

As Gordon Brown – New Labour's first Chancellor – makes clear:

> We reject equality of outcome not because it is too radical, but because it is neither desirable or feasible. Predetermined results imposed, as they would have to be, by a central authority and decided irrespective of work, effort or contribution to the community, is not a socialist dream but other people's nightmare of socialism.

> What angers people is that millions are denied the opportunity to realise their potential and are powerless to do so. It is this inequality that must be addressed. (Brown, 1997)

Brown, like others, favours what has come to be known as endowment egalitarianism, namely, providing fair opportunities for all citizens to acquire the necessary education, skills and training which will permit them to compete in a changing and uncertain labour market (Kay, 1996; McCormick, 1997). The role of government is not to provide or guarantee employment but rather to maximise the employability skills of all citizens by measures such as its first flagship policy *Welfare to Work* (Cm 3805, Ch. 3).

Crucially, as the first major welfare document of the Blair government – *New Ambitions for Our Country: A New Contract for Welfare* (Cm 3805, 1998) makes clear, paid work is now seen as the best way to improve the position of the socially excluded rather than 'dependency creating' welfare payments or services. Accordingly, emphasis will be given to education and training programmes and the development of a tax and benefits system which will make work 'pay.' Moreover, citizens will be encouraged to take increased responsibility for their own welfare needs which could herald a decisive shift towards what Klein and Millar (1995) have termed the 'do-it-yourself' welfare state.

According to New Labour it is no longer feasible to attempt to reduce inequalities in market incomes by traditional forms of egalitarian social policy. Instead, it is hoped that by upgrading the marketable skills of all citizens, those at the bottom end of society will be able to find their material salvation through paid work. In essence, as Pollard (1998) notes, New Labour is relying on an 'evolutionary' form of social mobility rather than overt egalitarianism to mitigate prevailing disadvantages. Despite some recent evidence that the growing inequality in the distribution of incomes in the 1980s and early 90s has been temporarily halted (Hills, 1998) without explicitly proactive welfare policies, it seems questionable whether a 'one club' employment strategy of this kind will reduce inequalities over the longer term (Goodman, *et al.*, 1997).

This rejection of an overt egalitarian strategy – which some contend was never really a part of Labour's postwar vision (Hindess, 1987) – has led commentators such as Kellner (1997) and Gray (1997b) to 'redefine' equality (see Franklin, 1997). According to Kellner (1997) it is not equality of opportunity or outcome which is required but equality of access:

> Equality of access casts its net far wider than equality of outcome and equality of opportunity. It is concerned with information, power, security, health and justice. It is about rights at work and the freedom to walk through streets without fear. Equality of access proposes that a mature democracy should strive as a matter of principle for a range of equal membership rights for all its citizens. (p. 20)

John Gray (1997b) contends that New Labour needs to engage with the New Liberalism of Green and Hobhouse in order to find 'a modern, post-social democratic conception of social justice' (p. 8) which recognises that citizens are concerned about the diminution of social cohesion but not inequality. Gray (1997b) believes that the public are concerned about the plight of the poor but they have no appetite for 'levelling down' tax policies.

> This means that redistribution should be implemented in the priorities adopted in public expenditure, not by taxation. A radical post-social democratic government will be concerned to direct resources where it judges human needs to be most urgent. It will want to assist the social groups which are most excluded and to give most help to those whose talents are most at risk of going to waste. The spending policies of such a government could – and should – be consistently redistributive. Yet its tax policies need not be more than very moderately progressive. (p. 9)

It may be the case that we are witnessing a return to what Powell (1995) has termed the non-egalitarian citizenship approach to welfare based on a social minimum and universalism rather than redistribution of income and wealth. For Sassoon (1997) this more modest goal is still well 'worth fighting for':

The difference in income which allows the rich to purchase a diamond as big as the Ritz might be vexing to destitute diamond-lovers. But it is not as iniquitous as the private purchase of a life-saving operation to the exclusion of others who cannot afford it. (p. 149)

Crucially, though, this citizenship approach is now likely to be of a conditional, rather than unconditional, kind. As Plant (1998) points out this contingent variant:

places much less emphasis on rights, and focuses instead on obligation, virtue and contribution. On this view citizenship is not a kind of pre-existing status, but rather something that is achieved by contributing to the life of society. The ideas of reciprocity and contribution are at the heart of this concept of citizenship: individuals do not and cannot have a right to the resources of society unless they contribute to the development of that society through work or other socially valued activities, if they are in a position to do so. (p. 30)

Welfare to Work is based firmly on conditional citizenship. While New Labour accepts that government has a duty to provide appropriate training and education they also believe that citizens have a corresponding obligation to avail themselves of the opportunities provided. Indeed those who fail to meet their obligations will be penalised by benefit reductions.

New Labour's willingness to impose tough sanctions on the 'recalcitrant poor' is indicative of its desire to shift away from the alleged non-judgementalism of leading postwar thinkers on the left such as Titmuss (Deacon, 1993) and Galbraith (Reisman, 1995).

Angels, Knights, Serpents, Knaves, and Pawns

Frank Field has proved to be one of the most influential critics of non-judgementalism in social policy. He contends that welfare measures should work with, rather than against, the grain of human nature. According to Field (1995) self-interest is a far more powerful motivating force than selflessness. As such the task for social policy is to ensure that the pursuit of self-interest and self-improvement can be fostered in ways which do not undermine the common good. Field is not opposed to altruism *per se*. However, the fact that this principle has proved so difficult to operate in families (not least in Titmuss' own, according to Oakley, 1996) or small communities leads him to reject it as a basis for state welfarism (Field, 1997a). The strength of Field's antipathy towards 'welfare altruists' such as Titmuss should not be understated:

The sanitised post-Christian view of human character held by Titmuss resulted in an approach to welfare which helped make Labour unelectable for so much of my political career. It has been the Titmuss legacy which I have opposed as being as dangerous as it is futile. Again. I stress that I do not see this as a minor issue. Nor do I feel that I have blown it out of all proportion. The Titmuss legacy lingered about the political debate with such force that I, for one, felt that it covered me with a form of intellectual treacle which made movement difficult. It precluded a proper discussion of fraud and this alone helped destroy Labour's credibility with street-wise voters who consequently did not consider Labour a party fit for the task of governing. Much worse, it immobilised Labour thinking as the political curtain began to sweep across the stage of state collectivism. (Field, 1997b, pp. 150–1)

For Field, the failure to recognise that within each citizen there are elements of both 'serpent' and 'angel' has blighted the post-1945 welfare state project. What is now required is a welfare strategy based on a principle which will resonate with the majority of citizens – namely self-interest rather than altruism. Field (1995) favours a twenty-year 'programme of reconstruction' which will include the phased dismantling of means-tested benefits (which he believes only serves to encourage dishonesty); the reform of the National Insurance Scheme and the introduction of compulsory universal second tier private pension provision. While Field is supportive of collectivism he doubts whether the state can perform this role given its declining popularity with the public. Instead he favours what he terms social collectivism under which 'national insurance rights will be vested with each individual member' and pension funds will be 'owned by the contributors' (p. 171). As he states:

No one now believes that the current National Insurance scheme is theirs, and that the future benefits they are currently paying for are safe. Taking unemployment benefit alone, while contributors have been asked to pay more, the earnings-related supplement to unemployment benefit has been abolished, the eligibility rules have been severely tightened, and, with the Jobseekers' Allowance, the 12 month duration of benefit halved. A new National Insurance scheme controlled by the contributors must be established for voters to believe that their contributions will be safe and that the eligibility rules will not be changed against their interest. (Field, 1996b, p. 21)

It should be noted there is space for a modicum of altruism in Field's plans. Those who are unable to engage in paid work for good reason, such as carers, will have their contributions met out of progressive taxation. Crucially, though, Field is at pains to stress that even this limited form of 'altruism' will be eroded if taxpayers consider the eligibility requirements to be lax.

Taxpayers are likely to stump up a contribution for poorer stakeholders only if they approve of the behaviour of those for whom they are contributing. (Field, 1997b, p. 147)

For Field this requires a proactive benefits agency which will assist 'all non-pensioner claimants in the development of career plans needed for re-entering the labour market' (ibid, p. 171.) The historic problem with agencies of this kind though is that there remains 'a fine line between measures which seek to do something *for* the unemployed and those which seek to do something *to* the unemployed' (Deacon, 1997, p. 10).

Julian Le Grand (1997) has also given consideration to assumptions about human motivations which underpin state welfarism. According to Le Grand the post-45 democratic socialist welfare strategy assumed that the providers and funders of state welfare were altruistic (knights) and that consumers would be passive recipients (pawns).

> it is not implausible to describe the bundle of implicit assumptions concerning human behaviour that characterised... the democratic socialist welfare state as one designed to be financed and operated by knights, for the benefit of pawns. (p. 157)

Le Grand questions the accuracy of these assumptions. As he notes 'public choice' economists and political scientists have suggested that the actions of welfare professionals can be better understood if they are regarded as self-interested rather than selfless practitioners while middle-class welfare funders often overlook the substantial personal benefits they derive from collective provision. Moreover, some commentators (Field, 1996b; Murray, 1994) contend that the behaviour of some welfare consumers such as recipients of means-tested benefits are self-interested or even selfish.

Le Grand (1997) accepts there is not enough information to predict how producers, funders or consumers will behave in 'welfare-relevant situations' (p. 161). In this 'situation of ignorance', Le Grand contends that:

> it would be safest to adopt public policies based on the knaves strategy. For a knave's strategy will do little harm if people are actually knights; but a knight's strategy could be disastrous if people are actually knaves. (p. 161)

However, Le Grand remains sceptical about the efficacy of adopting a knavish strategy not least because it might, in practice, undermine the public good (see also Goodin, 1988).

Le Grand also considers, but ultimately rejects, the possibility of continuing with a more proactive knightly strategy – that is, encouraging exemplary behaviour by means of exhortation or example (a strategy that has much in common with Etzioni's, 1993, 1997 brand of communitarianism) or by more 'coercive' legal measures (minimum wage legislation, compulsory child support payments).

Given the deficiencies in both these approaches, Le Grand opts for what he terms a 'robust' strategy – 'strategies or institutions which are robust to what-ever assumption is made about human motivation' (ibid., p. 163). In practice, this could lead to greater emphasis being given to 'partnership' or 'matching' schemes. In the case of long-term care, public funding would be available for a basic care package but this could be supplemented by individuals or relatives making contributions which would be matched pound for pound by public funds. Although less progressive than a means-tested scheme Le Grand contends 'matching' would appeal:

> to both the knight and the knave. It appeals to self-interest because it encourages people to provide for themselves. However, it also encourages relatives and friends to contribute resources to help people in need; and it appeals to a more collectivist spirit of altruism through the use of public money to provide the matching funds. (Le Grand, 1997, pp. 165–6)

New Labour's desire to distance itself from the collectivism of the golden age has led them to embrace what some regard as a more 'traditional' pluralistic welfare strategy (Finlayson, 1994).

The case for welfare pluralism has been advanced by a number of leading commentators on British social policy (Hadley and Hatch, 1981; Judge, 1987; Knapp, 1989) who contend that the deficiencies of state welfare could be remedied by the introduction of more decentralised, community orientated public services which would complement rather than replace voluntary and informal sources of care. New Labour would appear to be persuaded by Klein and O'Higgins' (1985) suggestion that welfare pluralism represents the most pragmatic welfare strategy in an age of uncertainty. A commitment to welfare pluralism enables politicians to shed any 'inflexible' ideological baggage position and be guided instead by the principle of purposeful opportunism – having some clear ideas about the direction in which you wish to proceed but being flexible in relation to the precise means to achieve these objectives. Instead of being wedded to specific policy 'instruments' governments can seek to meet their objectives, such as the establishment of a minimum income or the countering of health inequalities, in the most flexible and creative ways.

This commitment to welfare pluralism will also permit New Labour to endorse public/private partnerships. For example, the new Labour government has decided to continue with the Private Finance Initiative (PFI) which was established under a former Conservative administration. Under this scheme the capital costs of say a new public hospital will be met by a private company, who then lease back the buildings to the state over the medium to long term. While such schemes limit the need for short-term government borrowing the level of future repayments may leave little room for manoeuvre in the expenditure plans of subsequent administrations (Terry, 1996).

The non-state sector is also likely to have an expanded role in areas such as retirement pensions and long-term care given New Labour's commitment to provide basic rather than optimal levels of state support. This strategy is also fraught with dangers given the mis-selling of personal pensions in the 1980s and 90s (Waine, 1995) and the fact that collectively financed provision has advantages in terms of security, equity and efficiency (Townsend and Walker, 1995; Lynes, 1996; Burchardt and Hills, 1997).

New Labour's scepticism about 'tax and spend' policies coupled with its acceptance of New Right criticisms about the self-interested motivations of public sector workers has also led them to focus on measures which can enhance the quality and quantity of service delivery without the continued need for additional expenditure. For example, in the case of education it is accepted that some schools in deprived neighbourhoods might require some additional resources. However, New Labour believes that the performance of schools can generally be enhanced through better organisation and higher quality teaching. All schools will be expected to ensure that a high proportion of their pupils attain national standards in numeracy and literacy. To this end, a New Standards and Effectiveness Unit has been established to improve the performance in all British schools. In addition a National Schools Standards Task Force has been formed to deal with 'failing schools' and a Pathfinder Summer Literacy Scheme for pupils who have fallen behind with their reading and writing has been selectively introduced prior to more widespread use. Moreover, the government plans to introduce a new qualification for headteachers and to speed up the process of 'weeding out' underperforming teachers.

The advance of welfare pluralism has led to renewed interest in the voluntary sector which, contrary to the expectations of some earlier commentators (Owen, 1965), did not fall into terminal decline as a result of the growth of post-1945 state welfare (Deakin, 1995). However the much vaulted independence of the voluntary sector has been challenged in recent years by a series of Conservative initiatives which undermined their independence and weaned them away from partnerships with local authority. Indeed, many voluntary organisations have been forced to accept highly questionable funding and administrative arrangements demanded by central government sponsors in order to survive (Waine, 1992). Although some have highlighted the positive potential of such developments (Mulgan and Landry, 1995), there are real dangers that a greater acceptance of managerialism and a contract culture within high profile voluntary bodies will undermine public confidence in this sector (Taylor, 1995) heralding a return, perhaps, to more cynical perceptions of voluntary activity (Humphreys, 1995).

The lack of concerted opposition to the direction of New Labour's social policy might lead one to conclude that alternative welfare strategies have now been supplanted (Giddens, 1998). However, welfare ideologies tend to wax and wane rather than disappear completely. As such the resurgence of say a democratic socialist welfare strategy at some future point in time cannot, as some commentators suggest, be categorically ruled out (Gray, 1998).

Any consideration of the future for welfare in Britain must also take account of developments in other comparable nation states and the impact of influential supranational institutions such as the International Monetary Fund, the World Bank and the International Labour Organization (Deacon with Hulse and Stubbs, 1997). Certainly, there would appear to be a possibility of greater convergence in terms of the welfare arrangements operating within the member states of the European Union arguably along reformed corporatist lines (Esping-Andersen, 1990, 1996; Leibfried and Pierson, 1995). However, the fact that some member states have proved less than enthusiastic in their desire to embrace monetary union would seem to suggest that, in the absence of some seismic economic shock, diverse rather than uniform welfare regimes will continue to operate in the EU well into the next millennium. Indeed, the commitment to the principle of subsidiarity (Spicker, 1991) may even lead to greater diversity within a nation state as localities press for the right to offer 'non-standard' services which are deemed to be better suited to the needs of their residents. While there may be some advantages with developments of this kind there are also risks of increased social fragmentation (Marquand, 1998). Although the influence of supranational institutions is likely to increase, this does not necessarily mean that the influence of the nation state will decline significantly. While some might welcome a shift towards a more integrated global social policy on 'progressive' grounds (Deacon with Hulse and Stubbs, 1997), others are likely to be more circumspect given the possibility that such an occurrence might lead to a situation in which the emancipation of the few is dependent on increased 'immiseration' for the many (Gray, 1998). In particular the idea that paring back some of the corporatist 'welfare' structures operating in the European Union might prove beneficial in the battle to redistribute global resources from richer to poorer regions should be treated with caution. Indeed, growing fears about social and economic insecurity in many EU nations may well lead to a groundswell of support for governments which promise to enhance the level of social and economic protection and security.

In his overview earlier in this volume John Stewart referred to the 'highly contested and politicised nature of social policy during the twentieth century'. As we approach the millennium there are clear indications that the current Labour administration wishes to develop a new welfare consensus based around a reciprocal 'contract' between the individual and the state. Individuals who can undertake paid work will be expected to do so while those with 'legitimate' reasons for non-participation will be guaranteed a level of security. It is believed that this work orientated strategy for social policy coupled with cooperative partnerships between the public, private, voluntary and informal welfare sectors will lead to less discord in the area of social policy. While such a development cannot be ruled out it seems rather more plausible to conclude, not least given the dynamism of economic and social change and the diverse interests of the citizenry, that the area of welfare will continue to generate as many conflicts about principle and practice in the next century as it did in this.

Notes

Chapter 2 Paying for Welfare in the Twentieth Century

1. On the widespread purchase and significance of burial insurance, see Johnson, 1985.
2. Some exemptions to unemployment insurance continued for groups with low incidence of unemployment, so that between the wars the Unemployment Insurance Fund was weakened by the exclusion of these low risk groups.
3. Although the Fabian Society in its evidence to Beveridge suggested that the spreading of the income tax down the income scale during the war might make it best to finance welfare from general taxation.
4. The NHS, then as now, derived a small fraction of its income from National Insurance Contributions.
5. Economic growth, it should be emphasised, increases the demand for welfare spending, especially in the case of education and health where, as people get better off, they expect higher standards of provision.
6. Note that, contrary to a common perception, these cuts began long before the visit of the IMF to Britain in the autumn of 1976, and it was the introduction of the 'cash limit' system for public spending in the budget of 1976 that brought about the sharp reductions of succeeding years.
7. These cuts in capital spending on housing began under the Labour government, but the big change in spending came from the Conservative policy of subsidising individuals rent payments rather than subsidising housing provision by local authorities. (Hills, 1990, Ch. 5).
8. Combined with changes in the labour market and the squeeze on benefit levels, this change in tax incidence led to most remarkable of the Conservative period in office, the striking increase in the inequality in the distribution of income.
9. There are also redistributions from high to low unemployment occupations.

Chapter 3 Neoclassicism, the New Right and British Social Welfare

1. A number of extreme libertarians or 'anarcho-capitalists' reject the whole idea of the state. They are mainly American and although they have some followers in Britain they do not appear often in the literature.

2. Public goods cannot be supplied by the market because of the 'free rider' problem, that is, they are available for consumption by those who have not paid for them.
3. Conventional welfare goods are not public goods, like defence or clean air, because their consumption is an entirely private experience: although richer members of the community might feel better off if they knew the deprived were being taken care of.
4. See his *Voluntary Action* (1948).
5. President Johnson introduced Medicare (1965), health care for the over-65s, partly paid for by the pay-roll tax; and Medicaid (1965), zero-priced medical treatment for the poor.
6. Invalidity Benefit was changed to Incapacity Benefit in 1993. The latter is harder to obtain.
7. This was one of Thomas Malthus's complaints against poor relief.
8. The implication of all this is that welfare spending should be concentrated on those goods and services which the poor have to consume, for example primary education.
9. There is some case for the symmetry of civil rights and welfare rights since protection of the former does involve public spending (and therefore redistribution).
10. American private health spending has increased because of such things as litigation and the consequent heavy costs of insurance for doctors against malpractice suits.
11. The 'internal market' for health in Britain was established by legislation in 1990.
12. The problem is compounded in 'anonymous' market societies which are characterised by high mobility of labour.
13. Social Security Act (1986).

Chapter 11 Voluntary and Informal Welfare

1. The term was resuscitated by the Seebhom Committee in 1968, whose report led to the setting up of the new Social Services Departments. Prior to the Second World War, entries for social administration were cross-referenced with entries for social service in the *London Bibliography of the Social Sciences*. *Personal* social service was increasingly cross-referenced with social work. The concept of social service can therefore be seen as linking social administration and social work.

Chapter 12 Commercial and Occupational Welfare

1. 'Proxy' purchasers such as employers can, moreover, also provide their own 'in-house' services, thus adding to the complexity of welfare transactions in different markets. Proxy purchasing can also be undertaken by state agencies, though only limited reference can be given such interventions in this chapter.
2. Space pre-empts discussion of the welfare services provided by unions and professional associations.
3. Berridge (1990) provides some insight into the prevalence of another form of private provision, over the counter medication. Upper- and middle-income groups could also rely on the support provided by domestic servants, of whom there were 1,700,000 in 1914.
4. Relief was first granted when income tax was first introduced in 1799 and reinstated by Gladstone in 1853 as a means of easing savings for retirement. Glad-

stone also sponsored the 1864 Government Annuities Act which established a state life insurance scheme administered through the Post Office. This was little used and wound up in 1926.

5. Raised to £250 in 1920 and £420 in 1942.
6. Over the counter remedies also remained significant; working-class households spent an average of 3 per cent of their expenditure on medicines and medical services in addition to NHI contributions in the 1930s (Cherry 1996).
7. The inclusion of proprietary carriers was based on the condition that they set up separate provident units that were subject to members' control. Widows and orphans benefits were eventually introduced on a contributory basis in 1925.
8. Nearly a third of the smaller friendly societies went out of business between 1918 and 1936 (Cherry, 1996). Despite the manifold criticisms, the approved societies have been defended (Whiteside, 1983; Whiteside and Krafchik, 1983).
9. Beveridge had hoped to retain the friendly societies' administrative role, but found many were moribund or had lost their local associative role. He also planned to recruit industrial assurance agents to staff the new social security scheme.
10. Taxation was first introduced in the 1994 budget and raised in 1996. The parallel introduction of tax relief on health insurance for over-60s in 1994 appears to have had little impact on overall sales.
11. This is best illustrated by the building societies which have fallen from over 2,000 at the beginning of the century to around 80 today and the friendly societies which have fallen from 27,000 registered societies to 340, only 80 of which are open to new members.
12. This is exemplified in the Labour Party's own personal accident protection scheme. Underwritten by AIG, this offers party members and their families discounted insurance against permanent injury or death.

Bibliography

Abel-Smith, B. (1958) Whose welfare state? In Mackenzie, N. (ed.), pp. 55–73.

Abel-Smith, B. (1964) *The Hospitals 1800–1948*. London, Heinemann.

Abel-Smith, B. (1980) The welfare state: breaking the post-war consensus, *The Political Quarterly*, **51**: pp. 17–23.

Abel-Smith, B. and Townsend, P. (1965) *The Poor and the Poorest*. London, Bell & Sons.

Abercrombie, N. and Hill, B. (1976) Paternalism and patronage, *British Journal of Sociology*, **27**(4): 413–29.

Addison, P. (1975) *The Road to 1945*. London, Quartet.

Addison, P. (1994) *The Road to 1945*, rev. edn. London, Pimlico.

Addy, T. and Scott, D. (1988) *Fatal Impacts? The MSC and Voluntary Action*. Manchester, William Temple Foundation.

Adonis, A. (1996) For New Labour read New Liberals, *Observer* 8 September.

Aitken, I. (1992) Raising a glass amid the gloom, *Guardian* 13 March.

Alcock, P. (1987) *Poverty and State Support*. London, Longman.

Alcock, P. (1995) Social security and social insurance: a social policy perspective. In Silburn, R.L. (ed.).

Alcock, P. (1996) *Social Policy in Britain: Themes and Issues*. London, Macmillan.

Alcock, P. (1997) *Understanding Poverty*, 2nd edn. London, Macmillan.

Alcock, P., Erskine, A. and May, M. (eds) (1998) *The Student's Companion to Social Policy*. Oxford, Blackwell.

Aldcroft, D.H. (1992) *Education, Training and Economic Performance 1944 to 1990*. Manchester, Manchester University Press.

Anderson, M. (1977) The impact on the family relationships of the elderly since Victorian times on government income maintenance provision. In Shanas, E. and Sussman, M.B. (eds) *Family Bureaucracy and the Elderly*. Durham NC, Duke University Press, pp. 1–16.

Anderson, P. and Blackburn, R. (eds) (1965) *Towards Socialism*. London, Fontana.

Anderson, P. and Mann, N. (1997) *Safety First: The Making of New Labour*. London, Granta.

Anheier, H.K. and Seibel, W. (eds) (1990) *The Third Sector: Comparative Studies of Nonprofit Organizations*. New York, de Guyter.

Arber, S., Evandrou, M., Gilbert, N. and Dale, A. (1986) Gender, household composition and receipt of domiciliary services by the elderly disabled. Paper presented at the British Sociological Annual Conference, Loughborough.

Artis, M. and Cobham, D. (eds) (1991) *Labour's Economic Policies, 1974–79*. Manchester, Manchester University Press.

Association of British Insurers (1995) *Risk, Insurance and Welfare*. London, ABI.

Association of Metropolitan Authorities (1990) *Contracts for Social Care. The Local Authority View*. London, AMA.

Atkinson, A.B. (1972) Inequality and social security. In Townsend. P. and Bosanquet, N. (eds) *Labour and Inequality*. London, Fabian Society, Ch.2.

Atkinson, A.B. (1975) *The Economics of Inequality*. Oxford, Oxford University Press.

Atkinson, A.B. (1995) *Public Economics in Action: The Basic Income/Flat Tax Proposal*. Oxford, Oxford University Press.

Bacon, R. and Eltis, W.A. (1976) *Britain's Economic Problem: Too Few Producers*. London, Macmillan.

Balchin, P. (1995) *Housing Policy: An Introduction*, 3rd revised edn. London, Routledge.

Baldwin, P. (1990) *The Politics of Social Solidarity*. Cambridge, Cambridge University Press.

Baldwin, S. (1937) *On England*. London, Penguin.

Ball, M. (1983) *Housing Policy and Economic Power*. London, Methuen.

Ball, M. (1990) *Under One Roof: The International Financial Revolution and Mortgage Finance*. Hemel Hempstead, Harvester Wheatsheaf.

Banting, P. (1979) *Poverty, Politics and Policy: Britain in the 1960s*. London, Macmillan.

Barnett, S.A. and Barnett, Mrs S.A. (1894) *Practicable Socialism*. London, Longman.

Barnett, C. (1986) *The Audit of War*. London, Macmillan.

Barnett, C. (1995) *The Lost Victory*. London, Macmillan.

Barnett, C. (1996) *The Audit of War*, new edn. London, Pan.

Barr, N (1990) *Economic Theory and the Welfare State: A Survey and Interpretation*. London, Suntory Toyota/LSE.

Barr, N. and Coulter, F. (1990) Social security: solution or problem? In Hills, J. (ed.), Ch. 7.

Barry, N. (1985) The state, pensions and the philosophy of welfare, *Journal of Social Policy*, **14**(4): 467–90.

Barry, N. (1990) *Welfare*. Buckingham, Open University Press.

Barry, N. (1993) The New Right and provision for the elderly. In Jordan, G. and Ashford, N. (eds) *Public Policy and the Nature of the New Right*. London, Pinter, pp. 251–67.

Barry, N. (1995) Friedman. In George, V. and Page, R.M. (eds), Ch. 2.

Barry, N. (1997) Conservative thought and the welfare state, *Political Studies* **45**: pp. 331–45.

Baumol, W.J. (1986) Productivity growth, convergence and welfare: what the longrun data show, *American Economic Review*, 76: 1072–85.

Beenstock, M. (1994) Unemployment insurance, *Economic Affairs*, 14: 27–30.

Bellamy, R. (ed.) (1990) *Victorian Liberalism: Nineteenth-Century Political Thought and Practice*. London, Routledge.

Benjamin, D.K. and Kochin, L.A. (1979) Searching for an explanation of unemployment in interwar Britain, *Journal of Political Economy*, 87: 441–78.

Beresford, P. and Croft, S. (1995) It's our problem too! Challenging the exclusion of poor people from poverty discourse, *Critical Social Policy*, **44/45**: 75–95.

Berlin, I. (1969) *Four Essays*. Oxford, Oxford University Press

Berridge. V. (1990) Health and medicine 1750–1950. In Thompson, F.M.L. (ed.), Ch. 4.

Berthoud, R., Brown, J. and Cooper, S. (1981) *Poverty and the Development of Anti-Poverty Policy in the UK*. London, Heinemann.

Best, G. (1964) *Temporal Pillars*. Cambridge, Cambridge University Press.

Beveridge, W.H. (1909) *Unemployment: a Problem of Industry*. London, Allen & Unwin.

Beveridge, W.H. (1943) *The Pillars of Society*. London, Allen & Unwin.

Beveridge, W.H. (1944) *Full Employment in a Free Society*. London, Allen & Unwin.

Beveridge, W.H. (1948) *Voluntary Action*. London, Allen and Unwin.

Biagnini, E.F. and Reid, A. (1991) *Currents of Radicalism, Organised Labour and Party Politics in Britain, 1850–1914*. Cambridge, Cambridge University Press.

Billis, D. (1989) *A Theory of the Voluntary Sector: Implications for Policy and Practice*, Working Paper no. 5. Centre for Voluntary Organisation, LSE.

Billis, D. (1993) *Organising Public and Voluntary Agencies*. London, Routledge.

Birch, J. (1996) *Votes for Homes: The Roof Guide to British Housing Politics*. London, Coopers and Lybrand/Roof.

Bleaney, M.F. (1985) *The Rise and Fall of Keynesian Economics*. London, Macmillan.

Bock, G. and Thane, P. (eds) (1991) *Maternity and Gender Policies: Women and the Rise of the European Welfare States*. London, Routledge.

Boddy, M. (1980) *The Building Societies*. Basingstoke, Macmillan.

Boddy, M. (1989) Financial deregulation and UK housing finance, *Housing Studies*, **4**(2): 92–104.

Boleat, M. (1994) Private insurance and sick risks since World War II. In Silburn, R.L. (ed.).

Booth, A. (1978) An administrative experiment in unemployment policy in the 1930s, *Public Administration*, **56**(2): 139–57.

Booth, A.F. (1989) *British Economic Policy, 1931–1949: Was There a Keynesian Revolution?* Hemel Hempstead, Harvester Wheatsheaf.

Booth, A.F. and Pack, M. (1985) *Employment, Capital and Economic Policy in Great Britain 1918–1939*. Oxford, Blackwell.

Booth, C. (1889a) *The Life and Labour of the People*. London, Williams & Northgate.

Booth, C. (1889b) *Labour and Life of the People of London*. London, Macmillan.

Booth, C. (1894) *The Aged Poor*. London, Macmillan.

Booth, T. (1985) *Home Truths. Old Peoples' Homes and the Outcome of Care*. Aldershot: Gower.

Bosanquet, B. (ed.) (1895) *Aspects of Social Reform*. London, Macmillan.

Bosanquet, B. (1899) *The Philosophical Theory of the State*. London, Macmillan.

Bosanquet, B. (1901) The meaning of social work, *International Journal of Ethics*, **11**: 291–306.

Bosanquet, B. (1909) The Reports of the Poor Law Commission I. The Majority Report, *Sociological Review*, **II**(2): 109–26.

Bosanquet, H. (1903) *The Poverty Line*. London, Charity Organisation Society.

Bosanquet, H. (1906) *The Family*. London, Macmillan.

Bowlby, J. (1951) *Maternal Care and Maternal Health*. Geneva, WHO.

Bowley, M. (1945) *Housing and the State 1919–1944*. London, Allen & Unwin.

Bradley, H. (1990) Change and continuity in history and sociology: the case of industrial paternalism. In Kendrick, S., Shaw, P.S. and McCrone, D. (eds) *Interpreting the Past: Interpreting the Present*. London, Macmillan/BSA.

Bradley, I. (1985) *The Strange Rebirth of Liberal Britain*. London, Chatto & Windus/The Hogarth Press.

Bradshaw, J. and Lynes, T. (1995) *Benefit Uprating Policy and Living Standards*. York, University of York.

Braithwaite, C. (1938) *The Voluntary Citizen: an Enquiry into the Place of Philanthropy in the Community*. London, Methuen.

Braithwaite, W.J. (1957) *Lloyd George's Ambulance Wagon Being the Memoirs of William J. Braithwaite, 1911–1912*. London, Methuen.

Bramley, G. (1995) *Too High a Price: Homeless Households, Housing Benefit and the Private Rented Sector*. London, Shelter.

Briggs, A. (1961a) The Welfare State in historical perspective, *Archives Européene de Sociologie*, **2**(2): 221–58.

Briggs, A. (1961b) *Social Thought and Social Action: A Study of the Work of Seebohm Rowntree, 1871–1954*. London, Longmans.

Brittan, S. (1975) *Second Thoughts on Full Employment Policy*. London, Centre for Policy Studies.

Brittan, S. and Webb, S. (1993) *Beyond the Welfare State*. Aberdeen, Aberdeen University Press.

Broadberry, S.N. (1986) *The British Economy Between the Wars: a Macroeconomic Survey*. Oxford, Oxford University Press.

Broadberry, S.N. (1990) The emergence of mass unemployment: explaining macro-economic trends in Britain during the trans-world war I period. *Economic History Review* **XLIII**: 71–82.

Brody, E. (1981) 'Women in the middle' and family help to older people, *The Gerontologist*, **21**: 471–90.

Brooke, S. (1992) *Labour's War*. Oxford, Clarendon Press.

Brooke, S. (ed) (1995) *Reform and Reconstruction*. Manchester, Manchester University Press.

Brown, G. (1997) Why Labour is still loyal to the poor. *Guardian* 2 August.

Brown, J. and Cooper, S. (1981) *Poverty and the Development of Anti-Poverty Policy in the UK*. London, Heinemann.

Brown, K. (1971) *Labour and Unemployment, 1900–1914*. Newton Abbot, David & Charles.

Bruce, M. (1968) *The Coming of the Welfare State*, 4th edn. London, Batsford.

Brunsdon, E. (1997) Private welfare. In Alcock. P., Erskine. S. and May, M. (eds) Ch. III.2.

Buchanan, J. (1968) *The Contradictions of the National Health Service*. London, Institute of Economic Affairs.

Buchanan, J.M. and Tulloch, G. (1962) *The Calculus of Consent: Logical Foundations of Constitutional Democracy*. Michigan, University of Michigan Press.

Bulmer M., Lewis J. and Piachaud D. (eds) (1989) *The Goals of Social Policy*. London, Unwin Hyman.

Bunbury, H. (ed.) (1970) *Lloyd George's Ambulance Wagon*. London, Methuen.

Burchardt, T. and Hills, J. (1997) *Private Welfare Insurance and Social Security: Pushing the Boundaries*. York, Joseph Rowntree Foundation.

Burke, K. (1982) *War and the State*. London, Allen & Unwin.

Burke, P. (1992) *History and Social Theory*. Cambridge, Polity Press.

Butler, E. and Pirie, M. (1995) *The Fortune Account*. London, Adam Smith Institute.

Butler, E. and Young, M. (1996) *What's Wrong with the Welfare State?* London, Adam Smith Institute.

Butt, J. (1984) Life assurance in war and depression: the Standard Life Assurance Company and its environment 1914–1939. In Westall, O.M. (ed.) *The Historian and the Business of Insurance.* Manchester, Manchester University Press.

Cairncross, A.K. (1992) *The British Economy Since 1945: Economic Policy and Performance 1945–90.* Oxford, Blackwell.

Cairncross, A.K. and Burk, K. (1992) *Goodbye Great Britain.* London, Yale University Press.

Calder, A. (1965) *The People's War.* London, Paladin.

Calnan, M., Cant, S. and Gabe, J. (1993) *Going Private: Why People Pay for Their Health Care.* Buckingham, Open University Press.

Challis, D. and Davies, B. (1986) *Case Management in Community Care.* Aldershot, Gower.

Chandler, A.D. (1990) *Scale and Scope: the Dynamics of Industrial Capitalism.* Cambridge, MA, Harvard University Press.

Chandra, J. and Kakabadse, A. (1985) *Privatisation and the NHS.* Aldershot, Gower.

Chappell, E. (1988) *Pensions and Privilege: How To End the Scandal, Simplify Taxes and Widen Ownership*, Policy Study 96. London, Centre for Policy Studies.

Charity Organisation Society (1870) *Report of a Sub-Committee on House to House Visitation.* London, COS.

Cherry, S. (1992) Beyond national health insurance: the voluntary hospitals and hospital contributory schemes, *Social History of Medicine*, **5**: 455–82.

Cherry, S. (1996) *Medical Services and the Hospitals in Britain 1860–1939.* Cambridge, Cambridge University Press.

Child, J. (1969) *British Management Thought.* London, Allen & Unwin.

Childs, D. (1995) *Britain since 1939: Progress and Decline.* London, Macmillan.

Clark, C. (1937) *National Income and Outlay.* London, Macmillan.

Clegg, H. (1985) *A History of British Trade Unions since 1889, 1911–1933.* Oxford, Clarendon.

Clegg, H., Fox, A. and Thompson, A.F. (1964) *A History of British Trade Unions since 1889*, Vol.1. 1889–1910. Oxford, Clarendon.

Clotfelter, C. (1996) *Buying the Best, Cost Escalation in Elite Higher Education.* Princeton, Princeton University Press.

Coates, K. and Silburn, R. (1983) *Poverty: The Forgotten Englishmen*, 4th edn. Nottingham, Spokesman.

Coates, K. and Topham, T. (1991) *The Making of the Transport and General Workers Union*, Vol.1, Parts I and 2. Oxford, Blackwell.

Cole, I. and Furbey, R. (1994) *The Eclipse of Council Housing.* London, Routledge.

Commission on Social Justice (1994) *Social Justice.* London, Vintage.

Commission on Wealth Creation and Social Cohesion (1995) *Report on Wealth Creation and Cohesion in a Free Society.* London, Commission on Wealth Creation and Social Cohesion.

Conservative Party (1947) *The Industrial Charter: A Statement of Conservative Industrial Policy.* London, The Conservative Party.

Crafts, N.F.R. and Thomas, M. (1986) Comparative advantage in LTK manufacturing trade 1910–1936, *Economic Journal*, **96**: 629–45.

Cranston, M. (1969) John Locke and government by consent. In Thomson, D. (ed.) *Political Ideas*. Harmondsworth, Penguin, Ch.5.

Cronin, J. (1984) *Labour and Society*. London, Batsford.

Crosland, C.A.R. (1952) The transformation of capitalism. In Crossman, R.H.S.

Crosland, C.A.R. (1956) *The Future of Socialism*. London, Jonathan Cape.

Crosland, C.A.R. (1975) *Socialism Now*. London, Jonathan Cape.

Crossman, R.H.S. (1952) *New Fabian Essays*. London, Turnstile Press.

Crossman, R.H.S. (1976) The role of the volunteer in the modern social services. In Halsey, A.H. (ed.) *Traditions of Social Policy*. Oxford, Blackwell.

Crowther, M.A. (1982) Family responsibility and state responsibility in Britain before the welfare state, *The Historical Journal*, **25**(1): 131–45.

Crowther, M.A. (1988) *Social Policy in Britain 1914–1939*. London, Macmillan.

Cullingworth, J. (1979) *Essays on Housing Policy*. London, Allen & Unwin.

Curtice, J. (1992) Labour's slide to defeat. *Guardian* (13.4.92).

Cutler, T., Williams, K. and Williams, J. (1986) *Keynes, Beveridge and Beyond*. London, Routledge & Kegan Paul.

Damer, S. (1974) Wine alley: the sociology of dreadful enclosure, *Sociological Review*, **22**(2): 221–48.

Damer, S. (1980) State, class and housing: Glasgow 1885–1919. In Melling, J. (ed) *Housing, Social Policy and the State*. London, Croom Helm.

Dangerfield, G.F. (1966) *The Strange Death of Liberal England*. London, MacGibbon & Kee.

Daunton, M. (1983) *House and Home in the Victorian City*. London, Edward Arnold.

Daunton, M. (1987) *A Property-Owning Democracy?: Housing in Britain*. London, Faber.

Daunton, M. (1990) Housing. In Thompson, F.M.L. (ed.), Vol. 2.

Davies, B. and Challis, D. (1986) *Matching Resources to Needs in Community Care*. Aldershot, Gower.

Davin, A. (1978) Imperialism and Motherhood, *History Workshop Journal*, Spring, pp. 9–65.

Deacon, A. (1976) *In Search of the Scrounger: The Administration of Unemployment Insurance in Britain 1920–1931*. London, Bell & Sons.

Deacon, A. (1993) Richard Titmuss: twenty years on, *Journal of Social Policy*, **22**(2): 235–42.

Deacon, A. (1997) The case for compulsion, *Poverty*, Autumn, pp. 8–10.

Deacon, A. and Bradshaw, J. (1983) *Reserved for the Poor: the Means-Test in British Social Policy*. Oxford, Basil Blackwell/Martin Robertson.

Deacon, B. with Hulse, M. and Stubbs, P. (1997) *Global Social Policy: International Organizations and the Future of Welfare*. London, Sage.

Deakin, N. and Page, R.M. (eds) (1993) *The Costs of Welfare*. Aldershot, Avebury.

Deakin, N. (1994) *The Politics of Welfare*. Hemel Hempstead, Harvester Wheatsheaf.

Deakin, N. (1995) The perils of partnership; the voluntary sector and the state, 1945–1992. In Davis Smith, J., Rochester, C. and Hedley, R. (eds) *An Introduction to the Voluntary Sector*. London, Routledge, Ch. 2.

Dendy, H. (1895) The children of working London. In Bosanquet, B. (ed.) Ch. 3.

Dennis, N. (1997) *The Invention of Permanent Poverty*. London, Institute of Economic Affairs.

Dennis, N. and Halsey, A.H. (1988) *English Ethical Socialism*. Oxford, Clarendon.

Department of Social Security (1996) *Social Security Statistics 1996*. London, Stationery Office.

Digby, A. (1989) *British Welfare Policy: Workhouse to Workforce*. London, Faber & Faber.

Digby, A. (1996) Medicine and the English State, 1901–1948. In Green, S.J.D. and Whiting, R.C. (eds) *The Boundaries of the State in Modern Britain*. Cambridge, Cambridge University Press, pp. 213–30.

Dilnot, A.W. and Walker, I. (eds) (1989) *The Economics of Social Security*. Oxford, Open University Press.

Dilnot, A.W., Kay, J. and Morris, C. (1984) *The Reform of Social Security*. Oxford, Oxford University Press.

Dimsdale, N.H. (1984) Employment and real wages in the inter-war period, *National Institute Economic Review*, 110: pp. 94–103.

Ditch, J. (ed.) (1999) *Poverty and Social Security: Issues and Research*. London, Routledge.

Dixon, J. and Macarov, D. (eds) (1998) *Poverty: A Persistent Global Reality*. London, Routledge.

Dorling, D. (1995) *A New Social Atlas of Britain*. Chichester, John Wiley.

Douglas, J.W.B. (1964) *The Home and the School*. London, Macgibbon & Kee.

Doyal, L. and Gough, I. (1991) *A Theory of Human Need*. London, Macmillan.

Durbin, E. (1940) *The Politics of Democratic Socialism*. London, The Labour Book Service.

Durbin, E. (1985) *New Jerusalems: The Labour Party and the Economics of Democratic Socialism*. London, Routledge & Kegan Paul.

Dutton, D. (1991) *British Politics Since 1945: The Rise and Fall of Consensus*. Oxford, Blackwell.

Eccleshall, R. (1986) *British Liberalism: Liberal Thought from the 1640s to 1980s*. London, Longman.

Edgeworth, F.Y. (1922) Equal pay to men and women for equal work, *Economic Journal*, 32, December: 431–57.

Edwards, R. (1995) Making temporary accommodation permanent, *Critical Social Policy*, 43: 60–75.

Englander, D. (1983) *Landlord and Tenant in Urban Britain 1838–1918*. Oxford, Clarendon Press.

Equal Opportunities Commission (1982) *Caring for the Elderly and Handicapped: Community Care Policies and Women's Lives*. Manchester, EOC.

Ermisch, J. (1983) *The Political Economy of Demographic Change*. London, Heinemann.

Esping-Andersen, G. (1990) *The Three Worlds of Welfare Capitalism*. Cambridge, Polity.

Esping-Andersen, G. (1996) Positive-sum solutions in a world of trade-offs? In Esping-Andersen, G. (ed.) *Welfare States In Transition*. London, Sage.

Etzioni, A. (1993) *The Spirit of Community*. New York, Simon & Schuster.

Etzioni, A. (1997) *The New Golden Rule*. London, Profile.

Evans, M., Piachaud, D. and Sutherland, H. (1994) *Designed for the Poor – Poorer by Design: the Effects of the 1986 Social Security Act on Family Incomes*. LSE/STICERD WSP/105.

Evers, A., Pijl, M. and Ungerson, C. (1994) *Payments for Care: A Comparative Overview*. Aldershot, Avebury.

Fabian Society (1896) *Fabian Society News* (November). London, Fabian Society.

Falkingham, J. and Hills, J. (1995) Redistribution between people or across the life cycle? In Falkingham, J. and Hills, J. (eds) *The Dynamics of Welfare: the Welfare State and the Life Cycle*. Hemel Hempstead, Harvester Wheatsheaf.

Falkingham, J., Hills, J. and Lessof, C. (1993) *William Beveridge versus Robin Hood: Social Security and Redistribution over the Life Cycle*. LSE/STICERD WSP/88.

Falkingham, J. and Johnson, P. (1993) *A Unified Funded Pension Scheme (UFPS) for Britain*. LSE/STICERD WSP/90.

Feinstein, C.H. (1994) Success and failure. British economic growth since 1948. In Floud, R. and McCloskey, D. (eds) *The Economic History of Britain Since 1700*. Cambridge, Cambridge University Press, Vol. 3, Ch. 4.

Field, F. (1982) *Poverty and Politics: the Inside Story of the CPAG's Campaigns in the 1970s*. London, Heinemann.

Field, F. (1987) *Freedom and Wealth in a Socialist Future*. London, Fontana.

Field, F. (1995) *Making Welfare Work: Reconstructing Welfare for the Millennium*. London, Institute of Community Studies.

Field, F. (1996a) *Stakeholder Welfare*. London, IEA.

Field, F. (1996b) Making welfare work: the underlying principles. In Deacon, A. (ed.) *Stakeholder Welfare*. London, Institute for Economic Affairs.

Field, F. (1997a) Frank Field's response to Alan Deacon. In Morton, A.R. (ed.) *The Future of Welfare*. Edinburgh, Centre for Theology and Public Issues.

Field, F. (1997b) The welfare debate; managing self-interest, self-improvement, altruism. In Askonas, P. and Frowen, S.F. (eds) *Welfare and Values*. London, Macmillan, Ch. 15.

Field, F., Meacher, M. and Pond, C. (1977) *To Him Who Hath*. Harmondsworth, Penguin.

Fielding, S. (1992) What did the people want?: The meaning of the 1945 general election, *The Historical Journal*, 35(3): 623–39.

Fielding, S., Thompson, P. and Tiratsoo, N. (1995) *England Arise*. Manchester, Manchester University Press.

Finch, J. and Groves, D. (eds) (1983) *A Labour of Love: Women, Work and Caring*. London, Routledge & Kegan Paul.

Finlayson, G. (1994) *Citizen, State and Social Welfare in Britain 1830–1990*. Oxford, Oxford University Press.

Fitzgerald, R. (1988) *British Labour Management and Industrial Welfare 1846–1939*. London, Croom Helm.

Fitzhugh, W.A. (1996) *The Fitzhugh Directory of Independent Healthcare and Long-term Care*. London, Health Care Information Services.

Floud, J. (1954) The educational experiences of the adult population of England and Wales as at July 1949. In Glass, D.V. (ed.) *Social Mobility in Britain*. London, Routledge, Ch. 5.

Floud, J., Halsey, A.H. and Martin, F.M. (1956) *Social Class and Educational Opportunity*. Bath, Chivers.

Foot, M. (1997) *Aneurin Bevan*. London, Victor Gollancz.

Foote, G. (1986) *The Labour Party's Political Thought: a History*. London, Croom Helm.

Ford, J. (1995) *Which Way Out?: Borrowers with Long-Term Mortgage Arrears*. London, Shelter.

Ford, J., Kempson, E. and Wilson, M. (1995) *Mortgage Arrears and Possessions*. London, HMSO.

Ford, J. and Wilcox, S. (1994) *Affordable Housing, Low Incomes and the Flexible Labour Market*. London, National Federation of Housing Associations.

Fox, D. (1986) *Health Policies Health Politics: The British and American Experience, 1911–1965*. Princeton, Princeton University Press.

Fox, E. (1993) District nursing and the work of district nursing associations in England and Wales, 1900–1948. Unpublished PhD thesis, University of London.

Fox, E. (1996) Universal healthcare and self-help: paying for district nursing before the National Health Service, *Twentieth Century British History*, 7: 83–109.

Francis, M. (1997) *Ideas and Policies Under Labour, 1945–1951*. Manchester, Manchester University Press.

Franklin, J. (ed.) (1997) *Equality*. London, IPPR.

Fraser, D. (1984) *The Evolution of the British Welfare State*, 2nd edn. London, Macmillan.

Fraser, M. (1987) British politics 1945–1987: four perspectives. In Hennessy, P. and Seldon. A. (eds) *Ruling Performance: British Governments From Attlee to Thatcher*. Oxford, Blackwell, Ch. 10.

Freeden, M. (1978) *The New Liberalism: an Ideology of Social Reform*. Oxford, Oxford University Press.

Freeden, M. (ed.) (1990) *Reappraising J.A. Hobson: Humanism and Welfare*. London, Unwin Hyman.

Friedman, M. and Schwartz, A.J. (1963) *A Monetary History of the United States 1857–1960*. Princeton, Princeton University Press.

Friedman, M. (1962) *Capitalism and Freedom*. Chicago, University of Chicago Press.

Furniss, N. and Tilton, T. (1979) *The Case for the Welfare State*. Bloomington, Indiana University Press.

Garraty, J.R. (1978) *Unemployment in History*. New York, Harper.

Garside, W.R. (1980) *The Measurement of Unemployment: Methods and Sources in Great Britain 1850–1979*. Oxford, Blackwell.

Garside, W.R. (1990) *British Unemployment 1919–1939: a Study in Public Policy*. Cambridge, Cambridge University Press.

Gatrell, V.A.C. (1990) Crime, authority and the policeman state. In Thompson, F.M.L. (ed.), Chap. 5.

George, V. and Miller, S. (1994) *Social Policy Towards 2000: Squaring the Welfare Circle*. London, Routledge.

George, V. and Page, R.M. (eds) (1995) *Modern Thinkers on Welfare*. Hemel Hempstead, Harvester Wheatsheaf/Prentice Hall.

George, V. and Wilding, P. (1976) *Ideology and Social Welfare*, rev. edn. London, Routledge & Kegan Paul.

George, V. and Wilding, P. (1985) *Ideology and Social Welfare*, rev. ed. London, Routledge.

Giddens, A. (1994) *Beyond Left and Right*. Cambridge, Polity.

Giddens, A. (1996) There is a radical centre-ground, *New Statesman* 29 November, pp. 18–19.

Giddens, A. (1998) After the left's paralysis, *New Statesman* 1 May, pp. 18–21.

Gilbert, B. (1966) *The Evolution of National Insurance in Great Britain: The Origins of the Welfare State*. London, Michael Joseph.

Gilbert, B. (1970) *British Social Policy 1914–39*. London, Batsford.

Gillis, J.R. (1975) The evolution of juvenile delinquency in England 1890–1914, *Past and Present* **67**, May, pp. 96–126.

Ginsburg, N. (1979) *Class, Capital and Social Policy*. Basingstoke, Macmillan.

Ginsburg, N. (1983) Home ownership and socialism, *Critical Social Policy*, **3**(1): 34–53.

Ginsburg, N. (1992) Racism and housing: concepts and reality. In Braham, P., Rattansi, A. and Skellington, R. (eds) *Racism and Antiracism*. London, Sage.

Ginsburg, N. (1995) The impact of rising rents on housing benefit and rented housing, *Benefits*, **14**: 6–10.

Ginsburg, N. (1996) Recent changes in social housing. In May, M., Brunsdon, E. and Craig, G. (eds) *Social Policy Review 8*. London, Social Policy Association, Ch. 8.

Gladstone, F. (1979) *Voluntary Action in a Changing World*. London, Bedford Square Press.

Glendinning, C. and McLaughlin, E. (1993) *Paying for Care: Lessons from Europe*, Social Security Advisory Committee Research Paper 5. London, HMSO.

Glennerster, H. (ed.) (1983) *The Future of the Welfare State*. Oxford, Blackwell.

Glennerster, H. (1991) The radical right and the future of the welfare state. In Glennerster, H. and Midgley, J. (eds) *The Radical Right and the Welfare State*. Hemel Hempstead, Harvester Wheatsheaf, Ch. 9.

Glennerster, H. (1992) *Paying for Welfare, The 1990s*. Hemel Hempstead, Harvester Wheatsheaf.

Glennerster, H. (1994) Health and social policy. In Kavanagh, D. and Seldon, A. (eds) *The Major Effect*. London, Macmillan. Ch. 18.

Glennerster, H. (1995) *British Social Policy Since 1945*. Oxford, Blackwell.

Glennerster, H. (1997) Paying for Welfare. In Alcock, P., Erskine, A. and May, M. (eds), Ch. III.

Glennerster, H. and Evans, H. (1994) Beveridge and his assumptive worlds: the incompatibilities of a flawed design. In Hills, J. *et al.* (eds).

Glennerster, H. and Hills, J. (eds) (1998) *The State of Welfare*, 2nd edn. Oxford, Oxford University Press.

Glennerster, H. and Wilson, G. (1970) *Paying For Private Schools*. London, Allen Lane.

Glynn, S. (1991) *No Alternative? Unemployment in Britain*. London, Faber.

Glynn, S. and Booth, A. (eds) (1987) *The Road to Full Employment*. London, Allen & Unwin.

Glynn, S. and Booth, A. (1996) *Modern Britain: an Economic and Social History*. London, Routledge.

Glynn, S. and Howells, P.G. (1980) Unemployment in the 1930s: the 'Keynesian solution' reconsidered, *Australian Economic History Review* **20**: 28–45.

Glynn, S. and Shaw, S. (1981) Wage bargaining and unemployment, *Political Quarterly*, **52**: 115–16.

Godley, W. (1978) Britain's chronic recession: can anything be done? In Beckerman, W. (ed.) *Slow Growth in Britain: Causes and Consequences*. London, Heinemann.

Golding, P. and Middleton, S. (1982) *Images of Welfare: Press and Public Attitudes to Welfare*. Oxford, Basil Blackwell/Martin Robertson.

Goldthorpe, J.H. in collaboration with Llewellyn, C. and Payne, C. (1980) *Social Mobility and Class Structure in Modern Britain*. Clarendon: Oxford.

Goodin, R. and Le Grand, J. (1987) *Not Only the Poor*. London, Allen and Unwin.

Goodin, R.E. (1988) *Reasons for Welfare*. New Jersey, Princeton University Press.

Goodlad, R. and Gibb, K. (1994) *Housing and Social Justice*. London, the Commission on Social Justice.

Goodman, A., Johnson, P. and Webb, S. (1997) *Inequality in the UK*. Oxford, Oxford University Press.

Gosden, P.H.J.H. (1961) *The Friendly Societies in England 1815–1875*. Manchester, Manchester University Press.

Gosden, P.H.J.H. (1966) *The Development of Educational Administration in England and Wales*. Oxford, Basil Blackwell.

Gospel, H.F. (1992) *Markets, Firms and the Management of Labour in Modern Britain*. Cambridge, Cambridge University Press.

Gould, B. (1992) Speech on the launch of his campaign for the Labour Party leadership.

Gough, I. (1979) *The Political Economy of the Welfare State*. London, Macmillan.

Graham, H. (1983) Caring: a labour of love. In Finch, J. and Groves, D. (eds), Ch. 1.

Graves, J. (1943) *Policy and Progress in Secondary Education 1902–1942*. London, Nelson.

Gray, J. (1989) *Limited Government: A Positive Agenda*. London, Institute of Economic Affairs.

Gray, J. (1992) *The Moral Foundations of Market Institutions*. London, Institute of Economic Affairs.

Gray, J. (1997a) *Endgames*. Cambridge, Polity.

Gray, J. (1997b) Goodbye to Rawls, *Prospect*, November, pp. 8–9.

Gray, J. (1998) *False Dawn*, London, Granta.

Green, D.G. (1985) *Working-Class Patients and the Medical Establishment*. Aldershot, Gower.

Green, D.G. (1987) *The New Right*. Brighton, Wheatsheaf.

Green, D.G. (1993) *Reinventing Civil Society*. London, Institute of Economic Affairs.

Green, D.G. (1996) *Community Without Politics*. London, Institute of Economic Affairs.

Green, F., Hadjimatheou, G. and Smail, R. (1984) *Unequal Fringes*. London, Bedford Square Press.

Green, S. (1979) *Rachman*. London, Michael Joseph.

Green, T.H. (1986) Liberal legislation and freedom of contract. In Harris, P. and Morrow, J. (eds) *T.H. Green, Lectures on the Principles of Political Obligation and Other Writings*. Cambridge, Cambridge University Press.

Greenleaf, W.H. (1983) *The British Political Tradition Volume Two. The Ideological Heritage*. London, Methuen.

Grieve Smith, J. (1997) *Full Employment: a Pledge Betrayed*. London, Macmillan.

Hadley, R. and Hatch, S. (1981) *Social Welfare and the Failure of the State*. London, Allen & Unwin.

Hailsham, Lord. (1959) *The Conservative Case*. Harmondsworth, Penguin.

Halevy, E. (1928) *The Growth of Philosophical Radicalism*. London, Faber & Faber.

Hall, M.P. (1952) *The Social Services of Modern England*. London, Routledge & Kegan Paul.

Hall, P. (1974) *Urban and Regional Planning*. Harmondsworth, Penguin.

Halsey, A.H. (ed.) (1972) *Trends in British Society Since 1900: A Guide to the Changing Social Structure of Britain*. London, Macmillan.

Halsey, A.H., Heath, A.F. and Ridge, J.M. (1980) *Origins and Destinations*. Oxford, Clarendon.

Ham, C. and Hill, M. (1993) *The Policy Process in the Modern Capitalist State*. Hemel Hempstead, Harvester Wheatsheaf.

Hammond, J. and Hammond, B. (1911) *The Village Labourer*. London, Longman Green & Co.

Hammond, J. and Hammond, B. (1917) *The Town Labourer*. London, Longman Green & Co.

Hamnett, C. (1994) Restructuring housing finance and the housing market. In Corbridge, S., Thrift, N. and Martin, R. (eds) *Money, Power and Space*. Oxford, Blackwell, Ch. 12.

Hamnett, C. (1995) *Inheritance in Britain: The Boom That Never Happened*. Stratford upon Avon, PPP Lifetime.

Hamnett, C. and Rudolph, B. (1988) *Cities, Housing and Profits*. London, Hutchinson.

Hancock, W.K. and Gowing, M.M. (1949) *British War Economy*. London, HMSO.

Hannah, L. (1986) *Inventing Retirement: The Development of Occupational Pensions in Britain*. Cambridge, Cambridge University Press.

Hansmann, H. (1987) Economic theories of non-profit organisations. In Powell, W.W. (ed.).

Harloe, M. (1995) *The People's Home: Social Rented Housing in Europe and America*. Oxford, Blackwell.

Harman, H. (1992) NHS: *The Threefold Tory Threat – Underfunding, Commercialisation, Privatisation*. London, Labour Party.

Harrington, W. and Young, P. (1978) *The 1945 Revolution*. London, Davis Poynter.

Harris, J. (1972) *Unemployment and Politics*. Oxford, Clarendon Press.

Harris, J. (1977) *William Beveridge: A Biography*. Oxford, Clarendon Press.

Harris, J. (1981) *Unemployment and Politics: a Study of English Social Policy*. Bristol, University of Bristol Library Folio.

Harris, J. (1986) Political ideas and the debate on state welfare, 1940–45. In Smith, H.L. (ed.), pp. 233–63.

Harris, J. (1989) The Webbs, the Charity Organisation Society and the Ratan Tata Foundation: social policy from the perspective of 1912. In Bulmer, M., Lewis, J. and Piachaud, D. (eds), Ch. 2.

Harris, J. (1990a) Society and state in twentieth century Britain. In Thompson, F.M.L. (ed.), Ch. 2.

Harris, J. (1990b) Enterprise and welfare states: a comparative perspective, *Transactions of the Royal Historical Society*, 5th Series, **40**: 175–95.

Harris, J. (1991) Enterprise and the welfare state: a comparative perspective. In Gourvish, T. and O'Day, A. (eds) *Britain since 1945*. London, Macmillan, Ch. 3.

Harris, J. (1992) Victorian values and the founders of the welfare state. In Smout, T.C. (ed.) *Victorian Values*. Oxford, Oxford University Press/British Academy, pp. 165–82.

Harris, J. (1993) *Private Lives, Public Spirit. A Social History of Britain, 1870–1914*. Oxford, Oxford University Press.

Harris, J. (1996) 'Contract' and 'citizenship'. In Marquand, D. and Seldon, A. (eds) *The Ideas That Shaped Post-War Britain*. London, Fontana, Ch. 6.

Harris, R.W. (1946) *National Health Insurance in Great Britain, 1911–1946*. London, George Allen & Unwin.

Harrison, T. (1978) *Living Through the Blitz*. Harmondsworth, Penguin.

Hart, R. (1984) *The Economics of Non-Wage Labour Costs*. London, Allen & Unwin.

Hattersley, R. (1989) Afterword. In Hoover, K. and Plant, R. *Conservative Capitalism*. London, Routledge.

Hawksworth, J. and Wilcox, S. (1995) The PSBR handicap. In Wilcox, S. (ed.) *Housing Finance Review 1995/96*. York, Joseph Rowntree Foundation.

Hay, J.R. (1975) *The Origins of the Liberal Welfare Reforms 1906–1914*. London, Macmillan.

Hay, J.R. (1978) Employer's Attitudes to Social Policy and the Concept of 'Social Control 1900–1920'. In Thane, P. (ed.) *The Origins of British Social Policy*. London, Croom Helm.

Hay, J.R. (1983) *The Origins of the Liberal Welfare Reforms 1906–1914*, 2nd edn. London, Macmillan.

Hayek, F.A. (1944) *The Road to Serfdom*. London, Routledge & Kegan Paul

Hayek, F. A. (1960) *The Constitution of Liberty*. London, Routledge & Kegan Paul.

Hayek, F.A. (1967) *Studies in Philosophy, Politics and Economics*. London, Routledge.

Heald, D. (1983) *Public Expenditure: its Defence and Reform*. Oxford, Martin Robertson.

Health Education Council (1988) *Inequalities in Health*.

Held, D. (1995) *Democracy and the Global Order*. Cambridge, Polity.

Hendrick, H. (1994) *Child Welfare: England 1872–1989*. London, Routledge.

Hennock, E.P. (1987) *British Social Reform and German Precedents: The Case of Social Insurance, 1880–1914*. Oxford, Clarendon Press.

Herbert, S.M. (1939) *Britain's Health*. London, Penguin.

Hicks, U.K. (1958) *British Public Finances*, Oxford, Oxford University Press.

Higgins, J. (1992) Private Sector Health Care. In Beck, E., Lonsdale, S., Newman, S. and Patterson, E. (eds) *In the Best of Health? The Status and Future of Health Care in Britain*, London, Chapman Hall.

Hill, M. (1990) *Social Security Policy in Britain*, Aldershot, Edward Elgar.

Hill, M. (1993) *The Policy Process*, Hemel Hempstead, Harvester Wheatsheaf.

Hill, M. (1996) *Social Policy: A Comparative Analysis*. Hemel Hempstead, Prentice Hall.

Hill, O. (1877) *Our Common Land*. London, Macmillan.

Hills, J. (ed.) (1990) *The State of Welfare: the Welfare State in Britain Since 1974*. Oxford, Clarendon Press.

Hills, J. (1991) *Unravelling Housing Finance*. Oxford, Clarendon Press.

Hills, J. (1993) *The Future of Welfare: a Guide to the Debate*. York, Joseph Rowntree Trust.

Hills, J. (1995) *Joseph Rowntree Foundation Inquiry into Income and Wealth*, Vol. 2. York, Joseph Rowntree Foundation.

Hills, J. (ed.) (1996) *New Inequalities: The Changing Distribution of Income and Wealth in the United Kingdom*. Cambridge, Cambridge University Press.

Hills, J. (1998) *Income and Wealth: The Latest Evidence*. York, Joseph Rowntree Foundation.

Hills, J., Ditch, J. and Glennerster, H. (eds) (1994) *Beveridge and Social Security: An International Retrospective*. Oxford, Clarendon Press.

Hills, J., Glennerster, H. and Le Grand, J. (1993) *Investigating Welfare: Final Report of the ESRC Welfare Research Programme*. ESRC/Suntory–Toyota WSP, Discussion Paper 92. London, London School of Economics.

Hilton, J. (1944) *Rich Man Poor Man*. London.

Himmelfarb, G. (1985) *The Idea of Poverty*. London, Faber & Faber.

Himmelfarb, G. (1995) *The De-moralization of Society*. London, Institute of Economic Affairs.

Hindess, B. (1987) *Freedom, Equality & the Market*. London, Tavistock.

Hirst, P. and Thompson, G. (1996) *Globalization in Question*. Cambridge, Polity Press.

Hobhouse, L.T. (1898) The Ethical Basis of Collectivism, *International Journal of Ethics*, **8**:

Hobson, J.A. (1909) *The Crisis of Liberalism: New Issues of Democracy*. London, P.S. King & Son.

Hobson, J.A. (1914) *Work and Wealth: A Human Valuation*. London, Macmillan.

Hobson, J.A. (1938a) *Imperialism: A Study*, 3rd edn. London, Allen & Unwin.

Hobson, J.A. (1938b) *Confessions of an Economic Heretic*. London, Allen & Unwin.

Hodson, A.L. (1909) *Letters from a Settlement*. London, Edward Arnold.

Holmans, A. (1987) *Housing Policy in Britain: A History*. London, Croom Helm.

Holmans, A. (1995) *Housing Demand and Need in England 1991–2011*. York, Joseph Rowntree Foundation.

Holmans, A. (1996) Meeting housing needs in the private rented sector. In Wilcox, S. (ed.).

Holton, S. (1986) *Feminism and Democracy: Women's Suffrage and Reform Politics in Britain, 1900–1918*. Cambridge, Cambridge University Press.

Honigsabaum, F. (1979) *The Division in British Medicine: A History of the Separation of General Practice from Hospital Care 1911–1968*. London, Kogan Page.

Hopkins, E. (1995) *Working Class Help in Nineteenth Century England*. London, UCL Press.

Howe, G. (1965) *In Place of Beveridge*. London, Conservative Political Centre.

Hughes, J.J. and Perlman, R. (1984) *The Economics of Unemployment*. Brighton, Wheatsheaf.

Humphries, J. and Rubery, J. (1992) The legacy for women's employment: integration, differentiation and polarisation. In Michie, J. (ed.) *The Economic Legacy, 1979–1992*. London, Academic Press.

Humphreys, R. (1991) The Poor Law and Charity. The COS in the Provinces, 1870–1890, unpublished PhD thesis. University of London.

Humphreys, R. (1995) *Sin, Organised Charity and the Poor Law in Victorian England*. London, St. Martin's Press.

Hutton, W. (1995) *The State We're In*. London, Jonathan Cape.

Hutton, W. (1997) *The State To Come*. London, Vintage.

Hyde, R. (1968) *Industry Was My Parish*. London, Industrial Society.

Income Data Services (1995) *The Nanny Firm*. London, IDS.

Industrial Life Offices (1944) *Industrial Assurance Explained*. London, Industrial Life Offices.

Industrial Life Offices (1949) *Twenty Questions About Industrial Life Assurance*. London, Industrial Life Offices.

Industrial Welfare Society (1934) *Works, Sickness and Benevolent Funds*. London, IWS.

Inequalities in Health (1988) *The Black Report The Health Divide*. Harmondsworth, Penguin.

Jackson, P. (1994) A qualified defence of the welfare state, *Economic Affairs*, **14**: 8–11.

James, C. (1984) *Occupational Pensions: The Failure of Private Welfare*. London, Fabian Society.

Jefferys, K. (1987) British politics and social policy during the second world war, *Historical Journal*, **30**(1): 123–44.

Jefferys, K. (1991) *The Churchill Coalition and Wartime Politics 1940–45*. Manchester, Manchester University Press.

Jeffreys, K. (1992) *The Attlee Governments 1945–1951*. London, Longman.

Jewkes, J. (1947) *Ordeal by Planning*. London, Macmillan.

Jewkes, J. (1952) *A Return to Free Market Economics?* London, Macmillan.

Johnson, C. (1991) *The Economy Under Mrs Thatcher 1979–1990*. Harmondsworth, Penguin.

Johnson, N. (1987) *The Welfare State in Transition*. Brighton, Wheatsheaf.

Johnson, N. (1990) *Reconstructing the Welfare State: A Decade of Change 1980–1990*. Hemel Hempstead, Harvester Wheatsheaf.

Johnson, P. (1985) *Saving and Spending: The Working-Class Economy in Britain 1870–1939*. Oxford, Clarendon.

Johnson, P. (1986) Some historical dimensions of the welfare state 'crisis', *Journal of Social Policy*, **15**(4): 443–65.

Johnson, P. (1994a) The welfare state. In Floud, R. and McCloskey, D. (eds) *The Economic History of Britain since 1900* Vol. 3: 1939–1992, 2nd edn. Cambridge, Cambridge University Press.

Johnson, P. (1994b) The role of the state in twentieth century Britain. In Johnson, P., *Twentieth Century Britain, Economic, Social and Cultural Change*. London, Longman.

Johnson, P. (1996) Risk, Redistribution and Social Welfare in Britain from the Poor Law to Beveridge. In Daunton, M. (ed.) *Charity, Self-Interest and Welfare in the English Past*. London, UCL Press.

Jones, C. (1995) Now houses of ill repute are in red line districts, *Guardian* 25 June.

Jones, E. (1981) *The European Miracle: Environments, Economies and Geopolitics in the History of Europe and Asia*. Cambridge, Cambridge University Press.

Jones, H. (1994) *Health and Society in Twentieth-Century Britain*. London, Longman.

Jones, H. (1996) The post-war consensus in Britain: thesis, antithesis, synthesis? In Brivati, B., Buxton, J. and Seldon, A. (eds) *The Contemporary History Handbook*. Manchester, Manchester University Press, pp. 41–9.

Jones, H. (1998) The people's health. In Jones, H. and MacGregor, H. (eds) *Social Issues and Party Politics*. London, Routledge.

Jones, H. and Kandiah, M. (eds) (1996) *The Myth of Consensus: New Views on British History, 1945–64*. London, Macmillan.

Jones, K. (1991) *The Making of Social Policy in Britain 1830–1990*. London, Athlone.

Jones, R. (1987) *Wages and Employment Policy 1936–1985*. London, Allen & Unwin.

Jones, T. (1996) *Remaking the Labour Party: From Gaitskell to Blair*. London, Routledge.

Joseph. K. and Sumption, J. (1979) *Equality*. London, John Murray.

Joseph Rowntree Foundation Enquiry Into Income and Wealth (1995). York, Joseph Rowntree Foundation.

Joyce, P. (1980) *Work, Society and Politics: The Culture of the Factory in Later Victorian England*. Brighton, Harvester.

Judge, K. (1984) Private financing in social policy, *Economic Affairs*, April–June, pp. 29–32.

Judge, K. (1987) The British welfare state in transition. In Friedmann, R.F., Gilbert, G.N. and Sherer, M. (eds) *Modern Welfare States*. Brighton, Wheatsheaf, Ch. 1

Kanthack, E. (1907) *The Preservation of Infant Life*. London, H.K.Lewis.

Kavanagh, D. (1992) Debate: the postwar consensus, *Twentieth Century British History*, 3(2): 175–90.

Kavanagh, D. and Morris, P. (1989) *Consensus Politics From Attlee to Thatcher*. Oxford, Blackwell.

Kavanagh, D. and Seldon, A. (1989) *The Thatcher Effect*. Oxford, Oxford University Press.

Kay, J. (1996) The good market, *Prospect*, May, pp. 39–43.

Kazamias, A.M. (1966) *Politics, Society and Secondary Education in England*. Philadelphia, University of Pennsylvannia Press.

Keegan, W. (1984) *Mrs Thatcher's Economic Experiment*. London, Allen Lane.

Kellner, P. (1997) More equal than others, *New Statesman* 17 October, pp. 20–3.

Kendall, J. and Knapp, M. (1996) *The Voluntary Sector in the United Kingdom*. Manchester, Manchester University Press.

Keynes, J.M. (1926) *The End of Laissez-faire*. London, Hogarth.

Keynes, J.M. (1936) *The General Theory of Employment, Interest and Money*. London, Macmillan.

King, A. (ed.) (1976) *Why is Britain Becoming Harder to Govern?* London, BBC.

King, D.S. (1987) *The New Right*. London, Macmillan.

King, D.S. (1995) *Actively Seeking Work?* Chicago, University of Chicago Press.

Kinnock, N. (1985) *The Future of Socialism*. London, Fabian Society.

Kinnock, N. (1987) Speech to the Welsh Labour Party Conference at the opening of the general election campaign.

Kirby, M.W. (1981) *The Decline of British Economic Power Since 1870*. London, Allen & Unwin.

Klein, R. (1973) *Complaints Against Doctors*. London, Charles Knight.

Klein, R. (1995) *The New Politics of the NHS*, 3rd edn. London, Longman.

Klein, R. and Millar, J. (1995) Do-it-yourself social policy: searching for a new paradigm? *Social Policy & Administration*, 29(4): 303–16.

Klein, R. and O'Higgins, M. (eds) (1985) *The Future of Welfare*. Oxford, Blackwell.

Knapp, M. (1984) *The Economics of Social Care*. London, Macmillan.

Knapp, M. (1989) Private and voluntary welfare. In McCarthy, M. (ed.) *The New Politics of Welfare*. London, Macmillan, Ch. 9.

Knight, B. (1993) *Voluntary Action*. London, HMSO.

Koven, S. and Michel, S. (eds) (1993) *Mothers of a New World*. Maternalist Politics and the Origins of Welfare States. London, Routledge.

Kramer, R.M. (1990) Non-profit organizations and the welfare state. In Anheier, H.K. and Seibel, W. (eds).

Kuhnle, S. and Selle, P. (1992) Government and voluntary organisations – a relational perspective. In Kuhnle, S. and Selle, P. (eds) *Government and Voluntary Organisations*. Aldershot, Avebury.

Kymhka, W. (1995) Liberalism. In Honderick, T. (ed.) *The Oxford Companion to Philosophy*. Oxford, Oxford University Press.

Labour Party (1923) *Manifesto*. London, Labour Party.

Labour Party (1950) *The Future of Industrial Assurance: Labour's Proposals for Mutual Ownership by the Policy-Holders*. London, Labour Party.

Labour Party (1989) Policy Review Document (Health). London, Labour Party.

Labour Party (1990) *A Fresh Start for Health*. London, Labour Party.

Labour Party (1996) *Cut the Waste Cut the Waiting*. London, The Labour Party.

Labour Party (1997) *New Labour Because Britain Deserves Better*. London, The Labour Party.

Lafitte, F. (1945) *Britain's Road to Social Security*. London, Pilot Press.

Laing, W. (1992) *Laing's Review of Private Health Care 1992*. London, Laing & Buisson.

Laing, W. (1995) *Care of Elderly People Market Survey 1995*. London, Laing & Buisson.

Laing, W. (1996a) *Laing's Review of Private Health Care 1996*. London, Laing & Buisson.

Laing, W. (1996b) *Care of Elderly People Market Survey 1996*. London, Laing & Buisson.

Land, H. and Parker, R. (1978) Family policy in Britain: the hidden dimensions. In Kahn, A. and Kamerman, S. (eds) *Family Policy in Fourteen Countries*. New York, Columbia University Press, pp. 331–66.

Land, H. and Rose, H. (1985) Compulsory altruism for some or an altruistic society for all? In Bean, P., Ferris, J. and Whynes, D. (eds) *In Defence of Welfare*. London, Tavistock, Ch. 4.

Law, I. (1996) *Racism, Ethnicity and Social Policy*. Hemel Hempstead, Prentice Hall.

Lawson, N. (1992) *The View From No.11*. London, Bantam.

Layard, R. (1997) *What Labour Can Do*. London, Warner.

Laybourn, K. (1988) *The Rise of Labour: The British Labour Party 1890-1979*. London, Edward Arnold.

Laybourn, K. and Reynolds, J. (1984) *Liberalism and the Rise of Labour*. London, Croom Helm.

Leather, P. and Morrison, T. (1997) *The State of UK Housing: A Factfile on Dwelling Conditions*. Bristol, Policy Press.

Lee, J. (undated) *The integrity of the family: a vital issue*. COS Report, Bosanquet Paper, Trunk II, Box H, University of Newcastle Library.

Lee, M. (1971) *Opting Out of the NHS*. London, P.E.P.

Lees, D.S. (1961) *Health Through Choice*. London, Institute of Economic Affairs.

Lees, D.S. (1969) Health through choice. In Harris. R. (ed.) *Freedom or Free for All?* London, Institute of Economic Affairs, pp. 9–16.

Le Grand, J. (1982) *The Strategy of Equality*. London, Allen & Unwin.

Le Grand, J. (1991) *Equality and Choice*. London, Harper Collins.

Le Grand, J. (1997) Knights, knaves or pawns? Human behaviour and social policy, *Journal of Social Policy*, 26(2): 149–69.

Le Grand, J. and Bartlett, W. (1993) *Quasi-Markets and Social Policy*. Basingstoke, Macmillan.

Le Grand, J., Propper, C. and Robinson, R. (1992) *The Economics of Social Problems*. Basingstoke, Macmillan.

Le Grand, J. and Winter, D. (1986) The middle classes and the welfare state under Conservative and Labour governments, *Journal of Public Policy*, 6(4): 399–430.

Leibfried, S. and Pierson, P. (eds) (1995) *European Social Policy*. Washington, The Brookings Institute.

Leira, A. (1992) *Welfare States and Working Mothers: The Scandinavian Experience.* Cambridge, Cambridge University Press.

Levin, E., Sinclair, I. and Gorbach, P. (1983) *Supporters of Confused Elderly Persons at Home.* London, NISW.

Levy, H. (1937) *Industrial Assurance: An Historical and Critical Study.* Oxford, Oxford University Press.

Lewis, J. (1984) *Women in England, 1870–1950: Sexual Divisions and Social Change.* Brighton, Wheatsheaf.

Lewis, J. (1993) Developing the mixed economy of care: emerging issues for voluntary organisations, *Journal of Social Policy*, **22**(2): 173–92.

Lewis, J. (1994) Voluntary organizations in 'new partnerships' with local authorities: the anatomy of a contract, *Social Policy and Administration*, **28**(3): 206–20.

Lewis, J. (1996) The boundary between voluntary and statutory social service in the late nineteenth and early twentieth centuries, *Historical Journal*, **39**(1): 155–77.

Lewis, R. and Maude, A. (1949) *The English Middle Classes.* Penguin, Harmondsworth.

Liberal Party (1928) *Britain's Industrial Future being the Report of the Liberal Industrial Inquiry.* London, Benn.

Lindsay, A.D. (1945) Conclusion. In Bourdillon, A.F.C. (ed.) *Voluntary Social Services. Their Place in the Modern State.* London, Methuen, pp. 298–306.

Lister, R. (1987) *There is an Alternative – Reforming Social Security.* London, CPAG.

Lister, R. (1995) Dilemmas in Engendering Citizenship, *Economy and Society*, **24**: 1–40.

Little, A. and Westergaard, J. (1964) The trend of class differentials in educational opportunity in England and Wales, *British Journal of Sociology*, **15**: 301–16.

Llewellyn-Smith, H. (1910) Economic Security and Unemployment Insurance, *Economic Journal*, **20**(4): 513–29.

Llewelyn Smith, H. (1937) *The Borderland Between Public and Voluntary Action in the Social Services*, Sidney Ball Lecture. London, Oxford University Press.

Lloyd, T.O. (1986) *Empire to Welfare State.* Oxford, Oxford University Press.

Lloyd George, D. (1911) *The People's Insurance.* London, Liberal Publications.

Loch, C.S. (1923) *A Great Ideal and its Champion.* Papers and Addresses by the late Sir C. S. Loch. London, Allen & Unwin.

Locke, J. [1690] (1960) *Two Treatises.* Cambridge, Cambridge Press.

Lowe, R. (1989) Resignation at the treasury: the social services committee and the failure to reform the welfare state, 1955–57, *Journal of Social Policy*, **18**(4): 505–26.

Lowe, R. (1990) The second world war, consensus and the foundation of the welfare state, *Twentieth Century British History*, **1**(2): 152–82.

Lowe, R. (1993) *The Welfare State in Britain since 1945.* London, Macmillan.

Lowe, R. (1994a) The Welfare State in Britain since 1945. *ReFRESH*, **18**: 1–4.

Lowe, R. (1994b) Lessons from the past: the rise and fall of the classic welfare state in Britain, 1945–76. In Oakley, A. and Williams, A.S. (eds) *The Politics of Welfare.* London, UCL, Ch. 2.

Lowndes, G.A.N. (1969) *The Silent Social Revolution 1895–1965.* Oxford, Oxford University Press.

Lynes, A. (1996) *Our Pensions: A Policy For A Labour Government.* London, Eunomia.

Mabbett, D. (1997) *Pension Funding: Economic Imperative or Political Strategy?* Brunel University, Department of Government, Discussion Paper 97/1.

Macadam, E. (1934) *The New Philanthropy. A Study of the Relations between the Statutory and Voluntary Social Services*. London, Allen & Unwin.

McBriar, A.M. (1987) *An Edwardian Mixed Doubles/The Bosanquets versus the Webbs: A Study in British Social Policy 1890–1929*. Oxford, Clarendon Press.

McCormick, J. (1997) Mapping the stakeholder society. In Kelly, G., Kelly, D. and Gamble, A. (eds) *Stakeholder Capitalism*. London, Macmillan, Ch. 11.

McCrone, G. (1969) *Regional Policy in Britain*. London, Allen & Unwin.

McCulloch, G., Jenkins E. and Lawton, D. (1985) *Technological Revolution? The Politics of School Science and Technology in England and Wales since 1945*. Brighton, Falmer Press.

M'Gonigle, G. and Kirby, J. (1936) *Poverty and Public Health*. London, Gollancz.

Mackenzie, N. (ed.) (1958) *Conviction*. London, MacGibbon & Kee.

Mackenzie, N. and Mackenzie, J. (1984) *The Diary of Beatrice Webb* Vol. 3, *1905–1924: The Power to Alter Things*. London, Virago.

McKibbin, R. (1978) Social class and social observation in Edwardian England. *Transactions of the Royal Historical Society*, **28**: 175–99.

Macleod, I. and Powell, J.E. (1949) *The Social Services – Needs and Means*. London, Conservative Political Centre.

Macmillian, H. (1938) *The Middle Way*. London, Macmillan.

Macnicol, J. (1980) *The Movement for Family Allowances, 1918–45: A Study in Social Policy Development*. London, Heinemann.

McSmith, A. (1996) *Faces of Labour: The Inside Study*. London, Verso.

Malpass, P. (1990) *Reshaping Housing Policy*. London, Routledge.

Malpass, P. and Murie, A. (1994) *Housing Policy and Practice*. Basingstoke, Macmillan.

Mandelson, P. and Liddle, R. (1996) *The Blair Revolution*. London, Faber.

Mann, K. (1992) *The Making of the English Underclass? The Social Division of Welfare and Labour*. Milton Keynes, Open University Press.

Mann, K. and Anstee, J. (1989) *Growing Fringes: Hypotheses in the Development of Occupational Welfare*. Leeds, Armley.

Marchant, J. (ed.) (1946) *Rebuilding Family Life in the Post War World*. London, Odhams.

Markham, V. (1911) The Problem of Poverty, *Spectator* 26 August.

Marquand, D. (1989) The decline of post-war consensus. In Gorst, A., Johnman, L. and Lucas, W.S., *Post-war Britain, 1945–64: Themes and Perspective*, London, Pinter.

Marquand, D. (1998) The Blair paradox, *Prospect*, May, pp. 19–24.

Marris, R. (1997) *How to Save the Underclass*, London, Macmillan.

Marshall, A. (1892) Poor law reform, *Economic Journal*, **2**: 371–9.

Marshall, A. (1907) *Principles of Economics*. London, Macmillan.

Marshall, T.H. (1950) *Citizenship and Social Class*. Cambridge, Cambridge University Press.

Marshall, T.H. (1963a) Citizenship and Social Class. In Marshall, T.H., *Sociology at the Crossroads and Other Essays*. London, Heineman, Ch. 4.

Marshall, T.H. (1963b) *Class, Citizenship and Social Development*. London, Allen & Unwin.

Marshall, T.H. (1981) *The Right to Welfare*. London, Heinemann.

Marshall, T.H. and Bottermore, T. (1993) *Citizenship and Social Class*. London, Pluto.

Marsland, D. (1996) *Welfare or Welfare State?* London, Macmillan.

Martin, J. and Roberts, C. (1984) *Women and Employment. A Lifetime Perspective.* London, HMSO.

Marwick, A. (1968) *Britain in the Century of Total War: War, Peace and Social Change.* London, Bodley Head.

Marwick, A. (1982) *British Society Since 1945.* Harmondsworth, Penguin.

Marwick, A. (ed.) (1988) *Total War and Social Change.* London, Macmillan.

Marx, K. (1974) *Capital.* London, Lawrence & Wishart.

Marx, K. and Engels, F. (1968) *On Britain.* London, Lawrence & Wishart.

Mason, D. (1995) *Race and Ethnicity in Modern Britain.* Oxford, Oxford University Press.

Mason, T. and Thompson, P. (1991) Reflections on a revolution? In Tiratsoo, N. (ed.) (1991) *The Attlee Years.* London, Pinter, Ch. 4.

Massey, P. (1937) *Portrait of a Mining Town*, Fact No. 8. London,

Masterman, C.F.G. (1909) *The Condition of England.* London, Methuen.

Masterman, C.F.G. (1920) *The New Liberalism.* London, Methuen.

Matterson, A. (1981) *Polytechnics and Colleges.* London, Longman.

Matthews, R.C.O. (1968) Why has Britain had full employment since the war? *Economic Journal*, **78**: 555–69.

Matthews, R.C.O., Feinstein, C.H. and Odling Smee, J.C. (1982) *British Economic Growth, 1856–1973.* Oxford, Oxford University Press.

Maugham, W.S. (1915) *Of Human Bondage.* London, Heinemann.

Maurice, E. (ed.) (1928) *Octavia Hill: Early Ideals.* London, Allen & Unwin.

May, M. and Brunsdon, E. (1994) Workplace care in the mixed economy of welfare. In Page, R.M. and Baldock, J. (eds) *Social Policy Review* 6. Canterbury, Social Policy Association, Ch. 8.

May, M. and Brunsdon, E. (1996) Women and Private Welfare. In Hallett, C. (ed.) *Women and Social Policy.* Hemel Hempstead, Harvester Wheatsheaf, Ch. 11.

Mead, L.M. (1986) *Beyond Entitlement: The Social Obligations of Citizenship.* New York, Free Press.

Mead, L.M. (1992) *The New Politics of Poverty.* New York, Basic Books.

Meadows, P. (1996) I spend, therefore I am, *Prospect*, December, pp. 14–15.

Means, R. and Smith, R. (1985) *The Development of Welfare Services for Elderly People.* London, Croom Helm.

Melling, J. (1979) Industrial strife and business welfare philosophy: the case of the south Metropolitan Gas company from the 1880s to the War, *Business History*, **11**: 152–66.

Melling, J. (1980) Clydeside housing and the evolution of state rent control. In Melling, J. (ed.) *Housing, Social Policy and the State.* London, Croom Helm.

Melling, J. (1981) Employers, industrial housing and the evolution of company welfare policies in Britain's heavy industry: west Scotland 1870–1920, *International Review of Social History*, **26**(3): 255–30.

Melling, J. (1983) *Rent Strikes: People's Struggles for Housing in West Scotland, 1890–1916.* Edinburgh, Edinburgh University Press.

Melling, J. (1991) Industrial capitalism and the welfare of the state: the role of employers in the comparative development of welfare states. A Review of Recent Research, *Sociology*, **25**: 219–39.

Melling, J. (1992a) Welfare capitalism and the origins of welfare states: British industry, welfare and social reform, 1870–1914, *Social History*, **17**: 454–78.

Melling, J. (1992b) Employers, workplace culture and workers politics. British industry and workers' welfare programmes 1870–1920. In Melling, J. and Barry, J. (eds) *Culture in History: Production, Consumption and Values in Historical Perspective.* Exeter, Exeter University Press.

Merrett, S. (1979) *State Housing in Britain.* London, Routledge.

Merrett, S. (1982) *Owner Occupation in Britain.* London, Routledge.

Middlemas, K. (1965) *The Clydesiders.* London, Hutchinson.

Middlemas, R.K. (1986) *Power, Competition and the State*, Vol. I., *Britain in Search of Balance*, 1940–61. London, Macmillan.

Middleton, R. (1996a) *Government Versus the Market.* Aldershot, Edward Elgar.

Middleton, R. (1996b) The size and scope of the public sector. In Green, S.J.D. and Whiting, R.C. (eds) *The Boundaries of the State in Modern Britain*, Cambridge, Cambridge University Press, pp. 89–145.

Mikardo, I. (1948) *The Second Five Years – A Labour Programme for 1950.* London, Fabian Society.

Miliband, R. (1969) *The State in Capitalist Society.* London, Weidenfield & Nicolson.

Mill, J.S. (1976) *Principles of Political Economy.* New Jersey, Fairfield.

Ministry of Housing and Local Government (1953) *Houses: The Next Step.* London, HMSO.

Mitch, D. (1992) *The Rise of Popular Literacy in Victorian England.* Philadelphia, University of Pennsylvania.

Mitchell, D. (1991) *Income Transfers in Ten Welfare States.* Aldershot, Avebury.

Moggridge, D.E. (1976) *Keynes.* Glasgow, Fontana/Collins.

Mohan, J. (1991) Privatisation in the British health sector: a challenge to the NHS? In Gabe, J., Calnan, M. and Bury, M. (eds) *The Sociology of the Health Service.* London, Routledge.

de Montmorency, J.E.G. (1902) *State Intervention in English Education.* Cambridge, Cambridge University Press.

Moore, J. (1989) The End of the Line for Poverty, Speech to Greater London Area CPC, 11 May.

Morah, D. (1955) *A History of Industrial Life Assurance.* London, Allen & Unwin.

Morgan, G. and Knights, D. (1992) Constructing consumers and consumer protection: the case of the life insurance industry in the United Kingdom. In Burrowes, R. and Marsh, C. (eds) *Consumption and Class.* London, Macmillan.

Morgan, K.O. (1984a) Labour In Power, 1945–51. Oxford, Oxford University Press.

Morgan, K.O. (1984b) Aneurin Bevan 1897–1960. In Barker, P. (ed.) *Founders of the Welfare State.* London, Heinemann, pp. 105–13.

Moroney, R.M. (1976) *The Family and the State: Considerations for Social Policy.* London, Longman.

Morris, B. and Smyth, J. (1994) Paternalism as an employer strategy 1800–1960. In Ruberry, J. and Wilkinson, F. (eds) *Employer Strategy and the Labour Market.* Oxford, Oxford University Press, Ch. 6.

Mount, F. (1983) *The Subversive Family.* London, Allen & Unwin.

Mulgan, G. (1996) Union future is in mutual satisfaction, *Guardian* 3 September.

Mulgan, G. and Landry, C. (1995) *The Other Invisible Hand: Remaking Charity for the 21st Century.* London, Demos.

Murray, B.K. (1980) *The People's Budget.* Oxford, Clarendon Press.

Murray, C. (1984) *Losing Ground.* New York, Basic Books.

Murray, C. (1990) *The Emerging British Underclass*. London, Institute of Economic Affairs.

Murray, C. (1994) *Underclass: The Crisis Deepens*. London, Institute of Economic Affairs.

National Committee to Promote the Break-up of the Poor Law (1909) *The Minority Report of the Poor Law Commissioners*. London.

National Consumer Council (1976) *Means-Tested Benefits: a Discussion Paper*. London, NCC.

National Council for Voluntary Organisations (1990) *Working Party Report on Effectiveness and the Voluntary Sector*. London, NCVO.

Nevitt, A. (1966) *Housing, Taxation and Subsidies*. London, Nelson.

Newton, J. (1994) *All in One Place: The British Housing Story 1973–1993*. London, Catholic Housing Aid Society.

Nesbitt, S. (1992) *The Politics of Pensions Policy-Making in the 1980s*. Edinburgh, Edinburgh University Press.

Nicholson, P.P. (1990) *The Political Philosophy of the British Idealists: Selected Studies*. Cambridge, Cambridge University Press.

Niskanen, W. (1978) *Bureaucracy: Servant or Master?*. London, Institute of Economic Affairs.

Nissel, M. and Bonnerjea, L. (1982) *Family Care of the Handicapped Elderly: Who Pays?* Research Report No. 602. London, PSI.

Niven, M.M. (1967) *Personnel Management 1913–1963*. London, Institute of Personal Management.

Novak, T. (1988) *Poverty and the State*. Buckingham, Open University Press.

Oakeshott, M. (1975) *On Human Conduct*. Oxford, Clarendon Press.

Oakley, A. (1974) *The Sociology of Housework*. Oxford, Martin Robertson.

Oakley, A. (1986) *Social Welfare and the Position of Women*. Richard Titmuss Memorial Lecture, Hebrew University of Jerusalem.

Oakley, A. (1996) *Man and Wife*. London, Harper Collins.

Obelkevich, J. (1990) Religion. In Thompson, F.M.L. (ed.) Ch. 6.

Offer, A. (1981) *Property and Politics 1870–1914*. Cambridge, Cambridge University Press.

One Nation (1950) London, Conservative Political Centre.

One Nation Group (1959) *The Responsible Society*. London, Conservative Political Centre.

Oppenheim, C. (1993) *Poverty The Facts*, 3rd edn. London, Child Poverty Action Group.

Owen, D (1965) *English Philanthropy, 1660–1960*. Massachusetts, Harvard University Press.

Page, R.M. (1996) *Altruism and the British Welfare State*. Aldershot, Avebury.

Papadakis, E. and Taylor-Gooby, P. (1987) *The Private Provision of Public Welfare*. Brighton, Wheatsheaf.

Parsons, T. and Bales, R.F. (1955) *Family, Socialization and Interaction Process*. Glencoe, IL, Free Press.

Paton, C. (1993) Devolution and centralism in the national health service, *Social Policy and Administration*, 27(2): 83–108.

Pawley, M., Winstone, D. and Bentley, P. (1991) *UK Financial Institutions*. London, Macmillan.

Peacock, A. and Barry, N. (1986) *The Political Economy of Welfare Provision*. Edinburgh, David Hume Institute.

Peacock, A. and Wiseman, J. (1967) *The Growth of Public Expenditure in the U.K.* London, Allen & Unwin.

Peach, C. and Byron, M. (1994) Council house sales, residualisation and Afro Caribbean tenants, *Journal of Social Policy*, **23**(3): 363–83.

Peden, G.C. (1988) *Keynes, the Treasury and British Economic Policy*. London, Macmillan.

Peden, G.C. (1991) *British Economic Policy: Lloyd George to Margaret Thatcher*, 2nd edn. Hemel Hempstead, Phillip Allen.

Pedersen, S. (1993) *Family, Dependence and the Origins of the Welfare State: Britain and France 1914–1945*. Cambridge, Cambridge University Press.

Pelling, H. (1954) *The Origins of the Labour Party 1880–1900*. London, Macmillan.

Pelling, H. (1968a) *Popular Politics and Society in Late Victorian Britain*. London, Macmillan.

Pelling, H. (1968b) *A Short History of the Labour Party*, 3rd edn. London, Macmillan.

Pember Reeves, M.S. (1915) *Round About a Pound a Week*. London, Bell.

Perkin, H. (1989) *The Rise of Professional Society, England since 1880*. London, Routledge.

Phelps Brown, E.H. (1981) *Egalitarianism and the Generation of Inequality*. Oxford, Oxford University Press.

Piachaud, D. (1991) Revitalising social policy, *The Political Quarterly*, **62**(2): 204–24.

Pilgrim Trust (1938) *Men Without Work*, A Report made to the Pilgrim Trust. Cambridge, Cambridge University Press.

Pimlott, B. (1988) The myth of consensus. In Smith, L. (ed.) *The Making of Britain: Echoes of Greatness*. London, Macmillan.

Pimlott, B. (1989) Controversy: is the 'postwar consensus' a myth? *Contemporary Record*, **2**(6): 12–14.

Pinker, R. (1966) *English Hospital Statistics*. London, Heinemann.

Pinker, R. (1991) *Social Theory and Social Policy*. London, Heinemann.

Pinker, R. (1992) Making sense of the mixed economy of welfare, *Social Policy and Administration*, **26**(4): 273–84.

Pinker, R. (1993) Social Policy in the Post-Titmuss Era. In Page, R.M. and Baldock, J. (eds) *Social Policy Review 5*. Canterbury, Social Policy Association.

Pinker, R. (1995a) Marshall, T.H. In George, V. and Page, R.M. (eds), Ch. 6.

Pinker, R. (1995b) The place of freedom in the concept of welfare. In Barker, E. (ed.) *LSE on Freedom*. London, LSE Books.

Pirie, M. (1994) Reforming the welfare state. In Bell, M., Butler, E., Marsland, D. and Pirie, M., *The End of the Welfare State*. London, Adam Smith Institute.

Plant, R. (1998) So you want to be a citizen? *New Statesman* 6 February, pp. 30–2.

Political and Economic Planning (1937a) *Report on the British Health Services*. London, PEP.

Political and Economic Planning (1937b) *Report on the British Social Services*. London, PEP.

Political and Economic Planning (1953) The Cost of Social Services 1938–52 *Planning*, **19**: 1–12.

Pollard, S.G. (1962) *The Development of the British Economy 1914–1950*. London, Edward Arnold.

Pollard, S.G. (1969) *The Development of the British Economy 1914–1967*, 2nd edn. London, Edward Arnold.

Pollard, S. (1998) It's all about moving on up, *New Statesman* 10 April.

Pond, C. (1980) Tax expenditures and fiscal welfare. In Sandford, C., Pond, C. and Walker, A. (eds), pp. 47–63.

Powell J.E. (1977) *Joseph Chamberlain*. London, Thames & Hudson.

Powell, M. (1995) The strategy of equality revisited, *Journal of Social Policy*, **24**(2): 163–85.

Powell, M. and Hewitt, M. (1998) The end of the welfare state? *Social Policy & Administration*, **32**(1): 1–13.

Powell, W.W. (ed.) (1987) *The Non-Profit Sector. A Research Handbook*. New Haven, Yale University Press.

Pratt, J. and Burgess, T. (1974) *Polytechnics, a Report*. London, Pitman.

Prochaska, F. (1980) *Women and Philanthropy in Nineteenth Century England*. Oxford, Oxford University Press.

Prochaska, F. (1988) *The Voluntary Impulse. Philanthropy in Modern Britain*. London, Faber & Faber.

Pugh, M. (1993) *The Making of Modern British Politics*, 2nd edn. Oxford, Blackwell.

Qureshi, H. and Walker, A. (1988) *The Caring Relationship*. Basingstoke, Macmillan.

Radice, L. (1984) *Beatrice and Sidney Webb Fabian Socialists*. London, Macmillan.

Rae, J. (1981) *The Public School Revolution, Britain's Independent Schools 1964–1979*. London, Faber.

Raynsford, N. (1986) The 1977 Housing (Homeless Persons) Act. In Deakin, N. (ed.) *Policy Change in Government*. London, Royal Institute of Public Administration

Reddin, M. (1982) Occupational Welfare and Social Division. In Jones, C. and Stevenson, J. (eds) *The Year Book of Social Policy in Britain 1981–82*. London, Routledge.

Reeder, D. (1987) The reconstruction of secondary education in England 1869–1920. In Mueller, D.K., Ringer, F. and Simon, B. (eds) *The Rise of the Modern Educational System*. Cambridge, Cambridge University Press.

Reisman, D.A. (1995) Galbraith. In George, V. and Page, R.M. (eds), Ch. 7.

Report of the Commission on Social Justice (1994) *Social Justice: Strategies for National Renewal*. London, Vintage.

Richmond, M. (1899) *Friendly Visiting Among the Poor. A Handbook for Charity Workers*. New York, Macmillan.

Richter, M. (1964) *The Politics of Conscience: T.H.Green and his Age*. London, Weidenfeld & Nicolson.

Riddell, P. (1991) *The Thatcher Era and its Legacy*. Oxford, Blackwell.

Ritschel, D. (1995) Macmillan. In George, V. and Page, R.M. (eds), Ch. 7.

Roberts, D. (1960) *Victorian Origins of the British Welfare State*. New Haven, Yale University Press.

Robertson, J. (1990) The legacy of Adam Smith. In Bellamy, R. (ed.).

Rose, H. (1981) Re-reading Titmuss: the sexual division of welfare, *Journal of Social Policy*, **10**(4): 477–501.

Rose, M. (1972) *The Relief of Poverty 1834–1914*. London, Macmillan.

Ross, E. (1993) *Love and Toil. Motherhood in Outcast London 1870–1918*. Oxford, Oxford University Press.

Rowntree, B.S. (1901) *'Poverty': A Study of Town Life*. London, Macmillan.

Rowntree, B.S. (1941) *Poverty and Progress: a Second Social Survey of York*. London, Longman.

Rowntree, B.S. and Lavers, G. (1951) *Poverty and the Welfare State*. London, Longman.

Russell, A. (1991) *The Growth of Occupational Welfare in Britain*. Aldershot, Gower.

Salamon, L.M. (1987) Partners in public service: the scope and theory of government – nonprofit relations. In Powell, W.W. (ed.).

Salamon, L.M. (1990) The non-profit sector and government in the US. In Anheier, H.K. and Seibel, W. (eds).

Salter, B. (1994) Change in the British National Health Service: policy paradox and the rationing issue, *International Journal of Health Services*, **24**: 45–72.

Sanderson, M. (1988) Education and economic decline, 1890 to the 1990s, *Oxford Review of Economic Policy*, **4**: 38–50.

Sanderson, M. (1991) Social equity and industrial need; a dilemma of English education since 1945. In Gourvish, T.R. and O'Day, A. (eds) *Britain Since 1945*. London, Macmillan.

Sanderson, M. (1994) *The Missing Stratum, Technical School Education in England 1900–1990s*. London, Athlone Press.

Sanderson, M. (1995) French influences on technical and managerial education in England 1870–1940. In Cassis, Y., Crouzet, F. and Gourvish, T. (eds) *Management and Business in Britain and France*. Oxford, Oxford University Press.

Sandford, C., Pond, C. and Walker, R. (eds) (1980) *Taxation and Social Policy*. London, Heinemann.

Sassoon, D. (1997) *One Hundred Years of Socialism*. London, Fontana.

Saunders, P. (1990) *A Nation of Home Owners*. London, Unwin Hyman.

Saxon Harrold, S. (1990) Competition, resources and strategy in the British non-profit sector. In Anheier, H.K. and Siebel, W. (eds).

Scott, S. (ed.) *Post-war Britain, 1945–64: Themes and Perspectives*. London, Institute of Contemporary British History.

Seldon, A. (ed.) (1961) *Agenda For a Free Society*. London, Institute of Economic Affairs.

Seldon, A. (1981) *Wither the Welfare State?* London, Institute of Economic Affairs.

Seldon, A. (1990) *Capitalism*. Oxford, Blackwell.

Seldon, A. and Gray, H. (1967) *Universal or Selective Benefits?* London, Institute of Economic Affairs.

Shaw, G.B. (1893) *The Impossibilities of Anarchism*. London, Fabian Society.

Shorter, E. (1977) *The Making of the Modern Family*. London, Fontana.

Sherington, G. (1981) *English Education, Social Change and War 1911–20*. Manchester, Manchester University Press.

Silburn, R.L. (1995a) Beveridge. In George, V. and Page, R.M. (eds), Ch. 5.

Silburn, R.L. (1995b) *Social Insurance the Way Forward*. University of Nottingham/DSS.

Silburn, R.L. and Coates, K. (1970) *Poverty: The Forgotten Englishman*. Harmondsworth, Penguin.

Simey, T.S. and Simey, M.B. (1960) *Charles Booth: Social Scientist*. Oxford, Oxford University Press.

Simon, B. (1965) *Education and the Labour Movement 1870–1920*. London, Lawrence & Wishart.

Simon, B. (1974) *The Politics of Educational Reform 1920–1940*. London, Lawrence & Wishart.

Simon, B. (1991) *Education and the Social Order 1940–1990*. London, Lawrence & Wishart.

Sinclair, J.G. (1932) *Evils of Industrial Assurance*. London, A. Rivers.

Sinfield, A. (1978) Analyses of the Social Divisions of Welfare, *Journal of Social Policy*, 7(2): 129–56.

Smith, D. (1987) *The Rise and Fall of Monetaryism*. Harmondsworth, Penguin.

Smith, E. (1996) *Employer-provided Training in the UK*. London, IFF Research Ltd.

Smith, G. (1987) Whatever happened to educational priority areas? *Oxford Review of Education*, 13(1): 23–38.

Smith, H.L. (ed.) (1986a) *War and Social Change: British Society in the Second World War*. Manchester, Manchester University Press.

Smith, H.L. (1986b) Introduction. In Smith, H.L. (ed.), pp. vii–xi.

Smith, H.L. (ed.) (1996) *Britain in the Second World War*. Manchester, Manchester University Press.

Spencer, H. (1876) *Principles of Sociology*, 3rd edn. London, Williams & Norgate.

Spicker, P. (1991) The principle of subsidiarity and the social policy of the European Community, *Journal of European Social Policy*, 1(1): 3–14.

Spicker, P. (1993) *Poverty and Social Security*. London, Routledge.

Stedman-Jones, G. (1984) *Outcast London*. Harmondsworth, Peregrine.

Stevenson, J. (1977) *Social Conditions in Britain Between the Wars*. Harmondsworth, Penguin.

Stevenson, J. (1984) *British Social History 1914–1945*. London, Penguin.

Stewart, J. (1996) The children's party therefore the women's party. In Digby, A. and Stewart, J. (eds) *Gender, Health and Welfare*. London, Routledge, pp. 167–88.

Stewart, M. (1967) *Keynes and After*. Harmondsworth, Penguin.

Stewart, W.A.C. (1989) *Higher Education in Postwar Britain*. London, Macmillan.

Sullivan, M. (1996) *The Development of the British Welfare State*. Hemel Hempstead, Harvester Wheatsheaf.

Sullivan, M. (1987) *Sociology and Social Welfare*. London, Allen & Unwin.

Sullivan, M. (1990) Communities and social policy. In Edwards, A. and Jenkins, R. (eds) *One Step Forward...?* Llandysul, Gomer.

Sullivan, M. (1991) The Labour Party and Social Reform (PhD thesis), University of Wales.

Sullivan, M. (1992) *The Politics of Social Policy*. Hemel Hempstead, Harvester Wheatsheaf.

Supple, B. (1984) Insurance in British history. In Westall, O.M. (ed.) *The Historian and the Business of Insurance*. Manchester, Manchester University Press.

Supple, B. (1994) Fear of failing, economic history and the decline of Britain, *Economic History Review*, XLVII, 3: 441–58.

Sutherland, G. (1990) Education. In Thompson, F.M.L. (ed.), Ch. 3.

Swenarton, M. (1981) *Homes Fit for Heroes*. London, Heinemann.

Tawney, R.H. (1921) *The Acquisitive Society*. London, Unwin.

Tawney, R.H. (1952) *Equality*. London, Allen & Unwin.

Tawney, R.H. (1977) *Religion and the Rise of Capitalism*. Harmondsworth, Penguin.

Taylor, A.J. (1972) *Laissez-Faire and State Intervention in Nineteenth Century Britain*. London, Macmillan.

Taylor, M. (1995) Voluntary action and the state. In Gladstone, D. (ed.) *British Social Welfare*, London, UCL, Ch. 9.

Taylor, M. and Hoggett, P. (1993) *Quasi-markets and the transformation of the independent sector*, paper presented at the conference on Quasi-Markets in Public Sector Service Delivery: the Emerging Findings. Bristol, SAUS.

Taylor-Gooby, P. (1986) *The Future of the British Welfare State*. Unpublished paper. Canterbury, University of Kent.

Taylor-Gooby, P. and Dale, J. (1981) *Social Theory and Social Welfare*. London, Edward Arnold.

Tebbut, M. (1983) *Making Ends Meet. Pawnbroking and Working-Class Credit.* Leicester, Leicester University Press.

Terry, F. (1996) The private finance initiative – overdue reform or policy breakthrough? *Public Money and Management*, 16(1): 9–16.

Thain, C. and Wright, M. (1995) *The Treasury and Whitehall: the Planning and Control of Public Spending, 1976–1993.* Oxford, Clarendon Press.

Thane, P. (1978) Non-contributory versus insurance pensions 1878–1908. In Thane, P. (ed.) *The Origins of the Welfare State*. London, Longman, pp. 84–106.

Thane, P. (1982) *The Foundations of the Welfare State*. London, Longman.

Thane, P. (1984) The working class and state welfare in Britain 1880–1914, *The Historical Journal*, 27(4): 877–900.

Thane, P. (1989a) Old-age: burden or benefit. In Joshi, H. (ed.) *The Changing Population of Britain*. Oxford, Blackwell.

Thane, P. (1989b) The British Welfare State: Its Origins and Character. In Digby, A. and Feinstein, C. (eds) *New Directions in Economic and Social Policy*. London, Macmillan, pp. 143–54.

Thane, P. (1990a) The debate on the declining birth-rate in Britain: the 'menace' of an ageing population, 1920s–1950s, *Continuity and Change*, 5(2): 283–305.

Thane, P. (1990b) The Historiography of the British Welfare State, *Social History Society Newsletter*, 15(1): 12–15.

Thane, P. (1993) Women in the British Labour Party and the construction of state welfare. In Koven, S. and Michel, S. (eds).

Thane, P. (1996) Gender, Welfare and Old Age in Britain, 1870s–1940s. In Digby, A. and Stewart, J. (eds), pp. 189–207.

Thatcher, M. (1995) *The Downing Street Years*. London, Harper Collins.

Thomson, M. (1992) The Problem of Mental Deficiency in England and Wales, c. 1913–46. Unpublished D.Phil. thesis, Oxford University.

Thompson, F.M.L. (1963) *English Landed Society in the Nineteenth Century.* London, Routledge & Keegan Paul.

Thompson, F.M.L. (ed.) (1990) *The Cambridge Social History of Britain, 1750–1950*, Vol. 3. Cambridge, Cambridge University Press.

Thompson, N. (1996) *Political Economy and the Labour Party*. London, UCL.

Thompson, W. (1997) *The Left In History*. London, Pluto.

Timmins, N. (1995) *The Five Giants*. London, Harper Collins.

Tiratsoo, N. (ed.) (1997) *From Blitz to Blair.* London, Weidenfeld & Nicolson.

Tiratsoo, N. and Tomlinson, J. (1993) *Industrial Efficiency and State Intervention, 1939–1951.* London, Routledge.

Titmuss, R.M. (1950) *Problems of Social Policy*. London, HMSO.

Titmuss, R.M. (1955) Pension systems and population change, *Political Quarterly,* **26**(2): 152–66.

Titmuss, R.M. (1962) *Income Distribution and Social Change*. London, Allen & Unwin

Titmuss, R.M. (1963) *Essays on 'The Welfare State'*, 2nd edn. London, Unwin.

Titmuss, R.M. (1968) *Commitment to Welfare*. London, Allen & Unwin.

Titmuss, R.M. (1974) *Social Policy: An Introduction*. London, Allen & Unwin.

Titmuss, R.M. (1976a) The social division of welfare. In Titmuss, R.M. (ed.) *Essays on 'the Welfare State'*, 3rd edn. London, Allen & Unwin, pp. 34–53.

Titmuss, R.M. (1976b) The National Health Service in England: Appendix. In Titmuss, R.M. (ed.) *ibid.*, pp. 203–14.

Tomlinson, J. (1987) *Employment Policy: the Crucial Years, 1939–55*. Oxford, Clarendon.

Tomlinson, J. (1990) *Public Policy and the Economy Since 1900*. Oxford, Clarendon Press.

Tomlinson, J. (1995) Welfare and the economy: the economic impact of the welfare state, 1945–1951, *Twentieth Century British History*, **6**(2): 194–219.

Tomlinson, J. (1998) Why so austere? The British welfare state of the 1940s, *Journal of Social Policy*, **27**(1): 63–77.

Tooley, J. (1996) *Education Without the State*. London, Institute of Economic Affairs.

Townsend, P. (1957) *The Family Life of Old People*. London, Routledge & Kegan Paul.

Townsend, P. (1958) A society for people. In MacKenzie, N. (ed.), pp. 93–112.

Townsend, P. (1979) *Poverty in the UK*. Harmondsworth, Penguin.

Townsend, P. (1984) *Why Are the Many Poor?* London, Fabian Society.

Townsend, P. and Davidson, N. (eds) (1982) *Inequalities in Health*. Harmondsworth, Penguin.

Townsend, P. and Walker, A. (1995) *New Directions for Pensions: How to Revitalise National Insurance*. Nottingham, Spokesman.

Treble, J.H. (1979) *Urban Poverty in Britain*. Oxford, Oxford University Press.

Trevelyan, G. (1944) *English Social History*. London, Longman Green & Co.

Vaizey, J. and Sheenan, J. (1967) *Resources for Education*. London, Allen & Unwin.

Venables, Sir P. (1978) *Higher Education Developments: the Technological Universities 1956–76*. London, Faber.

Vincent, A. and Plant, R. (1984) *Philosophy, Politics and Citizenship*. Oxford, Blackwell.

Vinson Lord (1994) Can the Nation Afford Pensions? *Economic Affairs*, October, pp. 46–8.

Vlaeminke, M. (1990) The subordination of technical education in secondary schooling 1870–1914. In Summerfield, P. and Evans, E.J., *Technical Education and the State since 1850: Historical and Contemporary Perspectives*. Manchester, Manchester University Press, Ch. 3.

Waine, B. (1992) The voluntary sector – the Thatcher years. In Manning, N. and Page, R. (eds) *Social Policy Review 4*. Canterbury, Social Policy Association, Ch. 5.

Waine, B. (1993) *The Rhetoric of Independence. The Ideology and Practice of Social Policy in Thatcher's Britain*. Oxford, Berg.

Waine, B. (1995) A disaster foretold? The case of the personal pension, *Social Policy and Administration*, **29**(4): 317–34.

Walker, A. and Walker, L. (1991) Disability and financial need: the failure of the social security system. In Dalley, G. (ed.) *Disability and Social Policy*. London, Policy Studies Institute.

Walker, A. (1986) Community care: fact and fiction. In Walker, A., Ekblom, P. and Deakin, N. (eds) *The Debate about Community: Papers from a Seminar on Community in Social Policy*. London, PSI.

Ware, A. (1989) *Between Profit and State. Intermediate Organisations in Britain and the US*. Cambridge, Polity.

Ware, A. (1990) Meeting needs through voluntary action: does market society corrode altruism? In Ware, A. and Goodin, R.E. (eds) *Needs and Welfare*. London, Sage, Ch. 10.

Warde, A. (1992) Industrial discipline, factory regime and politics in Lancashire. In Sturdy, A., Knight, D. and Wilmott, H. (eds) *Skill and Consent: Contemporary Studies in the Labour Process*. London, Routledge.

Wates, N. (1980) *Squatting: The Real Story*. London, Bay Leaf Books.

Watkin, B. (1978) *The National Health Service: The First Phase, 1948–74 and After.* London, Allen & Unwin.

Weaver, R. (1950) Taxation and redistribution in the UK, *Review of Economics and Statistics*, **32**(3): 201–13.

Webb, B. (1948) *Our Apprenticeship*. London, Allen & Unwin.

Webb, B. and Webb, S. (1897) *Industrial Democracy*. London, Unwin.

Webster, C. (1988a) Confronting historical myths, *The Health Service Journal* 19 May, pp. 2–3.

Webster, C. (1988b) *The Health Services Since the War*, Vol. 1: *Problems of Health Care. The National Health Service before 1957*. London, HMSO.

Webster, C. (1990) Conflict and consensus: explaining the British health service, *Twentieth Century British History*, **1**(2): 115–51.

Webster, C. (1994) Conservatives and consensus: the politics of the National Health Service, 1951–1964. In Oakley, A. and Williams, A.S. (eds) *The Politics of the Welfare State*. University College London Press, pp. 54–74.

Webster, C. (1998) *The National Health Service: A Political History*. Oxford, Oxford University Press.

Weightmann, G. and Humphries, S. (1984) *The Making of Modern London 1914–1939*. London, Sidgwick & Jackson.

Weisbrod, B.A. (1988) *The Nonprofit Economy*. Cambridge, MA, Harvard University Press.

Welshman, J. (1996) Physical education and the school medical service in England and Wales, 1907–1939, *Social History of Medicine*, **9**(1): 31–48.

Whitehead, C. (1994) Markets in the United Kingdom: introduction and update, *Housing Policy Debates*, **5**: 231–40.

Whitehead, M. (1988) *The Health Divide in Inequalities in Health*. Harmondsworth, Penguin.

Whiteside, N. (1980) Welfare legislation and the unions during the first world war, *Historical Journal*, **23**(4): 857–74.

Whiteside, N. (1983) Private agencies for public purposes: some new perspectives on policy making in health insurance between the wars, *Journal of Social Policy*, **12**(2): 165–93.

Whiteside, N. (1987) Counting the cost: sickness and disability among working people in an era of industrial recession, 1920–30, *Economic History Review*, **40**(2): 228–46.

Whiteside, N. and Krafchik, M. (1983) Interwar health insurance revisited: a reply to Frank Honigsbaum, *Journal of Social Policy,* 12(4): 525–30.

Wilcox, S. (ed.) (1996) *Housing Review 1996/97.* York, Joseph Rowntree Foundation.

Wilding, P. (1972) Towards exchequer subsidies for housing 1906–1914, *Social Policy and Administration*, 6(1): 3–18.

Wilding, P. (1973) The Housing and Town Planning Act, 1919 – a study in the making of social policy, *Journal of Social Policy*, 2(4): 317–34.

Wilding, P. (1983) The Evolution of Social Administration. In Bean, P. and MacPherson, S., *Approaches to Welfare*. London, Routledge & Kegan Paul.

Wilding, P. (1992) Social Policy in the 1980s: An Essay on Academic Evolution in *Social Policy and Administration*, 26(2):107–15.

Wilkinson, R.G. (1989) Class mortality differentials, income distribution and trends in poverty, 1921–1981, *Journal of Social Policy*, 18(3): 307–35.

Wilkinson, R.G. (1994) Health, redistribution and growth. In Glyn, A. and Miliband, D. (eds) *Paying for Inequality: The Economic Cost of Social Injustice*. London, IPPR/River Orams Press.

Willetts, D. (1992) *Modern Conservatism*. Harmondsworth, Penguin.

Willetts, D. (1997) Conservatism now, *Prospect*, October, pp. 16–17.

Williams, K. and Williams, J. (1995) Keynes. In George, V. and Page, R.M. (eds), Ch. 4.

Williams, P. (1995) A shrinking safety net for a shrinking market. In Wilcox, S., *Housing, Finance Review 1995/96*. York, Joseph Rowntree Foundation.

Williams, R.G. (ed.) (1968) *May Day Manifesto to 1968*. Harmondsworth, Penguin.

Willmott, P. (1986) *Social Networks, Informal Care and Public Policy*, Research Report 655. London, Policy Studies Institute.

Wilson, A. and Levy J.H. (1937) *Industrial Assurance: An Historical and Critical Study*. Oxford, Oxford University Press.

Winch, D. (1969) *Economics and Policy: a Historical Study*. London, Hodder & Stoughton.

Winnicott, D.W. (1957) *The Child and the Family: First Relationships*. London, Tavistock.

Winter, J.M. (1986) *The Great War and the British People*. London, Macmillan.

Winter, J. and Joslin, D. (eds) (1972) *R.H. Tawney's Commonplace Book*. London, Cambridge University Press.

Wistow, G., Knapp, M., Hardy, B. and Allen, C. (1994) *Social Care in a Mixed Economy*. Buckingham, Open University Press.

Wohl, A. (1977) *The Eternal Slum: Housing and Social Policy in Victorian London*. London, Edward Arnold.

Woolfe, W. (1975) *From Radicalism to Socialism*. New Haven, Yale University Press.

Wray, D. (1996) Paternalism and its discontents: a case study, Work, *Employment & Society*, 10: 201–15.

Wright, T. (1996) *Socialisms Old and New*. London, Routledge.

Wrigley, C. (1971) *David Lloyd George and the British Labour Movement*. Hassocks, Harvester Press.

Wrigley, C. (ed.) (1987) *A History of British Industrial Relations*, Vol 2, *1914–1939*. Brighton, Harvester.

Yeo, S. (1979) Working class associations, private capital and the state in the late nineteenth and early twentieth centuries. In Parry, N., Rustin, M. and Satyamati, C. (eds) *Social Work, Welfare and the State*. London, Edward Arnold, pp. 48–71.

Young, H. (1991) *One of Us: A Biography of Margaret Thatcher*. London, Macmillan.

Official and Other Documents

Command Papers

441 (1868) *Special Report from the Select Committee on the Married Women's Property Bill*. London, HMSO.

Cd 4499 (1909) Royal Commission on the Poor Laws and Relief of Distress (Majority and Minority Reorts). London, HMSO.

Cmd 6404 (1942) *Report of the Committee on Social Insurance and Applied Services* (The Beveridge Report). London, HMSO.

Cmd 9333 (1954) *Report of the Committee on Economic and Financial Problems of Provision for Old-age* (The Phillips Committee). London, HMSO.

Cmnd 2154 (1963) *Higher Education* (The Robbins Report). London, HMSO.

Cmnd 2605 (1965) *Report of the Committee on Housing in Greater London* (The Holland Report). London, HMSO.

Cmnd 3623 (1968) *Royal Commission on Trade Unions and Employer's Associations* (The Donovan Report). London, HMSO.

Cmnd 6851 (1977) *Housing Policy: A Consultative Document*. London, HMSO.

Cmnd 8173 (1981) *Growing Older*. London, HMSO.

Cm 849 (1989) *Caring for People*. London, HMSO.

Cm 3805 (1998) *New Ambitions for Our Country: A New Contract for Welfare*. London, Stationery Office.

Departmental Documents and Official Reports and Publications

Board of Education (1944) *The Public Schools and the General Educational System* (The Fleming Report). London, HMSO.

Central Statistical Office (1996) *Social Trends 26*. London, HMSO.

Department of the Environment (1995) *Our Future Homes*. London, Department of the Environment, HMSO.

Department of Health and Price Waterhouse (1991) *Implementing Community Care Purchaser, Commissioner and Provider Roles*. London, HMSO.

Department of Health (1991) *On the State of the Public Health*. London, Department of Health.

Department of Health (1992) *On the State of the Public Health*. London, Department of Health.

Department of Health (1994) *On the State of the Public Health*. London, Department of Health.

Department of Health (1996) *Statistical Bulletin: Community Care Statistics, 1995*. London, Government Statistical Service.

Department of Health (98/050) *Our Healthier Nation*. Publication of Green Paper on Public Health. Press release.

Department of Health (98/051) *Dobson Unveils Cross-Government Drive to Improve Public Health*. Press release.

Department of Social Security (1993) *The Growth of Social Security*. London, HMSO.

Department of Social Security (1995a) *Households Below Average Incomes: a Statistical Analysis 1979–1992/3*. London, HMSO.

Department of Social Security (1995b) *Income Related Benefits: Estimates of Take-up in 1993/4.* London, HMSO.

Ministry of Education (1954) *Early Leaving, Report of the Central Advisory Council for Education.* London, HMSO.

Ministry of Education (1959) *Fifteen to Eighteen, Report of the Central Advisory Council for Education* (The Crowther Report) 1959. London, HMSO.

Ministry of Health (1939) *National Health Insurance.* London, HMSO.

Ministry of Housing and Local Government (1953) *Houses: The Next Step.* London, HMSO.

Hansard and Parliamentary Papers

Hansard (1911) XXV, c. 609, May, 1911.

Hansard (1944) Vol. 398 cols 427–518; 535–633, 16–17 March.

Hansard (1948) Vol. 449 cols 164–6, 7 April.

House of Commons (1995) *Social Services Committee, Review of Expenditure on Social Security*, HCP 132. London, HMSO.

PP 1904 vol. XXXII *Report of the Interdepartmental Committee on Physical Deterioration* vol.1 report and appendix.

PP 1955–56 vol. XX *Report of the Committee of Enquiry into the Cost of the NHS.* HMSO Cmd 9663. Chairman C.W. Guillebaud.

Other Papers

Public Record Office (1925) PIN 3/19, Wilson, H., *Pensions at 65 and Widows Pension* 23 February.

Churchill College, University of Cambridge, Willink papers Box 2 file IV. Unpublished autobiography.

Index

A

Abbey Life 284
Abel-Smith, B. 30, 207, 215, 273, 304
Abercrombie, N. 290
Addison, P. 7, 28, 210, 301
Addy, T. 266
Adonis, A. 103
Adverse selection 60–1
Age of austerity 40, 42
Aitken, I. 129
Albert, Prince 180
Alcock, P. 11, Chapter 9
Aldcroft, D.H. 144
Altruism 56, 59, 69, 78, 86, 100, 250, 261, 265, 309–12
Anarcho-capitalists 315
Anderson, M. 263
Anderson, P. 306
Anstee, J. 217
Anti-psychiatry 100
Arber, S. 263, 265
Army Bureau for Social Affairs 118
Artis, M. 188–9
Asquith, H. 84, 88, 91
Assisted Places scheme
  see under Education
Association of British Insurers 284
Association of Carers 263
Association of Metropolitan
  Authorities (AMA) 266
Assurance Companies Act (1909) 275
Atkinson, A.B. 181, 208, 221
Attendance Allowance 210
Attlee, C. 205, 208, 301
Audit Commission 175
Austria, welfare in 164
Aves Committee 266

B

Babies of the Empire Society 20
Backhouse, R. 86
Bacon, R. 188, 304
Baker, K. 144

Balchin, P. 235, 272
Baldwin, P. 18
Baldwin, S. 291
Bales, R.F. 258
Balfour, A. 90, 161
Ball, M. 232–5, 283
Banting, P. 209
Barbour, M. 227
Barnett, C. 30, 41, 147, 182, 301
Barnett, S. Canon 259–60
Barr, N. 180, 209, 297
Barry, N. 10, Chapter 3
Bartlett, W. 102
Basic income 58, 65, 221
Baulmol, W.J. 192
Bed and breakfast accommodation 244
Beenstock, M. 61
Belgium, welfare in 164
Bellamy, R. 81–2
Benjamin, D.K. 193
Benn, T. 194
Bentham, J. 81 82 155
Beresford, P. 305
Berlin, I. 104
Berridge, V. 316
Berthoud, R. 216
Besant, A. 111
Best, G. 256
Bevan, A. 105, 159, 169–71, 230, 302
Beveridge, W.H. 4, 15, 21–2, 24, 28, 40, 42–4, 46, 48, 50–1, 60, 62–3, 73, 84, 95–7, 103, 105, 116, 124–5, 127–9, 168, 179, 182, 185–6, 189, 195, 204–8, 249, 252, 261–2, 279–81, 315, 317
  and *Full Employment in a Free Society* 195
  and Report on Social Insurance 17, 24, 29, 40, 42–4, 46, 55, 62, 73, 96–7, 168, 195, 204–7, 209–12, 215, 222, 249, 279–81
  and Voluntary Action 22, 252, 262, 316

Bevin, E. 292
Biagnini, E.F. 87
Billis, D. 269
Birch, J. 245
Bismarck, O.E.L. 60, 201–2, 205
Black Report on Health Inequalities, 174
Blackburn, R. 101
Blair, T. 103, 129, 152, 157, 191, 196, 246, 297, 307
Bleaney, M.F. 195
Bock, G. 21
Boddy, M. 235, 238
Boer War 25 87–8, 161, 259, 290
Boleat, M. 284
Bolshevism 329
Bonnerjea, L. 264
Booth, A.F. 39, 183, 185–7, 194–5
Booth, C. 85, 201–2, 215, 257, 260
Booth, T. 269
Bosanquet, B. 83, 84, 254–5, 257–9, 262
Bosanquet, H. 90, 201, 250, 253–4, 257–9, 262
Bowen. J. (Child 'B') 175
Bowlby, J. 263–4
Bowley, M. 229
Bradley, H. 290
Bradley, I. 91–2
Bradshaw, J. 203, 208–9, 218–19
Braithwaite, C. 261
Braithwaite, W.J. 160–1, 164, 166
Bramley, G. 242–3
Briggs, A. 25–7, 85
Bright, J. 81
Bristol Contributory Welfare Association 277
British Medical Association 18, 165, 168–9
British Provident Association 277
British United Provident Association (BUPA) 285–6
Brittan, S. 58, 188
Broadberry, S.N. 193
Brody, E. 265
Brooke, S. 40, 301
Brown, G. 307
Brown, K. 38

Bruce, M. 26
Brunsdon, E. 11, Chapter 12
Bryce, 134
Bryon, M. 238
Buchanan, J.M. 73, 195
Building Societies 224–5, 232–5, 279, 283–4, 297, 317
Building Societies Act (1939) 234, 238
Building Societies Act (1986) 238
Bulmer, M. *et al.* 2–4
Burchardt, T. 286, 297, 313
Burk, K. 44
Burke, P. 6, 185, 192
Burns, J. 164
Butler, E. 18, 72, 77
Butler, R.A.B. 136–8, 142–3, 303
Butskellism 30
Butt, J. 275, 278

C

Cairncross, A.K. 44, 188
Calder, A. 118–19
Callaghan, J. 98–9, 189, 249
Calnan, M. 285
Campbell-Bannerman, H. Sir 88
Capital, International mobility of 44
Carers, 263–5, 268–9, 310
Carey, G. Archbishop 147
Caring for People (1989) 268
Carson, E. Sir 89
Castle, B. 76
Challis, D. 102
Chamberlain, J. 87, 88
   and Tariff Reform League 88
Chamberlain, N. 232
Chandler, A.D. 184
Chandra, J. 277
Chappell, E. 294
Character 37, 55, 81, 84, 257–8
Charity
   see Philanthropy
Charity Organisation Society 83, 162, 201–2, 253–5, 257–9, 262
Chartism 88
Cherry, S. 277, 317
Child Benefit 60, 78, 127, 209, 212, 216

Child, J. 289
Child Poverty Action Group 22, 207, 209, 266
Childs, D. 29
Chile, welfare in 77
Christian Socialism
  see Socialism
Church of England 108, 147
Churchill, W. 17, 184
Churning 69
Citizens' income
  see Basic income
Citizenship 26, 70, 101, 119, 255, 258, 302, 308–9
City Technology Colleges 139, 144
Clark, C. 48
Clarke, K. 173
Classic welfare state
  see Welfare state, classic
Clegg, H. 88
Clinton, W.J. President 129
Clotfelter, C. 153
Coates, K. 89
Cobden, R. 81
Cobham, D. 188–9
Cockerton Judgement 140, 147
Cohen Committee (1932) 280
Cole, G.D.H. 95
Cole, I. 230
Cole, M. 95
Colleges of Advanced Technology (CATS) 145
Commercial welfare
  see Private welfare
Commission of Inquiry into Industrial Unrest (1917) 228
Commission on Social Justice 146–7, 214, 306
Commission on Wealth Creation and Social Cohesion 196
Communism 25
Communist party 95
Communitarianism 67, 129, 311
Community care 35, 176–7, 266, 287
Comprehensive schools
  see Education, comprehensive
Conscription 92
Consensus
  see Welfare, post-1945 consensus

Conservatism 17–18, 55, 57–8, 78, 93
Conservative Party 15, 17–18, 22, 24, 28–30, 32, 35–7, 42, 45–6, 50, 55, 78, 88, 91, 94, 98, 104, 124–5, 138, 149–51, 154–7, 164, 167–77, 188–91, 193–6, 208, 210–13, 224–5, 228–39, 241–5, 265–6, 269, 282–4, 286, 293–4, 296–7, 303–4, 312, 315
Consultative Council on Medical and Allied Services 166
Cooke, A. 148
Corn Laws 81
Coulter, F. 180, 209
Council house sales 238, 241,
Coupon election (1918) 88
Crafts, N.F.R. 185
Cranston, M. 80
Cripps, S. 95
Critical social policy 101
Croft, S. 305
Cronin, J. 116
Crosland, A.R. 98–9, 105, 115, 119–25, 128, 137, 151, 303
Crossman, R.H.S. 106, 120, 262
Crowther, M.A. 16, 21, 25, 39, 52, 179, 185
Crowther Report on Education for 15- to 18-year olds 151
Cullingworth, J. 235
Curtice, J. 129
Cutler, T. 205

D

Dale, J. 101
Damer, S. 227, 231
Dangerfield, G.F. 89, 92
Daunton, M. 224–5, 233–4
Davidson, N. 304
Davies, B. 102
Davin, A. 19
Dawson, Lord 166
Deacon, A. 203, 208, 218–19, 309, 311
Deacon, B. 314
Deakin, N. 35, 52, 210, 266, 303, 313
Dearing, R. Sir 144, 153, 157

Defence of the Realm Act (1914) 92
Demographic trends 43, 179, 191, 200
Dendy, H. 257
Denmark, welfare in 164, 250
Dennis, N. 79, 101
Dentistry 165, 177, 280, 286–7
Department of the Environment 243, 245
Department of Health 174, 178, 267, 288
Department of Social Security 213, 218, 304
Dependency culture 30, 58, 180, 192, 210–11
Digby, A. 17, 19, 24, 27, 32, 185, 292
Dilnot, A.W. 50, 190, 221
Dimsdale, N.H. 193
Disability Living Allowance 210
District Health Authorities (DHAs) 126, 173
Ditch, J. 200
Do-it-yourself welfare 308
Dobson, F. 177–8
Dorling, J. 239
Dorrell, S. 175–6
Douglas, J.W.B. 150
Dunkirk 167
Durbin, E. 85, 95, 101
Dutton, D. 170, 303
Duty 58, 114

E

Earnings-related benefits 208–9
Eccles, D. Sir 143
Eccleshall, R. 86–7, 92–3
Economic growth 44, 50, 121–3, 139, 142, 146, 157, 180–1, 186–8, 190, 203, 214, 262, 282, 303, 315
Economic theory 16, 56, 85, 93, 180–1, 195
Eden, A. Sir 234
Edgeworth, F.Y. 254
Education 11, 25, 36, 45, 68, 108–9, 122, Chapter 6, 272–3, 288–9, 296–7, 302, 307, 313
  and Assisted Places Scheme 149–50, 154, 288, 297

Comprehensive schools 137, 142, 152, 155
Direct grant schools 138, 152
and Early Leaving Report 151
Elementary schools 140–1
Grammar schools 135–6, 140–1, 143, 148, 150–2
Grant maintained 144, 157
Higher 135, 138–9, 144–6, 148, 153, 155–7, 279, 288
Higher grade schools 140–1, 147–8
Independent schools 140, 149–50, 157, 279, 288
Junior technical schools 143
Secondary modern schools 150
Secondary Technical Schools 143
Education Act (1902) 134–5, 139–41, 147, 272
Education Act (1918) 135, 139
Education Act (1944) 18, 136–9, 141, 143, 146–7, 150–1
Education Act (1980) 149
Education Act (1988) 139, 288
Education Priority Areas 137–8
Education (Provision of Meals) Act (1906) 258–9
Educational Action Zones 157
Edwardian Guilds of Help 255
Edwards, R. 244
Efficiency 37, 47, 55, 85, 90, 134, 149, 162, 184, 197, 290
Egoism 57, 100
El Alamein 204
Eleven-plus examination 135–6, 148, 150–2
Eltis, W.A. 188, 304
Emergency Medical Service 118
Employment 11, 24, 30, 43, Chapter 8
Employment training 143
Enfranchisement 17
Engels, F. 107
Englander, D. 225, 227
Enthoven, A. 173
Equal Opportunities Commission (EOC) 263
Equality 66, 114, 120–4, 303, 307–8
Ermisch, J. 263

Esping-Andersen, G. 18–19, 250, 314

Essex man 129

Ethical Socialism
see Socialism Christian/Ethical

Ethnic minorities and housing 238–40, 243

Etzioni, A. 311

European Economic Community
see European Union

European Social chapter 196

European Union 98, 190, 284, 314

European welfare state 70, 71, 75

Evans, M. 44, 212

Evers, A. 268

Evidence-based medicine 175

F

Fabian Society and Fabianism 3, 30, 95, 101, 110–14, 116–17, 119, 125, 128, 161, 201–2, 215, 257, 271, 315
and the role of the expert administrator 112

Factory Acts 133

Falkingham, J. 214–15, 217

Falklands War 190

Family Allowances 20, 60, 94, 166, 204, 206–7, 209

Family Credit 45, 50, 60, 208, 212, 218

Family Income Supplement (FIS) 208, 212

Family Welfare Association 262
see also Charity Organisation Society

Feinstein, C.H. 187

Feminism 4, 8, 10, 100,

Field, F. 43, 48, 50, 52, 71, 79, 196, 210–11, 214, 222, 283, 293, 297, 309–311

Fielding, S. 301–2

Finance Act (1915) 278

Finance Act (1916) 278

Finance Act (1947) 293

Financial Intermediarists, Managers and Brokers Regulatory Association (FIMBRA) 284

Financial Services Act (1986) 284

Finch, J. 250

Finlayson, G. 23, 312

First World War 24–5

Fiscal welfare 27, 33, 44, 46, 249, 294

Fisher, H.A.L. 93, 135

Fitzgerald, R. 290

Fitzhugh, W.A. 287

Fleming Committee on The Public Schools (1944) 149

Floud, J. 141, 150

Foot, M. 99, 117–18

Foote, G. 107–8, 110

Ford . J. 239–40, 242

Forder, A. 2

Fordism 224

Formal welfare 33

Fowler, N. Sir 30, 212
Fowler Review on Social Security 30, 213

Fox, D. 163

Fox, E. 262, 277

France, welfare in 73, 135, 148–9, 155, 251, 264

Francis, M. 301

Franklin, J. 308

Fraser, D. 8, 27

Fraser, M. 303

Fraternity 274

Fraud 71

Free rider problem 316

Freeden, M. 23, 85–6

Freedom 56–7, 80–1, 84, 93

Freeman, J. 171

Friedman, M. 57–8, 98, 195, 304

Friendly Society Act (1876) 273

Friendly Society Act (1896) 273

Friendly Societies 23, 38, 41, 60, 72, 88, 107, 109, 160, 165, 201–2, 205, 250, 252, 261, 273–4, 276–7, 279, 290, 317

Full employment 19, 43, 49, 93, 95, 97–8, 103, 120, 123, 182, 186

Furbey, R. 230

Furniss, N. 122

G

Gaitskell, H. 98–9, 124

Galbraith, J.K. 309

Garden Cities movement 229

Garraty, J.R. 192
Garside, W.R. 182, 185
Gatrell, V.A.C. 146
Geddes, E. 136
General Certificate of Secondary
Education (GCSE) 156, 289
General Household Survey 263
General National Vocational
Qualification (GNVQ) 144, 157,
289
General Practitioners 160, 165, 167,
169–70, 173–4, 176–7, 273–4, 277,
280, 282, 287
and fundholding 74, 173–4, 176–7
General Strike (1926) 91, 94, 185,
291
George, V. 101, 103, 117, 123, 190
Germany, welfare in 25–7, 60, 69, 73,
75, 90, 134–5, 155, 163–4, 183–4,
201–2
Gibb, K. 246
Giddens, T. 305, 313
Gilbert, B. 18, 23, 37, 51–2, 163–4,
252
Gillis, J.R. 146
Gingerbread 266
Ginsburg, N. 11, Chapter 10
Gladstone, D. 266
Gladstone, W. 85–6, 317
Gladstonian Liberalism 85–6
Glendinning, C. 268
Glennerster, H. 3, 16,18, 21, 44, 52,
68, 174, 280, 282, 288, 296, 303
Globalisation 51, 190, 196, 284, 305
Glynn, S. 11, Chapter 8
Godley, W. 194
Golding, P. 221
Goldthorpe, J. 304
Goodin, R. 47, 67–8, 102, 311
Goodlad, R. 246
Goodman, A. 308
Gosden, P.H.J.H. 135, 273
Gospel, H.F. 184, 190, 194, 289,
293, 295
Gough, I. 101
Gould, B. 129
Government Annuities Act (1864)
317

Graham, H. 264
Graves, J. 279
Gray, H. 98
Gray, J. 68, 98, 102, 305, 308,
313–14
Green, D.G. 60, 67, 72, 98, 160,
222, 252, 297, 304
Green, F. 293
Green, S. 228
Green, T.H. 82–3, 84, 308
Greenleaf, W.H. 92, 97
Grey, E. Sir 84
Grieve Smith, J. 196
Groves, D. 250
Growing Older (1981) 265
Guaranteed minimum income
see Basic income
Guillebaud Committee on the NHS
42, 171–2

H

Hadley, R. 102, 266, 312
Hadow, H. Sir 136–7, 140–1
Hailsham, Lord 303
Haldane, R.B. 84, 134
Halevy, E. 81, 82
Hall, M.P. 2
Hall, P. 234
Halsey, A.H. 101, 141–2, 150, 179,
304
Ham, C. 102
Hammond, J. and Hammond, B. 2, 8
Hamnett, C. 225, 227, 283, 287
Hannah, L. 278, 289–91, 293
Hansmann, H. 251
Hardie, J.K. 164
Harloe, M. 224, 231
Harman, H. 152, 174
Harrington, W. 118
Harris, J. 17, 22–4, 30, 41, 49, 84,
96, 116–17, 133, 179–80, 184,
195, 202, 250–1, 274, 301–2
Harris, R.W. 164
Harrison, T. 301
Harrod, R.F. 93
Hart, R. 293
Hatch, S. 102, 266, 312
Hattersley, R. 128

Hawksworth, J. 245
Hay, J.R. 17, 25, 290
Hayek, F.A. 60–1, 98, 282, 304
Heald, D. 35, 52
Health 11, 41, 72–5, Chapter 7, 296
  Inequalities 177
  Of the nation 174
  Private provision 160, 171–3
  Rationing 175–6
  see also National Health Service
Health Action Zones 176
Health Education Council 174
Health Maintenance Organisations
  (HMO) 74
Health and safety 291
Health Service White Paper (1944)
  167–8
Healthcare 2000 175
Heath, E. Sir 98, 138, 188
Hegel, G.W.F. 83
Held, D. 305
Help the Aged 217
Hendrick, H. 20, 32
Hennock, E.P. 25, 90, 164
Herbert, S.M. 277
Hewitt, M. 303
Hicks, J. 95
Hicks, U.K. 146
Higgins, J. 285–6
Hill, B. 290
Hill, M. 30, 35, 102, 200, 208, 218,
  221
Hill, O. 254–7
Hills, J. 48–9, 52, 78, 102, 214–5,
  235, 286, 296–7, 308, 313, 315
Hilton, J. 281
Himmelfarb, G. 64–5, 79, 81
Hindess, B. 271, 308
Hirst, P. 51, 305
Hobhouse, L.T. 84–6, 103, 308
Hobson, J. 85–6
Hodson, A.L. 258
Hoggett, P. 269
Holmans, A. 229, 243–4
Holton, S. 89
Homelessness 224, 228, 236–7, 241,
  243–6
Homes fit for heroes 228, 230

Honigsbaum, F. 274
Hopkins, E. 274
Hospital Savings Association 277, 285
Hospitals
  Poor Law 160
  Voluntary 160, 166, 168–9, 261,
    273, 277, 280, 282
Housing 197, Chapter 10, 272, 302
  and ethnic minorities 236, 238,
    240, 243
  Improvement grants 234–5
  Local authority 22, 25, 78, 97,
    224–6, 228–32, 236–8, 241–6
  Owner occupied 223–6, 231–40,
    244–5, 272, 279, 282–3, 287
  Privately rented 223–9, 231,
    233–5, 237, 242–3, 245–6, 272,
    279, 282
  Repossessions 240
  'Right to buy' 45, 238, 282
  Subsidies 231–2, 237, 242, 315
  Unfit 223, 227, 230
Housing Act (1923) 232–3
Housing Act (1924) 229, 231
Housing Act (1949) 234
Housing Act (1980) 238
Housing Act (1988) 241
Housing Act (1996) 243, 245
Housing Associations 223, 241–2,
  244
Housing Benefit 45, 208, 212,
  236–7, 241–3
Housing (Homeless Persons) Act
  (1977) 236
Housing and Town Planning Act
  (1919) 225, 228–9
Howe, G. 303
Howells, D. 191
Hughes, J.J. 181
Hulse, M. 314
Human nature 58, 63, 65–6, 70, 309
Human resource management 294–5
Humphreys, R. 250, 313
Humphries, J. 190
Humphries, S. 279
Hutton, W. 191, 193, 306
Huxley, T.H. 84
Hyde, R. 291

Hyndman, H.M. 107

I

Idealism 82–3
Incapacity Benefit 316
Income Data Services 294
Income Support 60, 76, 211–12, 218
Income Support for Mortgage Interest
(ISMI)
see Housing subsidies
Independent Labour Party 95,
113–14, 227
Independent schools
see under Education
Industrial Assurance Board 281
Industrial Fatigue Research Board
291
Industrial Life Offices 281
Industrial Welfare Society 291
Inequality 101, 114, 172, 174, 191,
214, 222, 304, 315
Inflation 187–9, 194, 196, 235
Informal welfare sector 11, 15, 21–2,
33, 173, 217–8, Chapter 11, 271,
304, 312, 314
Institute of Economic Affairs 97, 153
Institute of Labour Management 291
Institute of Personnel Management
292
Inter-Departmental Committee on
Physical Deterioration (1904) 161
Inter-War years 24
International Labour Organisation
(ILO) 314
International Monetary Fund (IMF)
24, 236, 314–15
Invalid Care Allowance 264, 268
Invalidity Benefit 50, 63, 71, 316
Irish Home Rule 87–9
Italy, welfare in 164

J

Jackson, P. 60, 69
James, C. 294
Japan, welfare in 75–6, 143, 156
Jeffreys, K. 167–8, 302
Jewkes, J. 98, 282

Job Seekers Allowance 191, 197, 212,
310
Johnson, C. 190, 193,
Johnson, L.B. President 316
Johnson, N. 102, 210
Johnson, P. 31, 35, 37, 52, 133, 214,
274, 276, 315
Jones, C. 240
Jones, Harriet 29, 97
Jones, Helen 11, 16, 20, 25, Chapter
7
Jones, K. 200–1
Jones, R. 104, 189, 192, 194
Jones, T. 25, 104, 303
Joseph, K. 211
Joseph Rowntree Foundation 67, 214
Joslin, D. 114
Jowell, T. 178
Joyce, P. 289
Judge, K. 274, 312
Judgementalism 302, 309

K

Kahn, R.F. 86
Kakabadse, A. 277
Kaldor, N. 95
Kandiah, M. 97
Kanthack, E. 256
Kavanagh, D. 27, 98, 170, 303
Kay, J. 307
Kazamias, A.M. 134
Keegan, W. 189–90, 195
Kekewich, G. Sir 147–8
Kellner, P. 308
Kendall, J. 288
Keynes, J.M. 24, 28, 86, 93–7, 105,
116, 124–5, 181, 195, 204
Keynesianism 4, 16, 24, 94–6, 119,
121–2, 194–5, 306
Kindercare 288
King, A. 188
King, D.S. 25, 98
Kinnock, G. 128
Kinnock, N. 99, 128
Kirby, J. 231
Kirby, M.W. 184
Klein, R. 29, 102, 252, 308, 312
Knapp, M. 102, 288, 312

Knight, B. 270
Knights, D. 278
Kochin, L.A. 193
Koven, S. 21
Krafchik, M. 317
Kramer, R.M. 269
Kuhnle, S. 250–1

L

Labour exchanges 90, 184
Labour market 44, 46, 163–4,
  Chapter 8, 264
  Women's participation in 44, 264
Labour party 15,17, 23–4, 28, 35,
  38, 40, 42, 44, 85, 87–8, 91, 94–9,
  103, Chapter 5, 138, 149, 154, 157,
  159, 161, 164, 167–71, 174–8,
  184, 187, 189, 192, 194, 196–7,
  201, 204–5, 207–10, 213–14, 225,
  227–32, 235–7, 241, 245–6, 249,
  260, 280–2, 286, 288, 293, 297–8,
  301–3, 308, 310, 315, 317
  and Clause 4 95, 98
Labour Representation Committee
  87–8
Labourism 108–10, 230
Lafitte, F. 281
Laing, W. 285, 287
Laissez-faire
  see New Right
Land, H. 251, 264
Landlords 225, 227
Landry, C. 313
Lavers, G. 207, 215
Law, I. 16, 29
Lawson, N. 238
Layard, R. 289, 307
Laybourn, K. 108
Le Grand, J. 18, 47, 67–8, 102, 304,
  311–12
Leather, P. 283
Lee, J. 259
Lee, M. 287
Lees, D. 73, 98, 303
Legal and General 285
Leira, A. 250
Levellers 86–7
Levin, E. 268

Levy, J.H. 278, 280
Lewis, J. 11, 22–3, 183, Chapter 11
Lewis, R. 303
Liberal Democrat Party 99–100,
  103–4, 245
Liberal Party 23–4, 36–7, 85–94, 95,
  97, 99, 105, 108–9, 160, 225, 230,
  275, 290
  and Lib–Lab pact (1977–78) 99
  and 'People's budget' (1909) 37
  and welfare reforms (1906–1914)
    5, 7, 16–17, 23, 25, 34, 36, 59,
    160, 179, 184, 258, 276
Liberty
  see Freedom
Liddle, R. 305, 307
Liebfried, S. 314
Life Assurance and Unit Trusts
  Regulatory Organisation
  (LAUTRO) 284
Life Assurances Companies Act
  (1870) 274–5
Life expectancy 160
Life insurance 274, 296
Lindsay, A.D. 262
Lister, R. 221, 268–9
Llewellyn-Smith, G. 38, 185, 261
Lloyd George, D. 38–9, 88, 91, 93,
  159–61, 163–5, 184, 228
Lloyd, T.O. 110
Local authorities
  see Local government
Local government 22, 35, 151,
  154–5, 163, 216
Local government Board 20
Local Management of Schools (LMS)
  139
Loch, C. 254–5, 262
Locke, J. 80, 82
London Association for Hospital
  Services
  see Private Patients Plan
London County Council 229
London School of Economics 202,
  204–5, 207, 254
Lone parent families 44, 49, 58, 63,
  65, 71, 78, 191, 239, 304
Low Pay 180, 206

Lowe, R. 18, 27–8, 30–1, 42, 48, 52, 89, 179, 303, 306
Lowndes, G.A.N. 134
Lynes, A. 209, 313

M

M'Gonigle, G. 231
Mabbett, D. 50, 52
Macadam, E. 261–2
McBriar, A.M. 83, 85, 90, 259
McCormick, J. 307
McCrone, G. 188
McCulloch, G. *et al.* 143
MacDonald, R. 94, 203
Mackenzie, J. 162
Mackenzie, N. 162
McKibbin, R. 257
McLaughlin, E. 268
Maclean, J. 227
Macleod, I. 97
MacMillan, H. 31, 94–5, 98, 103, 194, 230, 303
  and The Middle Way 94
MacMillan, M. 167
McNichol, J. 167
McSmith, A. 104, 193
Major, J. 29, 35, 45, 193, 196, 237, 284, 286, 296–7
Malpass, P. 236, 244
Malthus, T. 80, 316
Manchester School 81
Mandelson, P. 305, 307
Mann, K. 89, 107–8, 217, 293
Mann, N. 306
Mann, T. 89, 107
Manpower Services Commission (MSC) 266
Marchant, J. 260
Markham, V. 259
Marquand, D. 170, 314
Married Women's Property Act (1870) 254
Marris, R. 197
Marshall, A. 85, 260
Marshall Aid 230
Marshall, T.H. 26, 70, 101–3, 115
Marsland D. 63, 67, 77, 301
Martin, F.M. 141

Martin, J. 263
Marwick, A. 118, 185–6
Marx, K. 106–7, 110, 120
Marxism 4, 8, 45, 95, 100, 106–8, 111, 114, 120, 271
Mason, D. 243
Mason, T. 301
Mass Observation 118, 147
Massey, P. 278
Mastermann, C.F.G. 85
Matthews, R.C.O. 146, 187, 195
Maude, A. 303,
Maugham, S. 256
Maurice, E. 256
Maxwell scandal 294
May, M. 11, Chapter 12
Mead, L.M. 64–5, 304
Meade, J. 95
Meadows, P. 304
Means, R. 264
Means-test and Means-testing 9, 29–30, 37, 60, 69–72, 75, 97, 205–6, 208–12, 214, 219, 273, 279, 310, 312
  Household means test 39, 203–4
Medicaid 316
Medicare 316
Melling, J. 227, 290
Merrett, S. 231–3, 235
Metropolitan Life of New York 292
Michel, S. 21
Middle Way Chapter 4
Middlemas, K. 194, 229
Middleton, R. 16, 24, 52
Middleton, S. 221
Mikardo, I. 281
Miliband, R. 101, 105
Militant 99
Mill, J.S. 82, 83, 104
Millar, J. 308
Miller, S. 190
Milner-Holland Report on Housing in Greater London 228
Minimum wage 94, 103
Ministry of Health 166, 277
Ministry of Labour 292
Mishra, R. 1–2
Mitch, D. 133

Mitchell, D. 47
Mobility Allowances 210
Moggridge, D.E. 93
Mohan, J. 286
Mond-Turner talks 291
Monetarism 16, 189
De Montmorencey, J.E.G. 133
Moore, J. 173, 211
Morah, D. 278
Moral hazard 63–6, 69, 72, 74
Morant, R. Sir 134–6, 140–2, 147–9
Morgan, G. 278
Morgan, K. 169–70, 194, 302
Moroney, R.M. 264
Morris, B. 290
Morris, P. 170, 303
Morris, W. 107–8
Morrison, H. 169
Morrison, T. 283
Mortgage interest tax relief 235–6,
    238–9, 245
Mortgage protection 217, 286
Mount, F. 265
Mulgan, G. 297, 313
Murie, A. 244
Murray, B.K. 37
Murray, C. 79, 304, 311
Mutualism 91, 250, 252–3, 256, 259,
    261

N

National Assistance 29, 36, 42, 60,
    204, 206–7
National Birthday Trust Fund 167
National Commission on Education
    142
National Committee to Promote the
    Break-Up of the Poor Law 162
National Consumer Council 209
National Council for Carers and their
    Elderly Dependants 263
National Council for Voluntary
    Organisations (NCVO) 266–7
National efficiency
    see Efficiency
National Health Service 16, 18, 20,
    28–9, 31, 35–6, 41–2, 45, 55, 68,

72–3, 116, 125–7, 129, Chapter 7,
    169, 204, 302, 315
    and pay beds 170–1, 286
    and prescription charges 171, 208
    Trusts 74, 173–7, 285, 287
    and waiting lists 285
National Health Service Act (1946)
    18, 169–70, 282
National Health Service and
    Community Care Act (1990) 126,
    173, 268
National Institute of Industrial
    Psychology 291
National Insurance 20, 30, 33, 39–40,
    42–3, 46, 48, 51, 55, 59–61, 166,
    184–5, 193, 202–3, 205–13, 221,
    252, 277–8, 291, 310, 315, 317
    and 'Approved' status 277, 280
    Fowler Review 30
    Fund 30, 39 40, 42–3, 48
National Insurance Act (1911) 18,
    23, 36, 38–9, 41, 59, 90, 159,
    163–7, 202–3, 252, 260, 277
National Insurance Act (1946) 301
National Liberal Federation 87
National Medical Aid Company 274
National Schools Standards Task Force
    313
National Society for the Prevention of
    Cruelty to Children (NSPCC) 22
National Vocational Qualification
    (NVQ) 289
Nationalisation 41, 98, 103, 112, 194
Need 66
Negative equity 239–40
Negative Income Tax (NIT) 58, 65,
    221
Neo-classicism
    see New Right
Nesbitt, S. 294
Nevitt, A. 227
*New Ambitions for our Country: A New
    Contract for Welfare* 307
New Jerusalem 24, 41, 114
New Labour 103–4, 126, 129–30,
    246, 297–8, 305–9, 312–13
    and the 'Third Way' 298, 305
New Left 100

New Liberalism 23, 34, Chapter 4, 225–6, 259, 308
New Right 10, 23–24, 30,45–6, Chapter 3, 78–9, 97–100, 104, 152, 185, 194, 257, 271, 303–4, 313
New unionism 88–9
New universities 139, 145
Newton, J. 242
Nicholson, P.P. 83
Niskanen, W. 56
Nissel, M. 264
Niven, M.M. 291–2
Norway, welfare in 164, 250–1
Norwich Union 285
Novak, T. 200
Nuffield Nursing Home Trust 286

O

Oakeshott, M. 61–3
Oakley, A. 250, 263, 309
Occupational welfare 33, 49–50, Chapter 12
Offer, A. 225
Office for Economic Co-operation and Development (OECD) 142, 156, 190
Office for Fair Trading (OFT) 297
OFSTED 154, 156
O'Higgins, M. 102, 312
Old age 64, 75–7, 176
Old age pensions 20–1, 35, 37–8, 40, 42–3, 45, 49, 62, 75, 163, 202, 206–8, 216, 312
Old Age Pensions Act (1908) 20, 38, 42, 59, 75, 90, 163, 202
Oliver, S. 111
One Nation Group 97, 303
OPEC oil crisis 44, 188–9
Oppenheim, C. 304
Opportunity State 128
Our Healthier Nation 178
Outdoor relief 45,
Owen, D. 313
Oxfam 217, 266

P

Pack, M. 194
Page, R.M. 52, 103, Chapter 13

Pankhurst, C. 89
Pankhurst, R. 89
Pankhurst, S. 89
Papadakis, E. 271, 288
Parker, R. 251
Parmoor Committee (1920) 280
Parsons, T. 258
Participation 305
Paternalism 256, 290
Pathfinder Summer Literacy Scheme 313
Patient's Charter 129
Paton, C. 174
Patten, J. 144
Pawley, M. 284
Pay-As-You-Go (PAYG) 50, 76–7, 206
Pay beds 277
Peach, C. 238
Peacock, A. 35, 76
Peden, G. 24, 184, 195
Pedersen, S. 20–1
Pelling, H. 92, 95, 108–9
Pember-Reeves, M.S. 257
Pensions Act (1996) 294
Perkin, H. 18, 155
Perlman, R. 181
Personal social services 253–8, 265, 268, 316
Personal Social Services Research Unit 102
Phelps-Brown, E.H. 180
Philanthropy 19, 22, 72, 84, 202, 249–50, 252, 254–5, 257–61, 304
Phillips Committee on the Economic and Financial Problems of Provision for Old-Age (1954) 43
Piachaud, D. 304
Pierson, P. 314
Pilgrim Trust 278
Pimlott, B. 7, 303
Pinker, R.A. 10, Chapter 4, 277
Pirie, M. 63, 77–8
Planning 61, 93, 94, 98, 120–1, 194
Plant, R. 84, 309
Plowden Committee 137
Pluralism 80
    see also Welfare, pluralism
Political and Economic Planning 52, 165

Political economy 80
Pollard, S. 308
Pollard, S.G. 233, 292
Pollitt, H. 118
Pond, C. 33
Poor Laws 5, 8, 22–3, 37, 64–5, 81,
    84, 88–9, 108, 160–1, 163, 184–5,
    200–1, 203, 205, 211, 216–7, 221,
    249–50, 252, 254–5, 260, 273
    Boards of Guardians 16
    Poor Law Amendment Act (1834)
        2, 5, 16, 45, 64, 90, 184, 192
    Royal Commission on the Poor
        Laws (1905–9) 85, 90, 108,
        161–3, 201–3, 259–61
Poor Relief 35, 57, 70, 85, 89–90,
    254
Popular Front 95
Positivism 110–11
Poverty 11, 26, 66, 72, 81–2, 85–6,
    89–90, 101, 108, 114, 123, 134,
    137, 177, 180, 183, 186–7, 189,
    191, Chapter 9, 250, 257–8, 261,
    304
    Line 257
    Prevention 219
    Rediscovery of in the 1960s 22,
        29–31, 43, 207–9
    Trap 71, 212, 218–9, 242, 245
Powell, J.E. 87
Powell, M. 303, 308
Prentice, R. 137
Price Waterhouse 267
Private Finance Initiative 175, 312
Private Patients Plan 285
Private welfare 22, 24, 33, 36, 49, 57,
    61–2, 72–3, 96, 127, 149, 157,
    205–6, 213–14, 217, 222, 239,
    Chapter 12, 304, 314
Privatization 63
Procedural justice 66
Prochaska, F. 19, 250, 261
Protection From Eviction Act (1924)
    227
Prudential 275, 278, 284
Public Assistance and Public
    Assistance Committees 203, 205
Public choice theory 56, 69, 311

Public opinion 127
Public Schools Commission 149
Pugh, M. 23

Q

Quasi-markets 74–5, 102, 126, 316
Qureshi, H. 263

R

Race and racism 5, 9, 16, 19–20, 29,
    103, 236
Race Relations Act (1976) 236
Rachman, P. 228
Rachmanism 224, 228
Radice, G. 161–3
Rae, J. 149–50, 288
Rathbone, E. 166
Raynsford, N. 236
Reciprocity 57, 75
Red Clydesiders 227
Reddin, M. 293
Redistribution
    Horizontal 60, 181, 216–7, 220–1
    Vertical 47–8, 100, 109, 129,
        215–7, 220–1, 308–9
Reeder, D. 140–1
Reform Act (1867) 17
Reid, A. 87
Reisman, D. 309
Relative deprivation 66
Rent 242, 272
    control 192, 226–8, 236, 279
    and Rate rebates 208, 212
    and social security 207
    Strikes 227
Rent Act (1915) 227
Rent Act (1957) 228, 235
Rent Act (1965) 228
Rent and Mortgage Interest (War
    Restrictions) Act (1915) 226–7
Repossession of housing 239–40
Representation of the People Act
    (1918) 17
Reynolds, J. 108
Ribbon development 234
Ricardo, D. 80
Richmond, M. 256

Richter, M. 84
Riddell, P. 174
Ritschel, D. 94
Robbins Report on Higher Education
138–9, 145
Roberts, C. 263
Roberts, D. 7–8
Robertson, J. 81
Robinson, J. 95
Rose, H. 5, 264
Rose, M. 200
Ross, E. 254
Rousseau, J-J. 83
Rowntree, B.S. 85, 90, 180, 183,
201, 203, 205, 207, 214–6, 220,
258, 260, 275, 278
Royal Commission on Elementary
Education (1888) 109
Rubery, J. 190
Rudolph, B. 225, 227
Russell, A. 293

S

Salmon, L.M. 251, 269
Salter, B. 174
Samuel, H. 84, 91
Sanderson, M. 11, Chapter 6, 183
Sandford,C. 52
Sassoon, D. 309
Saunders, P. 232, 296
Savings 37–8, 218
Saxon Harrold, S. 267
School Boards 133, 148
School Meals 90, 125, 135, 161, 208,
242, 259–60
School medical service 90, 135, 161,
260
Schwartz, A.J. 195
Scott, C.R. 93
Scott, D. 266
Scottish Nationalists 99
Second World War 96–7
Secondary Technical Schools 143
Securities and Investment Board 284
Seebohm Committee 266, 316
Seldon, A. 73, 98, 282, 304
Selectivity 9, 19, 26, 30, 37, 62,
68–9, 197, 230, 302, 307

Self-help 23, 90, 96, 107, 109, 197,
202, 205, 211, 280
Self-interest 56–7, 86, 220, 261,
309–11
Selle, P. 250–1
Shaw, G.B. 110–11
Shaw, S. 185
Shelter 22, 266
Shepherd, G. 144, 154
Sherington, G. 135
Shore, P. 237
Shorter, E. 254
Sick Pay 274, 291, 293–4
Sickness benefit 50
Silburn, R.L. Introduction, 96, 205,
222
Simey, M. 85
Simey, T.S. 85, 262
Simon, B. 109, 136, 146–7
Sinclair, J.G. 278
Sinfield, A. 33, 293–4
Slum clearance 226–7, 230–1, 279
Smith, A. 80–1
Smith, E. 295
Smith, G. 138,
Smith, H.L. 7, 25, 183, 186, 301
Smith, R. 264
SmithKline Beecham 153
Smyth, J. 290,
Snowden, P. 164
Social Administration
see Social Policy, academic
developments in
Social conscience thesis of welfare 2
Social contract 98–9, 189
Social Democratic Federation (SDF)
106–8, 110, 113
Social Democratic Party (SDP) 99
Social Democracy 105, 303, 305
Social division of welfare 249
Social efficiency
see Efficiency
Social exclusion 197, 307
Social Exclusion Unit 178
Social Insurance
see National Insurance
Social Justice 66–9

Social Policy
  Academic developments in 1–11,
    Comparative 4, 19–20, 102
  and economic policy 16, 24, 30
  and the impact of war
    see War – impact on welfare policy
Social problems 164, 254, 260
Social Security 11, Chapter 9, 287
Social Security Act (1986) 284, 294,
  316
Social solidarity 25
Social wage 189
Social work
  see Personal Social services
Socialism 96
  Christian/Ethical 3, 87, 101, 103,
    113–16, 129
  Democratic 10, 95, 98, 100,
    Chapter 5, 134, 303, 305, 311,
    313
  Guild 95
  Liberal 305
  Municipal 87
  Parliamentary 105
  State 101
  Supply-side 306
Socialist Medical Association 116
Sociology 2–3, 5–6, 85, 258, 263
Speenhamland 64–5, 184
Spencer, H. 250
Spens, W. Sir 137, 140
Spicker, P. 220, 314
Stakeholding 306, 310
State Earnings-Related Pensions Scheme
  (SERPS) 76, 208, 213–4, 284
Steadman-Jones, G. 5–6, 183–4
Stevenson, J. 230, 272
Stewart, J. 10, Chapter 1, 138, 314
Stewart, M. 195
Stewart, W.A.C. 138
Stigma 137
  and Poor Law 17, 29, 39, 65, 108,
    160, 184, 203, 205–8, 273
  and social housing 245
Stopes, M. 166
Stubbs, P. 314
Subsidiarity 314
Suffragette movement 89, 92

Sullivan, M. 10, Chapter 5, 204
Sumption, J. 211
Supple, B. 142, 274
Supplementary benefits 43, 208, 211–2
Sweden, welfare in 25, 57, 69, 191,
  250
Swenarton, M. 229

T

Taff Vale judgement 87
Take-up of social security benefits
  208–9, 218
Tariff Reform League 88
Tawney, R.H. 84, 103, 114–15
Taxation 36–7, 43–4, 46–8, 59, 95,
  103, 123–4, 152, 181, 209, 235,
  292, 316–7
Taylor, A.J. 23
Taylor, M. 23, 269, 313
Taylor-Gooby, P. 101, 271, 288
Tebbut, M. 257
Tenants movements 224–5, 227, 229,
  236
Terry, F. 312
Thain, C. 52
Thane, P. 21, 26–7, 37–8, 42, 87, 90,
  107–9, 116–17, 179, 184–5, 200,
  251, 276
Thatcher, M. 28–30, 35, 45, 73, 76,
  98, 103, 129, 137, 155, 159,
  172–3, 195–6, 210, 224, 236–8,
  241, 249, 265, 296
Thatcherism 24, 39, 44, 155, 190,
  195, 210–11, 224, 236–7, 241
The Future of the NHS 177
Thomas, M. 185
Thompson, F.M.L. 180
Thompson, G. 51, 305–6
Thompson, N. 306
Thompson, P. 301
Thomson, M. 262
Thorneycroft, P. 31
Tilton, T. 122
Timmins, N. 22, 28, 30, 303
Tiratsoo, N. 194, 301
Titmuss, R.M. 1, 7, 18, 25, 27, 33,
  42, 52, 100–2, 117, 119, 166–7,
  186, 249, 291–4, 301, 304, 309–10

Tomlinson, J. 10, 22, Chapter 2, 194–5, 301
Tooley, J. 153
Topham, T. 89
Town and Country Planning Act (1947) 234
Townsend, P. 186–7, 207, 209, 214–5, 219, 264, 304, 313
Toynbee, A. 84
Toynbee Hall 259
Trade Disputes Act (1906) 88
Trades Disputes and Trade Union Act (1927) 94
Trade Union Act (1913) 88
Trade Unions 38, 41, 87–9, 98–9, 103, 107, 109, 113, 120, 122, 165, 182, 185, 187, 189–90, 192, 194, 201, 225, 250, 252, 290
Trades Union Congress (TUC) 87
Training and Enterprise Councils (TECS) 143, 157
Training Opportunities Schemes (TOPS) 143
Treasury 24, 38, 40, 42–3, 47, 195, 230, 279
Treble, J.H. 183
Trevelyan, G. Sir 2, 140–1
Trickle down theory 67, 211, 214
Tudor Walters Report (1918) 229
Tulloch, G. 195

U

Ulster 89
Underclass 16, 58, 65, 77, 79, 253, 304
Unemployed Assistance Board 39, 203
Unemployed Workers Union 204
Unemployment 11, 16–17, 34–5, 38–9, 44, 46, 72, 93, 98, Chapter 8, 155
Unemployment insurance *see* National Insurance
Unemployment trap 218
Unison 175
United States of America
    Welfare in 19, 25, 57–8, 62, 64, 73–5, 129, 153, 191, 195, 251, 316

Universalism 9, 19–20, 26, 29–30, 68, 96, 123, 197, 230–1, 281, 301–3, 307, 309
University Grants Committee (UGC) 145
University for Industry 137
Urwick, L. 254, 259
Utilitarianism 64, 81–3, 155

V

Vaizey, J. 146
Vincent, A. 84
Vinson, Lord 294
Visiting societies 254–8, 289
Vlaeminke, M. 148
Voluntary Services Unit 266
Voluntary Welfare 10–11, 15, 22, 56, 62, 71–2, 96, 167, 201, 222, Chapter 11, 271, 276, 295, 312–4
    and contract culture 266–70
Volunteer Centre 266

W

Waine, B. 37, 284, 213, 313
Walker, A. 210, 214, 263, 265, 313
Walker, C. 210
Walker, I. 190
War, Impact on welfare policy 25–7, 116–19, 161, 167, 185
Warde, A. 290
Ware, A. 252, 261
Wates, N. 236
Watkin, B. 171
Weaver, R. 48
Webb, B. and Webb, Sidney 8, 90, 95, 110–14, 134, 161–2, 185, 201, 261
Webb, Steve 58
Webster, C. 28–31, 42, 170–1, 302
Weightman, G. 346
Weimer Republic 27
Weisbrod, B.A. 251
Welfare
    Definition of 33, 59
    Expenditure 10, 16, 24, Chapter 2, 191
    Pluralism 22, 80, 96, 100, 102–4, 126, 212–13, 249–51, 266, 312

Post-1945 consensus 16, 25–31,
   97–9, 170, 210, 303
Public opinion on 127
Rights 9, 69–72, 101, 114
and women 19–20
Welfare State
   Classic 17, 27, 29, 301, 306
   Definitional issues 16, 26–7, 31
   Economic burden of 40–1, 67
   Explanations for the development of
      26
   Institutional 62, 102
   Middle class capture of 68–9
   Residual 19, 62, 68–9, 102
Welfare to Work 129, 180, 307, 309
Welshman, J. 25
Western Provident Association (WPA)
   285
Wheatley, J. 229, 231
Whigs 4, 21, 86–7
Whitehead, C. 283
Whitehead, M. 304
Whiteside, N. 39, 50, 317
Wilcox, S. 238, 240, 242, 244–5
Wilding, P. 1, 4–5, 101, 103, 123,
   225, 228
Wilkinson, R. 174, 180
Willetts, D. 65, 304
Williams, J. 93, 96
Williams, K. 93, 96
Williams, P. 239
Williams, R.G. 101
Willink, H. Sir 168–9
Willmott, P. 263

Winch, D. 195
Winnicott, D.W. 264
Wilson, A. 278
Wilson, G. 288
Wilson, H. 98, 171
Winter, D. 18
Winter, J. 185
Winter, J.M. 114
Wiseman, J. 35
Wistow, G. 103
Wohl, A. 225
Women's Royal Voluntary Service 217
Womens' Social and Political Union
   89
Woolfe, W. 111
Woolworth 280
Wootton, B. 118
Work ethic 180
Workers Welfare Association (WWA)
   291
Workfare 57, 64–5, 191, 193, 197
Workmen's National Housing Council
   225
Wray, D. 290
Wright, T. 52, 104, 304–5
Wrigley, C. 160–1, 185, 192

Y

Yeo, S. 252, 273–4
Young, H. 190, 195
Young, M. 72, 78
Youth Opportunities Programmes
   (YOPS) 143
Youth Training Schemes (YTS) 143